—ACTING OUT—

THEORETICAL AND CLINICAL ASPECTS

Edited by

Lawrence Edwin Abt, Ph.D.

Stuart L. Weissman, Ph.D.

SECOND EDITION

JASON ARONSON INC.
Northvale, New Jersey
London

For
Zachary David Jones

THE MASTER WORK SERIES

First softcover edition 1996

Copyright © 1996, 1987 by Jason Aronson Inc.

Copyright © 1976 by Lawrence E. Abt and Stuart L. Weissman

All rights reserved. Printed in the United States of America. No part of this book may be used or reproduced in any manner whatsoever without written permission from Jason Aronson Inc. except in the case of brief quotations in reviews for inclusion in a magazine, newspaper, or broadcast.

ISBN 1-56821-778-1
Library of Congress Catalog Number: 87-71546

Manufactured in the United States of America. Jason Aronson Inc. offers books and cassettes. For information and catalog write to Jason Aronson Inc., 230 Livingston Street, Northvale, New Jersey 07647.

Contents

FOREWORD vii
By Leopold Bellak, M.D.

PREFACE TO THE SOFTCOVER EDITION xi
By Stuart L. Weissman, Ph.D.

PREFACE xiii
By Lawrence Edwin Abt, Ph.D., and Stuart L. Weissman, Ph.D.

PART I
THEORETICAL AND DYNAMIC CONSIDERATIONS OF ACTING OUT

1. THE CONCEPT OF ACTING OUT: THEORETICAL CONSIDERATIONS ... 3
   By Leopold Bellak, M.D., Larchmont, New York.
2. THE CONCEPT OF "ACTING-IN" 20
   By John N. Rosen, M.D., Clinical Professor of Psychiatry, Temple University Medical Center, Philadelphia, Pennsylvania.
3. ACTING OUT AND THE CREATIVE IMAGINATION: ANDRE GIDE ... 30
   By Mark Kanzer, M.D., New York, New York.
4. "ACTING OUT" OR "WORKING THROUGH?" 40
   By Richard C. Robertiello, M.D., New York, New York.

PART II
CLINICAL MANIFESTATIONS OF ACTING OUT

5. THE ACTING OUT CHILD 48
   By Paul Kay, M.D., Great Neck, New York.
6. THE ACTING OUT ADOLESCENT 68
   By Irene Josselyn, M.D., Phoenix, Arizona.
7. SUICIDE: A CLINICAL MANIFESTATION OF ACTING OUT 76
   By Robert E. Litman, M.D., Chief Psychiatrist, Suicide Prevention Center, Los Angeles, California.
8. SUICIDE IN CHILDREN AND ADOLESCENTS 87
   By Kurt Glaser, M.D., Clinical Director, Rosewood State Hospital, Owings Mills, Maryland.
9. DELINQUENCY AND CRIMINALITY: AN ACTING OUT PHENOMENON 100
   By Jacob Chwast, Ph.D., Postgraduate Center for Mental Health, New York, New York.

PART III
SPECIAL FORMS OF ACTING OUT

10. DRUG ADDICTION: AN ACTING OUT PROBLEM 110
    By Robert W. Rasor, M.D., Medical Officer in Charge, U. S. Public Health Service Hospital, Lexington, Kentucky.
11. ALCOHOLISM AS A FORM OF ACTING OUT 119
    By Ruth Fox, M.D., Medical Director, National Council on Alcoholism, Inc., New York, New York.
12. PSYCHOSOMATIC ILLNESS: A BODY LANGUAGE FORM OF ACTING OUT 129
    By Shervert H. Frazier, M.D., Chairman, Department of Psychiatry, Baylor University College of Medicine, Texas Medical Center, Houston, Texas.
13. ACTING OUT, OBESITY, AND EXISTENCE 135
    By Samuel V. Dunkell, M.D., Attending Psychiatrist, Payne Whitney Psychiatric Clinic, New York Hospital, New York, New York.
14. ACTING OUT IN HOMOSEXUALITY 142
    By Toby B. Bieber, Ph.D., New York, New York.
15. LEARNING INHIBITION: A PROBLEM OF ACTING OUT 152
    By Robert Melniker, Ph.D., Long Beach, New York.

PART IV
TREATMENT AND MANAGEMENT OF ACTING OUT

16. GENERAL TREATMENT PHILOSOPHY OF ACTING OUT 162
    By Rudolf Ekstein, Ph.D., Director, Project on Childhood Psychosis, Reiss-Davis Clinic for Child Guidance, Los Angeles, California.
17. ACTING OUT IN GROUP PSYCHOTHERAPY: A TRANSACTIONAL APPROACH 173
    By Lawrence Edwin Abt, Ph.D., The New School for Social Research, New York, New York.
18. PROBLEMS OF THERAPEUTIC MANAGEMENT OF ACTING OUT WITH HOSPITALIZED PATIENTS 183
    By Howard P. Rome, M.D., and Maurice J. Barry, Jr., M.D., Section of Psychiatry, Mayo Clinic and Mayo Foundation, Rochester, Minnesota.

19. ACTING OUT IN FAMILY PSYCHOTHERAPY 189
    By Carl A. Whitaker, M.D., Professor of Psychiatry, University of Wisconsin School of Medicine, Madison, Wisconsin.
20. ACTING OUT AND THE SUICIDAL PATIENT: TREATMENT AND MANAGEMENT 198
    By Harry Joseph, M.D., Assistant Clinical Professor of Psychiatry, Downstate Medical School, State University of New York, Brooklyn, New York.
21. MANAGEMENT OF ACTING OUT ADOLESCENTS 208
    By Ernst Papanek, Ed.D., Professor of Education, Queens College, University of the City of NewYork, Flushing, NewYork.
22. MANAGEMENT OF ACTING OUT PROBLEMS IN SCHOOL 233
    By Julia Vane, Ph.D., Associate Professor of Psychology, Hofstra University, Hempstead, New York.

PART V
PREDICTING ACTING OUT BY MEANS OF PSYCHOLOGICAL TESTS

23. THE WECHSLER SCALES AND ACTING OUT 242
    By Sidney Blatt, Ph.D., School of Medicine, Yale University, New Haven, Connecticut.
24. ACTING OUT INDICATORS ON THE RORSCHACH TEST 252
    By Joseph Levi, Ph.D., Chief Psychologist, Maimonides Hospital (Coney Island Division), Brooklyn, New York
25. DETECTION OF SUICIDAL RISKS WITH THE RORSCHACH 257
    By Marguerite R. Hertz, Ph.D., Professor of Psychology, Western Reserve University, Cleveland, Ohio.
26. PREDICTING ACTING OUT BY MEANS OF THE THEMATIC APPERCEPTION TEST 271
    By Zygmunt A. Piotrowski, Ph.D., Professor of Psychology, The Jefferson Medical College of Philadelphia, Philadelphia, Pennsylvania.
27. ACTING OUT AND ITS PREDICTION BY PROJECTIVE DRAWING ASSESSMENT 288
    By Emanuel F. Hammer, Ph.D., New York, New York.
28. THE BENDER GESTALT AND ACTING OUT 320
    By Fred Brown, Ph.D., Head, Division of Psychology, Department of Psychiatry, The Institute of Psychiatry, The Mount Sinai Hospital, New York, New York.

INDEX 333

Foreword

IT IS A TRUISM that all science has to concern itself with the understanding, prediction, and control of process. The behavioral sciences are especially concerned with man's interaction. Freud outstandingly contributed the hypothesis which permits us to view human behavior in terms of the continuum from childhood to adulthood—from dream to waking life, from relatively normal to relatively disturbed behavior. He bridged the previously-existing gap by showing the interrelationships in a variety of ways but, above all, by postulating and demonstrating that some of the links are unconscious: not apparent to subject or observer, but receptive to lawful inference.

With the help of Freudian and a few other hypotheses we can understand a broad spectrum of man's behavior. However, too much is still not specific enough a knowledge to permit desirable prediction and control: from the relatively banal problems of employee selection to the problems of raising children in such a way as to get predictably desirable results (if one knows what is desirable), there is much left to be done.

Acting out, as discussed in this volume, touches on many problem areas in human behavior, ranging from relatively technical, very narrowly defined behavior to a point where it becomes almost synonymous with action, being.

Even in its narrower definition, acting out is of great social importance. The character disorder, be it as a carrier of emotional contagion within a small family group, or as a demagogue of national scale, is a serious problem. The delinquent, the adult criminal, the drug addict, the ordinary psychotic, as well as the political lunatic, are problems of great social import which demand solutions. We need to know how to prevent the development of such bad actors, understand them well enough to control them therapeutically or socially, and we need to know right now most urgently how to predict who is likely to act out and when. This is not an academic problem. Every day hundreds of clinicians are faced with the decision as to whether a patient who has been hospitalized with serious emotional disorders will or will not act out his paranoid delusion and will or will not harm or kill people he fancies as enemies. The newspapers often carry the stories resulting from wrong decisions. Yet, the solution cannot be to play it safe in every case. Our hospitals could not hold half the people who might act out their delusions or respond to their hallucinations. Aside from this practical viewpoint, it has to be kept in mind that these patients are also people, suffering people who are somebody's child, somebody's brother or sister, or father or mother. They also have individual rights, and the question of the protection of society runs into the problem of the protection of the rights of the individual.

On the broader scene, the tragic assassination of President Kennedy comes easily to mind. Could Oswald have been diagnosed definitively as potentially dangerous? If so—and there are suggestions that he could have been—what can society do about it if the patient, or in his case, the patient's mother, refuses treatment? There is another social and legal problem: can legislation enforcing psychiatric treatment be enacted without seriously interfering with individual rights? In the case of the minor, how much of the parental prerogative can society usurp without seriously encroaching even more on personal freedom?

I am sure there are many different opinions on this subject, and it cannot be a matter of black and white. My personal opinion is that there is little room for argument and that no established dogma about rights is likely to prove useful. Law and mores change with the needs of society, and those change with technological development and other processes. It may be regrettable—and I myself find it unquestionably so—but the increased interaction between people makes increasing social legislation of many kinds inevitable.

Employers do not own their factories any more. If their decision to discharge employees, or close their firm, or lower wages can affect a whole community, the community steps in by means of a series of legal provisions. Most of the time one has to wait for electronic gadgets to have the right of way. The handwashing of foodhandlers is controlled by law lest they propagate infectious disorders. The California frontier is protected against importation of flora, and the celestial space is becoming subject to regulation. There is no question that the control of socially dangerous behavior will become increasingly a matter of public health legislation, much as vaccination and reportable diseases are already.

Whether one likes it or not, someone will have to take responsibility for those children who are being brought up by grossly incompetent parents in such a way that they become social dangers engaged in criminal acting out, or, even more dangerously, in political acting out. The political lunatic fringe is increasingly becoming the main danger in our world!

Are we actually equipped to assess dangerous potential? A number of excellent chapters in this volume discuss the various forms of acting out, with or without immediate social significance, diagnosing, predicting, and therapeutically controlling acting out.

I suspect that, as is so often the case, we know more than we systematically put into practice, or than society lets us put into practice. There is no doubt, however, that a great deal more must be known before the clinician can decide who is safe to discharge, who will or will not commit suicide, or relapse into drug addiction, alcoholism, sexual deviation, or political lunacy. We need to know more before we can safely presume to tell which children should be taken from the jurisdiction of the parents, and which person is beyond the expression of personal convictions and indeed primarily a social liability rather than an honest politician.

In the election of 1964, a small magazine queried the opinions of thousands of psychiatrists with regard to their opinion about one of the candidates. When some of the beliefs were published, there was much pious outcry and exhortation that psychiatrists were led astray and should adhere closely to clinical evidence. Maybe so, but if a person's public statements and written material are ever primary data for clinical inference—and they often are—the question is whether it is not easier to be academic and safe rather than politically and socially responsible. If it is correct that our criteria may not have been good enough for reliable judgment of a political personality, we had better get to work to be ready next time potential disaster threatens.

The present volume is, to my knowledge, the first one to address itself exclusively to acting out in its many facets. It is an excellent beginning and the editors should be congratulated on their timely service. Let us hope that it will not only spread the knowledge we have so far, but will also encourage significant research into the many pressing problems which acting out presents.

It may well be that acting out is one of those problems of such complexity and national significance that more than individual initiative in research is indicated. Like schizophrenia and alcoholism, for instance, acting out might be best dealt with by establishing a group of experts, possibly under the auspices of the National Institute of Mental Health, which will address itself to the many facets systematically. Such a study group, complemented by fulltime personnel, could accumulate all already available information, map out possible avenues of inquiry and management of the problem, and parcel out work and grants to suitable individuals and institutions. Thereafter, the study group would have to function also as clearing house, integrator, and controller of research findings, and eventually make recommendations to professional and legislative bodies.

It is likely that only by some such judicious mixture of overall integration and individual creativity that acting out, like other urgent clinical and social problems, will be brought to a reasonable solution.

—*Leopold Bellak, M.D.*

Preface to the Softcover Edition

The aim of this book remains as important as when the first edition was published. It is to explore the numerous forms of acting out from the psychoanalytic situation to everyday social action. Anyone who has endeavored to do reading or systematic research in the area of acting out has to be impressed with the fact that the subject, although extensively covered in scattered texts and journals, had never until the publication of this book been brought together in one volume.

The conception of this book is, like most conceptions, difficult to time with precision. The original edition was inspired by the assassination of President Kennedy. He stood for reason and sanity during a time of war, domestic violence, and bigotry. Since that time we have seen the end of the Vietnam war and the dismantling of the Soviet Union, yet violence and bigotry remain a constant threat to our national well-being. One has only to scan our daily newspapers or tune in the 6 o'clock news to experience the various forms of social pathologies that pervade our daily lives. Recent studies suggest that domestic crime and violence have replaced global nuclear war as the primary concerns of most Americans. Are these social problems special forms of "acting out"? Has our survival as a nation shifted from external destruction by foreign powers to internal self-destruction? Indeed, our very survival may to a large extent depend on the understanding, prediction, and control of acting out individually and on a national level. This book is dedicated to that end.

As with any symposium of this size, there are some disagreements among the writers. In many cases their viewpoints do not coincide with our own. But in all cases their papers are presented with such clarity of thought that the reader cannot help detecting a certain conceptual unity throughout, namely, that acting-out individuals, like all individuals, are attempting to communicate—and they differ only in their choice of "language."

In conclusion, I should like to extend to our contributors our warmest gratitude. They represent some of the finest minds from the fields of psychiatry, psychoanalysis, and psychology, and without their cooperation and precision of thought this book could not have materialized.

Sadly, my co-editor, Dr. Larry Abt, died in the fall of 1995. He was a wonderful guy with great organizational skills and a fertile mind. Without him this book would never have been a reality. I'll miss him.

S.L.W.

Washington Township, NJ

Preface

Since the appearance of the second edition of this book, the geography of the psyche has been under continuous exploration, moving toward greater understanding of the deeper motivations and their primary and secondary process expressions. It is increasingly clear, as a result of such efforts, that a person's past, like society's itself, is another country—frequently a *terra incognita*—with a sometimes frightening landscape of unknowable boundaries.

Some imaginative explorers are beginning to see more clearly that *patterns of acting out* reveal images of selfhood, in both content and style, that may not otherwise be discerned. In this light, acting out—which some psychoanalysts believe has been generalized too far beyond its original conceptualization to be clinically useful—has become a path to a deeper understanding of wide-ranging psychic processes.

Meanwhile, developments on the social landscape continue to demonstrate trends that we noted in our earlier Preface—further *erosion of confidence* in the American political process, *deceit of the Establishment*, and *political perfidy*. All of these we regard as evidences of *social acting out*, with unhappy consequences that cannot now be fully known.

In the delicate balance between reason and nonreason, the acting-out potential on the social scene has clearly moved in the direction of nonreason, to the point that we may realiably speak of an *assault on reason* of growing magnitude and importance. In many locales, wide-ranging and unremitting efforts are being carried forward to reject reason and to enthrone nonreason in our affairs.

We regard this situation as dire—and we see it as social acting out with unforseen outcomes. Individual security, anchored in societal security, thus stands deeply threatened by the rising tide of anti-intellectualism sweeping the shores of the approaching twenty-first century.

June 1987

L. E. A.
S. L. W.

About the Editors

Lawrence Edwin Abt received his B.S. from New York University, his M.S. from Columbia University, and his Ph.D. from New York University. He taught clinical psychology at Brooklyn College, the New School for Social Research, and, for five summers in Switzerland, Florida Institute of Technology. A member of Sigma Xi and a fellow of the American Psychological Association, Dr. Abt was in private practice as a clinical psychologist and psychoanalyst over a span of forty years. Editor and author of 22 books on psychology, Dr. Abt retired to Santa Barbara, California, in 1988 and died there in August 1994.

Stuart L. Weissman, Ph.D., is a graduate of Yeshiva University and completed his analytic training at the Postgraduate Center for Psychotherapy in New York City. Formerly Chief Psychologist at Bergen Pines Hospital in Paramus, New Jersey, Dr. Weissman is currently adjunct professor of psychology at Pace University in Pleasantville, New York. He maintains a private practice in Hackensack, New Jersey.

ACTING OUT

ACTING OUT

PART I
THEORETICAL AND DYNAMIC CONSIDERATIONS OF ACTING OUT

To integrate a section on the theory of acting out is no easy task. Like the biblical Tower of Babel, one is confronted with many different languages as well as points of view. Authors differ in terms of definition, narrowness or broadness of scope, and general position with respect to the psychopathological or adaptive nature of the process. To emphasize any one viewpoint would not do justice to the phenomenon, for the concept of acting out is so multifaceted and complex that little agreement on *definition,* much less a *dynamic* conceptualization, can be found in an intensive review of the literature.

Two main divergencies involve the psychopathological versus the adaptive or creative nature of acting out. Writers who have tended to emphasize the latter position are strongly in the minority. To avoid placing the concept entirely into the hands of the psychopathologists, we invited Drs. Kanzer and Robertiello to contribute papers which would complement the positions taken by Drs. Bellak and Rosen. Yet we felt it appropriate to present Dr. Bellak's paper first, for in it he touches on the genetic, dynamic, structural, economic, topographic, and even adaptive aspects of the process, and offers, as well, some treatment considerations. It is, in our opinion, the finest systematic review of the concept yet presented. Bellak views acting out as the "non-verbal translation of an unconscious statement," and as such emphasizes an externalization of internal conflicts, ranging from such mild episodic acts as overeating, to the more serious and destructive forms, such as suicide and homicide.

Whereas Bellak makes little dynamic distinction between the neurotic or psychotic form, Rosen strongly emphasizes the difference in his coinage of the term "acting in." To Rosen, "acting in" characterizes the psychotic whose external actions are merely the response to internal "dreaming, wishing for impossible or incompatible satisfactions." While both authors emphasize the *internal environment,* Rosen feels that in psychotics it is more "dream-like" and less a function of external events.

Although Kanzer emphasizes the more adaptive aspects of acting out, he parallels Rosen's thinking in viewing acting out as a search for "substitute fulfillments" of inner desires from which one takes flight.

Tracing the life of Andre Gide, his homosexual and masturbatory fantasies, Kanzer bridges the author's internal experiences and those of his characters, such as in *The Counterfeiters,* in which the main character is seen clearly as a representation of Gide's early years. Yet Kanzer feels that Gide's problems prevented him from exploring character deeply for ". . . . true motivation had to be hidden from himself as well as others."

Robertiello, taking a decidedly "humanistic" position, feels that much of what is erroneously labeled "acting out" is essentially an attempt at "working through" conflict. His is a bold and new theoretical approach in which he feels that true acting out is in the service of maintaining repression, while working through involves those forces of expression which lead to *mastery.* Such expression is considered necessary for development of ego strength and may indeed be *essential* for change. He cautions that many patients are fashioned into "dead, controlled, conforming people" as a result of the acting out fears of their analysts, and he further makes the controversial point that such attitudes help to maintain patients as "asexual little children."

1. The Concept of Acting Out: Theoretical Considerations

By LEOPOLD BELLAK, M.D.

In a very genuine sense, the systematic and comprehensive theoretical statement that Leopold Bellak offers in the chapter that follows may be regarded as setting the tone for both the theoretical and therapeutic portions of Acting Out. *It is well known that Dr. Bellak has done as much as any person to clear away the conceptual underbrush and open up the paths to larger theoretical and practical understanding of the whole process of acting out, and readers of this volume will feel an indebtedness to him as they consider not only his chapter but many of the others in this volume in relation to the propositions which Bellak offers so clearly and well.*

ACTING OUT, in a broad sense, is one of the most important problems of our society: to translate impulses into action comprises the problems of delinquency as well as those of sociopathy generally. The problems of acting out include the lunatic fringe of politics as well as the fellow who might endanger the world by pulling the atomic trigger. In a narrower clinical sense, it involves some of the most awesome decisions one has to make daily: will the person with homicidal or suicidal fantasies and impulses act on them or not? Will the patient hospitalized for paranoid problems be safe now to be discharged into the community, or may he still translate his ideas into action?

To develop reliable and valid differential criteria for the person, or for certain of his personality features, who will act out surely seems one of the most urgent tasks. Except for some research on the problem of suicide, little if anything of systematic nature has been done along these lines.

Looking for established definitions of "acting out," we find that English and English[6] have defined acting out briefly as *manifesting the purposive behavior appropriate to an older situation in a new situation which symbolically represents it.* Hinsie and Campbell[14] have defined it as *the partial discharge of instinctual tension that is achieved by responding to the present situation as if it were the situation that originally gave rise to the instinctual demand.* Whereas both definitions are useful, neither fully encompasses the scope of this phenomenon. It is my purpose to explore the concept both descriptively and metapsychologically in the hope of arriving at a theoretically sound understanding which will permit a more consistent therapeutic management.

CLINICAL VARIETIES OF ACTING OUT

The usage of the term and concept of acting out in clinical discussions covers a wide range of phenomena. Sometimes the term is used to characterize brief acts of circumscribed and merely episodic nature; e.g., an obese person is sometimes said to be acting out his sense of frustration and his need for gratification by overeating. Of course, the dynamics may be much more complex, but the essential implication here is that such a person, feeling frustrated, disappointed, and unloved, translates these usually unconscious feelings into the act of feeding himself. The act of eating, symbolically represents the unstated verbalization, "Nobody loves me, nobody feeds me. Therefore I have to feed myself," or "I feel empty, I feel deflated. I wish to have the feeling of being full and solid." It is obvious that drinking may have the same unverbalized meaning. One may say, in such instances, that the term acting out is used when certain behavior seems to make a simple unconscious statement. It is this quality of making an unconscious statement that differentiates acting out from other neurotic behavior with phobic or obsessive activity, as well as the fact that acting out is usually ego-syntonic, at least at the moment of action. (Overeating, however, as a simple form of acting out, is often ego-alien and may be perceived as compulsive by sophisticated people.)

Another conceptually simple use of the term acting out is frequently encountered in discussions of psychotic behavior. An assaultive attack may be considered as the acting out of delusional and hallucinatory distortions: the behavior is consistent with and caused by the distortions, and has little or nothing to do with reality. When we ask ourselves, in dealing with psychotics, "Is this patient likely to act out?" we are wondering what the chances are that he will act upon his unrealistic perceptions and impulses. The question is one that has enormous therapeutic and social import, and it is an urgent task that we understand and develop reliable criteria why certain individuals are able to sustain indefinitely paranoid feelings and vicious notions without ever doing harm, and others are sometimes pressed and overrun by similar impulses into the performance of dreadfully destructive acts. Fortunately, only a small percentage of psychotics translate their distorted perceptions into action.

Another rather simple form of acting out is also characteristic of the hysterical personality. What impresses one most strongly about such individuals is the tremendous mood swing, from love to hate, from depression to elation, with actions correspondingly extremely different, in rather short time intervals.

In a sense, some of the behavior typical of fugues and multiple personalities belongs in the area of acting out: in these major dissociated states, one split-off part of the personality is permitted to act out ordinarily unacceptable impulses.

Psychopaths or sociopaths, unlike psychoneurotics, are characterized by alloplastic reactions. They tend to translate their conflicts and drives into behavior rather than into the symptoms of the autoplastic neurotic. Addiction, among other things, a form of acting out, leads to further acting out under the influence of the drug.

The nuclear concept of acting out, however, may perhaps best be seen in the behavior of often apparently normal people suffering from character disorders who tend to react to certain situations in a nearly stereotyped way. Their behavior patterns do not appear stereotyped to them, but do to the observant onlooker. There are those who act in an inappropriate or ill-advised way as an unconscious invitation for aggression against themselves. There are others who persistently respond pathologically and self-destructively by being greatly attracted to those whose main aim is to exploit them sadistically; there are men and women whose empty promiscuity is an acting out of certain childhood conflicts and frustrations in their lives. It is as if all these individuals, when presented with a certain set of stimuli, respond with a whole sequence of behavior wrongly programmed by an electronic computer. Although discordant to everyone but themselves, their behavior is concordant with their unconscious subjective set of realities, and therefore does not change with realistic experience: they do not see a cause-and-effect relationship between their behavior and its manifest results, since they ascribe the results to accident or fate and therefore do not profit from ordinary learning. In effect, the situation works out entirely as it is supposed to according to the unconscious set, and the defenses make their maladaptive behavior appear appropriate and ego-syntonic to them. This clinical situation has often been misconceived as a "repetition compulsion," though there is no more or less compulsion in it than in any other act related to a mental set. The manifest absurdity of this acting out behavior made it appear like a compulsion.

In these character neuroses, the acting out is less episodic, more woven into the entire "life-style." To borrow a useful phrase from Adler, one can say that their character structure evolves around some "fictive, unconscious goal." Similar to the simpler forms of acting out, their entire behavior seems to make a statement, e.g., "I am going to be bigger than anybody else," or "I will show everyone what a self-effacing person I am." A special and serious form of acting out in terms of the whole character structure is seen in the so-called "fate neurosis" (or "success neurosis"): the individual always seems the unwitting victim of apparently uncontrollable circumstances, is always disappointed, always fails. Analysis reveals that such an individual actually constructs his life in order to fail, in order to inflict self-harm, in order to suffer. Like the colloquial *Schlemiehl,* he always finds a banana peel to slip on, even if he has to place it there for the purpose.

Some people make acting out a style of life by which they become, to some extent, known: for example, the playwright best remembered for his drinking excesses and uninhibited statements, the actress who remains an *enfant terrible* well into old age, the absent-minded professor who actually lives that particular conception of his role.

Another type of personality, related to the one just discussed but much less well-integrated, is the one found in excitable people, who constantly blow off one kind of affect or another, in one form or another: from ticlike twitches to volatile verbal expressions to hasty acts of all kinds. These people's behavior is not identical with the impulse disorder in its usual sense. In the case of the impulse disorder, there are often long quiescent periods, if anything, often characterized by seeming calm bfore the blow-off. The excited person has no quiet period, and acting out is but one of the many overactivities.

It becomes apparent, then, that acting out involves phenomena of somewhat different complexity, different clinical syndromes and may have episodic or more diffuse temporal characteristics, and has tremendous variation in the extent to which it dominates a personality.

THE METAPSYCHOLOGY OF ACTING OUT

Before we enter upon a strictly schematic consideration of our topic, it is useful to review briefly the main contributions to our considerations.

Freud first mentioned acting out in *The Psychopathology of Everyday Life,*[10] in which he describes various kinds of symptomatic and faulty actions within the range of normal behavior. In his "Fragment of an Analysis of a Case of Hysteria,"[11] the well known study of Dora, he refers to her premature termination of her analysis as an acting out of certain childhood recollections and fantasies. In 1914, in a paper on technique,[12] he uses the term acting out in still a third context, that of its relationship to transference and resistance.

Some time later, Fenichel[7] attempted a more systematic discussion of acting out. He describes people in whom "an unconscious misunderstanding of the present in the sense of the past is extraordinarily strong; the patients repeatedly perform acts or undergo experiences, identical or very similar ones, that represent unconscious attempts to get rid of old instinctual conflicts, to find a belated gratification of repressed impulses (instinctual demands as well as guilt feelings), or at least to try to find relief from some inner tension.[11] For these persons the "environment is only an arena in which to stage their internal conflicts." The patients appear as restless, hyperactive personalities, or their activity may be hidden and their life history may give the impression that they are the toys of a malicious fate, the repetitions being experienced passively and rationalized as occurring against the person's will. In another context (in the same volume), Fenichel describes these patients as having an intolerance for tension, as being unable to perform the step from acting to thinking: they exhibit an immediate yielding of reasonable judgment to all impulses. He feels that their aim is the avoidance of displeasure rather than the attainment of pleasure; that oral fixations and early traumata play a significant role; and that acting out is often associated with cyclic moods. He quotes Alexander as stating that this type of problem is closely related to what Alexander first described as "neurotic character."

In another paper,[8] Fenichel emphasizes that the *quality* of action in itself is especially conspicuous in acting out as compared to other neurotic activity, that it is generally a fairly organized activity and not merely a single movement, gesture, or mimicked expression. Fenichel further characterizes acting out as being ego-syntonic, and as being alloplastic rather than autoplastic defenses. People who act out tend to change their environment rather than themselves, and whereas their behavior seems appropriate to them, it seems implausible and inappropriate to others.

After herself reviewing Fenichel, Greenacre[13] brings forward major considerations of her own. She says that in acting out "there may be special problems in accepting and understanding current reality either because of (1) specific problems in the immediate real situation; (2) special persistence of memories of earlier disturbing experiences; or (3) an inadequate sense of reality. . . . In the case of acting out there is a compulsion to reproduce repetitively a total experience or episode rather than to select some small part of it as a token representation." She notes that acting out is relatively more frequent in persons undergoing analysis, and as such, constitutes a special technical problem. Acting out creates reality situations of a detrimental nature and discharges tensions outside of the therapeutic milieu which makes it impossible to analyze them. She limits her discussion to habitual neurotic acting out which she sees as a selective distortion of reality. In contrast, she sees psychotic acting out as characterized by a complete taking over of the current situation by early unconscious memories which severely affect reality perception and bar conscious memories and attitudes. She also differentiates "isolated, occasional, really symptomatic acting out during the course of analysis from those conditions in which the acting out is frequent, habitual, or characteristic of tendencies evident in the entire life of the patient." According to her, "the impulsiveness is based on an inability to tolerate frustration, a special disturbance of reality and of self-criticism, the quality of marked motility or activity often of a dramatic character—all especially characteristic of the extremely severe neuroses, which sometimes appear close to psychoses and the psychopathies."

Both Greenacre and Fenichel consider part of the genesis of habitual acting out an oral fixation, a great narcissistic need, an intolerance of frustration, a constitutionally heightened motility, and the presence of severe early traumata which cause repetitive abreactive acting out similar to that found in the traumatic neuroses. Greenacre, however, adds a special emphasis on visual sensitization which produces a bent for dramatization (she sees it as related to exhibitionism and scoptophilia), and on an unconscious belief in the magic of action. She thinks that the need for dramatization may be crucial in converting plain neurotic action into acting out. She feels that the important role of acting is due to disturbances of the development of speech in the second year. When such is the case, motor action is used to take over some of the communicative functions. She feels that this also accounts for the prevalence of body language in people who act out. The capacity to verbalize and to think in verbal terms (which she sees as having an important function in the integration of emotions with appropriate content of thought) is interfered with and therefore an inadequate ability to organize and control emotion results.

In order to discuss acting out more systematically, it may be useful to consider it genetically, dynamically, adaptively, structurally, economically and topographically, even at the risk of being repetitive.

Genetic Aspects. Fenichel says that oral fixations and marked traumatic experiences play a large role in this phenomenon. Greenacre adds that difficulties in the second year of life, specifically interference with speech development and compensatory motility as a substitute for verbal communication, also play a part. She considers visual sensitization, which may derive from exhibitionism and scoptophilia, as producing a bent for dramatization and an unconscious belief in the magic of action. *Expression* of impulse and emotion rather than *organization* carries over into the secondary process.

I believe that multiple diverse identification coupled with a lack of synthesis of ego-nuclei also plays a role. Some patients intermittently act out highly diverse roles which seem patterned on identification with one or the other parent. Low frustration tolerance, which is also considered as a dynamic aspect of acting out, is frequently related to a developmental interference: inconsistent rearing, over-indulgence, insufficient discipline, general over-charging with sexual and aggressive impulses (beyond those specifically mentioned by Greenacre) predispose to low frustration tolerance and acting out.

Blos,[5] in a recent paper, discusses acting out in the adolescent as operating in the service of ego synthesis as a phase-specific mechanism. He states that "the adolescent process proceeds from a progressive decathexis of primary love objects through a phase of increased narcissism and autoerotism to heterosexual object finding." He goes on to say that these changes are "accompanied by a profound sense of loss and isolation, by a severe ego impoverishment which accounts for the adolescent's frantic turn to the outside world, to sensory stimulation and to activity." In the sense that action and motion are normal adolescent means for resisting the surrender to primal passivity, "action assumes the quality of a magic gesture: it averts evil, it denies passive wishes, and it affirms a delusional control over reality." Still discussing normal adolescent development, Blos says "the adolescent process can be accomplished only through synthesizing the past with the present and the anticipated future . . . (through) constantly striving to bring the past into harmony with the terminal stage of childhood, with adolescence. Is it surprising to find among the instrumentalities of remembering the one called acting out?"

In the more diffuse type of acting out a much broader genetic basis than the ones mentioned so far needs to be considered. In their lives, we find not the subtlety of mere visual sensitization described by Greenacre, but a general overstimulation and sensitization for all stimuli—in the sense of a much lowered threshold both for input and output. It may be that the concept of lower stimulus barrier advanced by Escalona, et al.[4] describes some congenital differences. More often, such people seem to have been exposed to tremendous overstimulation of nearly all sense modalities and zones, starting out with a mother with hypermotility during rocking and nursing and continuing into frequent exposure to aggressive and sexual stimulation. Much as I believe that an infant needs a certain amount of sensory input for development (best conceptualized by means of Magoun's concept concerning the function of the ascending reticular system) it also seems that a "system" may get a permanent overload; such a person then has a lifelong excessive stimulus hunger matched only by the inability for containment and the constant need for discharge.

Dynamic Aspects. Both Fenichel and Greenacre agree that the acting out individual permits past experience to dominate his perception of contemporary stimuli. The more rigidly such distortions occur and the broader the scope of contemporary stimuli so affected, the more serious is the condition.

Some authors have discussed the defensive aspects of acting out as a cathartic and abreactive experience: the patient blows off steam and reduces the tension. Sometimes acting out, even when violent or self-harming, wards off the more anxiety-laden feeling of depersonalization.[1] The defensive function of acting out lies in keeping certain forms of behavior ego-syntonic with the help of denial and repression. Jacobson,[15] writing on denial and repression, says that the resistance against remembering effected by acting out constitutes a form of denial. "Acting out," Jacobson says, "appears to be regularly linked up with a bent for denial. That this persistent denial goes hand in hand with a distortion of reality is borne out convincingly by patients of this kind. The function of acting out is denial through action; the magic of action and of gesture appear in such cases in great clarity."

In the very complex forms of acting out, though, as in character neuroses, I would think that repression also plays a large role. The complex forms of acting out are highly overdetermined, and are unconscious (not preconscious, as in denial). One sequence of patterns is actually often designed defensively to counteract another sequence of behavior patterns; a series of masochistic and passive seductive acts may be followed consistently by active sadistic reactions, and vice versa.

An interesting proposition, although in part a genetic one, deserves some thought. Fries and Woolf[9] have suggested that there are definite congenital activity types, and that the more active type may be predisposed to a choice of alloplastic rather than autoplastic defenses. One wonders, then, if some of the dynamic determinants of acting out behavior may not be predicated on a congenital basis.

As yet, we have no information on the possible relationship of imprinting to acting out and other forms of character development.

Adaptive Aspects. Sometimes acting out which is not directly in the interest of the individual may have certain social advantages. Revolutionary behavior, which may contain instances of individual acting out, is an example. Needless to say, when individual acting out features become predominant, the "cause" suffers by hindrance of realistic goals.

Blos has pointed out the adaptive aspects of acting out in adolescence.

A controlled use of acting out is not infrequent among actors, perhaps especially among "method acting" devotees. The relationship between dramatic acting and acting out may account for the higher incidence of this phenomenon in the theatrical world. The same features of dramatization, scoptophilia, and exhibitionism Greenacre mentions as being related to a tendency to act out are also related to dramatic performances on the stage. Depersonalization, often related to acting out, is met among theatrical people: some actors feel "real" only when acting on the stage, and feel depersonalized at other times. Such people have a tendency to carry over stage roles into real life. On the other hand, certain highly-typecast performers, e.g., the villain, the tough guy, the milksop, portray often only those roles which they act out in real life.

Structural Aspects. A lack of fusion of ego-nuclei has been mentioned from a genetic standpoint. In acting out individuals, it is often as if the left hand knows not what the right hand is doing. The actions of one move bear apparently little relationship to those of another. Indeed, it is almost as if one were dealing with different individuals at different times. A deficiency in the synthetic function of the ego seems crucial.

Other ego functions are involved in the poor impulse control, low frustration tolerance, and poor reality testing which all are integral aspects of acting out. An inability to attain object constancy or a reasonable degree of sublimation and neutralization also plays a major role. The logic implicit in secondary process functioning and the detour behavior which is essential in the hierarchical relationships of goals are other structural defects related to acting out.

Economic Aspects. Fenichel and Greenacre have pointed out the general role of narcissism in acting out. Action is overinvested in acting out: it has magic connotations, subjective symbolic meaning, and thus remains highly personalized and non-communicative; the statement the acting out person seems to convey fails in its communicative purpose by virtue of the highly subjective nature of the expressed act. Along with the narcissistic overinvestment of certain ego functions including those of action and motility, there is also often a narcissistic overinvestment of the self.

Topographical Aspects. Complex acting out is usually largely unconscious. In those instances where it is part of a rapidly fluctuating hysterical behavior or of brief episodic nature, it is preconscious, with denial related to the instability of the performance. A combination of preconscious denial and unconscious repression respectively plays a role in the immediate triggering and the basic programming.

Sociological Aspects. It is frequently overlooked that the manifest forms which acting out assumes are often determined by cultural milieu, social factors, and other contemporary determinants. Certainly metapsychological considerations determine the predisposition and potentiality for acting out, yet social factors may be critical with regard to the form it follows or even to its actual emergence. Drug addiction may be the symptom of choice among the Spanish population in New York City, alcoholism among the Irish. Relatively crude forms of acting out may be consistent with one socio-economic level, whereas more subtle forms characterize a higher level. War and mob situations may lead to acting out of a socially contagious nature in otherwise reasonably controlled people. Foreign and other unaccustomed settings may facilitate acting out which is carefully controlled in the familiar milieu.

CRIMINOLOGICAL ASPECTS

"The criminal law defines a crime as a prohibited act to which is applied a sanction in some form of penalty. A further qualification specifies that to establish a crime, two elements must concur, namely, a prohibited physical act (e.g. in action, participation in the act itself, or an omission to act), and a non-physical or subjective element, the mental component (*mens rea*) designated as intent. Anglo-American jurisprudence is a carrier of a long tradition that mental disability deprives the person of this mental ingredient of intent. From the 13th century, the law has held that an insane person does not know what he is doing, is lacking in mind and reason and in such condition of altered *mens rea* is not held culpable. The insane person who does not possess the requisite 'knowing' of his doings is also lacking in the requisite 'intent' to commit a crime. This doctrine reached its final development in 1843 with the adoption of the McNaughton Rule which is the prevailing test of insanity as a criminal defense to a crime. This is known as the 'right and wrong' rule."[16]

Roche goes on to point out that a number of recent developments have broadened the conception of responsibility for criminal acts. Among them he cites the recognition and role of some of the sociological aspects mentioned above. He also discusses the broadened recognition of mental illness embodied in the Durham Rule of 1954, that an accused is not criminally responsible if his unlawful act was the product of "mental disease or mental defect."

The special role of acting out in the judgments of responsibility for criminal acts is not sufficiently appreciated. By the McNaughton Rule, extremes of impulsive acting out, usually lumped under the poorly defined concept of "temporary insanity," are accepted as mitigating or exculpating circumstances. Psychotic acting out or other severe disturbances are covered by the Durham Rule.

In either instance, it appears likely that "ego-alien" acting out would fare much more favorably than ego-syntonic acting out of character disorders or psychotic characters, or the more traditionally conceptualized psychopathic character. It is understandable enough that a judge or jury would feel that no irresistible act or defect in judgment due to mental illness was involved, as the accused does not give that impression, and the act does not feel like an ego-alien one to the judge and jury themselves. One curious exception to this legal situation has existed in Austrian jurisprudence: There, a man or woman might be adjudged to have committed a criminal act as a consequence of "Hörigkeit;" that is, as a consequence of a state of thralldom or bondage to the spouse or lover. In such a case, the state of bondage was considered a mitigating circumstance.

It is luckily quite easy to illustrate this concept of bondage by reference to a well-known book by Somerset Maugham, appropriately called *Of Human Bondage*. In it he describes in probably autobiographical form the seemingly involuntary, hopeless, and helpless infatuation and subservience of a man to a woman. While many of the man's acts involve irrational behavior, none of it is clearly criminal. The point is, however, that in similar characterological acting out, criminal acts can also be committed. Thralldom hardly deserves extensive discussion here, as it is but a special subtle instance of the relationship of acting out in its many forms to criminal acts and the concept of responsibility.

Acting out is not only of the broadest relevance for the consideration of all criminal acts: it is also of paramount significance from the standpoint of "punishment," or what should be called *correctional measures*.

Three aspects seem obvious:

(1) Such offenders as seem to have been motivated by personality characteristics which may lend themselves to presently existing and available therapeutic measures be given an optimal and maximal chance for therapeutic change.

(2) This is hardly the case at present and needs change. Instead of purely legal consideration, eventually correction should be formulated by a mental health team, including penologists and sociologists, aside from psychiatrists and psychologists and social workers.

(3) It is in the nature of *some* acting out unfortunately that we seem at present unable to deal with it successfully therapeutically, as will be pointed out later in this chapter. Whether it involves paranoid psychotics, sex offenders, or murderers with organic brain defects one should not confound compassion with poor judgment. Although every attempt must be made to increase our therapeutic potential, society must be protected against the acting out of individuals whom we cannot help at present. To blur the distinction is a disservice to the mental health field as well as to society in general.

This does by no means imply condoning the currently barbarous and ill-informed and highly unsuccessful forms of punitive confinement in jails which breed more criminal behavior, sex deviation, and social burdens. Where removal from society is necessary, any number of means can be found which would be more humane as well as less costly and occasionally may be even more successful than our present jails.

THE THERAPEUTIC MANAGEMENT OF ACTING OUT

In view of the diverse complexity of behavior covered by the concept of acting out, and in view of the many psychological features and social aspects, the therapeutic management of this phenomenon will obviously vary a great deal from patient to patient. The strategy and tactics of a well-planned therapeutic program impose their own individual structure.[2]

Within this framework, it is often useful to differentiate between immediate and long-range techniques, though the need for one or the other may often overlap. Among the short-range measures[3] to be considered are:

1. *Removing the patient from the situation* which precipitates or triggers acting out. In some cases, a change of social milieu is possible and indicated; in others, plain prohibition of certain contacts may be indicated. However, Greenacre points out how limited the use of such prohibition is both from the standpoint of immediate effectiveness and because of its potentially detrimental effect on the conduct of the analysis or therapy.

Where environmental factors are important in sustaining the tendency to act out, it may be prerequisite for successful treatment to effect a change, if possible, before treatment begins. This may involve changing the geographic milieu, or insisting the patient move out of the parental home or business, or altering the arrangement by which a son works for his father-in-law, etc. I find it infinitely more useful to make such changes in advance, if necessary in consultation with the others involved, rather than to try to analyze in an untenable atmosphere.

2. *Cathartic interpretation* dealing directly with the drive expressed in acting out may sometimes be useful provided necessary precautions are kept in mind of the consequences of interpretation.

3. The attempt to make *the behavior ego-alien* is perhaps the most useful instrument. One points out the repetitive and harmful nature of the behavior patterns, and above all, indicates to the patient that he is really a victim of his unconscious distortions. By making apparent the passive role he plays in relation to his own impulses, one can remove much of the feeling of omnipotence and magic which is inherent in acting out.

4. Since immediate action is a large factor in all acting out, *any delay,* of itself, will tend to interfere with this behavior. The patient who wants to get married today, who wants to break off treatment now, who wants to initiate divorce proceedings instantly, may sometimes be deterred by an agreement to wait a day, a week, a month. The benefits of such an agreement are twofold: in the first place, the urgency of the moment may be bypassed; in the second place, one gains time to interpret usefully.

5. In extreme cases, it may be necessary to enlist the *help of others* to curb harmful acting out.

6. A *strengthening of the superego* may be immediately helpful. One appeals persistently to the patient's conscience and points out to him the social implications of his behavior and the detrimental effect it may have on others. One attempts to ally with the part of the patient's personality which wishes to control the impulses. At those times when the danger of acting out is acute, it is necessary to be available to the patient by telephone or personal contact in order to delay or deter the episode.

Long-range Measures. Among the long-range measures for dealing with acting out, Greenacre considers the three basic techniques of prohibition, interpretation, and strengthening the ego. She is highly cognizant of the shortcomings of prohibition as a long-range technique. She sees interpretation as the method of choice, but applicable primarily to those patients with a reasonably well-integrated ego and in whom acting out occurs only occasionally. It is her feeling that interpretation of id content is usually contra-indicated, but that extensive interpretations of narcissism are helpful. With a patient's strong positive transference, she feels that one can soon acquaint the patient with the relationship of his tendency to act and its use in warding off anxiety. She also feels that, in general, an early intellectual outlining of the meaning of the patient's behavior may be useful in increasing self-scrutiny and self-criticism. Her long-range goal is to gain relief by the conversion into verbal or thought-out expressions of the preverbal material that has been previously acted out. She reports success in changing the general manner of expressiveness from acting out to verbalization, although some patients may have to remain on guard always against the possibility of tensions that might become unbearable. Greenacre also takes cognizance of the important fact that occasionally a quality of the therapist's own behavior may encourage acting out. He himself may tend to act out either overtly or in more subtle form, or he may choose patients as a medium for his own acting out much as some parents trigger acting out in their children.

I have found a few other techniques useful additions in dealing with this problem therapeutically. One is the systematic and intentional use of prediction: if the therapist is able to tell the patient in advance that he is very likely to act out because of an approaching set of circumstances or situation, it will go a long way towards aborting the behavior. It may be pointed out to the patient that the purpose of the prediction is the hope of proving it false. If the analyst repeatedly predicts correctly, it will have a marked effect on the patient's conduct.

Another tactical procedure which has proved useful in my experience is to further the synthetic abilities of the patient by a great deal of reviewing and by routinely tying dissociated events together in interpretative statements. Acting out patients, particularly the hysterical ones, have a tendency to forget completely what mood they were in the day before, or what last week's most urgent problem was. Such patients must be reminded of the state of affairs of yesterday and the week before, and shown the relationship of today's need for action to those just past. To this effect, I have found it useful to insist that such patients start off their therapeutic hour recalling themselves the main dynamic gist of the previous, or maybe several previous sessions, and intentionally and actively relating current material to previous material. This technique, coupled with extra-frequent review and overview, seems useful for important integrative development.

I feel that it is important to prevent acting out as a form of repeating a wrong "learned" behavior pattern. I explain to the patient that in a sense, every act, every phase of acting out, fortifies the wrong response much as does the repetition of a poorly executed dance step or a wrong driving maneuver. I use a simple explanation of conditioning to drive home the importance of avoiding repetition of acting out both for short-range control and long-range therapeutic attainment. From the same standpoint, I consider the periodic use of appropriate drugs strongly indicated to avoid repetitions of acting out. Drugs that will decrease the predisposing anxiety and tension will give one the breathing spell necessary for therapeutic attainment, and at the same time hinder further strengthening of pathological patterns. It may be possible that some drugs, especially of the phenothiazine group, may interfere with acting out by decreasing the affective drive directly, and thus increasing the synthetic functions indirectly. It may also be possible that phenothiazines directly increase synthesizing capacities of the ego. It remains for future experimental approaches to establish the processes involved, but the clinical effects of anxiety reducers, tranquilizers, and energizers in different acting out patients seem evident.

In some patients, the amount of unlearning and relearning by the purely verbal means available in individual therapy is limited. In such cases, the judicious use of group therapy with its unique opportunity for learning and unlearning in actual social situations may prove a useful adjunct to individual psychoanalytic psychotherapy or analysis.

There are many instances in which acting out remains refractory: a large percentage of these patients do not enter treatment even if they have sought one consultation, or break off very soon, long before one has had a chance to make ego-alien what is ego-syntonic to them. Even if they stay in treatment, progress may be slow or not materialize.

The person who is constantly excited, who has had a sensory overload in early childhood and now lives on a high level of tension, with a great need for stimuli *and* immediate discharge, remains largely unreachable psychotherapeutically. Some totally new, possibly physiological, forms of therapy must be searched for.

Even for the control of some forms of acting out, in neurotics, some new and totally different treatment approaches may have to be devised; possibly a technique predicated upon a combination of learning theory with the understanding derived from psychoanalytic psychodynamics may be useful: that is, varieties of conditioning, not concerning manifest aspects of behavior but rather the unconscious sets we know about, techniques for acquiring frustration tolerance, etc.

Many of the difficulties in treating acting out are related to the fact that the genetic roots lie in preverbal experiences. No wonder that acting out shares its therapeutic problems with other pathological syndromes of non-verbal nature and preverbal origin, and is often even an exchangeable symptom: it is useful to keep in mind that acting out is often closely related to hypochondriasis, psychosomatic conditions, and hysterical phenomena. In all these instances, we deal with a variety of body language expressions rather than with verbal communication appropriate to the secondary process. Greenacre, in closing her paper, asks why symptomatic acting out is so very common in conversion hysteria. I believe the answer is that although sometimes acting out takes the complex form of interpersonal behavior patterns, at other times it makes its own preverbal statement in the form of migratory hypochondriacal concern over one organ or another, e.g., "there is something wrong with me; I find my body deficient, decaying, inferior, liable to invasion." Of course it is well known that the conversion symptom also makes a somatic statement of repressed material. It is by this common denominator of somatic statement of non-verbal content that I believe acting out, hypochondriasis, psychosomatic phenomena, and hysterical phenomena are linked.

If problems remain in the successful treatment of neurotic acting out, it seems to me appropriate to be pessimistic concerning the treatment of the more severe forms of acting out, involving major social pathology.

I often feel that it is wishful thinking to expect that addictions and major asocial and antisocial forms of acting out will respond to our current psychiatric therapeutic armamentarium, often very thinly spread, except with a relatively small percentage where the severity of acting out is not primarily related to the degree of psychopathology, but rather to social and other situational factors. In instances of sociopathic or psychotic acting out of major violence, I do not feel that psychiatric treatment alone can take the place of other forms of humane management which offer society more immediate protection until the effectiveness of our diagnostic and therapeutic attempts has increased generally or has been proven extensively in each individual case of a social offender.

SUMMARY

Acting out is a concept which includes a wide range of phenomena varying in complexity, dynamics, temporality and therapeutics. We have scanned a sampling of the clinical manifestations of this concept. We have considered its genetic, dynamic, adaptive, structural, economic, and topographical aspects. We have noted that social factors often determine the translation from potentiality into actuality, and also frequently determine the form the acting out will take.

Therapeutic management has been outlined in terms of the immediate preventative steps and the long-range goals. It is my conclusion that there are still serious limitations to the therapeutic management of acting out. Such limits must be realistically acknowledged, and action must be predicated with this in mind.

Finally, the close relationship of acting out to conversion hysteria, psychosomatic, and hypochondriacal conditions was pointed out, the common denominator being non-verbal statements, by action or somatic symptom.

REFERENCES

1. Bellak, L. Depersonalization as a variant of self-awareness. In *Unfinished tasks in behavioral science*. Inaugural Symposium, Institute for Research in Behavioral Science, Chicago Medical School. Baltimore: Williams and Wilkins, 1963.
2. ——. Methodology and research in the psychotherapy of psychoses. Psychiatric Research Report #17, Am. Psy. Assoc. Nov., 1963.
3. ——. The role and nature of psychotherapy in community psychiatry. In Bellak, L. (Ed.) *Handbook of community psychiatry*. New York: Grune & Stratton, 1963.
4. Bergman, P., and Escalona, S. Unusual sensitivities in very small children. *The psychoanalytic study of the child*. Vols. 3 and 4. New York: International Universities Press, 1949.
5. Blos, P. The concept of acting out in relation to the adolescent process. Presented at the New York Psychoanalytic Society meeting, September 25, 1962.
6. English, H. B., and English, A. C. *A comprehensive dictionary of psychological and psychoanalytic terms*. New York, London, and Toronto: Longmans Green, 1958.
7. Fenichel, O. *Psychoanalytic theory of neurosis*. New York: W. W. Norton, 1945.
8. ——. Neurotic acting out. *Psychoanal. Rev., 32,* 197, 1945.
9. Fries, M. E., and Woolf, P. Some hypotheses on the role of the congenital activity type in personality development. *The psychoanalytic study of the child*. Vol. 8, New York: International Universities Press, 1953.

10. Freud, S. *The psychopathology of everyday life.* Chapters 8 and 9, London: Ernest Benn, 1914.
11. ——. Fragment of an analysis of a case of hysteria (Dora). In *Standard edition,* Vol. 7, London: The Hogarth Press, 1953.
12. ——.Further recommendations in the technique of psychoanalysis: Recollection, repetition, and working through. In *Collected papers,* Vol. 2, Chapter 32.
13. Greenacre, P. General problems of acting out. *Psychoanal. Quart.* 1950. *19,* 455.
14. Hinsie, L. E., and Campbell, R. J. *Psychiatric dictionary,* (3rd Ed.) New York: Oxford University Press, 1960.
15. Jacobson, E. Denial and repression, *J. Am. Psychoanal. Ass.,* 1957, 5, 61.
16. Roche, P. Q. Psychiatry and law in the community. In Bellak, L. (Ed.) *Handbook of community psychiatry.* New York: Grune & Stratton, 1963.

2. The Concept of "Acting-In"

By JOHN N. ROSEN, M.D.

> *Dr. John N. Rosen, in a thoughtful and interesting paper, offers his concept of "acting-in" as one coordinate with the older conception of acting out which he feels extends and deepens our understanding of behavior. Rosen uses both concepts to describe and explain the irrationalities encountered in neurotic and psychotic behavior.*
>
> *It is clear from the material that follows that Rosen's "acting-in" refers to behavior that is observed rather than the more subjective processes of dreams.*
>
> *Readers of this chapter will find Rosen's ideas provocative, interesting, and helpful in understanding their own therapeutic encounters.*

"ACTING-IN" is a new psychoanalytic concept that takes its place with Freud's concept of "acting out,"[11] to describe and explain the apparent irrationalities we find in neurotic or psychotic behavior. Acting-in is coordinate with acting out, just as "primary process" is coordinate with "secondary process," or as "unconscious" is coordinate with "conscious." Together, the concepts of acting-in and acting out account for all varieties of human behavior in which the motivation can be traced back to early childhood experience: to an impulse, or wish, that has been repressed until recently and that is still unconscious. In their broadest application, accordingly, acting-in and acting out include not only neurotic or psychotic behavior—i.e., behavior of individuals who are clearly neurotic or psychotic, who require treatment—but also certain kinds of "normal" behavior—i.e., behavior of individuals who are *not* clearly neurotic or psychotic, who do not require treatment. In their more restricted application, however, acting-in and acting out are limited to individuals who are being treated for neurotic or psychotic conditions. Thus, in Hendrick's[16] definition:

> *Acting-out* [is] the neurotic gratification of a repressed wish by compulsive behavior, especially in reacting to another person; used chiefly for acting-out of transference phantasies during psychoanalysis or psychotherapy.

If the psychoanalyst or psychotherapist recognizes that it is psychologically arbitrary to define behavioral phenomena in terms of their occurrence or non-occurrence during treatment, we have no objection to such definitions; they are convenient, and they retain the essence of what a particular behavioral act means to the behaving individual. But it seems that some psychoanalytic writers have neglected or forgotten to show how irrelevant the treatment situation may be to an individual who acts out, or acts-in, during it. Consequently, these writers have described acting out as if it were a kind of non-verbal communication addressed specifically to the psychoanalyst or the psychotherapist,[14] as if the individual were thinking: "I am afraid to put this message into words, but I will enact some charades for you, and perhaps you will see what I mean." Whenever we encounter such representations of supposedly "neurotic" or even "psychotic" behavior, we may suspect that the writer has unconsciously—perhaps consciously—disavowed our psychoanalytic belief in the influence of the past upon the present. Other writers have described acting out as a repetition or re-enactment of some earlier behavior.[8] Although they have recognized the influence of the past upon the present, they seem to have confused cause with effect.

After all, in Freud's original concept of acting out,[12] the impulse is old or repetitious, but the action itself is immediate and more or less original. Unfortunately, even Anna Freud seems to have softened this distinction; in *The Ego and the Mechanisms of Defense,* she has stated:

> The patient ceases to observe the strict rules of analytic treatment and begins to act out in the behavior of his daily life both the instinctual impulses and the defensive reactions which are embodied in his transferred affects.[9]

More recently, Freud's concept has been obscured by the various restatements and redefinitions of his followers. As I remarked in an earlier paper, " 'Acting-Out, and 'Acting-In,' "[24] I will follow the primary definition that I understand to have been Freud's: acting out is an action arising from unconscious and infantile impulses, which are released from repression during psychoanalytic treatment. On the present occasion, I will add the qualifying point that psychoanalytic treatment is not the only situation in which acting out or acting-in can occur. Since *"transference"* is a universal phenomenon, and since it does not require a psychoanalyst or any other particular individual to be its object,[30] acting out and acting-in are also universal.

I introduced the concept of acting-in, originally, in *Direct Psychoanalytic Psychiatry.* There I compared the nightmare and the psychosis, and I went on to say:

> We understand by this concept that a psychotic individual tends to be preoccupied with happenings in an internal, dream-like environment. He acts and reacts with reference to this internal environment as though he were uninfluenced by the happenings of the external environment.[27]

If the psychotherapist has ever experienced a physical assault or other violence on the part of a psychotic individual whom he has been treating, he may object to this formulation. He may be convinced that the behavior was meant only for him, and he may have scars and other hard evidence to support his conviction. He may say, in effect: "The individual had an uncontrollable impulse to attack me, and he acted out his impulse instead of telling me about it." Yet I still say that the psychotherapist is mistaken in this reaction. I maintain that the individual was *acting-in;* he was acting in a dream, acting in reference to an internal environment of which the psychotherapist may have known nothing.

What is this internal environment? In a word, it is "mother." In Freud's structural terms, it is the superego; but for the psychotic individual, the superego is not simply a discrete organization, or structure, or libidinal object, or set of objects, with which the ego has certain kinds of relationships.[33] For the psychotic individual, the superego is more or less ubiquitous, and diffuse. It is a kind of envelopment, a kind of deadly but indispensable atmosphere. It smothers him, yet he cannot get along without it. In various behavioral manifestations of transference, we find expressions of his need for this indispensable, smothering "mother." In the more dramatic and violent instances of acting-in, we find expressions of his frustration and rage. My recent monograph, *The Concept of Early Maternal Environment in Direct Psychoanalysis,*[25] discusses these aspects of the individual's regressive dilemma, and relates them to his neo-natal experience with "the mother he knew"; i.e., the actual mother or the surrogates for her, perceived through the distortions and complications of need, frustration, terror, hallucination, and other occurrences in infancy. Although we can never know what the individual really did experience, during the neo-natal period, we can surmise that there must have been some terrible events, some reality-sources of the individual's life-long imaginations. Perhaps the mother did impose a double-bind upon the infant[1]; or perhaps she was merely insensitive to the infant's needs.[2] In our present state of psychological knowledge, we can only speculate. Eventually, however, our observations of maternal action[3] and of infantile reaction[32] may give us the prototypical pattern for acting out and acting-in.

For the time being, it is my opinion that acting out and acting-in are, basically, *reactions* to the individual's early maternal environment. In my original attempts to make therapeutic contact with individuals who were psychotic, I discovered that such contact necessitates a definite *counteraction* by the psychotherapist. If the psychotic is using his transference to externalize the early maternal environment—to get it "outside," so that he can deal with it as something concrete—then the psychotherapist must use his own feelings, his sympathy and concern for the individual's needs. He must assume the foster-parental responsibilities, the maternal role, in accordance with the governing principle of direct psychoanalysis. I[31] first formulated this principle, somewhat imprecisely, in a paper written nearly two decades ago:

> In the case of direct psychoanalysis the counter-transference [sic] must be of the nature of the feelings a good parent would have for a highly disturbed child. The therapist, like the good parent, must identify with the unhappy child and be so disturbed by the unhappiness of the child that he himself cannot rest until the child is again at peace. Then the parent can again be at peace. If this feeling is present, the patient will *invariably* perceive it unconsciously. This does not mean that the therapist may not react automatically to physical attack, but if the basic unconscious relationship is as described, any conscious reaction [to physical assault] on the part of the therapist will not be misunderstood by the patient as an alteration of the basically sound interplay of feeling.

I would now use the term, *counteraction,* instead of "counter-transference," which was incorrectly used in this formulation of the governing principle. "Counteraction" means a deliberate therapeutic response—sincere, but judicious and controlled—to the individual's dilemma; whereas "counter-transference," according to the *Dictionary of Psychological and Psychoanalytical Terms,* means the arousal of the analyst's repressed feelings by the analytic situation, especially the transference by the analyst of his repressed feelings upon the individual whom he is treating.

Direct psychoanalysis has undergone considerable refinement and sophistication during the past 20 years; however, its therapeutic aims have remained essentially the same as those stated or implied in my first formulations of the governing principle. As I have shown in a forthcoming paper, "The Therapeutic Aims of Direct Psychoanalysis,"[29] these aims can still be described in terms of the therapist's deliberate "foster-parent" attitude toward the psychotic or neurotic individual who has been entrusted to his care.

A few years after I had begun this work, I was able to formulate some additional "general principles" of direct psychoanalysis, and to describe more clearly the therapeutic reactions or counteractions to the psychotic behavior that I later designated as "acting-in." With regard to violent and possibly dangerous behavior, I said: "Having concentrated the patient's attention on the malevolent behavior of his real mother while he is still hazy as to who is who, the therapist often finds the full fury of this free energy turned against himself."[26] At the same time, I called attention to the importance of maintaining control over the treatment situation; for a therapist who lacks this control, or lacks the means of providing it, will inevitably back away from certain kinds of manifest content. He will try to avoid the therapeutic clues and cues that might lead to eruptions of unconscious material—to acting-in, acting out, "abreaction," or whatever he calls these occurrences. In "classical" psychoanalysis, for instance, the would-be therapist may invoke analytic *"rules"* against acting out, instead of providing therapeutic control over the individual's behavior. He may, in the words of Karl Menninger, "overlook and fail to deal with the patient's unconscious or dimly conscious wish to have the analyst interfere in his behavior."[19] This wish does not necessarily represent masochism, or any need to be punished; more often, it represents the universal need of the infant to be held, comforted, reassured that his malevolent rage is not magically destructive—to be protected, ultimately, from himself. Recognition of this need, and action to meet it, are therapeutic functions. In direct psychoanalysis, we deliberately attempt to fulfill these functions. In "classical" or indirect psychoanalysis, these functions are supposed to be beyond the call of analytic responsibility.

My recent monograph, *Psychoanalysis Direct and Indirect,*[28] has dealt extensively with the great contrast between a therapeutic response to an individual's needs, and a mere investigation of circumstances under which his needs might have arisen. Just what is analytic responsibility? Sometimes I get the impression that it is responsibility to psychoanalysis *per se,* or to the beloved memory of Freud, or to the analyst himself. In historical perspective, however, I can see that no self-indulgent psychologies have stood the test of time,[35] and I am encouraged to think that "classical" psychoanalysis will be superseded by semi-classical, *direct* psychoanalysis, if not by a popular psychotherapy for every human being who needs it, regardless of race, creed, national origin, or ability to pay. At this point, I am simply impatient with the timid revisions and the minute modifications of "classical" psychoanalysis.[18] And I am growing tired of periodic protests to the effect that "classical" psychoanalysis really is, or can be, somewhat flexible. A generation has grown old since Fenichel[5] observed:

> For psychotics and children as well as for certain character cases, the 'classical' method must be modified. That procedure is the best which provides the best conditions for the analytic task. A 'nonclassical procedure,' when the classical one is not possible, remains psychoanalysis. It is meaningless to distinguish an 'orthodox' psychoanalysis from an 'unorthodox' one.

Meaningless or not, the distinction has continued to be made; "schools" of psychoanalysis have been divided by it,[20] and members of these schools have been inhibited by it, in their explorations of new therapeutic possibilities.[22]

It is instructive to consider our immediate interests—acting out and acting-in—against this historical background. When Ferenczi and Rank proposed not only to permit acting out behavior, but also to permit a correspondingly active, therapeutic response, Freud[17] issued a circular bulletin to the leaders of the profession; he said in part:

> I find it hard to believe that in . . . four to five months, one can penetrate to the deepest layers of the unconscious and bring about lasting changes in the mind. Naturally, however, I shall bow to experience. Personally I shall continue to make 'classical' analyses, since . . . I am of the opinion that we still have very much to investigate and cannot yet, as is necessary with shortened analyses, rely solely on our premises.

That was forty years ago. *The Development of Psychoanalysis,* the joint monograph by Ferenczi and Rank,[7] has long since fallen into the limbo of psychoanalytic "curiosities." But Freud's objections—which were mild and judicious, under the circumstances, I think—have remained current. The new leaders of the psychoanalytic profession would say that we *still* have very much to learn, that we cannot *yet* rely solely on our premises. I agree. But I would ask these "classical" psychoanalysts if they will ever set a limit, a point of diminishing returns, beyond which they will give over their investigations and get down to the actual responsibilities of treatment. I would ask them, also, how they propose to learn very much about acting out, acting-in, and other kinds of behavior that they refuse either to recognize or to tolerate.

In the course of my own psychoanalysis, which was thorough to say the least, I was exposed to all of the customary, "classical" inhibitions and prohibitions. I was taught, for instance, that "the repetition compulsion is the last resort of the ego in the process of defense. What cannot be attained in any other way is acted out but *not remembered* until a temporary exhaustion of the instinctual energy occurs."[23] Fortunately for me, I did not altogether understand the meaning of such statements. My medical training and subsequent experience had inclined me toward specific cases, away from abstract formulations of "defenses," libido, and so on. When I became a resident in psychiatry, during the early 1940's, I continued to follow my pragmatic inclinations. I more or less stumbled upon the importance of paying close attention to what the psychotic individual says and does—his "manifest content." This was not my exclusive discovery, but it was a radical departure from the traditions of Brooklyn State Hospital, where I was working, and from the traditions of the New York Psychoanalytic Institute, where I had been taking courses. Once I had grasped the profound relevance of Freud's dream-psychology to psychosis, the "connection between a symbol and a symptom,"[10] then I was able to make therapeutic contact with some of the hundreds of state hospital patients. This was how *direct* psychoanalysis originated, far from the serene circumstances in which a "classical" psychoanalyst makes his living.

Essentially, direct psychoanalysis has continued to be a practical application of certain Freudian principles—with some modifications, derived from practical experience. I am still a pragmatist at heart; I have no interest in theoretical constructs or procedural postulates for their own sake. I have no vested interest in *any* construct or postulate. If an idea is clinically useful, I do not accept it or reject it on the basis of its "orthodox" or unorthodox sources. It may come from one extreme of psychoanalysis, in Hartmann's conservative ego-psychology,[15] or it may come from another extreme, in Ferenczi's whimsical formulations of psychical functioning.[6] In either instance, and in all instances, I simply put it to the one test that reliably separates sense from nonsense: the test of therapeutic effectiveness or ineffectiveness with a particular human being, a psychotic or neurotic individual in treatment.

The essential points of direct psychoanalytic theory, all closely related to the "early maternal environment" concept, have been developed along these lines. Component concepts, such as "acting-in," have been fitted one by one into my general understanding of psychosis, neurosis, and the psychotherapeutic relationship. Gradually, the picture becomes clear; the details begin to emerge; the connections between one part and another are apparent. I can see now the connection between psychotic acting-in and psychotherapeutic counteraction: it is not the connection between dreaming and being awakened—for the individual could be jolted awake by any kind of shock treatment. It is, rather, the connection between dreaming in vain and dreaming *not* in vain, between frustration and satisfaction. Ordinarily, the psychotic's dream, or his interminable nightmare, is unlike a normal dream; it is not a wish-fulfillment, but the endless repetition of wishes that can never be fulfilled. There is no wish-fulfilling "mother," in fact, and in the psychotic's fantasy the "mother he knew" is both indispensable and deadly. He cannot fulfill his wish to be reunited with her, unless his wish to survive is simultaneously frustrated. Now the therapeutic intervention of the direct psychoanalyst is properly to be regarded, in one sense, as a participation with the psychotic individual to achieve his wish-fulfillments. These are not wishes for any actual, substantial satisfactions —if they were, then "jelly-bean" therapy would be sufficient. The psychotic's wishes are for imaginary satisfactions; and the knowledgeable psychotherapist can fulfill them at that level. To a very large extent, he can do so verbally; the psychotic individual will accept words for deeds. When the psychotherapist says, for instance, "I am taking care of you," he needs only a few bits of realistic evidence to substantiate his claim; he describes the actual comforts that the individual has been enjoying in the treatment unit: "I give you good, warm food; I protect you from harm; I have these nice people taking care of you," and so on. Let it be clearly understood that the psychotherapist does not lie to the individual whom he is treating. Psychosis is not lying; neither is psychotherapy. Psychosis is acting-in; it is dreaming, wishing for impossible or incompatible satisfactions. Psychotherapy, for the psychotic individual, untangles these incompatibilities and makes possible—i.e., imaginable—these satisfactions.

Much more could be said about the connection between psychotic acting-in and psychotherapeutic counteraction. Yet it appears that something should be said, as well, about the mistaken representations of this connection. For instance, an attempt was made recently to represent this connection in terms of learning theory.[21] As a description, it was meager; as an explanation, it failed to illuminate. In some sense, the direct psychoanalyst is a kind of teacher: he educates or reeducates the individual concerning the parent-child relationship and the emotional problems related to it. But the psychotic individual is not, in any sense, a student. Like the drowning man who has no time for swimming lessons, the psychotic individual has no time for psychology lessons. He is desperate; he is devoting his full time and his full energies to finding an immediate solution of an insoluble problem. Accordingly, psychotherapeutic "teaching" is only a euphemism for rescue work and first aid. To stretch this euphemism, to say that the psychotherapist uses "rewards" and "punishments" as a behaviorist would do with a laboratory animal, is not to cover the fundamental characteristics of the therapeutic process. The better approach, and the more difficult one, is to take psychotherapy on its own terms—or to provide new and appropriate terms, if necessary—so that it can be evaluated scientifically. In this direction, some progress has been made.[4] Further progress awaits the psychologist or the behavioral scientist who is himself dedicated to the work at hand.

We would do well to remember that, for centuries, progress literally awaited the coming of Freud. Before him, many psychologists and philosophers had "discovered" the unconscious mind[34]; they had at least recognized its existence, and they had even managed to describe its general characteristics. But they failed, for various reasons, to approach it closely enough; it was within them, of course, yet they consciously kept their distance from it. These pre-Freudians treated the unconscious mind like an interesting, amusing, possibly dangerous pet. It remained for Freud to close this distance, to demonstrate the psychopathology of everyday life,[13] and to demonstrate the immediacy of the unconscious mind in all human life, sleeping or waking. After Freud, it remains for us to do relatively little. Our concepts and our hypotheses, all too often, are but footnotes in the great texts of his achievement.

REFERENCES

1. Bateson, G. Discussion of the "double-bind" concept. In C. Whitaker (Ed.) *Psychotherapy of chronic schizophrenic patients.* Boston: Little, Brown, 1958. Pp. 31-56.
2. Brody, Sylvia. *Patterns of mothering.* New York: International Universities Press, 1956.
3. Deutsch, Helene. *The psychology of women.* Vol. 2, *Motherhood.* New York: Grune & Stratton, 1945.
4. English, O. S. Clinical observations on direct analysis. In O. S. English, W. W. Hampe, Jr., Catherine L. Bacon, and C. F. Settlage (Eds.). *Direct analysis and schizophrenia.* New York: Grune & Stratton, 1961. Pp. 1-41.
5. Fenichel, O. *The psychoanalytic theory of neurosis.* New York: Norton, 1945.
6. Ferenczi, S. The psyche as an inhibiting organ [1922]. In *Further contributions to the theory and technique of psycho-analysis.* London: Hogarth Press and Institute of Psycho-Analysis, 1960. Pp. 379-383.
7. Ferenczi, S., and Rank, O. *The development of psychoanalysis* [1923]. New York and Washington: Nervous and Mental Disease Publishing Co., 1925.
8. Fliess, R. *Erogeneity and libido.* New York: International Universities Press, 1956.
9. Freud, Anna. *The ego and the mechanisms of defense* [1936]. New York: International Universities Press, 1946.
10. Freud, S. A connection between a symbol and a symptom [1916]. In *Collected papers,* Vol. 2. New York: Basic Books, 1959. Pp. 162-163.
11. ——. Further recommendations in the technique of psychoanalysis. Recollection, repetition and working through [1914]. In *Collected papers,* Vol. 2. New York: Basic Books, 1959. Pp. 366-376.
12. ——. *An outline of psychoanalysis* [1940]. New York: Norton, 1949.
13. ——. *The psychopathology of everyday life* [1901.] New York: Macmillan, 1914.
14. Fromm-Reichmann, Frieda. Psychoanalytic psychotherapy with psychotics: the influence of modifications in technique on present trends in psychoanalysis [1943]. In D. M. Bullard (Ed.) *Psychoanalysis and psychotherapy.* Selected papers of Frieda Fromm-Reichmann. Chicago: University of Chicago Press, 1959. Pp. 133-136.
15. Hartmann, H. *Ego psychology and the problem of adaptation* [1939]. New York: International Universities Press, 1958.
16. Hendrick, I. *Facts and theories of psychoanalysis* (3rd. Ed.). New York: Knopf, 1958.
17. Jones, E. *The life and work of Sigmund Freud,* Vol. 3. New York: Basic Books, 1957.
18. Lorand, S. Modifications in classical psychoanalysis. *Psychoanal. Quart.,* 1963, *32,* 192-204.
19. Menninger, K. *Theory of psychoanalytic technique.* New York: Basic Books, 1958.
20. Munroe, Ruth L. *Schools of psychoanalytic thought.* New York: Holt, 1955.
21. Murray, E. J. Direct analysis from the viewpoint of learning theory. *J. consult. Psychol.,* 1962, *26,* 226-231.
22. Nacht, S. The non-verbal relationship in psycho-analytic treatment. *Int. J. Psycho-Anal.,* 1963, *44,* 328-333.

23. Nunberg, H. *Principles of psychoanalysis* [1932]. New York: International Universities Press, 1955.
24. Rosen, J. N. "Acting-out" and "acting-in." *Amer. J. Psychotherapy,* 1963, *17,* 390-403.
25. ———. *The concept of early maternal environment in direct psychoanalysis.* Doylestown, Penna.: The Doylestown Foundation, 1963.
26. ———. Direct analysis: general principles. In *Direct analysis: selected papers.* New York: Grune & Stratton, 1953. Pp. 1-27.
27. ———. *Direct psychoanalytic psychiatry.* New York: Grune & Stratton, 1962.
28. ———. *Psychoanalysis direct and indirect.* Doylestown, Penna.: The Doylestown Foundation, 1964.
29. ———. The therapeutic aims of direct psychoanalysis. In A. R. Mahrer and J. R. Thompson (Eds.) *The goals of psychotherapy.* New York: Appleton-Century-Crofts. In press.
30. ———. Transference: a concept of its origin, its purpose and its fate. *Neth. Acta Psychotherapeutica,* 1954, *2,* 300-314.
31. ———. The treatment of schizophrenic psychosis by direct analytic therapy. *Psychiat. Quart.,* 1947, *21,* 3-37, 117-119.
32. Rubinfine, D. L. Maternal stimulation, psychic structure, and early object relations—with special reference to aggression and denial. In Ruth S. Eissler et al. (Eds.) *The Psychoanalytic Study of the Child,* Vol. 17. New York: International Universities Press, 1962. Pp. 265-282.
33. Sullivan, C. T. *Freud and Fairbairn: two theories of ego-psychology.* Doylestown, Penna.: The Doylestown Foundation, 1963.
34. Whyte, L. L. *The unconscious before Freud.* New York: Basic Books, 1960.
35. Zilboorg, G. *A history of medical psychology.* New York: Norton, 1941.

3. Andre Gide: Acting Out and the Creative Imagination

By MARK KANZER, M.D.

> *Dr. Mark Kanzer, in the material that follows, suggests that the specific form of romance that each individual wants to work out for himself may involve acting out, neurosis, or sublimation, and that commonly there are alternations and patterns among these possibilities. In studying the vicissitudes of romance, Kanzer chooses as his topic for exploration the literary works of Andre Gide, thus providing the reader with a deep and intuitive appreciation of Gide as a personality and also as the creator of important literary works.*
>
> *The result of Kanzer's inquiry is a fruitful marriage between what he knows about acting out and what he understands about the nature of the creative process.*

"EVER LET THE FANCY ROAM, pleasure never is at home," commented the poet. The flight into reality, whether in fancy or action, has always been an impetus to myth formation, to the adventure story, and to the wanderings of the adventuresome myth-makers themselves in self-imposed exile from one land to another. The "family romance" is inherently the point of departure for all these tendencies; the imaginary flight from family ties, which characteristically succeeds the frustrations of the oedipal phase in the growing child, may become the predisposition to outward displacements of dreams and actions in later years.

Characteristically, the family romance reveals its oedipal origins in the "birth of a hero fantasy"[12] whose basic ingredients are: (1) the departure of the hero on a more or less conscious mission; (2) the arrival in a strange land which is suffering from an oppressive monster; (3) a reward offered by the king including the hand of his daughter and half the kingdom, to the man who shall destroy the monster; and (4) the ordeal, victory, and triumphant home-coming of the hero. The precipitating cause of the fantasy is often the birth of a younger sibling. Details vary; the underlying unconscious theme combines the destruction of the unwanted sibling and the father and the winning of the mother. The mark of the superego is already deeply entrenched in these events; father and sibling are spared direct aggression and mother direct sexual conquest, so that at the end, the real family is portrayed as hailing proudly the offspring who has directed his menacing drives into socially approved channels.

The specific form of the romance that each individual works out for himself may involve acting out, neurosis, or sublimation[9]; more commonly, there are alternations and patterns among these possibilities. Such conflicting tendencies are commonly demonstrable in the lives of writers and bear significantly on the origin and meaning of their creative works. Sometimes, these are largely autobiographical reports of the drives that have compelled their wanderings and unconscious quests, as for example with Herman Melville, Jack London, Joseph Conrad, Eugene O'Neill, and Ernest Hemingway. The themes of good and evil, of sin and redemption, emerge more and more clearly from the adventures, along with a disposition to introspection and a questioning of the nature of the universe, which reveal their origins in infantile sex curiosity. The later works of such adventure writers may become increasingly philosophical and religious; the persons, places and actions of the earlier narratives then prove to have been symbols of internal conflicts that forced the author, Ulysses-like, to turn homeward for the last battle.

The real or imaginary wanderings of the writer and his succession of frustrated heroes may be less overtly adventuresome and more introspective from the start, as in the case of the self-exiled Henry James. Homer, Shakespeare, Dante, Dostoyevsky, Ibsen, and Joyce are among those who illustrate, in various ways, inherent relationships between homelessness and the creatively transformed dream of the return. Frequently, a journey may be the occasion for taking inner as well as outer distance from the self; subsequently, there are changes in personality and writings that attest to a crisis and transformation. Thomas Mann,[10] assaying Goethe's Italian trip from this standpoint, might well have provided the illustration from his own autobiographically conceived Aschenbach in *Death in Venice*.

The minutes of the Vienna Psychoanalytic Society[11] show an interesting discussion of this problem in a meeting on Feb. 6, 1907, devoted to a review by Wilhelm Stekel of a book by Dr. K. Williams, *On the Psychopathology of the Vagabond*. It was Otto Rank, already well advanced on his monumental work, *The Incest Motive in Poetry and Saga,* and soon to publish *The Myth of the Birth of the Hero,* who called attention to the vagrant tendencies of many writers and artists. He declared that inclination to become a writer often manifests itself first during travels, as does neurosis. Rank linked both these characteristics with the flight from family life and saw them as outwardly, as well as inwardly, directed defenses against the oedipal desires. Freud accepted this explanation and suggested that paranoia, disposing to a severance from objects (narcissism and projection), favored the recourse to travel, while the hysterically-inclined, clinging to his love objects, was more disposed to neurosis. Certainly, the typical adventure of the hero, with its underlying ambivalence and search for God, the Creator, tends to be dominated by the homosexual tendencies of superego formation during the latency period. The heroines have little real character; Theseus finally deserts Ariadne, Jason does the same with Medea, and the Western hero rides off into the sunset to find a different girl to rescue on the morrow.

The life and works of Andre Gide reveal, in much detail, the alternation between writing and travel as interrelated solutions of these tendencies. The nuclear role of unusually intense overt masturbation during the oedipal period, subdued only temporarily and with great difficulty during the latency phase, has been documented with remarkable thoroughness in the analytically insightful biography by Jean Delay.[3] The boy's severe childhood neurosis represented conflicting loyalties in a home where the superego was bound to be built about a domineering and puritanical Huguenot mother and the love object by a mild and undemanding father who died when the child was ten. There were no brothers or sisters to whom the lonely Andre could divert his interest; moreover, he was excluded from school and playmates because of his uncontrollable masturbation even before the father died. Predictably, he was left to nourish erotic and anxious fantasies that derived predominantly from the negative oedipus complex.

From spending most of his time in reading, he advanced to story-telling of his own. At 15, this took the form of attempting to seduce a friend through the proposition that each reveal to the other "everything" about himself. The other blushingly declined, and the friendship ended. Seductive exhibitionism was next deflected to the more indirect route of literature when Andre undertook to keep a diary, written on a desk set up before a mirror. "At that time I felt I could not write, I almost said think, except in front of that little mirror," Gide later reminisced[3]; "in order to become aware of my emotions, of my thoughts, I felt I had first to read them in my eyes. Like Narcissus, I bent over my own image; therefore, all the sentences I wrote at the time were also somewhat bent."

Thus began the magical maneuvers, the slightly modified masturbatory practices and fantasies that were aimed to conjure up for himself an externalized Double who would share with him directly, where a real boy would not, in his preferred gratifications. Certain modifications had to be made to suit the censor. Reliving the appropriately self-chosen application of the legend of Narcissus to himself, Andre found his nymph, Echo, in a first cousin, Madeleine, some two years older than himself. She was a Double whose reflection in the mirror would equip him with a female body and also with a successor to the mother with whom he more fundamentally identified.

She also offered a link, however insubstantial, between his fantasy life and the world of reality. At first, in a dreamy and impractical manner, he idealized her and, as he reached the age of 20, proposed marriage. Both Madeleine and his mother recognized his immaturity and scouted the idea. Out of this situation grew his first book, *The Journal of Andre Walter,* which was designed to prove his seriousness and overcome their opposition. It was thus a literary version of the traditional "ordeal" of the hero.

As its title implied, it was an exhibitionistic display of his real diary, somewhat romantically transformed. In essence, it described a young man who, deprived of his beloved by the taboo of a dying mother (so much for Mme. Gide!), cultivated his taste for literature, art, philosophy, and religion, but finally succumbed more and more to onanism until he lost his sanity and died as the pure snow was falling.

Even this cogent statement failed to move either Madeleine or the mother, though the latter was prevailed upon to pay for the cost of publishing the book. It was a success in Parisian literary circles and permitted Andre to venture a bit beyond the pond of Narcissus. In so doing, he left behind him the outworn personality of Andre Walter and adopted the pose of a youthful esthete, complete with long flowing hair and eccentric clothes. He would study his face in the same mirror before which he wrote and, to prepare himself for his public, "would gaze upon my features untiringly, study them, train them like an actor, and I searched my lips and my eyes for the expression of all the passions I hoped to feel."[3]

Many actors and artists share with the imposter the "as if" character and the search for identity, sexual and otherwise, as well as the exhibitionism of the perpetual teenager. Gide now completed his pose from the literary standpoint (along with more genuine self-searching that characterized him) in a new book, *An Essay on Narcissus,* which in the Oscar Wildean fashion of the time, celebrated art as an end in itself and a sufficient content in life. Simultaneously, however, his imagination was striking out in an entirely different direction in *Le Voyage d'Urien.* This pre-existentialist work on the experience of nothingness found him still onanistic and beset with fears of losing his mind. He had recently spent some months in Munich to savor new surroundings, but also, as it turned out, to prepare himself for a break with his mother. He refused to use letters of introduction she had procured for him, reproached her for coming between Madeleine and himself and, on his return to Paris, took up independent lodgings rather than continue to reside at home.

The voyage of "Urien," in the fashion of the family romance, portrays the hero in the company of friends, seeking to escape from study and "anguish" by setting forth on the ship Orion—named for the hunter who, coming upon the moon goddess, Artemis, bathing in a forest pool, was transformed into a deer and torn apart by her dogs. They sail on a succession of imaginary waters (in an apparent urinary fantasy): the Sargasso Sea, the Pathetic Ocean, the Sea of Ice. Dangerous temptresses appear, including an obligatory queen for the family romance; castrating symbols loom up in conjunction with these women: crabs, "cruel" crayfish, poisons and pestilence. Madeleine makes her appearance as "Ellis"; if not cruel, she is certainly exasperating and insubstantial, so that Urien deserts her (a plain warning). The voyage ends with Urien and his companions trapped in a cake of ice from which they seek to escape by digging corridors and staircases within it.

The following year, Andre was still seeking an escape from the ice when he wrote *La Tentative Amoureuse,* which proved again the impossibility of imagining a consummated love with a woman. It did, however, reveal the depths of his inner penetration, which in later years made him at least partially receptive to Freud's teachings. His successive books, he recognized, served essentially as "postponed temptations" which in the meantime molded his personality so that he was impelled to seek realistic satisfactions. Instead of age-specific action, as during the maturation of normal youth, he experienced a prolonged process of introversion, daydreaming, and the acting out of narcissistic fantasies. His drives, in the course of this, underwent too serious a distortion to find love objects in the real world other than those that externalized his infantile self.

Nevertheless, imagination, as experimental action, had prepared him for the last step. The *Voyage of Urien* materialized in the company of a friend, Paul Laurens, also something of a Narcissus, but with only conscious heterosexual goals. The course was now set opposite to the Sea of Ice; the young men chose Africa. They discovered abundant opportunities for sexual satisfaction; Andre at first shared a female dancer with Paul but finally settled for Arabian boys as "normal" for himself. This decision had been adumbrated in passages both in *Andre Walter* and *Urien* and materialized into a mutual onanism that seemed to solve the problem of Narcissus: at last he could touch himself.

Nevertheless, mother was involved in all this, too, and autoerotism was not the final inner goal. Mother (and her alter ego Madeleine) had been the involuntary witnesses to his exhibitionistic masturbation when he compelled them to read *Andre Walter*. Now mother was brought down to Africa, through a combination of circumstances that largely represented seductive maneuvers by Andre, so that his affair with the dancer could be flaunted before her. When she broke into tears, he gave up the only heterosexual activity that ever seemed to have given him satisfaction.

Mother had also been brought into his nascent homosexual development when, at his request, she was induced to send him quantities of toys from Paris with which he went about winning friendships among little Arabs in whom he was developing an interest. Two years later, on a second trip to Africa and with his sexual proclivities now well established, he wrote to Mme. Gide that he was bringing home a 15 year old Arab "servant." There ensued a crisis in which the mother wrote frantic letters arguing against this and encountered in return only obdurate insistence on the part of her son. Andre threatened to keep the boy in his room, if mother could find no other place in the house, or to move elsewhere with him. In addition to showing such preference for his young lover, he gave evidence of a still older oedipal triangle when he remarked that he did not understand how his father had put up with her. Returning with the boy would not only have restored a father-son union to the home and displaced mother sexually; it would also have fulfilled a "birth-of-the-hero fantasy" in which Andre, not mother, had produced the child. The resistances of reality were too great; the traveller returned alone.

Mme. Gide died soon after this episode, and Andre finally married Madeleine, taking her along thereafter on his wanderings in an unconsummated union. The desire to procreate children was transferred to his books, with which he sometimes described himself as being pregnant. Now it was the world, not just mother or Madeleine, that he sought to shake with his exhibitionistically displayed and even glorified adventures. This was accomplished with the next installment of his development history to which he gave the title *Fruits of the Earth* after an exhilarating night which he spent with Oscar Wilde and two young musicians they brought back to their hotel.

His reflected image in the new book was that of a nomadic sage who takes his delights without qualms wherever he finds them. This hero is, in fact, a messiah who preaches that it is man's duty to find pleasure, for therein lies salvation. The life and words of Christ, himself, provide the model for this precise inversion of Mme. Gide's puritanical teachings. Her son at last had found a superego that was "normal for him."

Gide also applied the new doctrine to his own craft, literature. Sensing correctly a bond between himself and Dostoyevsky, whose nomadic escapades had taken the form of gambling sprees to Germany, he found himself quoting with approval the Russian novelist's opinion that "improvement makes straight roads; but the crooked roads without improvement are roads of Genius".[8] To this Gide offered his own corollaries, phrased in aphoristic tones reminiscent of Wilde and Nietzsche: "Fine feelings are the stuff that bad literature is made on"; "The Fiend is a party to every work of art"; "There are no artists among the saints, no saints among the artists"; "There are three threads in the loom on which every work of art is woven: the lust of the flesh, the lust of the eyes and the pride of life." William Blake was also drawn upon for support: "The true Poet is of the

Devil's party without knowing it." Gide, of course, was insisting that the poet should know it, though he was obliged to admit certain limitations: "les motifs secrets de nos actes nous echappes."[4]

COMMENT

The hero and the criminal, Freud found,[5] were related as rebels against God. He especially had in mind Prometheus, whose defiance of Zeus was an oedipal act cloaked by social motives—the traditional revolt of the eldest son and the brother band against the tyrannical father who hoards for himself the sexual fire. The subsequent suffering of the hero terminates the family romance on a note of defeat and expiation, the typical fate of the neurotic son.

The writer, who dreams of himself as tragic hero, may share the disposition to crime. Freud emphasized the link between Dostoyevsky and his criminal heroes[6]; in safety, the writer may indulge for himself and his readers the antisocial daydreams that are actually carried out by the heroes. Freud implicated in the Russian his "boundless egotism," his oedipal fantasies, and the masturbatory conflicts that were displaced into a gambling mania which was also an appeal to his mother to save him from self-destruction by yielding herself sexually. We recognize this note in *Andre Walter* as well.

Kenneth Burke[1] commented that "a tragedy is not profound unless the poet imagines the crime—and in thus imagining it, symbolically commits it." For illustration, it was to Gide that he turned, the writer for whom "Thou shalt not" became compulsively transformed into the thought, "what would happen if"—a gateway that proved open to the return of the repressed not only for his fantasies but for his actions. Burke quite accurately called Gide "a specialist in the portrayal of scrupulous criminals, who has developed a stylistic trend for calling to seduction in the aspects of evangelism and who advises that one should learn to 'travel light.'"

Fowlie[4] speaks in a similar vein when he calls Gide's characters "surrealistic heroes whose goal is to commit a gratuitous act, without motivation" in order to express the schizoid split in his character. The lack of motivation is only apparent; the hero contrives to find the situation in which the "happening" is both wished and contrived without the need to accept guilt for planning it. His wandering is part of the disguise for the act which in his unconscious he is performing at home. In this instance, the repressed impulse was the heterosexual ingredient that was hidden in his homosexual behavior.

To state Gide's problem metapsychologically, it would seem to us that the masturbatory conflicts and fantasies of the young Gide were determined by excessively severe castration anxiety related to the dominating, yet alluring, figure of the mother. Resolution occurred along lines common among homosexuals: denial mechanisms were employed to convert her into a phallic female whom he could establish as the basis for his superego identifications. In turn, he projected his own oedipal self onto the boys that he seduced as he wished that his mother had seduced him. Alternately, the mother was superego and temptress, provided that her genitals could be regarded as masculine. Gide, as the nomadic messiah, was the phallic mother imperfectly desexualized for her superego function; the compulsive sexuality that she required was the result of the return of the repressed which she could not effectively ward off. When Gide looked in the mirror of onanism or homosexuality, he saw the oedipal boy he once had been; what he did not see—and here his vision and his understanding remained always "bent"—was his own disguise as the mother in the sex act, as the mother in the birth act, and the mother in the role of religious mentor.

The mirror-searching Gide provides us with the increasingly common example of the modern writer who has gathered some knowledge of psychoanalysis, and even dabbled in therapy, to supplement the forces that drive him to seek self-understanding. With the fragmenting that was characteristic of him, he sought analysis from Mme. Sokolnicka, described by Delay as a Czech disciple of Freud, who was living in Paris; after four sessions, he terminated treatment but safely permitted the analysis to continue in a book, *The Counterfeiters*.[8] Here Mme. Sokolniska was sufficiently idealized to be represented as Sophroniska (from the Greek root for wisdom) and was assigned the task of reliving a period in the life of young Andre to discover whether she might really have helped him at that time. The result was suicide.

In *The Counterfeiters*, the 13 year old Boris is depicted clearly enough as Andre, though perhaps with a year or two added to his age. He is an effeminate misfit in a boarding school, a former compulsive masturbator who has become a tangle of nervous symptoms since giving up his sexual habits. His mother had discovered his activities and reproached him severely; what had really been decisive was the death of his beloved father, which Boris came to believe was due to shock and grief over his masturbation. (This link between autoerotic practices and the idea of the father's death is a frequent disguise for a death wish toward the sexual rival for the mother.)

Sophroniska disapproves of Boris' mother and her unenlightened behavior, it is true, but possesses many of her driving qualities and her uncompromising sense of righteousness. We learn little of the "disciple's" professional qualifications or methods; child analysis as a specialty had scarcely dawned at the time, and there were few competent analysts except

Freud himself. We do not know on what basis "Sophroniska" claimed to be an analyst at all. Nevertheless, she does relieve Boris of his symptoms, and he falls in love with her daughter Bronja, two years older than himself (as Madeleine with Andre). The death of Bronja sets off a chain reaction which leads Boris to relapse into masturbation and then suicide. The final act occurs in the presence of his grandfather and with the latter's pistol. As the boy approaches the old man with the weapon following the death of Bronja, the parricidal motive comes close to the surface of consciousness; then Boris turns the weapon against himself in the context of a superego punishment for the all but uncontrollable oedipal drives. The pulling of the trigger is a substitute masturbatory act which converts his shameful practices into a gesture of noble and pitiable expiation; the exhibitionistic satisfaction is, however, retained.

Edouard, a young novelist and the narrator in *The Counterfeiters,* is the contemporary Gide, just as Boris is the revived image of his childhood. He, too, enters into discussions with Sophroniska, which probably resemble the real discussions of the novelist with Mme. Sokolnicka and bring up the habitual defense of the creative artist against psychoanalysis: reason alone will not satisfy the inner needs of man (as though analysis were merely an exercise of reason!). Yet one may suspect that it was less a matter of protecting his mysterious needs than of fleeing from them; the mother transference was already operative, and the relapse into masturbatory self-destruction, sublimated through art, seemed preferable to an analytic process that threatened to produce a Freudian substitute for the mother's Huguenot evangelism. Mme. Sokolnicka, a strange analyst indeed, even inveighs against masturbation because it promotes "laziness." Nevertheless, Boris, before his suicide, momentarily achieves an embrace within her maternal arms.

The suicidal sacrifices that Gide himself underwent "for art" exercised their deleterious effects upon his capacities for self-fulfillment in this medium as well as in sex. A need to present his diary to the public—the repetitious incentive for his ventures into print—made writing an appendage to perversity and sexual acts a preliminary to self-exposure through literature. Gide could not explore character deeply, for true motivation had to be hidden from himself as well as others. He became a natural pioneer of surrealism, and his hero, Lafcadio, longed "to commit a gratuitous act, an act having no motivation and no reason."[4] He is, in fact, "the unadaptable man, the wanderer," the split personality who seeks different guises and different partners in a perennial attempt to discover and affirm himself.

Yet this self was not allowed to come into being. Sexual action and literary elaboration are too intimately fused to permit the separate development of either. On the brink of sexual fulfillment, the artist in Gide causes him to "meet, in the moment of forgetting himself, the moment that recalls him to himself," while conversely in his art, as he drives toward "the extreme point of innovation, the strangest boldness of spirit, he meets a regret and a taste for measure and equilibrium" that ruins the experiment.[2] Perhaps it is more just to see in Gide, as does Fowlie, not an unsuccessful literary Eros but rather an authentic representation of the Narcissus myth and the form it assumes in art.

SUMMARY

Acting out of fantasy life has always been a fertile source of creative literature. Yet, the goal of the acting out can not be the external satisfactions that are imagined, experienced, and reported; it can only be the inner desire from which the adventurer flees to substitute fulfillments that can only leave him frustrated and confused. The heroes of the "family romance" like Ulysses, Theseus, and Jason shed their glamorous princesses as they painfully make their way home. Some of the chroniclers become more introverted and symbolic as they turn inward for the true self-discoveries that are so difficult to attain without assistance. The life and works of Andre Gide reveal in unusual detail the meaning of the Narcissus myth when applied to the arts in this connection.

REFERENCES

1. Burke, K. *The philosophy of literary form.* New York: Vintage Books, 1957.
2. Cook, A. *The meaning of fiction.* Detroit: Wayne State University Press, 1960.
3. Delay, J. *The youth of Andre Gide.* Chicago: U. of Chicago Press, 1963. P. 196.
4. Fowlie, W. *Age of surrealism, U.S.A.;* New York: The Swallow Press, 1950.
5. Freud, S. Civilized Sexual Morality and Modern Nervous Illness. *Standard Edition,* Vol. IX, pp. 177-204. London: Hogarth Press, 1959.
6. ———. Dostoevsky and Parricide. *Standard Edition,* Vol. XXI, pp. 175-198. Hogarth Press, 1961.
7. Gide, A. *Dostoevsky.* Norfolk, Conn.: New Directions, 1949.
8. ———. *The Counterfeiters.* New York: The Modern Library, 1955.
9. Kanzer, M. Acting Out, Sublimation and Reality Testing. *J. Amer. Psychoanalyt. Asso.,* Vol. V, Oct. 1957, pp. 663-684.
10. Mann, T. *Last essays.* New York: A. A. Knopff, 1959.
11. *Minutes of the Vienna psychoanalytic society,* Vol. 1, 1906-8. Edit. H. Nunberg and E. Federn. New York: Intern. Univ. Press, 1962.
12. Rank, O. *The myth of the birth of the hero.* New York: Robert Brunner, 1952.

4. "Acting Out" or "Working Through?"

By RICHARD C. ROBERTIELLO, M.D.

Dr. Richard C. Robertiello wishes to draw a sharp distinction between acting out and working through. It is his view that much of what one sees, both within therapy and in the larger area of living, is more clearly to be understood as working through than as acting out.

Robertiello sees working through as a process essential for personality growth and change and, in common with acting out, having to do with experiencing and repeating unconscious wishes from childhood that emerge into awareness. The distinction is an important one, and is useful to consider in relation to acting out itself.

LET US BEGIN with some definitions and clarifications. When a patient is in analysis, certain repressed childhood impulses begin to break out of the unconscious. One of the ways that this can occur is that the patient begins to see present situations in which he is involved as very similar to the past situations connected with his repressed impulse. "Acting out" occurs when a patient views a present situation as similar or parallel to a past one and then tries to gratify the unconscious wish from childhood in the present situation. An important element, however, is that his action in the present situation, though it may be quite inappropriate, is ego-syntonic and is usually rationalized as being appropriate. In this way the unconscious childhood wish is gratified, but at the same time the nature of the childhood impulse continues to be repressed, that is—kept out of consciousness. The past events are not remembered, and there is no insight gained—merely a repetition in the present of some past emotion.

Of course, this is what one expects to occur in transference to the analyst in the analytic situation prior to the analyst's interpretation of it. Thus the appearance of the repressed impulse is essential to the analytic process and to the patient's getting insight. However, it is valuable only if the patient is amenable to seeing the inappropriateness of his action and subsequently to uncovering the nature of the childhood situation that he is repeating. In "acting out" the repetition occurs outside of the transference to the analyst and is usually so strongly rationalized that the patient does not acquire consciousness of the inappropriateness, which in turn would lead him to the past events or feelings that he is reliving. The term "acting-in" has also been used to describe behavior that occurs and reoccurs within the transference to the analyst, but is still rationalized consistently by the patient and never seen as inappropriate, so that it does not lead to insight or a consciousness of the original childhood traumatic situation.

The important issues then in acting out are (1) the gratification of a childhood unconscious impulse in a present situation which has some parallels or similarities to the original situation and (2) the maintenance of the repression through the patient's not seeing the present day behavior as inappropriate, or at least, his viewing it as ego-syntonic and not connecting it with reliving a past situation. Both of these conditions are essential to calling a piece of behavior acting out. As we shall see later, one of the confusions is that a piece of behavior is sometimes mistakingly referred to as acting out even if it does not continue to maintain repression.

Now, what about "working through." "Working through" consists of demonstrating over and over again, the unconscious impulse from childhood in all its different forms and expressions. In the process of doing this, the impulse becomes conscious, the defenses against it are diminished since they are no longer needed, and the impulse falls under the control of the ego. "Working through," thus, is an essential part of growth and change in the analytic situation. Without it there can be no real change. "Working through" is somewhat parallel to the attempt to master an impulse through repetition that is seen in children's play or the repetitive dreams in the traumatic neuroses.

THEORY OF ACTING OUT

From this it is clear that the theoretical question that is posed is: Is a piece of behavior "acting out" or is it "working through." On the surface the answer would seem to be a simple one. If the impulse is conscious or at least very close to consciousness so that it can fairly easily be under the control of the ego, we have "working through." If it is unconscious and repression is maintained, we have "acting out." However, clinically it is often not so clear-cut as it would theoretically appear to be. Besides this, the same piece of behavior will be called "acting out" by one analyst and "working through" by another. Some analysts tend to encourage the patient's experiencing his impulses, as in experiential group therapy or psychodrama. Other analysts feel that the less dramatization and experiencing of impulses goes on, the more effective the therapy. The latter feel that all or at least most of the expression of the impulse should be limited to the transference between the patient and the analyst. This leads to radically different views in both therapy and practice. In general, the more classical and conservative approach has been to contain the impulses and restrict them as much as possible to the transference, no matter whether they are conscious or unconscious. But analysts using newer techniques feel that there is not enough expression of affect in the transference to the analyst alone. They feel that the "working through" that occurs in the transference is often too watered down and too intellectual. So they provide group therapy as a vehicle for expressing or experiencing the emotions or even openly encourage the patient to experience or express the irrational childhood emotions in his life situation up to the point where some irreversible harm might be done. With a relatively healthy neurotic patient, there can be a great deal of experiencing of irrational feelings without drastic deleterious effects on his real life situation.

Another problem in defining "acting out" versus "working through" is that "acting out" has become a rather standard cliché or "dirty word" among analysts to describe any behavior in a patient (or for that matter friend, relative, or popular figure) of which they disapprove on moral grounds. This is especially true of any non-conforming sexual behavior, but it also applies to non-conforming behavior in general. The analytic profession is rather strongly rooted in middle class morality and conservative behavior. Most analysts lead lives that are quite conventional. So the term "acting out" is applied to any piece of behavior that does not fit into their particular ways of living, regardless of whether it is connected with the expression of an unconscious childhood wish while simultaneously maintaining repression of it, or *not*.

For instance, *not* having a sexual relationship may be used in the service of expressing an unconscious wish from childhood in the same way that having an unconventional sexual relationship may be used. Let us take as an example a woman who avoids men and stays home to take care of her widowed mother. She rationalizes that men are not attractive to her and that her mother needs her. Actually she may be gratifying her infantile wish to stay close to mother and be protected by her while at the same time avoiding consciousness of this wish. The whole field is clouded by some rather transparent moralizing on the part of therapists. We must be very aware of our own submission to authority and our own tendencies to keep our patients well-behaved asexual little children as much as we must be aware of our encouraging them unconsciously to be the bad dirty little children we may have wanted to be. The latter is stressed frequently; the former much less so. We must remember that our aim is to help the patient uncover his unconscious and thus lift repression. This process often can be aided by the patient's experiencing feeling and indulging in action. Experiencing, however, may be therapeutic in more areas than repression alone.

Let me give an example of an incident in a group that brings out the contrast between "acting out" and "working through." A girl in one of my groups had been dealing in her individual therapy with feelings of penis envy and an idea that her body was ugly and deformed because she did not have a penis. This feeling also extended to her mind. Just as she felt her body was defective because of her lack of a penis, and this led to her being afraid to expose herself to men and to sexual involvements, similarly she felt her mind was also defective and that she had to hide herself from people's knowing her thoughts as well, or she would be rejected as defective. This led to her being very silent and not self-revealing in the group. She was this way for about a year until she uncovered the root of the problem in her accompanying individual therapy. One day in her group therapy she started talking about a desire to remove her clothes. She was aware that this was connected with her feelings of penis envy and consequent dislike of her body and need to hide it. She had a great impulse to take all her clothes off in group and proceeded to do so. In doing so, she faced her anxiety about exposure and to a certain degree conquered it. After that incident she was able to express herself better verbally and to be less closed and shy. This piece of behavior was to my mind "working through" *not* "acting out," despite the fact that it was unusual, sexual in a broad sense and, very unconventional. It was not used to maintain repression. The group's reaction to it was not a particularly sexual one. Most of the other members understood the symbolic meaning of the act and dealt with it on that level.

One of the other members in the group, a man, also undressed immediately after the girl did. For him, it was a piece of "acting out." He was not involved in any problem that had to do with exposure. He simply could not tolerate the idea of another group member's getting more attention than he. He rationalized his behavior along the lines of his being free and able to do what he felt like doing. However, he was rationalizing and maintaining repression of his impulse from childhood to defeat his sibling in a competition. This was interpreted to him, but he resisted the interpretation at that point.

I have dealt with the sexual aspects of experiencing because this is the area most analysts tend to view with the greatest suspicion. I would encourage experiencing other feelings just as strongly. For instance, two men in one of my groups are at this moment prepared to have a go at one another in the boxing ring. It will be a valuable experience for both of them. One of them sees the other as his feared oedipal rival father and is getting over his castration fears and the accompanying defenses. The other sees his opponent as his non-giving orally depriving mother. He has never been able to express his anger at her or even at a surrogate figure (like the analyst) very directly for very long. He has instead become a whiner and a complainer and is generally masochistic. I think a direct physical expression of his anger, which he has known about intellectually for years without major change, may be a breakthrough for him.

Obviously I take the position that there has been too much anxiety among analysts, in general, about the expression of irrational impulses from childhood. Because of their uneasiness about "rocking the boat," many analysts have tended consciously or unconsciously to squelch the expression of these impulses and to damn any expression of irrational impulses from childhood by calling it "acting out." Because of this, many of the impulses are expressed only in a very diluted, filtered, and controlled manner. This results in but a partial resolution of the problem, if any at all. Actually what may occur is that, when the impulses emerge, and, with the analyst's tacit encouragement are not able to be expressed fully and with great affect, the defenses that were erected to maintain repression of the impulses may be reinforced. Thus instead of freeing the psychic energy that is used to maintain the defenses for greater creative activity, just enough of the impulse is released to cause a backlash of increasing the defenses. So many people observe that former analytic patients are all alike—they are all rather dead, controlled, conforming people. If this is so, or it tends to be so, one of the main reasons for it may be the analyst's unconscious restriction on the patient's experiencing and expressing and actually affectively "working through" his emotions from childhood because of the analyst's fear of the disorder and emotional upheaval involved, so that he incorrectly labels the behavior as "acting out."

Another issue is whether we are entitled to apply the term "acting out" not only to a specific incident or situation that arises during a patient's analysis, but to his general life pattern of expressing his neuroses not, in terms of subjective symptoms, but in relation to his life pattern. We arrive here at another issue—the difference between a symptom neurosis and a character neurosis. First of all, it is obviously true that some people tend to internalize and express their neurosis in subjective symptoms, while others are relatively symptom-free but get themselves repeatedly into uncomfortable life situations. But can we really say the latter are necessarily "acting out" people? They may be, and many probably are, but we have to be careful not to overgeneralize because some of the behavior that may seem "acting out" to us may also be "working through." Some people seem to repeat the same behavior over and over without getting insight or increasing the strength of their egos. It is also true however, that other people *do* learn from repetitive kinds of behavior, and ultimately begin to develop some mastery and some ego strength as a result of it.

This points to the fact that there seems to be a general prejudice in the analytic world against people who express their conflicts through their behavior rather than through internalization and subjective symptoms. Thus we find analysts calling these people automatically "acting out" characters without a thought to the possibility that some "working through" also may be taking place. This prejudice also runs along the lines that symptom neurotics are easier to treat and are better patients than character neurotics. Actually there may be some truth in this, but it is not necessarily always true. Character neurotics may not respond well to classical analytic treatment, but may do exceptionally well with a treatment that is still basically analytic but has some modifications in technique.

This prejudice is also applied to therapists who use experiential techniques, especially in groups. They are accused of encouraging "acting out" or of "acting out" themselves, either directly or vicariously. Again on certain occasions and with certain therapists this may well be so. On the other hand, it may also be true that their choice of technique is not based on some neurotic compulsion but rather on a real conviction that a true resolution of a conflict requires much more of an affective experiencing of it than a more classical analytic approach generally permits. Experiential therapists may feel, as I do, that a childhood impulse must be strongly felt and fully savored over and over before it can really be "worked through" and gotten under control of the ego.

SUMMARY

In summary, my intention in this paper has been to point out the difference between "acting out" and "working through." The former is a resistance to insight and change whereas the latter is essential for change. Both have to do with experiencing and repeating unconscious wishes from childhood that are emerging from repression. In one instance, it is a meaningless blind repetition without insight or growth. In the other, it is part of a process of mastery and increasing ego strength. And yet clinically they may be and are often confused with one another. The analytic world, in general, seems to have a bias against experiential mastery of a problem and often tends to call a piece of behavior "acting out" when it is actually part of "working through." This especially applies to nonconforming types of behavior. The decision about this should not be dictated by the conformity of the behavior, but by whether or not it furthers awareness and consciousness. The theoretical and technical issues which hinge on this distinction are vast. They include the acceptance of such media of treatment as experiential group therapy and psychodrama. They also affect the analyst's attitude in both individual and group therapy in terms of generally encouraging the expression and experiencing of repressed wishes from childhood, including outside the transference proper, or generally discouraging this and trying to limit the expression of it to the transference itself.

PART II
CLINICAL MANIFESTATIONS OF ACTING OUT

Aggressive behavior in children and adolescents, suicide, crime, and delinquency are the most common forms of acting out that one observes in daily clinical practice. They occupy a good part of our evaluation of any patient, young or old, since the behaviors are often so dramatic and, when left unchecked, can destroy the therapeutic relationship, if not the patient himself.

Dr. Kay, a child analyst, is well suited to his task of describing the dynamics, course, and treatment of acting out in children. His illustration by means of the case of "Sammy" brings to life what might otherwise be vague and circumscribed theory. Seeing the essential task as building a "bridge" between the child's fantasies and overt expression in non-masochistic fashion, the author beautifully details the dynamics and treatment of the acting out child with special emphasis on the role of the parents.

Dr. Josselyn's paper on adolescence is a refreshing insight into the non-pathological aspects of acting out during this period of development. Acting out at this level is seen ". . . as normal a psychological phase in adolescence as sucking in infancy . . ." The author feels that such behavior is, in fact, necessary, representing the disintegration of "the psychological equilibrium of childhood . . ." and the facilitating of maturation. Dr. Josselyn's views are strongly influenced by developmental psychology and take into account the intensification of drive states and modification of former defenses for coping with current pressures of adolescence.

The two papers by Drs. Litman and Glaser on suicide and suicide in children and adolescents are offered with a certain logic to their sequence. In the general area of suicide, Dr. Litman details the essential fantasies in the suicidal person which become translated into overt action. Rather than take a single dimensional approach, the author outlines seven syndromes, ranging from the more common depressions to the less well-explored areas of "transference suicide," and those representing what he calls "special ego state."

Dr. Glaser's contribution is noteworthy in pointing out the surprisingly high rate of suicide among youth in this nation and in others.

In comparison with adult suicide in which depression plays a strong role in precipitating suicidal episodes, Dr. Glaser points out that classical depressive symptoms are rare in the young.

As he sees it, the crucial factor precipitating suicidal acting out is a breakdown in communication with significant persons in the child's environment owing to inability or lack of opportunity.

Dr. Glaser's extensive bibliography which covers statistical research from other countries should prove a handy reference for anyone investigating this critical area of human behavior.

Dr. Chwast's paper on delinquency and criminality is a psychosociogenic view of acting out. His view is a multidimensional one as contrasted to those who would postulate a linear, molecular relationship. The diverse ways in which acting out is manifested as well as the great number of specific etiological factors associated with the phenomenon are clearly spelled out in this paper with particular emphasis on cultural conflicts and values.

5. The Acting Out Child

By Paul Kay, M.D.

In "The Acting Out Child," Dr. Paul Kay sets forth in considerable detail his experiences with Sammy, whom he had for an extended period of time in child analysis. One feels in reading his contribution that Paul Kay has a deep affection for and understanding of the pre-school child and especially of the psychological meaning of acting out behavior that is so often encountered in this group of young children.

The reader, in taking the long therapeutic view that Dr. Kay affords him, will develop an understanding of how the child analyst approaches the difficult problem of understanding and resolving the child's deep human attachments which lie behind the translation of his play behavior into acting out.

IN COMPARISON TO ADULTS, children, especially those under six, will normally act, play out or act out* rather than think, feel, and speak. These normal tendencies are responsible for most of the usual difficulties inherent in the therapy† of children. At about three years of age, most children are able to curb their socially unacceptable drives because by that time "object relationships have begun to be more important than drive gratifications."[12] But this psychic state is new and precarious. Woolf[23] has reminded us that children normally lie and steal up to the fifth or sixth year. I think this estimate is too conservative. Mittelman,[19] referring to motility in general, has asserted that the motility urge, as such, declines after the age of five or six and that not until the age of ten does the child prefer verbal communications to play activity in psychotherapeutic sessions.

The acting out child, whether verbal or not,—and many such children are remarkably, indeed, seductively verbal—is, as a group, considered to be the most difficult of all child patients to treat for reasons which will be taken up in detail in the course of this chapter. My aim in this paper is to share with the reader my stormy analytic experience with Sammy, a four and a half year-old boy who not only acted out, but who spoke

---

*I use the phrase "acting out" so that it covers the traditional as well as the newer concepts. It refers, for example, to the idea of remembering through action as a result of the repetition compulsion which appears as transference resistance, as well as in daily life (Freud, S.,[9,10] Freud, A.,[7] and Fenichel[6]). It also refers to Ekstein's and Friedman's concept as "experimental, adaptive, recollection"; and finally, to a "mode of ego functioning which is related on the one hand to reality testing and, on the other, to sublimation or potential sublimation" in regard to the need for and control over the object.[16]

†Includes psychoanalysis and psychotherapy.

very little and then not clearly. The experience was checkered with successes and failures but the technical and theoretical considerations implicit in the successes and failures make for a worthwhile review of some of the basic aspects of acting out in children.

As far as the acting out tendency itself is concerned, Fenichel[6] has stressed a constitutional factor tending toward action, oral fixation with its accompanying narcissism and intolerance of frustrations and severe early traumata as the main genetic factors. Greenacre[13] has added to this list "visual sensitization producing a bent for dramatization," a belief in the "magic of action," traumata before or at the time of the onset of speech and delayed speech development as compared to that of motility. Along with Fenichel, she has stressed interpretation, prohibition, strengthening of the ego and, in particular, analyzing the patient's narcissism. Although all these points were made in reference to adults, they have, I think, validity in regard to children.

Most of the literature on acting out in children deals with delinquency in the late latency and older child. The first and classic statement on this subject was made by Aichhorn.[1] He stressed the impaired ego and superego development resulting from defective mothering as the cause of delinquency and the necessity of a preparatory phase before treatment proper can take place. The therapist must first establish a kind of corrective parent-child relationship with the delinquent so that the acting out can be halted out of "love" for the therapist and therapy of the underlying conflicts can take place. This statement has been repeatedly confirmed and, at times, enriched. Eissler[5] has noted the frequent occurrence of "frank dishonesty" perpetrated on the delinquent in early childhood by his parents. Lampl-De Groot[17] has stressed the pathognomonic element in the delinquent's superego as a "weak ego ideal."

Johnson[15] and Szurek[22] have added to the classic formulation a new dimension: the child's delinquency results from the acting out of his parent's unconscious, socially forbidden impulses. Johnson has remarked on the wish of such parents to see their children hurt. As a result of their formulation, Johnson and Szurek emphasize the absolute necessity of treatment or continued cooperation from the parents or they will destroy the treatment. Johnson, deviating somewhat from the traditional approach, advises the therapist to set "limits" for the delinquent even before an attachment develops and to carefully avoid giving the delinquent subtle invitations to act out.

Bird[3] has asserted that lack of individuation and the resulting tendency to overact to the unconscious wishes of others which had occurred originally with the mother brings about the type of acting out described by Johnson and Szurek.

Anna Freud[8] has pointed to the acting out of completely suppressed phallic masturbation fantasies as a major source of delinquency.

Ekstein and Friedman[4] view the tendency itself to act out as originating in the "baby's only means of gratification . . . calling the helper." Along with Greenacre,[13] they hypothesize that if the child learns language from parents he distrusts—or if he experiences traumata in the preverbal phase—he may prefer and easily regress to preverbal forms of communication under stress. Instead of conceptualizing acting out simply as transference resistance and dealing with it traditionally by means of interpretation and prohibition, if necessary, they accept it as the patient's only means of communication, as an "experimental recollection, a primitive mode of adaptation." In the analysis of a 13 year old boy who stole, carried dangerous weapons, truanted, and ran away, they concluded that the acceptance and deliberate use of the boy's acting out as his only means of communication made it possible eventually for the boy to imitate the therapist, identify with him, and give up acting out for problem solving on a secondary process dominated level of thinking and expression. This change was accompanied by a shift from the essentially narcissistic personality organization typically found in the acting out patient to more of an object seeking personality organization.

Primitive action they view as an attempt to master reality immediately and provide gratification. In "play action," real gratification is delayed and substitutive gratification is experienced. Resolution of conflict is attempted. Fantasy and thinking occur. Reality testing develops. The primary process is still dominant but to a lesser extent. "Play-acting" involves an "initial identification with a fantasied object, to master the future experimentally." Fantasy is a "higher form of play action in which the need for action is given up." In acting out, despite the occurrence of thought and speech, regression toward narcissism, action and the dominance of the primary process takes place.

In the scanty psychoanalytic literature on acting out in the young child, the concern over object loss tends to over-shadow other themes both as a basic cause of acting out and as the starting point for the development of a technique necessary for the treatment of such children. Freud[9] described a piece of play action in a toddler in which the latter acted out his attempt to master the anxiety over the absence of his mother. Ruben[20] has demonstrated through the analysis of a ten year old boy that his acting out of the impulse to steal "represented a repetition of a preoedipal trauma condensed into a . . . masturbation fantasy." The trauma consisted of loveless rearing and the loss of a love object at the age of three. The stolen objects represented both the lost object and reality. The analyst dealt with the boy's rejection of treatment by utilizing his acting out as communication and helping him to create a symbiotic tie with her.

Friedlander[12] has asserted that serious tendencies toward delinquency can be diagnosed as easly as four years of age* and effectively treated psychotherapeutically at that time. Frankl,[11] writing about the accident-prone child has shown that children with this tendency can be diagnosed and treated effectively as early as two years of age. She believes that such early treatment can prevent the development of a "fate neurosis."† She reports on the analysis of a two year old girl, Nella, who reacted to an insufficient emotional tie to mother in infancy by turning her regression against herself and hurting herself in various ways. In treatment, Nella tried to climb out the window. Frankl's interpretation of her wish for protection by the analyst or that she wanted to throw herself away was ineffective. The therapist had to lift her down from the window explaining why she was doing so. Physical intervention and other therapeutic techniques were necessary before Nella could develop an attachment to the analyst and verbal interpretation became effective.

The "relative deprivation of object love" in early life leading to a "lowering of the libidinal cathexis of the self," delayed or impaired fusion of aggression and libido, disturbance of the function of drive control, and the turning of aggression against the self may lead to accident proneness. Later, phase-specific conflicts and anxieties associated with the turning of aggression against the self and a preference for action rather than thought or fantasy may also lead to accident proneness.

Sterba[21] has reported on the therapy of a four year old girl, Sally, who stole, ran away, seduced other children, sucked boys' penises, fought continuously with other children, wet her bed and deliberately hurt herself. The interpretation and working through of her penis envy led to cessation of the acting out.

Sally had quickly established a positive relationship with the therapist. Sterba's conclusion as to why Sally's response to therapy was so good in spite of the poor home conditions and the meager cooperation of the mother was that Sally's "acting out of her waywardness in the . . . sessions gratified her . . . to the extent impossible with older delinquents."

Mahler's[18] basic technique in the analysis of a six year old boy, an "enfant terrible," who acted out violently in and out of the analysis his need to shock adults with erotic, aggressive behavior, was the interpre-

---

*Unmanageability, lying, running away, and a relationship of the mothering person to the child which has been characterized by separations prior to the age of three, "lack of interest," and "inconsistency" indicate potential delinquency in the child.

†Further explained by Bellak in Chapter 1 of this volume.

tation of his intense castration fears, his identification with father's phallus as an aggressive sexual organ, and his identification with the fantasied phallus of mother. Mahler indicates that, at times, she had to use physical restraint and prohibition.

Harley[14] has given the clearest and richest presentation of technique that I have yet to come across in the treatment of an acting out child. The three and a half year old boy she analyzed was described as "wild," "destructive," the "terror of the neighborhood" who would attack anyone without any provocation, and who was unable to withstand the slightest frustration without temper tantrums. For the first three months of treatment, she attempted to "strengthen the child's confidence" in her, "permitted him to be the young child he had not had a chance to be and did not attempt to discuss his problems with him"; in fact, she "discouraged verbalization and imaginative play." Instead, she "played with him with clay and water" and "engaged with him in a good deal of nonsense talk appropriate to his age." She told him that she would not let him bite her and gave him a rubber toy to bite, reassured him that she would help him with his fears through understanding, and gave him all the gratification she could, including extra time, food, candy, physical contact, and constant reassurance of her love. Then, with a strengthened ego, the boy could bring up his pregenitality for analysis.

What special techniques, if any, are necessary for the young child who acts out and is relatively non-verbal? What does one do with the parents of an acting out child? These have been, and still are, some of the questions in my mind as I have gone over the material on Sammy.

II

Sammy, a four and a half year old boy, was brought to me for a speech problem. He spoke little, rarely clearly and often in bursts with the words running together. At other times, he mumbled softly. He had begun speaking later than is usual, and until the age of two and a half he could barely make himself understood, even to his mother.

His parents were also concerned about his other tendencies which they tried to minimize. They described him as generally timid and nervous, preoccupied with death, hateful towards girls, often seclusive when with other children and unable to fight back even against his brother Freddy, two years his junior. Of his father, he was said to be terrified. The consultant who had referred the parents to me had stressed to them Sammy's "passivity" and its implications for the future. This opinion had alarmed them, especially the father. Both had immediately begun to urge Sammy to be aggressive, especially to his brother. They felt their urging had been successful. Soon after the analysis started, the mother reported how she had gotten Sammy to bite his brother when the latter bit him.

In contrast to this history of passivity, the parents reported two sudden, violent attacks Sammy had made on his brother, around the time of the latter's first and second birthdays. The first time, Sammy had thrown a rock at his brother and had hit him in the forehead. Suturing at the hospital was required for the resulting laceration. Up to that time, Sammy was said to have been unaware of his brother's existence. The mother recalled that the first time she could take a walk with Sammy after Freddy's birth he had surprised her by throwing sand at other children.

The other problem, one which the parents dismissed entirely because they had "cured" it themselves several months prior to seeing me, consisted of Sammy's inability because of pain to move his bowels sometimes for as long as a week. The symptom had started soon after Freddy's birth and had gotten worse a year later when Freddy had recovered from a chronic diarrhea. Laxatives, drugs, enemas, suppositories and digital manipulation of the anus by the physician had not helped. Finally, the parents had "cured" Sammy by giving him several enemas successively over a period of two days. The "dam broke". Sammy had three gigantic bowel movements, two on the parental bed, and had asked father if he "loved" him.

Sammy was further described as an "impatient," "quiet," unaffectionate child who had always been "extremely physically active." After Freddy's birth he had become quieter, almost "lethargic." Mother felt that she and Sammy had always gotten along well with one another and had never been separated until Freddy's birth. To her Sammy had been a good child who had developed well except for his speech. He had resisted her gentle efforts to get him to use the potty. Instead, he had defecated in his pants in a corner of the dining room. After he had been cured of his bowel trouble, he began to use the toilet in the bathroom. Other features of his history were his close attachment, since infancy, to a stuffed animal which he cared for as if it were his child and his hoarding and hiding of various objects in his room.

Mother had rarely spoken to Sammy during his early childhood. (Freddy, incidentally, had been spoken to quite freely since birth by parents, grandparents and others.) Sammy, because of various circumstances, one of which was father's long working hours, had had relatively little contact with anyone besides his mother until Freddy had come along.

Mother described herself as having been relaxed and happy during Sammy's infancy. (I question her statement.) Her difficulties began toward the end of the second pregnancy when she began to suffer from fatigue and dizzy spells. The "toughest period" came with the birth of Freddy and the move from an apartment into their own home. Her anxiety about taking care of Freddy and Sammy, the lack of help from her mother, and the constant demands by her husband to socialize regardless of her fatigue had finally led to "physical and mental exhaustion." She had lost 13 pounds during Freddy's first year and had only "come out of it" a few months before the start of Sammy's analysis.

Both parents stressed their wish to give Sammy the help which they had so desperately needed in their own childhood and had not gotten. They repeatedly asserted their guilt feelings about Sammy's difficulties. They prided themselves on their interest in Sammy and their attempt at giving him everything they could especially attention and affection. For this and other reasons, Sammy had often spent the night or part of it in the parental bed. Father enjoyed holding Sammy close to his body at such times with Sammy's buttocks fitting into the concavity offered by his hips and thighs.

The parents were both in their early thirties, intelligent, and each, in his way, ambitious. In the course of my contacts with them, I learned of the father's violent outbursts of temper over trivia and his demand that his wife yell at him to help him control himself instead of being silent and submissive. Mother kept her rages and fears to herself. Both had a strong need to deny unpleasantness. Father went into a "shell" and mother put her head "in a bag." Above all, they felt cheated out of an affectionate, rich childhood by their parents and still resented the deprivation. Father experienced the deprivation as coming from his father whom he feared, hated, and admired. To accept anything from father would be humiliating. Mother experienced her deprivation mainly in terms of her mother. Mother was especially bitter in that both her parents had always leaned on her and still did. Each parent was also concerned about the omissions and distortions in the report of the other parent to me and was anxious to give me a true and complete picture. Naturally, my picture remained incomplete especially in regard to Sammy's early development, weaning, training in bowel and bladder control and general aggressiveness. Father, for example, often referred vaguely to having to spank Sammy because mother was too lax and mother also spoke of Sammy's "rambunctiousness," but yet both constantly stressed how well Sammy was doing.

The parents were quite different in their appearance and manner. Father was stylishly and neatly dressed, exuberant, smiling and aggressive. He enjoyed talking. Mother dressed plainly, almost shabbily, rarely smiled, usually looked worn out and spoke continuously in a monotone as if the talking were just another great burden she could barely endure.

Sammy, in person, was a small, wiry, handsome boy who, for the first three sessions, was quite controlled. Now impassive, now sad or tremulous and uncertain, he darted about silently, asking "What's that?" from time to time. He accused me frequently of "fooling" him. He was demanding and whining. He paid no attention to me except as someone who would do something for him or refuse him. He showed concern about mother or father being in the waiting room or outside with Freddy by vague remarks of one or two words and quick dashes into the waiting room. He made or used mother, father and baby figures to play with. Sometimes, they were made of "duty." He injured, mutilated, or killed them repeatedly. He delighted in playing and smearing with water, paint and glue; at times, he smelled and tasted the mixture.

The sessions gradually began to take on a wild, chaotic atmosphere. He began to search my face rapidly as he tried out various ideas or impulses. He began to seem teasing and defiant. He set a glass near the edge of a table and touched it slightly. It fell. He smiled and said "accident." He began to run and jump about. Beginning with the fourth session, his excitement, so far barely contained, burst out. He messed, tried to bite, hit and kick me, and destroyed or attempted to destroy whatever came to hand. He jumped from chairs and tables onto the floor and ran about recklessly, frequently tripping on a toy or bench and falling although he was otherwise remarkably agile. He enjoyed running out of the office and building and then up and down the street, finally returning to the office.

These wild periods sometimes seemed to occur for no reason. Usually, they had been preceded by hurts and frustrations earlier in the day or just prior to a session. They frequently occurred when I frustrated one of his impulses or interpreted his jealousy, rage or wish to be cared for like a baby. At other times, they occurred when he could not perform as well as he wished, e.g., print, draw or use the scissors. They were accompanied mostly by a kind of joyless elation, sometimes by frank anger and sooner or later by a teasing, triumphant air. He often had to urinate or defecate. Occasionally he touched his genitals, indicating a definite sexual element. (Some of his play and behavior indicated strong anal and phallic masturbatory urges.)

In playing out his "superman," "magician," or "monster" identities, he often became excited and acted out his sado-masochistic impulses. In these identities he was omnipotent and omniscient. He created and killed babies and their parents. He made people disappear and reappear. He enjoyed attacking, tricking or trying to torment me. At such times, he often spoke in loud, clear tones and would fire away various commands or epithets at me such as "Get up!" "Sit down!" "Come here!" "Stupid!" As an animal or monster, he would also growl or make animal-like noises. He proudly indicated both in words and manner that this was being like father. At other times when silent and preoccupied, for example, he resembled mother but any reference on my part to such a resemblance was intolerable.

He lived in a magical world. If he feared animals, then they were "really" there about to attack us and he would be frightened despite his magical powers, my help and his residual sense of reality. There was little sustained make-believe. If he made "poison," it was "real poison." What he thought was "real." This magical world contributed in a major way to his masochism. He believed he could stand on the railroad tracks and when the train approached, he would run away in time. Once he almost ran away from me and headed for the tracks which were fairly near the office. As his mother's delivery date for a new child approached, he began to complain of various symptoms and then, when mother was frightened, laughed at her for being tricked. At the same time, he became more and more reckless in his general behavior. My interpretation of his wish to control mother and keep her near him (by being sick or hurting himself) was ineffective. He managed to fall down an escalator and fracture his radius.

He also became more and more interested in the real world and doing real things. His play-action, described later on in the chapter, indicates the meaning of this preoccupation with reality. It had to do with his central concern of controlling the object to prevent his being abandoned.

At times he acted and talked as if he were a baby and would actually hurt himself slightly or complain of being hurt stressing his discomfort and need for help. At such times he would often ask me to help him tie his shoelaces, after covertly untying them. The frequent obvious wish to be a baby and cared for was hotly denied and projected on to me, Freddy, and on various other people. To be a baby was as bad as being a girl. To be grown-up, like father, i.e., omnipotent, was the best of all things. His basic underlying wishes, however, were to be either mother or baby and both were equally unacceptable. Often he tried to sing a lullaby like "Rock-a-Bye-Baby" while he swung a suspended lamp back and forth as if he were a parent rocking a baby to sleep.

Denial, isolation, and projection formed the basis of his massive, almost impregnable defensive operations. Except in play action, where at times he permitted himself a rich, direct expression of his sadistic impulses, he was constantly referring to me or Freddy as the "bad" ones, "crook," destroyer or killer who had to be punished. Nothing unpleasant in his life was admissible during the sessions for a long time—if he could help it. The need to project and torment formed the basis of his need to lie.

In his "play action" and occasional "playing-out," both of which occurred more frequently as the analysis went on, he most enjoyed a hide-and-seek game, planting seeds, "going to bed at night" and "waking up in the morning" after putting out all the office lights, and the preparation and serving of food and beverages to me. He was preoccupied with looking and being looked at. He took the active, commanding role in our play activities. I had to be passive. To surprise, trick and scare me was often the point of the action, especially in the hide-and-seek game. He always had to find me easily but I could not find him or, if I did, it was only with his imperial permission and direction. A variant of the hide-and-seek game seemed to be one in which he or I tied to a long string. One end was held and manipulated by one player who could then pull in or let go the player at the other end which might be quite a distance away.

His pervasive need to surprise and scare me most likely stemmed from his experiences with his parents who prepared Sammy for an event, such as their departure for vacation, by telling him at the last minute in order to save him anxiety. Given the history and Sammy's communications, it is very likely that the main historical source of Sammy's compulsive need to surprise lay in his mother's sudden departure for the hospital one night to give birth to Freddy. Sammy had awakened, seemed to be aware for a moment that something was going on and had then returned to sleep. Later I could confirm this hypothesis partially.

The problem was how to transform this omnipotent, sado-masochistic little boy whose hold on reality was thin and fluctuating, whose language if not his main gratification (Sammy did well at camp, for example, because he was a daring and skillful athlete) was action, and who used rather than suffered from his troubles (most of which appeared to him to arise in others) into a boy who knew what a problem was, knew that he had one and understood the idea of getting rid of it through talking with me.

My attempts to curb his acting out as if it were neurotic in origin by verbal prohibition, interpretation and offering him substitute, inanimate objects as a target for his rage were unsuccessful. More than that, the verbalization of any aspect of his conflicts especially that pertaining to his rage at mother generally seemed to annoy him and stimulate acting out behavior. Attempts to make him aware of his defensive operations, especially his need to deny and project, appeared to have been entirely unsuccessful until he began to develop a trusting and somewhat affectionate attachment to me, based chiefly on his realization of my constant interest in him as well as my desire to help him. It was at that point that he began to listen. This attachment appears to have started when I had begun to convince him of my intention to curb his acting out.

I stopped his acting out only by stopping him physically; this measure, of course, was only temporarily successful. Along with the physical restraint, I voiced my determination not to let him hurt himself, me or any of my important possessions and to help him control himself.

I used such restraint gently and sparingly in order to minimize his perception of me as simply another edition of his overbearing, frightening and seductive father. Still considering the tactile and kinesthetic aspects of his relationship to his parents, especially his father, and later on his overt attempts at affectionate physical contact with me, I am quite certain that the physical restraint was a definite factor in helping him to establish an attachment to me that was acceptable to him in terms of his past experience. In avoiding the affectionate physical contacts he wanted at times, and in offering him instead a more neutral kind of care, i.e., helping him with his shoelaces or with drawing or with anything which coincided with my analytic aims (play-action rather than acting out or speaking, regardless of content, rather than action), I may well have succeeded in not adding to his prominent castration anxiety or reinforcing his strong feminine, masochistic wishes. Instead, I hope I had offered the energy of these wishes the pathways which led to increased awareness of himself and others, dependence on me, knowledge of reality and the advantages of verbal communication.

The physical restraint also appeared to play an important part in the development of our working relationship in that it represented a necessary piece of reality: I was a man and he was a little boy whom I could control.* Because of his sense of omnipotence, this was often difficult for him to accept or perceive.

At various times, depending on circumstances, I accompanied, preceded or followed the physical restraint with talking quietly† to him. I emphasized the reality of injuring me or himself in what he was doing or about to do, expressed my disapproval strongly, and urged him to talk or enact his feelings. I pointed out to him the various aspects of his difficulties as they came into view as his "worry" and how by talking we could find out what made the worry and that it would then gradually go away. In addition to stressing the reality and what I approved or rejected in his behavior, I tried in various ways to give his loss of control meaning in terms of being jealous, deprived or angry. I added to such comments the fact that all boys feel this way at times as they grow up. At times, I spoke in a general way so as not to disturb his need to be perfect.

Initially he generally tended to ignore my remarks completely unless I was responding to him. Then he began to react to them with impatience, irritability, and frank outbursts of anger. Later on, when I said something that struck home (e.g., his jealousy, wish to be a baby, hatred of brother, mother, and father), he would scream "Stop!" cover his ears with his hands and frantically involve us in some play action. Gradually, he came

---

*One is reminded of Axline's[2, p. 130] dictum: "The therapist establishes only those limitations which are necessary to anchor therapy to the world of reality and to make the child aware of his responsibility to the relationship."[11]

†There were times when I was also angry with him and showed it in my voice but, at all times, I made an effort to be clear and firm in my speech and manner. I was not always successful in these attempts.

to listen to me and finally, to respond verbally. He even grasped the idea of coping verbally and tactfully with an interruption to some pleasurable pursuit and sharing with me, the deferment, on his initiative, of a verbal exchange. Once, for example, while he was trying to print, I had begun to say something. In a friendly, dignified way he said, "Wait till I'm finished—then I'll talk with you." He carried out his promise.

This type of remark and behavior I had had occasion to express before and he had gotten to be like me in this and other instances. The process was like the imitative type of identification he showed in connection with his father.

After several months, I could manage, at times, to stop his sado-masochistic acting out by verbal prohibition or by simply reminding him of reality. Gradually, he began to pause and look at me as if for guidance before doing something potentially destructive. Finally, he began to use my words at such times saying: "I'll be careful, Dr. Kay. I won't jump" or "I won't break my neck" or ". . . my leg" and control himself. He could even ask, by the end of a year, for paint and promise to paint with it instead of smearing or throwing it at me or around the playroom. "Then you can give me more paint for tomorrow when we see how it goes," he would add. But along with the growing internalized appreciation of reality and ability to control himself, he still lost control occasionally and required physical restraint up to the very end of treatment.

Rather than quantities of direct, primitive and perhaps indiscriminate mothering or fathering to build up a relationship through candy, food, gifts, and putting myself at his disposal for all kinds of special, affectionate attentions during and between sessions, the traditional "non-analytic" preparation for the acting out child, especially the young child, I tried to give him the kind of gratification which fitted in most closely with both his needs and the requirements of the analytic situation. Praise, for example, delighted him. His need for it was insatiable. I used it generously to help him appreciate reality, control himself, accept troublesome interpretations, and be less than perfect. This permitted him to not only allow me to show him how to do something, but to work at something he could not do well initially, e.g. using a scissors. I stressed the interpretation of his narcissism and sense of omnipotence. He was impressed and then quite pleased at my telling him that grown-ups and children normally make mistakes even after they have learned something. Subsequently, on making an error, he repeated the idea very earnestly that "boys and even big people can make mistakes, can't they?"

To a far greater degree than with the neurotic child, I encouraged Sammy's play-action as a natural bridge between acting out and the direct verbal expression of conflict. By actively sharing the play with him and, in particular, by giving his need for omnipotent control some harmless gratification in ordering me around, we could begin to establish a bond in which he made me his helper, ally and protector, e.g., against the wild beasts that were out to attack us. Then I could safely bring up, for example, as part of the play action, if appropriate, the idea of boys who could be angry at their fathers but so afraid of their feelings that they would have to make up an animal and put the feelings in them. Such a comment about projection, if made directly, he would ignore or dismiss angrily, but he would listen to it within the confines of the play.

Encouraging him toward substitutive gratifications gradually came to be modestly successful partially because of his strong and varied interests (singing, acting, writing, reading, gardening, and understanding the real world) and made available opportunities for symbolic control of the object. Such symbolic control of the object in contrast to control of the object through acting out offered strong possibilities for sublimation. During the analysis, for example, he developed an interest in singing which was connected with his mother and the wish to be babied by her. Gardening, on the other hand, in the form of seed planting represented feelings not only about his mother and the birth of Freddy but also feelings of pride and joy in connection with actual gardening experiences with his father.

As the analysis went on, certain new tendencies in his functioning gradually appeared and flourished, although the old ones persisted. The acting out became less frequent; play-action increased, and direct verbal exchanges of ideas began to occur. He began to talk more slowly, more clearly and more loudly and finally achieved the ability to speak coherent sentences. His need to speak indistinctly and incoherently or just mumble could be and was repeatedly interpreted as partially due to his fear of his hostile thoughts and acts being discovered and leading to punishment. His silence had a similar meaning as well as other ones. He became far more responsive to me as a person and deliberately looked to me for specific help with his school work, standards of behavior in the community and knowledge of the world in general which I had been encouraging him to obtain from me. He needed to regard me as omnipotent. He was dismayed and unbelieving if I did not know something or could not order "the army" to do something for his sake.

His concept of a "worry" evolved from that of "scary dreams" within a few months after treatment started to "when you can't do something, you bang your head" (against the wall) at the close of treatment. By the time treatment came to an end, he clearly perceived me as one who could and would help him with his worries. Just prior to the cessation of treatment, his mother reported his suggestion that his friend Bruce should get help from me for his fighting and that she should send Freddy to me because Freddy made "duty" in his pants in order to be a baby like their new baby. But to the very end, he still denied his problems and projected them, at times, onto Freddy and other people.

He was quite inhibited in school generally, socially, and academically. (He enjoyed doing the school work at home.) After the birth of the baby, he temporarily acted out sadistic impulses meant for baby and mother against children in school. At home, the change in Sammy had been dramatic. He spoke often and very clearly. He not only had become so assertive toward Freddy that, at times, he hurt him in his speech and manner, but he quite frequently beat him up. Most of all, he had lost his fear of his father. When his father shouted at him, he now stood his ground. Instead of dreading his father's punishment on finding out any of the "bad" things that he had done during the day (one of the reasons for his secretiveness and silence in treatment), he now greeted father with something like this: "Daddy, I want to tell you about something bad I did today." He also gave up hating girls and announced at the dinner table that he had a girl friend.

As longer and longer fragments of analytic work began to take place, it was clear that the masturbatory and primal scene material, so much in evidence in his behavior and play action, could not be worked with. What could be worked with was his need to control the object and the fear which fed it: loss of the object.

Sammy's early rejection of me, his omnipotent attitude, and his oral and anal sadistic attacks on me represented, in distorted form, my greatest ally in the analysis: his craving for an object. Early in treatment, while ignoring me vigorously, he would suddenly ask when would I see him again and did I like him. A few months later, he began to speak of seeing me on weekends in various places and rejected my statements to the contrary.

A few months after the analysis started, I announced the dates of my vacation. He remained silent and impassive. He tied me to a chair and asked if I would return later. His manner began to suggest anger. He wanted to play hide and seek. Doughnut, his cherished, stuffed dog was in the game. He played it in the usual way: he was to find me easily, surprise and scare me but not the reverse. The more fear I simulated, the more he was delighted. I told him that his game was a wonderful one because if he was scared of being surprised that I would suddenly disappear and that he could never find me, he could now make believe that he was the one who did the scaring and surprising and I was the one who couldn't find him. Sammy then suggested that I send a card to Doughnut and himself, adding that "Doughnut would miss you."

In the next session, he made "poison" and insisted on my drinking it (poster paint). He sipped a little to entice me. I was finally able to persuade him that by making believe I was drinking it we would be able to play the game just as well, adding that anyway our main job was to find out why he was doing this. I suggested that maybe he wanted me to drink the poison as a punishment for going away and maybe my going away reminded him of his mother's going away when his brother Freddy was born. Maybe he wanted to punish mother at that time, too, even though he loved and needed her. He said nothing but gave up the game, insisting that we both go outside the building to water the seeds which we had planted there some weeks ago. We did.

After another hide-and-seek game in a subsequent session, he asked whether I was "scared" and if I was "lost" when he commanded me not to find him. I said that it looked as if he were still worried about my going away and probably it reminded him of how he felt when mother went away to the hospital to give birth to Freddy. Did he remember that time? He then mumbled something to the effect that "Marie, the nurse . . . took care of me."

When his mother gave birth to another sibling in the latter part of the analysis, he characteristically avoided any mention of the event. He began to act and talk like a baby, called me "baby" and "nothing" and attempted to punch me. He got more and more excited and began to twirl himself around, staggering, falling and laughing. He referred to himself as "drunk" and "dizzy." I said that maybe he didn't talk about the new baby because he felt so hurt and angry and that he was trying to forget about it but that his feelings were so strong that they were driving him "crazy" (from time to time he had begun to refer to himself as "crazy" isolated from any particular content). As soon as I had finished speaking, he blurted out, "You're right!"

Prior to his mother's hospitalization for the delivery, he played the string game with me. He commanded me to pull him in from various distances. The game excited and pleased him. I said how he must wish he could do the same with mother when she went to the hospital. He laughed and nodded. Then he had me cut and retie the string repeatedly, which I interpreted in terms of his wish to control the separation from mother.

Near the premature termination of the analysis, Sammy had shown for about one week an intermittent, unexplained interest in cave men. Sammy was eager for me to read to him portions of a book on cave men, discuss their way of life in detail, and help him make some of the implements and weapons that they used, insisting that we make them "real." One day he came in with some berries he had picked from a shrub outside the building, insisting that we get some water and some cooking utensils and make a real pie from the berries. I tried to find out why he was interested in making the pie and failed. Then I said that I had heard from his father that his parents planned to go to Europe this summer. He made no response and I commented on his omission of this important information from the analysis. After a pause, I added that his father and mother wanted him to go to camp while they were away in Europe and that it seemed that he hadn't liked that. I had also heard that if they went to Europe by plane he feared that they would crash and die and so he had insisted that they go by boat. He stopped what he was doing, walked about, and said he did not want to go to camp and then smiled in a wise, knowing way tapping his forehead several times. "I know him, I know him," he said, "He's a tricker, he's a cheater." He went on to clearly imply that he felt his father was sending him to camp in order to get rid of him so that he and mother could go to Europe and that he did not like it one bit.

I sympathized openly with his difficult position (which I knew was true). By this time, he had returned to the berries and had accepted my suggestion that we make a make-believe berry pie. It seems that he wanted to go to the North Pole and live with the Eskimos (cave men) and therefore he wanted to know just what to eat and how to live there. He thought that wild berries were one type of food that Eskimos ate. He would take his entire family with him.

When I interpreted his wish to get rid of his worry of being separated from mother and father by making believe that he was taking them all to the North Pole and that he wanted the "make believe" to be "real" because he was so worried about losing his parents, his face lit up as if he were pleased at my sharing a unique secret with him. "That's right," he said, and continued on with the play action.

III

So far as the preparatory phase went, the analysis was successful, basically because of Sammy's need for an object. But the analysis failed, indeed, was broken up by the parents because of the very same need in them.

On the surface, it was the mother's pregnancy occurring soon after the analysis started which led to the premature termination of the analysis more than a year and a half after its onset and several months after the birth of the baby. The mother complained of the impossibility of driving Sammy to my office because of her increased burdens at home intensified by the loss of her maid and Freddy's aggressive, infantile response to the new baby. In addition, she and her husband were satisfied with Sammy's improvement at home and in school. She was visibly exhausted and agitated. Her desire to stop treatment coincided with her husband's increasing reluctance to spend any more money on the analysis. The parents terminated treatment suddenly, and characteristically, by giving me only three sessions with which to help Sammy confront this unfortunate development.

I was finally able to find out from the parents that they had been enraged at me for some time because I was only interested in Sammy and I did not understand or appreciate mother's predicament. Father's reason for his rage was that I was "cold" to him.

Mother's inability to keep Sammy out of her bed in spite of my repeated discussions with her over the inadvisability of this practice and her need to talk to Sammy frequently about his troubles in the course of the analysis as if she, too, were treating him pointed to her great concern over maintaining a tight bond with him. During the last two months of treatment, she had stressed on one occasion that she was jealous of Sammy's close relationship to her husband (a clear reference to myself) and feared losing Sammy to him. The parents' decision, as a matter of fact, came within a week after the mother had reported to me a unique event: Sammy, on meeting her after school, had told her that he was anxious to see me and talk to me about some worries. She seemed quite impressed by Sammy's remark.

All these considerations point to the parents' rage at me as originating in the frustration of their wish that I be their parent and also in depriving mother of her (symbiotic?) relationship with Sammy. (When she was ill, she was delighted in Sammy's taking care of her just as she took care of him when he was ill.) Her probable concern over losing Sammy to me must have inspired the wish for another baby, and also to break up Sammy's treatment. She had rejected the pregnancy consciously.

While mother probably feared and resented my taking away her symbiotic partner, father apparently resented losing Sammy to me as a feminine love object in a relationship which seemed modelled on that of his relationship to his father. Sometime prior to the end of treatment, he had once lightly remarked that since Sammy was now better he did not have to be so gentle with him, i.e., he could spank him and shout at him again.

So far as father was concerned, giving him more "support" may well have been threatening to him in view of his concerns about passivity and receiving things from his father. I had suggested treatment to both but they had rejected the idea. I still do not know what more could be done for such parents so that they would not impair or interrupt treatment. For example, their continued stimulation of Sammy at night most likely was another although, in itself, not fatal blow at treatment by keeping him at a high pitch of excitement, overtaxing his limited ego functioning and thus reducing, I am certain, his capacity to form a therapeutic alliance.

In this regard, I had blundered in failing to appreciate early and fully enough Sammy's acting out problem and its implications for treatment. Attempting too early to deal with his problems verbally, as if they were those of a neurotic child, only increased his acting out. Much time and distress probably would have been saved for all concerned had I realized the significance of Sammy's acting out in terms of the specific impairments in his ego functioning, his dread of losing the pre-oedipal mother, and therefore, his uncontrolled need to de everything possible, including attempts at self-destruction to wrest constant concern and care from her. Conflicts, associated with sibling rivalry, masturbation, castration, primal scene fantasies, positive and negative oedipal wishes, all of which were condensed in his sado-masochistic behavior, were to make analytic work in emotional reality and primitive ego functioning to make analytic work in the usual sense possible without special preparatory work.

Greenacre,[13] Johnson,[15] and Bird[3] lay particular stress on the analyst as one important source of acting out in the acting out patient. My anger which, at times, grew to exasperation even though controlled either visibly stimulated him to further sadistic or masochistic acting out or tended to frighten him. Shades of his father!

The development of an attachment to me (even though basically narcissistic) seemed to have contributed significantly to his ability to speak and, in particular, to his wish to speak about his troubles. He had, it seems, introjected me as a speaking adult interested in using speech in a certain way unlike his parental introjects. In regard to his speech problem, incidentally, his mother stated that he had had an oral staphylococcal infection for three weeks after birth. This infection could certainly have sensitized the speech area to the traumata in his preverbal phase which I have already mentioned: the silent mother, the scarcity of human contact, her sudden disappearance at night to the hospital, the birth of Freddy and the loss of mother's attention, mother's depression and irritability, father's absence and temper outbursts, and the omnipresent seductiveness from both parents. "Constitution" need not be invoked to explain Sammy's delayed speech nor, for that matter, his great penchant for action. He must have been in a constant state of excitement and frustration since infancy and, in addition, he had an acting out father with whom to identify.

The literature tends to leave the reader with the impression that the acting out child has been "deprived." Yes, but in specific ways. It may also be the excessive stimulation and gratification in combination with the deprivation that is important.* Sammy, for example, apparently received considerable stimulation of a homosexual, sado-masochistic nature from

---

*See Bellak's point in "The Metapsychology of Acting Out," Chapter 1 of this volume.

father. He was deprived—undoubtedly of affect—but just as important, of the kind of rearing which would have permitted his ego to flourish independently. His parents, unfortunately, could neither protect Sammy from excessive stimulation nor let him use their ego functions consistently and steadily enough so that his own could get a good start. In this sense, the analysis was helpful to him in offering him a second chance to develop his speech, the ability to substitute fantasy and thinking for action, and the appreciation of inner and outer reality. His attempts to deal with the threat of object loss by realistically facing his feelings about his father as well as his concept of his father's character and by his primitive sublimation of the wish to control the needed object through a combination of dramatization and intellectual mastery of the external world are vividly and movingly demonstrated. Further, his wish and capacity to profitably share his secret solution with me is a far superior adaptation than was originally possible with his severely narcissistic, almost autistic personality organization at the start of the analysis. (Much of this growth must also have been due to maturation.)

IV

Technique, including the technique of dealing with the parents, must be based as vigorously as possible on the precise nature of the ego deficiencies as well as that of the conflicts of both child and parent in the analysis of an acting out child if technique is to be effective therapeutically and an instrument of research as well. I look forward to more clinical data and theoretical concepts derived from the treatment of such children so that better therapeutic techniques will become available for the therapist in private practice.

REFERENCES

1. Aichhorn, A. *Wayward youth,* New York: Viking Press, 1935.
2. Axline, V. *Play therapy,* Cambridge, Mass.: Houghton Mifflin Company, 1947.
3. Bird, B. A Specific Peculiarity of Acting Out, *J. Amer. Psa. Assoc.,* 1957, Vol. *V.*
4. Ekstein, R., and Friedman, S. W. Acting Out, Play Action, and Play Acting, *J. Amer. Psa. Assoc.,* 1957, Vol. *V.*
5. Eissler, K. R. Some Problems of Delinquency, In Eissler, K. R. (Ed.) *Searchlights on delinquency,* New York: Int'l. Univ. Press, 1949.
6. Fenichel, I. *Neurotic Acting Out,* from *The Collected Papers of* Otto Fenichel, Second Series, edited Fenichel H., & Rapaport, D., New York: Norton, 1954.
7. Freud, A. *The ego and the mechanism of defense,* New York: Int'l. Univ. Press, 1946.
8. ———. Certain Types and Stages of Social Maladjustment, In Eissler, K. R. (Ed.). *Searchlights on delinquency,* New York: Int'l. Univ. Press, 1949.

9. Freud, S. *Beyond the pleasure principle, St. Ed.* Vol. *VIII*, 1920-22, London: Hogarth Press, 1955.
10. ———. *Remembering, repeating and working through, St. Ed.,* Vol. *XII*, 1914, London: Hogarth Press, 1958.
11. Frankl, L. Self-Preservation and the Development of Accident Proneness in Children and Adolescents, *Psa. St. Child,* 1963. Vol. *XVIII,* New York.
12. Friedlander, K. R. Latent Delinquency and Ego Development, In Eissler, K. R. (Ed.) *Searchlights on delinquency.* New York: Int'l. Univ. Press, 1949.
13. Greenacre, P. General Problems of Acting Out, In Greenacre, P. (Ed.) *Trauma, growth and personality.* New York: Norton, 1952.
14. Harley, Marjorie. Analysis of a Severely Disturbed Three-And-A-Half Year Old Boy, *Psa. St. Child,* 1951. Vol. *VI.*
15. Johnson, A. M. Sanctions for Superego Lacunae of Adolescents, In Eissler, K. R. (Ed.) *Searchlights on delinquency.* New York: Int'l Univ. Press, 1949.
16. Kanzer, M. Acting Out, Sublimation and Reality-Testing, *J. Amer. Psa. Assoc.,* 1957, Vol. *V.* New York.
17. Lampl-De Groot, J. Neurotics, Delinquents, and Idea Formation in Eissler, K. R. (Ed.) *Searchlights on delinquency.* New York: Int'l. Univ. Press, 1949.
18. Mahler, M. Les Enfants Terrible. In Eissler, K. R. (Ed.) *Searchlights on delinquency.* New York: Int'l. Univ. Press, 1949.
19. Mittleman, B. Motility in Infants and Children and Adults. *Psa. St. Child,* 1954, Vol. *IX,* New York.
20. Ruben, Margarete. Delinquency: A Defense Against Loss of Objects and Reality. *Psa. St. Child,* 1957, Vol. *XII,* New York.
21. Sterba, E. Delinquent Mechanisms in a Four Year Old Girl, In Eissler, K. R. (Ed.) *Searchlights on delinquency.* New York: Int'l. Univ. Press, 1949.
22. Szurek, S. A. Some Impressions from Clinical Experiences with Delinquents, In Eissler, K. R. (Ed.) *Searchlights on delinquency.* New York: Int'l Univ. Press, 1949.
23. Woolf, M. The Child's Moral Development, In Eissler, K. R. (Ed.) *Searchlights on delinquency.* New York: Int'l. Univ. Press, 1949.

6. Acting Out in Adolescence

By IRENE JOSSELYN, M.D.

In "Acting Out in Adolescence" Dr. Irene Josselyn, who has had long experience in the therapy of adolescents, provides the reader with a developmental and largely non-pathological way of looking at the occurrence of acting out behavior in this age group.

Her treatment of the problems is balanced, clear, and will be of use to all of those who seek to see many of the problems in this area as peculiar to and growing out of many of the biological changes characteristic of adolescent behavior.

ACTING OUT IN ADOLESCENCE can not be evaluated except against the background of the general psychology of the adolescent phase of development. Without setting forth as an inherent part of this chapter the particular aspects of that background which have bearing on the behavior of an adolescent and which at first glance appear to justify the diagnostic term "acting out," any discussion of the particular syndrome would be meaningless. The first part of this chapter, therefore, is a review of certain points of the general psychological aspects of adolescence.

Adolescence, as a psychological term, has almost as many definitions as there are people interested in this phase of development. For the purpose of this discussion I would like to use a rather broad definition that encompasses a psychological constellation covering the span frequently referred to as early, middle, and late adolescence. In such a context adolescence is a phase of psychological development in which there is an intensification of inherent drives that results in two different components of the adolescent's psychological and behavioral constellation. On one hand there is an increased striving for maturation and the attainment of adulthood. On the other hand the defenses, formerly effective in handling the conflicts that were created by the inherent drives in early childhood, are inadequate to cope with the pressure that results from the intensification of those drives; during adolescence the psychological equilibrium of childhood partially disintegrates.

The striving for more rapid maturation and the disintegration of the former ego defense mechanisms are not entirely antagonistic. The disintegration actually facilitates maturation. The individual strives to find a manner in which to deal with his basic conflicts that will be different from those which he sees as characteristic of childhood and therefore adult-alien. To attain adulthood, it is essential that the dominance of the childhood defense patterns be tempered and that a new format of adaptation to, and integration of, the drives and of reality, as well as the structuralization of defense patterns compatible with an adult role, be developed. The relative weakening of the defenses under the onslaught of intensified impulses facilitates this. The ego, however, during this period of stress is often inadequate to the task of immediate mastery through mature mechanisms. As a result, the behavior of the adolescent is unpredictable. At times he appears surprisingly strong and mature; at times he appears to have regressed, rigidly utilizing defenses that were flexibly serviceable in childhood; at other times he presents the chaotic picture of a person who responds to all impulses without any integration of their primarily contradictory goals. The adolescent phase of psychological development is past when the chaotic state finally crystallizes into an adult personality, whether as a result of greater psychological maturation, and consequently more adequate adaptive patterns and integration of inherent drives, or as a result of a relinquishment of the urge towards maturation, and regression to the childhood format that had formerly proved adequate because at that time it was age-equivalent.

The basic psychological shift is initiated by the biological change that occurs in pre-puberty and immediate post-puberty. Until recent years, any discussion of adolescence had tended to stress the sexual aspects of this biological change and the inability of the adolescent to deal with the strength of sexual impulses. More recent writings stress equally the increase in other drives. The composite strength of all the stress is expressed in what I have referred to above as a surge toward maturation. Blos[1] refers to this as a striving to replace former passivity with activity.

It is important to bear in mind that a description of the manifestations of adolescence, as outlined above, is appropriate only to adolescents in cultures such as ours. For example, more primitive cultures prepare the child for the disintegration of his ego defenses by defining to a greater or lesser extent what the answer to the psychological state is. With and following the initiation rites, the young person can utilize the ego-surrogate that has been established by the laws of the tribe. He is told, in effect, at adolescence, "This is the time you act in this way." The individual enters the adult world of his tribe with conscious guide lines which he must follow until such time that adulthood becomes a part of his own effective ego, or suffer severe consequences. The tribal structure is thus perpetuated from generation to generation. One disadvantage of this pre-structuralization of the individual's adult life is the inability of most members of the tribe to make an effective adjustment to a major change in the tribal situation. Not to minimize the tragically insensitive role that our forefathers and ourselves have played in the destruction of the American Indian, perhaps one reason we were able to paralyze the inherent potentials of the Indians was the inflexibility of their adjustment patterns that were established by the tribe's inviolate mores.

In certain more complex cultures the dictum to the adolescent is, in effect, "Now is the time you become what you want to be, which should at least not be what we are, but what we say a person should be; but you must also be someone who thinks as an individual, acts as an individual, and who prepares himself not to perpetuate the tribal mores, but to improve them. Bear in mind, however, that anything you consider improvement may not conform to what we have considered improvement, and therefore we will disapprove." Our society, at least theoretically, urges an individualized pattern of maturation, criticizes when that pattern does not take an acceptable form, smiles indulgently at many clumsy steps taken by the maturing individual, and offers little in structured guidance for the attainment of adulthood.

The adolescent, in spite of the lack of definition provided him by the culture, and the half-hearted, inconsistent response of the adult world to his machinations unless his behavior becomes seriously threatening to the stability of his milieu or the rights of others, does have a built-in value system, originating from his childhood experiences, which remains intact even though at times it appears shaky. He may verbalize an abandonment of that value system, he may tentatively violate it, but its basic elements survive in spite of repeated waves of attack. The adolescent also has his own peer group that, in spite of the confusion of its individual members, serves as an ego-surrogate through the "tribal mores" of the group. These are tribal mores that the individual dares not ignore.

There may be a change occurring of temporary, or possibly permanent, nature in the experiences and the confusions of the adolescent. It may be simply that more sensitive studies are revealing that a greater number of adolescents than we had assumed in the past have sought and found rigid tribal mores in their own milieu that have enabled them to avoid the turbulence of adolescence. Sociologists and psychologists in some studies of groups of adolescents suggest that the present adolescent is more conforming to parental standards than our observation of certain individual adolescents and our theoretical formulation of the psychological phase of adolescence would indicate. If this is true, their findings suggest that it is urgent to consider the meaning of the degree of structuralization the adolescent responds to, and what, if any, implications such conformity and the nature of the structuralization have for the future of this culture.

For the purpose of this discussion I am assuming that, for the most part, the present day adolescent is still living in a culture that provides only broad and flexible directives for attaining adulthood and that he is able to tolerate a certain lack of structuralization. To summarize, during the adolescent phase the individual is responding to the impact of multiple impulses that are primary in nature and that have, as a result of biological changes, attained a greater intensity than they had during early childhood when certain defenses proved effective. The ego, during adolescence, is inadequate to the task of mastery of these impulses that are in some instances totally, probably more frequently partially, freed from the formerly effective restraint. Our culture does not offer a tribal initiation that would serve as an ego-surrogate, but does reinforce the urge to attain the ill-defined state of adulthood. There is great internal pressure in the individual adolescent to avoid regression or any direction to the pathways that, when sought in childhood, led to a state of relative equilibrium. The individual rather seeks, and to a certain extent seeks without guidance, new pathways that will lead to adulthood.

In this psychological and social confusion it is inevitable that confused behavior will result. It is commonly stated that adolescence is the time of acting out and that acting out is as normal a psychological phase in adolescence as sucking is in infancy. Such a description of adolescence is accurate only if one wishes to utilize the term acting out to describe any behavior that has its core in inherent impulses that find expression in action rather than in symbolic words or neurotic symptoms. By that definition the person who does not act out would be an individual who could sustain a mental state without body needs or desire for action, as well as with no urge to find expression in relationships to the external world for the thought processes that have woven themselves into a gestalt. It would seem preferable to reserve the term acting out for a more limited diathesis. Action in lieu of symbolic thinking, action as an alternative to remembering, and particularly action that deals with infantile conflicts by a repetitive pattern of behavior that is ego-syntonic because the ego avoids the tasks of evaluation of reality, integration of conflicting impulses, and the demands of the superego, would seem a more serviceable definition of the acting out syndrome. It suggests a differentiation between acting *out* and acting *upon* an impulse. In this sense acting out, it would be assumed, would have a goal of impulse expression with at least theoretically determinable nuclear root and with no additional aim. To this narrower definition of acting out the behavior of many adolescents would not conform. Rather, the behavior would appear to be a trial and error pattern which, because various end results are sought which have yet not been synchronized into a common goal, is not effective except at the moment.

Blos,[1] in discussing acting out in adolescence, pointed out that certain behavior that could be broadly considered acting out serves as a means of mastery for the adolescent. His discussion would suggest that, defining acting out in the more narrow sense, as I have suggested above, what is often evaluated as acting out behavior in adolescence is, in reality, acting *upon* an impulse. Because integrated behavior, in part for reasons discussed later, is not at times possible, when a need is felt, or an impulse presses for expression, the adolescent tries, perhaps after some thought, perhaps without evaluation, to find the gratification sought or to express the impulse in order to explore possible ways by which to gratify the need or deal with the impulse.

A case in point is that of John. He appeared during the diagnostic evaluation to be a typical acting out personality. Perhaps as an adult he will prove to be so; therapy was interrupted by his parents, and therefore the nature of his basic conflict was never uncovered, and much of his behavior cannot be explained. One piece of it, however, would conform to an unconscious seeking of gratification of a current desire that he had found no way to fulfill until a chance alternative proved at least temporarily effective. John had created for himself a telephone credit card number. He used it extensively when on vacation and at boarding school to call his friends, and sometimes his parents. He also was very generous in permitting his friends to use it when they expressed a desire to talk to some particular person. The telephone company finally traced the source of the false credit card.

As John discussed the difficulty he was in with the telephone company, he was quite matter-of-fact. He did not deny that he had initiated the plan for the false credit card, or that he was responsible for the greater part of the bill, close to $1,000.00, that finally accumulated. He did resent the fact that no one would believe that about $100.00 of the bill really represented charges that his friends, not he, had made. Most of his own calls were made to a friend of his who had moved to another city.

It became obvious in his discussion of this person whom he had called that the boy was the only one with whom John had been able to communicate. John's primary complaint about his parents was that he had never been able to talk to them. His parents stated that even as a small child he was always uncommunicative. John's recollection was that he couldn't talk to them, primarily because if he tried to do so, he pushed a button that released a long, either dull or censorous lecture. He had learned finally that he could sometimes get something across to his father if he telephoned him at the office. If a lecture resulted, he would not have to listen; his father would not know he was not listening so John could not be accused of being rude.

Convinced, after it was discovered, that his fabricated telephone number was not wise, he discontinued using it. Perhaps another factor in this renunciation was the ease with which he communicated in therapy. At about this time his parents sent him away to school. The telephone again became important. When a crisis arose at school, he called his therapist to discuss his difficulties. On those occasions, with the permission of the therapist, he called collect rather than reactivating his false credit card. However, the determinant of John's choice of his behavior pattern was, it appeared, primarily a need to talk to someone. He was a very confused individual who, at least in therapy, never wasted time on idle chatter. His attitude was one of not understanding himself, anxiety over his inability to do so, and a plea that his therapist try to organize what John saw as chaos into some form that John could understand. He commented many times that he never seemed to be able to judge the right or wrong of an act until after he did it. As far as the false credit card was concerned, he had not thought whether it was right or wrong until it became evident it was the latter, after his manipulations were discovered.

As the infant becomes increasingly mobile, he at first acts rather than thinks. He has no memory of experiences upon which to base any expression of his impulse that would be integrated into his total internal and external reality. Gradually in the normal sequence of maturation he becomes aware of who he is as a person and of his relationship to the external world. This crystallization of self is determined by his increasing ability, due to neurological development, to understand and integrate experiences, to an increasing capacity to relate to others, and to the incorporation into his own self-image of those concepts that are the reflection of the attitudes of others and become his superego. With the crystallization of the self, memory of past events serves to preserve the crystallization. Thus, between memory, current experiences, and a self-image there is a circular feedback that enables a developing psychic structure to achieve an integration of the multiple internal and external stimuli, an integration that leads to an adaptive pattern and to defense mechanisms, and thus a character and personality structure. If one link of this circular phenomenon is removed, the circle no longer remains. While many aspects of adolescence are significant, one that would seem to have bearing on the causation of adolescent behavior is the nebulous nature of the adolescent self-image. Why the child's self-image disintegrates during adolescence has been discussed by many,[1,2,3,4] and a recapitulation of the various factors is not within the scope of this paper. To the degree that there is a lack of a crystallized concept of the self in adolescence, memory fails to serve as a governing factor in determining the way in which an impulse can be handled.

Many memories are alien to any formulation of a new and mature identity. Often what is remembered is a threat to the adolescent's narcissism since it implies to him a demand to act as a child, and thus relinquish the goal of attaining an adult self-concept. Thus memories are often consciously discarded. Repressed memories are even a greater threat since they involve conflicts that, if recalled, would add additional strain to the already over-taxed ego. The childhood superego has certain archaic components that must be discarded. The adolescent senses this but is not certain which aspects are worth retaining, which should be abandoned, and how to be certain those components retained represent his own self-image rather than a mirror reflection of his parents.

During adolescence, memory and symbolic thought have only limited use because there is no clear-cut self to complete the circle. Since the adolescent does not know who he is, many memories are like stories about someone he knew, but with whom he feels he had little in common. As a result of his confusion as to his own identity, the adolescent tries to start all over again. This is manifested in his behavior by a series of trial runs; he experiments with different expressions of impulse and different modes of providing gratification. While conflicts at this developmental stage are characteristically the reactivation of earlier core conflicts, the adolescent's typical way of handling them is not in the nature of a repetition compulsion utilizing old ways, even though the old ways failed, to master conflict; it is rather to try new ways. This action does not act as a substitute for symbolic thinking; it is an experiment with a possible solution. His basic behavior pattern resembles, in many ways, the behavior of the toddler.

That there are adolescents whose behavior can be evaluated as typical of the acting out character at any age is certainly true. The behavior is then a solution to early conflicts rather than either the attainment of some resolution of those conflicts or the development of a neurosis. If fixed in that solution, adolescence, according to the definition upon which this chapter is based, has passed. The phase task has been completed, the individual has found a self-identity, unsatisfactory as it may be to others and as crippling as it may be to fulfillment of his own potential.

There are individuals who are not acting out characters, but rather act out under certain stresses that prove beyond their ego capacity to handle other than by action behavior that resembles more closely that of the adolescent. Their behavior, however, has no goal beyond relief of the immediate stress. The adolescent often has the additional goal of exploration and learning. However, under stress the adolescent may act out an impulse for the primary purpose of discharging tensions with which he can not cope in any other way. He recovers, as does an adult under similar circumstances. The uniqueness of adolescent behavior, which appears to resemble acting out patterns, is that phase of it which is determined by an urgency to learn who the self is, to establish memories for this self, and to provide the material, not a substitute, for symbolic thought.

REFERENCES

1. Blos, P. *On adolescence.* New York: Free Press of Glencoe, 1962.
2. Erikson, E. H. *Childhood and society.* New York: W. W. Norton, 1950.
3. Gitelson, M. Character synthesis: The psychotherapeutic problem of adolescence. *Amer. J. of Orthopsychiat.,* 1943, *18.*
4. Josselyn, I. *The adolescent and his world.* New York: Family Service of America, 1952.

7. Suicide: A Clinical Manifestation of Acting Out

By ROBERT E. LITMAN, M.D.

Dr. Robert E. Litman considers suicide as a clinical manifestation of acting out and cites, through a series of case examples that have come to his attention at the Suicide Prevention Center in Los Angeles, the kinds of unconscious problems and behavioral translations that issue in attempts at suicide, whether successful or not.

It is clear that this is a complex area of major importance, and one in which through Litman's help we are better able to work our way to an understanding.

ACTING OUT is an essential element of suicide. In some clinical situations, for example, the emergency evaluation of suicidal persons by Suicide Prevention Center* therapists, the potential of the patient for acting out is a critical factor in determining the therapeutic procedure.

The observations and conclusions described here are derived from two main methodological approaches to suicide. One is the "psychological autopsy" method of retrospective reconstruction of the life situation and suicidal behaviors of persons who have committed suicide in Los Angeles County during recent years. As part of the investigations, which were conducted in cooperation with the Chief Medical Examiner-Coroner's Office, we interviewed relatives, friends, employers, and physicians of the deceased.[4] The interviews included several hundred with psychotherapists of patients who committed suicide.

The second source of data has been the clinical experiences of the staff of the Suicide Prevention Center[5] at Los Angeles with almost 10,000 living suicidal persons. Slightly more than half of these persons called the around-the-clock emergency telephone service[6] for help for themselves. The other calls were initiated by relatives, friends, or professional persons who were worried about a patient or client.

These two approaches to suicide investigation are complementary. Each has advantages and disadvantages. Retrospective interviews about individuals who committed suicide are subject to the distortions and omissions of informants. On the other hand, inferences based on interviews with living suicidal patients can be applied to committed suicides only with

---

*The Suicide Prevention Center receives support from National Institute of Mental Health grants administered through the Medical School of the University of Southern California.

caution. Patients are slightly suicidal, moderately suicidal, or seriously suicidal. There are essential differences between slightly suicidal people and seriously suicidal people.[10] For example, therapists who deal with slightly suicidal patients tend to be impressed by their manipulations, exploitations, and hostility. By contrast, therapists who review cases of suicide or treat seriously suicidal patients tend to be impressed by their hopelessness, confusion, and terrible suffering.

The editors have defined acting out[1] as "any act which attempts to resolve an internal conflict by translating the unverbalized statement of conflict into action—the latter being ego-syntonic, although the consequence is alien," or, more briefly, "Acting out is a generally nonverbal translation of an unconscious conflict." In the next section I will briefly present three histories typical of suicide, with emphasis on the internal conflict and the process of translation into suicide action.

TYPICAL SUICIDES

Case 1: Mr. A, age 51, shot himself with a rifle through his heart, while sitting in his automobile, at approximately 8 A. M. He had been a real estate salesman who led a conventional life, ambitiously oriented toward financial success, which, to him, was especially important, since he felt inadequate at times because he lacked a college education. During a short period, about four months before his death, he lost three important business transactions which he had counted on, and following this loss he became morose, depressed, irritable, and despondent, and he began to drink, mostly beer, rather heavily. He became indecisive and began to talk about changing to some different type of work.

This disturbed his wife. Although there was no obvious marital disharmony, in recent years they had grown apart. The children were grown, and her main interest was religious. There had been almost no sexual intercourse for several years. The wife had Mr. A examined by a physician, who diagnosed high blood pressure and prescribed an anti-hypertensive drug. She tried to interest Mr. A. in church affairs, but he did not attend regularly.

One week prior to Mr. A's death his wife, concerned about his lethargy, sleeplessness, lack of appetite, and hopeless attitude, telephoned the physician, who said that the patient should have more activity. Two days before his death Mr. A went to a department store and bought a rifle, which he left in his car. The night before his death he talked to a clergyman for several hours, mostly about his failure and anxiety. He woke around 5 A. M. and went for a walk, during which he unwrapped the gun and loaded it. Then he returned for breakfast. At his wife's request, they prayed. Then he went for another walk, again to his automobile, and this time he shot himself.

Later, his wife found several notes, torn up in small pieces in the wastebasket. Apparently he wrote the notes before going for a walk at 5 A. M. and tore them up when he returned for breakfast at 7. When reassembled, the notes read, "Honey, I am unable to take this any longer. God have mercy on my soul. I'm sorry, but I am unable to go on living in the condition I am in. Please be brave. Sorry that life turned out this way. I hope you can find a better life without me. I know I must be nuts. Life isn't worth living, and I have to go through hell every day that I have been through."

After the death Mrs. A wondered if she had been in some way responsible. She herself had been feeling let down and depressed. She said they had no financial problems. Mr. A's father had died in an accident on the thirteenth of the month, which was the date Mr. A committed suicide.

We infer that the main internal conflict concerned Mr. A's feeling that he could not live up to the demands of his conscience, of God, and of his wife. There might have been an identification with his dead father involved in choosing the exact day of his death. He had evidently considered suicide for some time, gradually moving toward the final act.

Case 2: Mrs. B, age 47, died in her own home from an overdose of barbiturates. She had been a well-educated and extremely intelligent woman, who, for most of her life, was anxious and worried, especially about her health. She inherited a good deal of money from her father and never worked. She felt lonely and insecure, ostensibly because she was unable to establish stable relationships with men. She had been divorced twice. Over the years she had seen several psychiatrists, each time for a few consultations, and each time she terminated the therapy, usually, she said, because the doctor was too cold and impersonal. She had been taking sleeping pills for many years.

Each time a love relationship was severed, she went through a period of depression and twice had made suicide attempts with barbiturates. About a month before her death she consulted a psychiatrist because of weight loss, sleeplessness, and acutely depressive feelings, brought on, she thought, by news that her divorced husband had remarried. The psychiatrist recommended more consultations with him, but she failed to keep her appointment, and he did not call her. On the day of her death she consulted her family physician, who was alarmed by the serious weight loss and said that he would have to do a careful diagnostic study, since she might be suffering from some organic illness, possibly even a tumor. That night she took a fatal overdose of sleeping pills, leaving a note, which said she couldn't face a lingering death from cancer. An autopsy showed no tumor, and no particular organic illness.

This patient's main unconscious problem seemed to revolve around her need for love, which was in conflict with her fear of intimacy. Her life pattern seemed to act out a memory of briefly being close to someone and then separating. There was some evidence that she unconsciously hoped to be rescued from the last suicide action, as she had previously been rescued, for she communicated clues to suicide to several people. It was known that she had saved up a large number of pills over a long period of time, with the idea that some day she might use these pills for suicide.

Case 3: Individuals who have survived a very serious suicide action, which, in all probability, should have resulted in death, may be an exceptionally good source of information on the psychology of suicide. Mr. C, aged 62, shot himself in the head with a pistol. Apparently the shell was defective, for it produced very little power and the bullet, after breaking through the skull, lodged in the meninges, barely penetrating the brain, causing minimal damage. Mr. C had been a successful commercial artist. One year previously he suffered a small cerebrovascular accident. This did not impair his ability to walk, speak, or think, but it did leave him with a tremor, which disabled him as an artist. He had previously been divorced from his wife, and he lived with his aged mother.

During his year of unemployment Mr. C became increasingly depressed. He felt he was no good, that he was a burden on his mother, and he could not accept his status as an ex-artist. He rehearsed shooting himself with the pistol, unloaded.* Finally, he took a room in a motel, so that his mother would not be disturbed by the shot, and fired the bullet into his brain. He was shocked to find himself still alive. He staggered out of the room into the lobby, where help was summoned. When interviewed the next day, he was not suicidal. After his discharge from the hospital he obtained work as a gardener and made a good adjustment. He seemed to have completely lost his former identity as an artist. Two years later he was well and happy.

His internal conflict seemed to center around feelings of self-depreciation and guilt and an inability to accept loss of status. Unconsciously he was dissatisfied with living with his mother, but was unable to leave her. When he shot himself, he had a thought that it was like destroying a badly injured horse. After the suicide attempt he seemed to feel that he had been reborn, with a new identity.

THE PSYCHOLOGY OF SUICIDE ACTS

These case examples illustrate that suicide acts, as a general rule, are not sudden, unpredictable, impulsive, momentary, or random acts. In most cases, the suicide plan has been developed gradually and rehearsed in fantasy and preliminary action. In nearly every case of suicide there is

---

*From a prognostic standpoint, it would appear that the person who thinks through (or "rehearses") his intent in a "step-by-step" fashion is much more likely to act out than one who simply reflects on the possibility. This point needs further research.

evidence of crisis, conflict, ambivalence, mixed motivations, and multiple determinants.[3]

Emotional crises occur from time to time in all lives when people face problems, which temporarily are beyond their ability to solve. Situations which threaten the continuity of our mental, physical, and social equilibrium are powerful sources of stress. Confrontations with death, ill health, loss of love, or change in social status are typical examples. The person under stress feels restless, uneasy, painfully tense, and unable to adapt. At first, suicide is only one of many possible reactions. The individual tries Solution A, Solution B, Solution C, Solution D, and feels no improvement. He thinks of Solutions E, F, G, H, and I and imagines no improvement. Finally he comes to Solution S—suicide. He struggles against it, abandons it, tries other thoughts, other actions. Sometimes nothing helps. The person loses hope and returns repeatedly to thoughts of suicide. His thinking grows more distorted, constricted, confused, and desperate, and as the suicide act is rehearsed in fantasy and in preliminary actions, the act acquires momentum and an autonomous pressure for completion.[3]

Contributions to an act of suicide come from all psychological levels and structures and from the external environment. There is no simple or single psychological formula which applies to all suicides.

Some of the more important unconscious fantasy systems which contribute to suicide take the form of wishes, as follows: (1) A tired wish for surcease, escape, sleep, death; (2) a guilty wish for punishment, sacrifice, to make restitution; (3) a hostile wish for revenge, power, control, murder; (4) an erotic wish for passionate surrender, the greatest ecstasy, reunion with the loved dead; (5) a hopeful wish for life, for rescue, rebirth, a new start.

Suicide is usually associated with failure of important ego functions, such as orientation in the external world, understanding causes and effects, and the control of dangerous wishes. There tends to be a narrowing and constriction of ego span and ego capacity. Frequently the feeling of hopelessness is so severe as to amount to a cognitive defect.

Certain superego attitudes dispose toward suicide. Among these are inability to accept help because of pride, and an all-or-nothing view of life, which suggests suicide to a person who is losing. The histories of many suicides indicate that there were pathological identifications with hostile parents or nuclear identifications with loved persons who died.*

Finally, there is a social factor in every suicide. Some meaning is supplied by the cultural, religious, and sociological milieu which provides a context for suicide. More specifically, suicide ocurs within a nexus of interpersonal relations and communicates a message, most often a "cry for

---

*This is particularly true if the loved person's death was by suicide.

help."[22] The people around the potential suicide play an important role in the outcome, either by acts of commission, omission, or both.

Example: A husband came home at 3 A. M. to find his wife unconscious, an empty sleeping pill container in the waste paper basket, and on the table a note, "Wake me if you love me." He threw the note down and left. She died. Such acts of desertion, as well as acts of rescue, suggest a mutual acting out.

VARIETIES OF ACTING OUT

The acting out in suicide manifests itself somewhat differently in various clinical categories. Without attempting a complete survey, I will discuss briefly some aspects as follows: (1) Suicide with minimal acting out; (2) acting out in the transference; (3) malignant masochism and schizophrenia; (4) special ego weakness; (5) alcoholism; (6) symbiotic union; (7) depression.

Suicide with minimal acting out: Indications of minimal acting out would be an absence of crisis, personality change, and ego splitting; and the presence of adequate reality testing, verbalization of the essential conflicts, and a general sense of continuity between the total personality and the suicide act. By such criteria "appropriate" suicides do occur among the old and very sick, but are relatively rare. Some people leave careful notes, which indicate guilt over exhausting the resources of the family in a useless and painful survival. Often the aged have great ambivalence over killing themselves, on one hand wishing for surcease but, on the other hand, feeling paralyzed to act. For instance, an old man wrote, "I'm going to try to die of carbon monoxide. I hope it works this time." In terminal diseases suicide is often precipitated by an abrupt or unfeeling family decision to move the patient from his home to a nursing facility. The patient acts out his panic, loss of identity, and anger at being dispossessed.

Transference acting out: Approximately 10 per cent of suicides in Los Angeles have talked with a psychiatrist or other mental health specialist within two months before the death. For a few of the patients, the contact was only brief and meaningless, but for a majority there had been a therapeutic relationship with transference and countertransference aspects. The suicide of persons who were in therapy tended with great regularity to occur at a time of separation between patient and doctor. Frequently the separation was caused by an absence of the doctor due to travel or vacation, or it was brought about by an interruption or termination of treatment. Many of the patients had very recently been discharged from psychiatric hospitals. Therapists agreed that the transference feelings of the patients were "I have been abandoned." A subsidiary fantasy was "It is hopeless. Doctors cannot or will not help me."

That patients feel abandoned by their therapists is well known to the staff of the Suicide Prevention Center. Of approximately 1,700 night calls in 1963, almost a third were from persons who had a therapist. These people called the Suicide Prevention Center instead of their own therapists because of transference feelings, usually of being abandoned. They said, "My doctor is tired of me." "I don't want to impose on the doctor any longer." "He doesn't want to see me anymore." Sometimes the patient had abandoned the doctor. "He gets too personal and upsets me too much." The most seriously suicidal persons are not those who feel angry and want "to show the doctor" or make him "feel sorry." The most serious cases seem to be living out a memory-fantasy of being abandoned and left to die.

Malignant masochism: Some patients in therapy commit suicide as a form of negative therapeutic reaction. These cases are rare but extremely tragic, not only for the patient, but for the therapist. Superego pathology is especially prominent in these patients. They give a history of either a loved dead parent for whom they long, or an incorporated hostile parent who demands death as the only way of obtaining love.

Case 4: A young woman, diagnosed as a schizophrenic, had been a demon in a psychiatric hospital for many months because of her uncontrolled self-destructive behavior, which included repeated episodes of cutting up her arms and neck with broken glass, bottles, windows, or whatever she could use. Finally, one of the resident doctors took a special interest in her and began to see her every day. After a few months there was a dramatic change. She stopped cutting herself and began to wash regularly, dress neatly, and use make-up. One day he complimented her on the changes. That night she hanged herself* One element of her history was the story that her mother had savagely abused the girl when she was about three years old, and the mother had a psychotic break.

Schizophrenia: Schizophrenic patients who commit suicide usually have a history of previous suicide attempts or threats, and have had periods of confused behavior, with occasional outbursts of poorly organized action. Because schizophrenics misinterpret the actions of others and are dominated by their own fantasies, they may suicide unpredictably. They make up the only group of suicides which occur without any prior indication to the therapist of withdrawal, separation, or breaking off of communication. For example, a schizophenic ran away from a psychiatric hospital and jumped from a high building because he felt that his death would save

---

*One is reminded of Rogers'[a] keen observation that even a judgment of "good" can be threatening since it implies the power to make the judgment of "bad" at a later time.

his family from persecution by the FBI and the communists. Most of the bizarre suicides, such as jumping into a cement mixer, self-incineration, nailing self to a cross, and diving head first from a bridge onto a freeway are acts of schizophrenics. Since many suicidal schizophrenics are also potentially homicidal, there is some danger for rescuers who try to interrupt the destructive acts.

Ego weakness: Reports on individuals who committed suicide indicate that there was a change in the ego of the deceased. Informants say, "He was different." "Her whole personality changed." Patients who survive very serious suicide attempts often report, "It was like I was in a dream." "I couldn't think straight." "I felt I had to do it." A woman who cut her wrists said, "Usually I feel weak but at the moment I was cutting my wrists, I felt strong, purposeful and punishing. My arm seemed to belong to someone else. Then the blood came, and I was myself again."*

A few suicides, less than five per cent, result from impulsive panic behavior. For example, a man arrested after a homosexual act suddenly darted away in handcuffs from police officers and threw himself under the wheels of a passing truck. Such guilt-panic suicides occur once or twice a month in jails in Los Angeles. After a disaster there may be impulsive suicides. For instance, a husband whose wife was killed in an automobile accident slipped away from the crowd and hanged himself. The unconscious conflicts seem to center around guilt.

A substantial minority of suicides are catalyzed by the ego weakening action of alcohol and other drugs. Alcohol greatly reduces the self-preservative functions of the ego and allows latent suicidal fantasies to emerge into consciousness and latent actions to be acted out.

Alcoholism: Suicide actions occur frequently in alcoholic characters, not only because of the ego weakening effects of alcohol, but also because the alcoholic character contains strong self-destructive elements. Many chronic alcoholics become depressed, realizing that the years of alcoholism have cost them friends, love, and financial success. Some authorities say that the alcoholic must "hit bottom." This period of crisis is frequently associated with suicidal action, so that for any group of alcoholics, about five per cent may be expected sooner or later to commit suicide. In periodic alcoholics, suicide is most apt to occur toward the end of a binge and is associated with tremendous guilt and self-reproach. In chronic alcoholics who have come to the end of their psychological rope, failure and escape fantasies predominate.

Symbiotic union: Many people, including those who appear to have

---

*A frequent phenomenon among individuals who feel an increased sense of "loss of reality" or "depersonalization"—the primary purpose of the act being not to suicide, but to "snap back to reality."

made a normal life adjustment, have, in reality, never successfully completed the separation-individuation stage of development and retain a considerable parasitic need to lean upon the ego of others. If the symbiotic association is dissolved, the individual feels abandoned, helpless, and terribly threatened, and he feels an urge to take action, which may include suicide. Often the actions are addressed directly to the partner as a message, "You can't leave me, I need you, you must stay." Much depends upon how the partner responds. Often both partners in a symbiotic union become depressed and suicidal together,[7] each signaling by action but not by words the feeling, "I am terribly frightened of the impending breakup, but I can do nothing about it."

Depressive suicide: When depressives struggle to express their feelings, they report, "I feel empty, sick, dead, terrified." "I can't stand the suffering." "I feel hopeless that any improvement can occur." Four ominous signs of suicide potentiality in depressives are: (1) An impatient, agitated attitude that something must be done immediately; (2) a detailed, feasible, lethal suicide plan; (3) pride, suspicion, and hyper-independence as character traits; (4) isolation, withdrawal, living alone, or living with someone so emotionally removed from the suicidal person that the patient, in effect, is living alone. The act of suicide often expresses in action a conflict between wishes to fail, give up and rest on one side, and a demanding ambition on the other. The act says, "Leave me alone. I am sorry but I can't do what you want me to do. I have to do what I want to do."

IMPORTANCE OF SUICIDE PLAN

Depressions are characterized by exhaustion of energy, psychomotor retardation, and paralysis of will. How can the depressed, immobilized patient initiate and carry out a decisive self-destructive act? In my opinion, the essential mechanism is ego-splitting. A fragment of ego, dissociated from the preoccupied major part, becomes the nucleus for acting out. The unconscious conflicts are translated into acting out through the intermediary stage of the suicide plan.

During painful crises, thoughts of suicide provide temporary relief from tension. From such thoughts and numerous other psychic elements, including wishes, memories, fantasies, identifications, defenses, and partial adaptations, the suicide plan is formed. It is crystallized, strengthened, and reinforced by repetitions in imagination and by verbal extensions such as promises, threats, and declarations. At first the plan seems alien and dangerous to the individual himself and provokes anxiety. Gradually, the suicide plan acquires an autonomous structure within the ego, more or less dissociated from the rest of the self and tolerated as ego-syntonic.

Various preliminary actions are initiated. For example, a weapon is chosen or the suicidal act is rehearsed. Although further elaboration may be suspended for days or months, the suicide plan has acquired some of the qualities of an incomplete or interrupted on-going act. Such interrupted acts have an autonomous momentum toward completion.[3,9]

Case 5: A stable, middle-aged professional man became extremely disturbed when his wife asked for a divorce. He quit working, made vague threats toward her, and then developed over a period of months a complicated suicide plan with midnight, December 31st, as the deadline. Since the marriage had been unhappy and his wife lacked beauty and charm, I asked him why he felt she was indispensable. He answered that by now his wife had nothing to do with it. "I said I would kill myself, and I am going to do what I said I would do." He agreed that the plan sounded crazy; yet, "to myself, doctor, I just don't feel crazy." The patient acted out his plan, plunging a stiletto into his heart. His life was saved by open heart surgery, and he was no longer suicidal. The act had been completed.

The concept of a relatively autonomous suicide plan is of special importance to professional persons working in emergency centers, hospital admitting services, or wherever a therapeutic disposition must be determined for suicidal patients. In evaluating the danger of acting out, the details of the suicide plan: place, time, method, purpose, deadlines, and commitments, should be reviewed with the patient. Clinical techniques for interrupting on-going incomplete suicide acts are described elsewhere in this book and in other publications.[2,6]

SUMMARY

1. Acting out is an essential element of suicide.
2. The internal conflicts that are translated into suicide actions are varied, complex, and multidimensional. Id, ego, superego, and environment all contribute to each suicidal act.
3. Features of typical suicides are reported. Some specific suicide syndromes are reviewed. These include: Suicide with minimal acting out, transference suicide, schizophrenia, alcoholism, special ego states, neurotic symbiotic unions, and depression.
4. Suicide acts begin as fantasy attempts to resolve crises. The fantasies evolve gradually into a suicide plan, which is rehearsed in imagination and in anticipatory actions.
5. The suicide act itself acquires momentum and an autonomous pressure toward completion. This factor is of special importance for therapists who evaluate patients in emergency centers or hospital admitting units.

REFERENCES

1. Bellak, L. Acting-Out: Some Conceptual and Therapeutic Considerations. *Amer. J. Psychotherapy,* 1963, *17,* 375-389.
2. Farberow, N. L., and Shneidman, E. S. *The cry for help.* New York: McGraw-Hill Co., 1961.
3. Levy, D. M. The Act As A Unit. *Psychiatry,* 1962, *25,* 295-314.
4. Litman, R. E., Curphey, T., Shneidman, E. S., Farberow, N. L., Tabachnick, N. Investigations of Equivocal Suicides. *J.A.MA,* 1963, *184,* 924-929
5. Litman, R. E., Shneidman, E. S., and Farberow, N. L. Suicide Prevention Center. *Amer. J. Psychiat.,* 1961, *117,* 1084-1087.
6. Litman, R. E., Farberow, N. L., Shneidman, E. S., Heilig, S. M., and Kramer, J. A. Suicide Prevention Telephone Service. *JA.M.A.,* Accepted for Publication, 1965.
7. Litman, R. E. Immobilization Response to Suicidal Behavior. *J.A.M.A. Arch. Gen. Psychiat.* 1964, *11,* 282-285.
7a. Rogers, C. R. The Characteristics of a Helping Relationship. *Pers. Guid. J.,* 1958, 6-16.
8. Shneidman, E. S., and Farberow, N. L. *Clues to suicide.* New York: McGraw-Hill Co., 1957.
9. Spitz, R. A. The Derailment of Dialogue: Stimulus Overload, Action Cycles, and the Completion Gradient. *J. Amer. Psychoanalytic Assoc.,* 1965, *12,* 752-775.
10. Stengel, E. Some Unexplored Aspects of Suicide and Attempted Suicide. *Comprehensive Psychiat.,* 1960, *1,* 71-80.

8. Suicide in Children and Adolescents

By Kurt Glaser, M.D.

> *Dr. Kurt Glaser offers the reader a comparative approach to an understanding of the increasingly disturbing problem of suicide in children and adolescents. The incidence of suicide in this age group throughout the world is seen as increasing but varying from one country to another. Dr. Glaser is interested in studying the forms in which suicidal intent is expressed and the conflicts and disturbances within the family setting that so often are related to the development of suicidal wishes and the acting out of those wishes.*
>
> *His contribution is an important one which readers of this volume are certain to find significant, interesting, and still disturbing.*

SUICIDES, SUICIDAL THREATS, gestures, and attempts are severe forms of acting out. Although directed against the "self," the act has a symbolic significance that is often to hurt or destroy others. Because of the danger to life or the possibility of permanently crippling results, any intents at self-destruction constitute a psychiatric emergency which requires special therapeutic approaches and preventive measures.

A study of the psychodynamics of the suicidal patient and of the nature of the preceding psychopathology and warning signs may indicate the way toward preventive psychotherapeutic approaches. Since information obtained from the records of completed suicides can supply only deductive implications from historical data and lacks the reliability of personal communication from the patient himself, the present chapter confines itself to a discussion, based on a study of patients who had indicated, but not completed, their intent to destroy themselves.

The material was gathered from a study of a series of patients referred for private psychiatric consultation, and from the literature both in this country and abroad. Certain psychodynamic patterns were found to repeat themselves, and it is thought that their description may be helpful to those working with patients of a similar socioeconomic background.

INCIDENCE

The extent of the suicide problem varies from country to country. Ellis and Allen,[12] in their book, *The Traitor Within,* present a comprehensive statistical comparison of the incidence in various European countries. Other investigators have described the problem as it exists in England,[7,34] France,[17] Germany,[42] Austria,[26] Sweden,[8,13] and Japan.[23] Still others have published historical and sociological surveys and discussions of the problem of suicide among primitive people.[10,15,33,39]

The incidence of completed suicides in children and adolescents in the United States, based on *Vital Statistics* for the year 1962, is summarized in table I. It is interesting to note that in completed suicides, males outnumber females by a wide margin, while in attempted suicides the number of girls is generally reported as being considerably larger.[3,4,20,35]

Table I—Deaths and Death Rates* (In Parentheses) from Suicide in the United States—1962

	Under 10 yrs.	10-14 yrs.	15-19 yrs.	20-24 yrs.
Total	1 (0.0)	102 (0.6)	556 (3.8)	946 (8.2)
Male	1 (0.0)	89 (1.0)	409 (5.5)	706 (12.5)
Female	— —	13 (0.1)	147 (2.0)	240 (4.0)
White:				
Male	1 (0.0)	85 (1.1)	367 (5.8)	607 (12.5)
Female	— —	12 (0.2)	126 (2.0)	207 (4.1)
Negro & other:				
Male	— —	3 (0.3)	32 (3.7)	82 (12.6)
Female	— —	1 (0.1)	17 (1.9)	31 (4.3)

*Death rates per 100,000 estimated midyear population in specified group.
From *Vital Statistics of the United States, 1962.*[38]

Parrish[24] studied the causes of death among Yale University students between 1920 and 1955 and found that of 209 deaths which occurred in this period, 91 (43.8 per cent) were the results of accidents, with suicide the second leading cause at 12 per cent (25 students). Bakwin[2] reported that in 1954 suicide ranked fifth in frequency as a cause of death among 15-to-19-year-old youngsters.

Vital statistics for Baltimore City,[37] with a total population of 924,000, showed no deaths from suicide in children under 14 years of age for 1963, and four in the 15-19 year age group.

The frequency of threats and attempts is considerably higher but cannot be measured accurately since most of the milder forms are not taken outside the family circle and do not come to the attention of the physician or any authority.

Statistical estimates of attempts usually come from poison control centers or accident wards of hospitals and do not include "threats." In a study of cases reported to the New York City Poison Control Center between 1955 and 1958, Jacobziner[18] found the ratio of suicidal attempts to successful suicides to be 50 to 1. Tuckman and Connon,[36] who studied cases of attempted suicide that came to the attention of the Philadelphia Police Department and Poison Control Center over a two-year period in 1958-1959, found a ratio of 120 to 1 of attempted to successful suicides among persons under age 18. They consider even this figure an underestimate. Shochet[32] reported 267 cases of attempted suicide seen in the Emergency Service of Sinai Hospital in Baltimore over a three year period; 61 of these were under 19 years old, with no completed suicides in this age group at this hospital.

The cases which come to the attention of hospitals or police departments usually are the more serious attempts. But there is no doubt that the problem is more widespread than official figures indicate.

The private practitioner, who reaches patients in the socioeconomic groups which are more apt to seek help at the first indication of more serious behavior deviations, often observes milder, less dramatic symptoms of the potential suicide. But these cases generally do not appear in any official tabulations, especially since even in this group suicidal attempts may be consciously concealed in order to save embarrassment, or they may not be recognized as such by either the family, the physician, or even the patient himself, but interpreted as accidents or reckless behavior.

More covert signs of suicidal intent may be detected through psychological studies. An attempt to explore suicidal tendencies of college students at Cornell was made by Braaten and Darling,[6] who used the Minnesota Multiphasic Personality Inventory (M.M.P.I.) and the Mooney Problem Check List. In France, Zimbacca et al.[41] have used the M.M.P.I. and the Rorschach to study the psychopathological characteristics of a group of suicidal patients under 21 years of age. Sapolsky[27] used the Rorschach Test to discover suicidal ideation.

FORMS OF EXPRESSING SUICIDAL INTENT

Suicidal tendencies are expressed in various ways, ranging from a casual statement to the actual, completed suicide. Grouping by severity has been attempted in some studies.[6,22] The mode of expression, however, is not a reliable indicator of the magnitude and depth of the conflict, nor a gauge for the likelihood of repetition.

At times the *casual statement,* "If I don't get what I want, I'll kill myself," may only be a form of speech and not indicate a serious disturbance. At other times it may be a plea for help of a person in serious difficulties and, if not heeded, may be followed by more dramatic threats or possibly a fatal act.

Most casual statements of this nature are not reported to the physician, and parents usually pay little attention to them. But if they are repeated, or accompanied by symptoms of emotional imbalance, or made in the presence of a person usually identified as expert in the field of mental health—which may be a physician, psychologist, social worker, or school counselor—these statements take on a more serious character and should be considered as "threats," and usually require further study.

A boy of 11 years "mentioned killing himself," according to his mother. The parents did not consider his school performance satisfactory in view of his high intelligence, and felt that he was socially not active enough.

Further investigation showed that the boy had not had any recent mood changes, signs of depression, or change in personality. His school performance was average, although it did not correspond to the high demands of the parents. The boy was younger than his classmates since he had skipped a grade at the parents' insistence.

No other serious conflict could be detected. Parental counseling, removal from the highly competitive private school, and proper class placement led to satisfactory school and social adjustment.

Another boy of 12 had made a similar statement to his mother. This boy, however, refused to attend school, felt threatened by other students, and during the initial psychiatric interview indicated that he considered suicide as his "only way out."

He had a serious conflict over his rather unusual breast development which he could no longer hide when he was required to undress for showers, following sports activities. He also felt that he had made enemies among his classmates when, as a member of the school safety patrol, he had reported them for misbehavior.

This boy's conflicts were of a more serious nature, and he and the family needed more than just parental counseling. His "casual statement" had to be considered as a "threat" and a plea for help in conflicts which he could neither solve himself nor communicate without assistance to parents or school personnel.

A more serious warning signal is the *gesture*. It is characterized by a suicidal act, carefully planned to be noticed by someone important in the life of the youngster, but executed in such a way that serious harm is most certainly avoided. Such a patient does not take a serious risk on his life. The thinly veiled purpose of such a gesture is to influence a person and manipulate the environment.

A 17 year old girl told the therapist: "I just scratched my wrist—many do." After visiting an aunt she wanted to prevent or delay her return to her parents.

This girl was socially well adjusted; her school progress was satisfactory, and she had applied for and obtained college admission. The condition of this patient did not warrant prolonged treatment. A few interviews with the girl and counseling sessions with the parents were sufficient to bring about changes in the parent-child relationship, especially since the girl was soon to leave home for college.

A gesture, however, may be followed by more serious attempts if it does not succeed in altering the environmental situation, or if it is made by a person whose resistance to external or internal stress is reduced by emotional and physical ill health.

The next degree in severity is the *"threat."* While it may sound like the "casual statement" mentioned above, it has a more sincere flavor, and is accompanied by other symptoms such as mood swings, temper outbursts, characterological changes, sudden drops in school performance, or withdrawal from friends. If such a threat does not bring the expected results, the patient may then resort to a suicidal attempt.

Such *attempts* are strong, are often last and desperate calls for help, and involve the patient in a definite risk. The patient is often as seriously disturbed as the one who completes the suicide, with the outcome frequently depending on fortuitous circumstances not under his control. We thus may find psychiatrically very ill patients in the "attempt" group, while psychiatrically less disturbed patients may destroy themselves. Any patient in this group deserves a complete psychiatric evaluation, and most of them will be in need of treatment.

A 13 year old girl took phenobarbital, which she had available for the control of her epileptic seizures. She left a note indicating the number of pills she had taken, practically giving instructions for her own rescue. One may conclude that she had no serious intention of taking her life, but circumstances, such as a delay in her parents' return, may have foiled her rescue and the attempt, geared solely to influencing the environment, may have turned into a completed suicide.

Another patient, an 18 year old girl, technically falls into the same category of "attempted suicide" because she survived, but she did so only through immediate surgical intervention. She had been under psychiatric treatment with several psychiatrists and discontinued with all of them at her parents' insistence, the father being unwilling and unable to accept her need for treatment.

Hospitalization was recommended; she escaped from the admitting room, bought a gun, and inflicted herself with several penetrating wounds in the chest. Although classified as an attempt, she was a seriously disordered person who was sincere in her action and neither expected nor wished to survive.

There is still another group of patients who express their suicidal intents *in covert form,* such as accidents or reckless behavior.[21,30] Their numbers cannot be determined since, in many cases, the true motivation for their behavior never reaches the conscious level of the patient nor is it recognized by others. There are indications that many accidents fall into this category. Even if these patients have serious psychiatric disorders, their acts are usually not recognized or classified as suicides or suicidal attempts.

A 17 year old boy had made mild suicidal attempts and gestures. His mood swings, temper outbursts, and violent spells of anger were indications of a serious psychiatric disorder, but he was not given psychiatric help at that time. His subsequent driving at a speed of 100 miles per hour through the small town where his family lived strongly suggested the interpretation of a desperate attempt at self-destruction, destruction of others, or both, or a most inappropriate call for help.

This young man had difficulties in differentiating between hurting himself and hurting others. He was angry at his girl friend and at his parents, and felt misunderstood by the world around him and disappointed in his own inability to solve his conflicts or manage his own affairs. His behavior forced his environment—in this case the police—to action.

Whether the authorities and parents recognize the need for psychiatric help in such cases depends upon their sophistication. At times professional persons, such as the family physician, school psychologist, or social worker get involved and may be able to interpret to the family the deeper meaning of the boy's actions, and thus indicate to them the need for psychiatric help.

Although the above described forms of expression of suicidal intents may be indications of an emotional disturbance and an appeal for help, they cannot be used as reliable gauges for the seriousness of the disturbance, and each case should be investigated on its own merits.

CONFLICTS AND DISTURBANCES OF FAMILY INTRA-RELATIONSHIPS

Intra-family disharmony may reach a degree which seems so unbearable to the child that he seeks drastic means of attracting attention to his plight. Appelbaum[1] interprets suicide as a form of acting out with the intent of solving a psychological problem, even though the "solution" may mean biological destruction.

A controlling and domineering parent, most frequently the mother, stymies the adolescent's desire to attain independence, to rely on his own abilities, to practice the skills he has learned, and to experience his own successes and learn from his mistakes. Self-reliance and self-esteem are lowered, and anger develops toward himself and his parents. Eventually his actions may no longer be directed by logic, but only by his inner need to establish his identity through rebellion against the domineering attitude of his parent.

One teen-ager made this very clear by declaring, "Even if I know mother is right, I just can't give in." The suicidal act then becomes destruction of his own unworthy self and at the same time punishment of his parent. This was brought out by a young man who stated, "Wouldn't it be a nice anniversary present for my mother if I killed myself?" He thought that by this act he could most deeply hurt and punish his mother.

Emotionally detached parents do not meet the dependency needs of their children. The child thus feels rejected and unloved, and finds it impossible to turn to his parents for the solution of conflicts or for comfort in stressful situations. This situation in turn generates feelings of hostility toward the parents who failed the child in their parental role.

The combination of a controlling and domineering mother and a passive, emotionally detached father was found in several of our patients who had made suicidal attempts. Similar findings are reported in the literature, such as, for instance, the case of "Alec" in Bosselman's[5] *Self-Destruction*.

Almost any *inner conflict* in the child may reach proportions which make it seem impossible for the child to escape or solve his dilemma. The situation may be aggravated by a lack of supportive resources available to the child, especially if the parents are non-communicative, detached, or absent, or if the child is afraid to communicate with the parents, as in the case when the conflictual situation involves forbidden behavior. The child's intelligence, maturity, past experience, tolerance for anxiety will influence his choice of the coping mechanism. Here the direct purpose of the suicidal attempt may be to draw attention to the existence of a conflict. As in most neurotic behavior, the deeper aspects of the conflict-producing situation are concealed, rendering the defensive coping mechanism ineffectual.

While we associate suicidal ideation in the adult almost always with depression, this is not so in children. Schrut[29] found that only four of the 19 cases he studied were "chronically depressed, schizoid children," while 15 of this group were "hostile and aggressive, 'acting-out' or openly delinquent."

Overwhelming feelings of guilt may occasionally be the cause of a depressive reaction, although the typical symptoms of depression, as seen in the adult, are seldom present in the very young. In this age group we are more apt to find impulsive reactions to anger and hostility, with the full cycle of ensuing guilt for death wishes and need for punishment not in evidence or not discernible. In our series, classical signs of depression were rare, and those that were observed occurred in older teen-agers. (See case report below.)

While some investigators consider schizophrenic reaction as an important underlying psychopathology in suicidal adolescents,[3] others feel that depression is the most significant condition leading to suicide but that it may not be recognized as such. Toolan,[35] who studied 102 youngsters up to the age of 17 who had been admitted to Bellevue Hospital because of suicidal attempts and threats, writes: "It is our belief that suicidal thoughts and attempts are either ignored or undervalued in adolescents because of the erroneously accepted tenet that adolescents do not become depressed, ergo, suicide is unlikely. If we can successfully recognize the signs by which depression is manifested in younger persons we shall then be in a position to prevent many serious suicidal attempts."

The loss of a dear person can be the cause of intolerable guilt, especially if the patient had in some way felt responsible for his death. Feelings of hate, anger, or jealousy, with the ensuing death wishes, may underlie such self-accusations of responsibility.

> One of our patients, a 17 year old girl, indicated strong feelings of guilt over the death of her sister, who had received a bone marrow transfusion, with our patient as donor, shortly before the latter's death from leukemia.

Being unable to live up to mother's or father's high expectations and believing himself to be a disappointment to the parents may be another reason for low self-esteem and may produce guilt for not being able to reward the parents adequately. Parents not infrequently reinforce this guilt in their attempt to fire the child's ambition to perform. Such statements as, "We do everything for you, and you don't try to please us with good school grades," make the child feel helpless, incapable, and unworthy.

> One young lady, who had taken an overdose of aspirins in a suicidal attempt, expressed this by the statement, "I can never please my parents. I am a disappointment to them." When the situation was discussed between the parents and the child, it became clear that the parents were not consciously aware of the high demands which they made upon the young lady, nor were they cognizant of the realistic limitations of the child's abilities. The mother, in her pleading way, had reinforced guilt feelings in the girl by constantly pointing out the many sacrifices and efforts the parents had made in order to make their daughter happy.

Youngsters with low self-esteem may resort to a suicidal attempt in order to attract the attention and publicity which may give them the desired status. It would not be surprising, therefore, to find that "contagion" plays a certain role in choosing suicide as a means of getting the notoriety which another person had received. An element of suggestion is indicated by the

rather frequent occurrence, shortly before the patient's own attempt, of suicidal acts in the immediate environment of the patient. This has been an interesting feature in a number of our patients and has also been reported in the literature.[9,19,25,42]

PREVENTION AND TREATMENT

The fact that the majority of suicides or suicidal attempts are preceded by threats, in words or action, makes a study of these warning signals all the more important. Jacobziner[18] indicated that 35 per cent of the patients in his study had told someone of their plan prior to the attempt. Shneidman and Farberow[31] state that 75 per cent of persons in their study who committed suicide had previously threatened or attempted to take their lives. Lawler et al.,[20] in their report on 22 children who had been seen at the Winnipeg Children's Hospital following suicidal attempts, found that many of the youngsters had given previous warnings, and that these had gone unrecognized. In France, Gaultier et al.[16] reported that in their group of 47 adolescents many had given earlier indications of their disturbance through previous attempts. If these warnings and threats are recognized and heeded as genuine appeals for help, it has been thought that the repetition of suicidal attempts can be reduced considerably.[28]

This author believes that in order to prevent possible further suicidal acts, more than the triggering motives must be understood by the therapist, the patient, and his parents, and that a brief series of interviews, not necessarily on an in-patient basis, is usually needed for this clarification. Ettlinger and Flordh,[13] who studied 500 cases of attempted suicide in Sweden, pointed out that the assessment of motives yielded different results depending upon when the history was obtained. Immediate interrogation produced the more superficial trigger mechanism, while later interviewing disclosed the deeper and more significant disturbances. They emphasized the benefit of brief hospitalization in observation departments of hospitals. In their follow-up study 8-24 months after the attempts, they found that 16 patients had subsequently died through suicide. They felt that while some suicides may be inevitable, others are preventable. The physician's role in the prevention of suicide has been discussed in a number of studies.[11,22,40]

The basis for suicide prevention in the child is the acceptance of the warning signals as appeals for help on the part of a troubled youngster. Their genuineness and seriousness can be evaluated by means of a careful history obtained from parent and child, designed to elicit mood changes, increased temper outbursts, changes in school performance, withdrawal from friends, or other changes in attitude toward the environment.

Once the genuineness is established, an assessment of the nature of the stressful situation which had triggered the suicidal episode gives us an indication of the child's resistance to withstanding strain and his ability to cope with conflictual situations. The milder the stress which has led to the act, the weaker must be the defenses and coping mechanisms of the patient, and the greater are the chances for a recurrence of a similar situation which may again lead the patient to use a suicidal escape mechanism.

We then proceed to evaluate the nature and depth of the inner conflict experienced by the child and the degree of disharmony existing in the family. This involves an analysis of the child's inner resources in coping with conflictual situations, such as his physical and emotional health, his maturity as compared to his chronological resources and his ability to communicate with other persons; it further includes an evaluation of the resources available to the child, such as parents, friends, or other important people in the patient's life, and their ability and willingness to help.

Unless the severity of the suicidal threat or the absence of resource persons makes it mandatory, hospitalization of the suicidal child or adolescent may further contribute to his feelings of isolation, emphasize his helplessness, and in its degrading effect of physical restraint may increase the feeling of inadequacy. This author feels that while hospitalization may be necessary to prevent death, it is better avoided if the physician can assume with reasonable certainty that the individual can be influenced and if he can rely on the child's immediate environment for cooperation.

If it is found that the patient does not require hospitalization for his immediate protection, or removal from the conflict-producing environment, therapeutic measures can be initiated on an ambulatory basis. At times it may be indicated to assist the patient directly in the temporary avoidance of the source of conflict. This, in fact, may be a prerequisite to continued extramural therapy; on the other hand it may reduce the anxiety level to the extent that it may remove motivation for further therapy. The advisability of such assistance has to be evaluated in the light of this potential complication.

One common denominator for most acting out adolescents is their inability to communicate, or the lack of availability of persons with whom they can communicate meaningfully. It therefore seems that one of the main tasks in preventing a recurrence is the opening of verbal communication channels between physician and patient, and later between parents and patient, so that in the future conflicts may be expressed in words rather than in action. For this it will be necessary that the physician who sees a patient following a suicidal attempt or who suspects suicidal intentions in the patient make himself available to the patient on a 24-hour basis, with an assurance of confidentiality.

In some older adolescents it may be possible to treat only the patient, keeping the parents informed but basically excluding them from the treatment process. In the younger child and in most adolescents, especially those in strong dependency relationship to parents, counseling or treatment of the parents is necessary, depending on the depth of their involvement, the nature of the child's conflict, or the degree of the parents' own emotional health.

If the psychological conflict is of deeper nature, prolonged psychiatric treatment may be indicated. It might be pointed but here that while pediatricians may tend to underestimate the seriousness of suicidal intent and underlying conflict, psychiatrists are more apt to overrate the seriousness of the conflict or underestimate the self-adjusting powers of the individual.

In the first case, the patient may well have to resort to a second attempt in order to attract attention to his plight and impress his surroundings with the seriousness of his conflict. In the second situation, the insistence on prolonged therapy may have a detrimental effect on the patient who may feel that he can cope with or solve his conflicts himself, or who may not at the time wish to enter into prolonged treatment, possibly because he feels too threatened by the magnitude or nature of the conflict and may not be ready to expose it to the psychiatrist, his parents, or himself. In order to escape therapy, the patient then may have to resort to missed appointments or unsatisfactory excuses; and the psychiatrist loses his usefulness as a resource to this patient who is likely to be too embarrassed to return, or who may develop hostility toward what he interprets as the controlling attitude of the psychiatrist which, in the patient's eyes, may well resemble his mother's domineering attitude which he had tried to escape unsuccessfully in the past. Once the contact with the psychiatrist is severed, the patient loses an important safety valve he may need in times of future crises.

SUMMARY

Children and adolescents facing conflictual situations will seek solutions in a variety of ways. Depending on the emotional health and maturity of the child and the magnitude of the conflict in relation to the child's age and maturity, the youngster will seek solutions to the conflict in what may be considered appropriate or inappropriate ways.

One of the inappropriate coping mechanisms is "acting out" which can be directed against others or against one's self. The motivating emotions may be anger and hostility toward controlling parents, feelings of worthlessness and guilt, and frustration in the attempt to find solutions without resorting to dramatic actions.

Classical symptoms of depression are rare in the young. The crucial factor in determining the need for acting out through suicidal acts usually is the lack of ability or opportunity to communicate meaningfully with persons important to the child.

Preventive and therapeutic measures thus must at first be directed toward the establishment of communication channels between patient and therapist. The next step is a therapeutic approach toward the conflict within the child, and parental guidance with the goal of promoting understanding and establishing adequate communication channels between the parents and the child.

REFERENCES

1. Appelbaum, S. A. The problem-solving aspect of suicide. *J. Projective Techniques and Personality Assessment.* 1963, *27,* 259-268.
2. Bakwin, H. Suicide in children and adolescents. *J. Pediat.* 1957, *50,* 749-769.
3. Balser, B. H., and Masterson, J. F. Jr. Suicide in Adolescents. *Amer. J. Psychiat.,* 1959, *116,* 400-404.
4. Bergstrand, C. G., and Otto, U. Suicidal attempts in adolescence and childhood. *Acta Paediat.,* 1962, *51,* 17-26.
5. Bosselman, B. C. *Self-Destruction: a study of the suicidal impulse.* Springfield: Charles C Thomas, 1958. Pp. 25-29.
6. Braaten, L. J., and Darling, C. D. Suicidal tendencies among college students. *Psychiat. Quart.,* 1962, *36,* 665-692.
7. Carpenter, R. G. Statistical analysis of suicide and other mortality rates for students. *Brit. J. prev. soc. Med.,* 1959, *13,* 163-174.
8. Dahlgren, K. G. *On suicide and attempted suicide: a psychiatrical and statistical investigation.* Lund: A.-B.Ph. Lindstets Univ.-Bokhandel, 1945.
9. Derbyshire, R. L. Some social aspects of suicide in Baltimore City during the years 1954, 1955, and 1956. Unpublished Master's thesis, Univ. Maryland, 1959.
10. Dublin, L. I. *Suicide: a sociological and statistical study.* New York: The Ronald Press Co., 1963.
11. Elias, R. B. Is suicide preventable? *Calif. Med.,* 1959, *90,* 128-129.
12. Ellis, E. R., and Allen, G. N. *Traitor within: our suicide problem.* Garden City, N.Y.: Doubleday & Co., 1961.
13. Ettlinger, R., and Flordh, P. Attempted suicide: Experience of 500 cases at a general hospital. *Acta Psychiat. Neurol. Scand.,* 1955, Supp. 103.
14. Farberow, N. L., and Shneidman, E. S. (Eds.) *The cry for help.* New York: McGraw-Hill Book Co., 1961.
15. Firth, R. Suicide and risk-taking in Tikopia society. *Psychiatry,* 1961, *24,* 1-7.
16. Gaultier, M., Fournier, E., and Gorceix, A. A propos de 47 cas de tentatives de suicides chez des adolescents. *Hygiène Mentale,* 1961, *50,* 363-369.
17. Gaultier, M., Fournier, E., Gorceix, A., and Zimbacca, N. Etude clinique et statistique d'un groupe de mineurs suicidants. *Semaine des Hopitaux,* 1963, *50,* 2375-2384.
18. Jacobziner, H. Attempted suicide in children. *J. Pediat.,* 1960, *56,* 519-525.
19. Launay, C., and Col, C. Suicide et tentative de suicide chez l'enfant et l'adolescent. *Revue du Praticien,* 1964, *14,* 619-626.
20. Lawler, R. H., Nakielny, W., and Wright, N. A. Suicidal Attempts in children. *Canad. Med. Assn. J.,* 1963, *89,* 751-754.

21. Menninger, K. A. *Man against himself.* New York: Harcourt, Brace & Co., 1938. Pp. 318-336.
22. Motto, J. A., and Greene, C. Suicide and the medical community. *A.M.A. Arch. Neurol. Psychiat.*, 1958, *80,* 776-781.
23. Ohara, K. A study on the factors contributing to suicide from the standpoint of psychiatry. *Amer. J. Psychiat.*, 1964, *120,* 798-799.
24. Parrish, H. M. Causes of death among college students. *Publ. Hlth. Rep., Wash.*, 1956, *71,* 1081-1085.
25. Ringel, E. Ein Beitrag zur Frage der vererbten Selbstmordneigung. *Wien. Z. Nervenheilk*, 1952, *5,* 26-40.
26. Ringel, E., Spiel, W., and Stepan, M. Untersuchungen über kindliche Selbstmordversuche. *Prax. Kinderpsychol. Kinderpsychiat.*, 1955, *4,* 161-168.
27. Sapolsky, A. An indicator of suicidal ideation on the Rorschach Test. *J. Projective Techniques & Personality Assessment*, 1963, *27,* 332-335.
28. Schneer, H. I., Kay, P., and Brozovsky, M. Events and conscious ideation leading to suicidal behavior in adolescence. *Psychiat. Quart.*, 1961, *35,* 507-515.
29. Schrut, A. Suicidal adolescents and children. *J.A.M.A.*, 1964, *188,* 1103-1107.
30. Selzer, M. L., and Payne C. E. Automobile accidents, suicide and unconscious motivation *Amer. J. Psychiat.*, 1962, *119,* 237-240.
31. Shneidman, E. S., and Farberow, N. L. (Eds.) *Clues to suicide.* New York: McGraw-Hill Book Co., 1957.
32. Shochet, B. R. Attempted Suicide: Experience in a General Hospital emergency service. *Md. State Med. J.*, 1964, (March), 107-112.
33. Steinmetz, S. R. Suicide among primitive people. *Amer. Anthropologist*, 1894.
34. Stengel, E., and Cook, N. G. *Attempted suicide: its social significance and effects.* London: Chapman & Hall Ltd., 1958.
35. Toolan, J. M. Suicide and suicidal attempts in children and adolescents. *Amer. J. Psychiat.*, 1962, *118,* 719-724.
36. Tuckman, J., and Connon, H. E. Attempted suicide in adolescents. *Amer. J. Psychiat.*, 1962, *119,* 228-232.
37. Vital statistics, City of Baltimore. Annual report of the Department of Health, 1963.
38. *Vital Statistics of the United States, 1962.* U.S. Department of Health, Education, and Welfare, Public Health Service, National Vital Statistics Division.
39. Zilboorg, G. Suicide among civilized and primitive races. *Amer. J. Psychiat.*, 1936, *92,* 1347-1369.
40. Zilboorg, G. Differential diagnostic types of suicide. *Arch. Neurol. Psychiat.*, 1936, *35,* 270-291.
41. Zimbacca, N., Gorceix, A., and Lejeune, M. Étude psychometrique de la population précédente. *Semaine des Hopitaux*, 1963, *50,* 2384-2391.
42. Zumpe, L. Selbstmordversuche von Kindern und Jugendlichen: Persoenlichkeitsmerkmale und Entwicklungsverlaeufe anhand von 34 Katamnesen. *Z. Psychother. Med. Psychol.*, 1959, *9,* 223-243.

Note:

The literature on suicide and suicidal attempts in children and adolescents is not voluminous, and some of the reference material cited in this paper does not deal specifically with children. These references are included here because it is felt that the findings are to a certain extent applicable to children and adolescents. For an extensive collection of references on suicide in general the reader is referred to Farberow and Shneidman's book, *The Cry for Help,* published in 1961.

9. Delinquency and Criminality: An Acting Out Phenomenon

By Jacob Chwast, Ph.D.

In "Delinquency and Criminality: An Acting Out Phenomenon," Jacob Chwast offers us a panorama of the activity, both illegal and marginal, that young persons and adults engage in that may lead to their delinquency and criminality. In laying bare the whole range of delinquent and criminal behavior with which the chapter deals, Doctor Chwast writes from a background of twenty years as a member of the New York Police Department; and what he has to say grows out of not only his acute psychological understanding but also his many years of day to day wrestling with the problems of management of delinquency and crime in New York City.

He makes it clear that the typical offender runs the gamut of age in dereliction, pathology, and even the absence of pathology, and that he comes from all levels of American society. In seeking to understand these persons who have run afoul of the law, Chwast finds it most helpful to ask what is the form of their acting out, where does it take place, what is its direction, and what is its duration? The result of his inquiry is a contribution to psychological literature but also to an understanding of law enforcement problems.

DELINQUENCY AND CRIMINALITY have been regarded generally as forms of acting out behavior *par excellence*. An obvious reason for this is that a delinquent or criminal becomes identifiable as such by definition because of some overt act committed in violation of law. It is this, his acting against the standards of society as concretized in legal codes, that sets the offender, be he adult criminal or juvenile delinquent, apart from his fellow man.*

To a large degree, this acting against such social norms may reflect the resolution of unconscious conflicts within the individual and thus represent acting out, if the latter is so defined; to a large degree, it may not represent acting out in this sense and yet denote overt actions.

When one contemplates the entire panorama of illegal activity, one finds it difficult to generalize about all offenders, although some generalizations

---

*Generally, delinquency is defined as consisting of acts which if committed by an adult would be considered to be criminal. There is the exception to this rule, however, in that specified courses of action which are not deemed criminal *per se* such as incorrigibility, truancy, running away, etc., may also be deemed to be delinquent.

about some are possible. As a group, offenders consist of all kinds of people in all kinds of circumstances. The offender runs the gamut of ages, derelictions, pathologies, or even "non-pathologies." He is found in prison, the court, and the community. He operates by himself, within the family orbit, as a member of a clan, or in the gang peer-group. He may be under arrest, on probation, parole, or undetected as yet.

Although murder, assault, rape, robbery, burglary, and arson do strongly suggest acting out on an unconscious basis, this ought not be blithely assumed. Although this may be true for the acculturated offender who is the product of the dominant middle class in American society, it may not be true for that type of offender who is the product of what has been referred to as a "culture conflict."[14] In this situation, the reaction of a large group of dislocated people who have become the inhabitants of the ghettos in large urban centers usually may be less a reflection of unconscious conflicts than it is of unfamiliarity, confusion, or rebellion against dominant values and mores.

For this reason, a grasp of the nature of delinquency and criminality demands a deeper comprehension of the social forces underlying them than is necessary perhaps for any of the other forms of acting out. In saying this, one appreciates how cautiously one must tread in view of Durkheim's classic study of suicide: one in which he lays bare primarily the sociological factors involved.[8] In any event, for delinquency and crime, social considerations are at least of equal importance to those which are psychological in origin.

What becomes much more challenging is the specification of the ways in which these social factors or processes interact with the psychological processes within the individual to eventuate in acting out behavior of an illegal, antisocial (i.e., delinquent or criminal) nature. The complexity of this task becomes apparent when one observes that, in addition to the overall *Zeitgeist*, the subculture and peer group exert powerful pressures upon the individual toward deviance. The family or "under-the-roof culture," of course, scores high as a prepotent influence.[9]

Before discussing a number of causal factors which appear related to delinquent and criminal acting out, we find it useful to comment upon some parameters of this phenomenon, such as its form, locus, direction, and duration.

Forms of Acting Out

1. By the individual. The most common expression of acting out behavior is that seen in the individual. Some observers have contended

that most delinquency is the result of gang activity primarily,[7] but it is more likely that criminal and delinquent acts are overwhelmingly perpetrated by persons who operate by themselves.

2. *By dyads.* Many types of acting out require the participation of a partner. An already historic instance of this is the Leopold and Loeb case; other folie à deux situations come to mind. In dyadic acting out, two varieties are possible. In the first, both partners may be joined via interlocking pathology in achieving a similar antisocial objective as, for example, a robbery or other crime. In the second, the partners may be antagonistic yet reciprocally reinforcing the activity of the other. This undoubtedly occurs in many crimes of a sexual nature and, of course, one is reminded of the relationship between the criminal and the victim noted by Von Hentig.[16]

3. *By groups.* Acting out by groups is usually most dramatic. Ordinarily this occurs as a consequence of gang conflict. Here the actors are invariably adolescent peers who have joined forces in fairly durable relationships against other peer groups and adult society.

Larger numbers of persons can also merge their forces to act out. Under these circumstances, this may appear as mob action—an essentially transitory grouping unified for a single purpose—or the acting out may persist for a long time as is typical of the criminal combine. In the latter, clan relationships seem significant, and the impulse to act may be derived more from conscious, predetermined, predaceous motivation than from unconscious conflict.

4. *By the family.* Although this is not appreciated so much as it might be, the hearthside is often the place where much criminal acting out occurs. Most of this does not come to official attention because the tendency is for all of our social institutions to converge toward preserving family unity and functioning. Those familiar with the types of family situations dealt with in civil cases, however, are considerably impressed by the enormous number of acts which would be defined as criminal in other contexts: maiming, assault, larceny, extortion, and the entire range of sexual deviation.

Locus of Acting Out

The theatres of delinquency and criminality are rather diversified:

1. *The family.* As indicated above, the family is the site of considerable antisocial activity. Of course, in acting against the family, it is evident that this may occur in the actual household or outside. Although the family may well be implicated as a causal factor in much crime and delinquency, it is being referred to in this context merely as the actual setting in which the acting out occurs.

2. The peer group. While the peer group serves as a meeting ground for young people as they strive to gratify basic needs, it is also the scene of much conflict. This conflict generally occurs between rival groups of adolescents but often is enacted against other members of the community.

3. Against authority. In a special way, the acting out of children in school, in the social agency such as the community center, or directly against the police is to be seen as a manifestation of some unresolved problem with authority figures.

4. Within the community. Criminal and delinquent behavior which occurs in the community at large may be exhibited in two ways. In the first place, it may occur as an impersonal act against anybody who happens to become the target of the actor's hostility. Second, it may be seen as a personal act against a specific target.

Direction of Acting Out

Criminal and delinquent acting out can take place against a person, place, or object. Wilson[17] has observed that two elements contribute to the perpetration of a criminal act. First, the individual must possess the desire and, second, he must be presented with the opportunity to commit a crime, or must believe that the opportunity exists. Other than in the wholly adventitious crime, and even here one cannot be certain, the symbolic significance of the criminal target must be grasped in order to understand why it is that some opportunities are seized upon and others are not.

Duration of Acting Out

1. Transitory. Many offenses are essentially one-shot affairs. Indeed, most crimes are enacted by individuals who will never repeat their offenses. In this case, the individual is usually stimulated to the anti-social act because some crisis has erupted in his life with which he cannot cope other than by going out of bounds.[10]

2. Continuous. Among some persons, criminal acting out is a fairly constant occurrence. The basic orientation is anti-social at most times, under most circumstances.

3. Episodic Regular. Other persons are also subject to persistent anti-social impulses which they may not enact continuously but with a certain degree of periodicity. In these instances, the anti-social impulse manifests an ebb and flow which results in the commission of an offense at points at which the pressure reaches a peak.

4. Episodic irregular. It is also possible for some individuals who possess a lower loading of tension to act this out from time to time on an irregular basis.

Some Causal Factors

While the causes of acting out are linked to personality and/or socially pathological processes, a number of specific etiological factors appear delineable. Although no pretense is made that the following listing is exclusive or complete, it is offered as a beginning in this direction.

1. *Anti-social crisis:* Usually the delinquent act, and this holds to a large extent for a criminal act, flows from an anti-social crisis which may assume several forms.[10] Anti-social activity does not respect time or place usually, nor does it respect treatment so much as one would hope. The therapist may, therefore, observe the crises which constitute essentially reactions to the transference relationship or to the offender's real life situation. In the former, the offender may react to some alteration in his relationship with the therapist that explodes into acting out. In the latter, the offender might be reacting to some acute stress which occurs in his life situation and over which he has no control.

During the course of therapy, the therapist may observe other overlapping types of crises which can be accompanied by acting out. These are the presenting crisis, continuous crisis, and terminal crisis, each of which is essentially defined by its name.

2. *The malevolent transformation.* This phenomenon has been described by Sullivan[15] as one wherein the individual who has felt himself to be rejected and hated throughout his life turns this feeling around into a feeling of hatred for other persons. At this time, he is unable to tolerate any feelings of tenderness or dependency, and strikes out aggressively when such feelings are stirred up within him. The anxiety aroused at the rejection which they portend is too much for him to bear, and his aggression serves as a signal repudiation of his need for affection.[4] This mechanism is one which appears to fit the psychopath or character disorder extremely well and in their cases the reaction is probably irreversible.[5] It also occurs among gang children, in whose case there seems to be considerable hope that it can be reversed.[13]

3. *Desensitization.* Closely linked to the malevolent transformation is the process of desensitization. Here the individual who is unable to tolerate feelings of tenderness gradually constructs for himself emotional callouses. In this fashion, he can insulate himself against feelings of loyalty, sympathy, kindness, or concern so that his actions become increasingly inhuman and brutalized. This mechanism undoubtedly typifies the offender who joins the organized criminal syndicate and executes its predatory decrees unswervingly. In such cases, it often happens that the criminal progressively marches from malicious mischief to murder in a negative testing out style. Each small crime, successfully accomplished and then absorbed emotionally without a response of guilt or other counter balancing compensatory reaction, leads the criminal to the next larger antisocial venture.[12]

4. *Overpowering instinctual drives.* For some individuals, the pressure of instinctual drives is so great that neither they nor society has the capacity for containing them. Such individuals are almost invariably inaccessible to therapeutic intervention because their feelings and fantasies are not appeased by ordinary gratifications or rewards. One observes antisocial acting out on this basis occurring frequently in the case of drug addicts and psychopaths.

This phenomenon probably also accounts for the difficulty usually encountered in the treatment of adolescent delinquents, and it contributes considerably to sexual acting out.[5]

5. *Alienation.* A common malaise of our times is alienation. Most people today wall themselves off from their feelings because the threat implicit in a society such as ours, which is becoming increasingly technological at a frightening pace, is too much to bear.* When these feelings are confirmed by experiences at home, among peers, or within the community, the tension for anti-social acting out becomes greatly reinforced.[2] The effects of alienation are evidenced by people at all levels and in all forms. It is especially pronounced among the socially deprived members of society among whose numbers delinquents figure high.

6. *Guilt.* The relationship between guilt and acting out is rather complex. Usually guilt enters the lists as an ally of anxiety, whether casually, concomitantly, or sequentially, and thus serves to suppress rather than to excite an actional response. In some instances, however, guilt does precipitate acting out, and such instances may be classified under two headings. First, when guilt is so excessive that it cannot be tolerated internally any longer, it may become transformed into a state of tension which leads to agitated, rather non-discriminating, randomized activity. The second class of responses to guilt is one in which the individual has become so preoccupied with an avoidance of significant relationships and responsibility that when even the slightest twinge of guilt threatens to appear, he acts swiftly to destroy its source. This mechanism is similar to what has been described above in the malevolent transformation and in desensitization.

Mention must also be made here of the point of view held by Bergler,[1] that psychopathic acting out is usually the consequence of massive unconscious guilt against which the psychopath reacts. It should be stressed, however, that the quality of such guilt must differ considerably from that which leads to purposeful ameliorative behavior. Whereas the former constitutes a primitive response, the latter is much more sophisticated and civilized.[6]

7. *Control.* Control is probably the most critical factor in determining whether acting out does or does not occur. This may be stated more

---

*Bellak has referred to this phenomenon as "impersonalization" as contrasted to "depersonalization"—a more frequent clinical symptom 20 to 30 years ago.

explicitly in this form: anti-social acting out takes place under circumstances in which controls, inner or outer, are not strong enough to restrain the individual from overtly discharging certain of his impulses, i.e., those which may be dangerous to life or limb or the possessions of others.

To some extent, the foregoing discussion has dealt with a number of considerations which determine whether an individual can build up adequate inner control developmentally, or can determine why they may be broken down, if previously present. Within the individual, controls are built up gradually and generally emerge from two sources.[3] In the first place, the individual, if he feels loved by the significant others surrounding him, particularly in his younger years, will identify with their values and ideals, and willingly submit himself to the demands for appropriate behavior implicit therein. The other pressure upon the individual to control himself so that he does not act out in disapproved ways is by punishment or by the deliberate inculcation of guilt feelings within himself. The use of guilt in this way assures that socialized conduct results from the individual's interaction with his environment without recourse to more sereve alternatives such as corporal punishment, or deprivation in the case of child, fines, imprisonment, banishment, or even execution in the case of the adult offender.

There is an intimate connection between inner and outer, or personal and social, controls. If the outer controls are too rigid, too loose, or inconsistent, the individual's inner controls may not develop appropriately; and acting out may become an essential means of escaping unbearable anxiety or tension.

Outside Value Supports

As one's personality is molded, one responds to all of the stimuli about him, whether obvious or not. The manner in which these stimuli, or messages from the outside environment, are transmitted or communicated to the individual is of the essence in determining the way and extent to which the person will respond to them. If the message is direct and uncluttered, the individual can receive it without confusion and react accordingly. If, however, he receives a message at one level, which is contradicted at another level, the individual's response is bound to emerge in an unanticipated manner. This may well happen frequently where the delinquent child is concerned. With him, Johnson[11] has suggested that he acts out the unconscious impulses of his parent. This formulation can be extended beyond the familial orbit, as stressed by Johnson, although the latter is probably most significant for the child.

The family itself is exposed to the open and covert cues of society as is the child. These open and covert cues are largely determined by society's explicit and implicit values. These values influence the family tremendously, and oftentimes the net result in actual behavior is that although some individuals may partially control their impulses in order to achieve certain approved objectives, they may not control these or related impulses partially because they are being encouraged simultaneously on another level to gratify them. This process of encouraging the enactment of impulses and concomitantly inhibiting their enactment is one which pervades the entire range of human relationships. It takes place between the child and his parents; between the child and his peers; between the child, his family, and the subculture; and between the child, his family, and the larger society (primarily perceived in the newspapers, radio, television, moving pictures and other media of mass communication) about him.

From this it seems that acting out cannot be understood as dependent primarily upon intrapsychic causes, but it also is related to reality factors. It is evident that the outer world, in most significant ways, reinforces or inhibits impulses which lead to acting out behavior of a criminal or delinquent nature.

If violence is extolled as a national or regional policy, or even locally, one can hardly expect the young and immature to withstand the impulse to strike out. If, on the other hand, peaceable solutions are sought in conflict situations at all levels of our social structure, one can legitimately expect that acting out behavior will diminish. This becomes particularly clear in the lower socio-economic levels, whether old brownstone or new red brick. The child from the lower socio-economic neighborhood will oftentimes reflect, by aggressive actions, the bitterness and hostility he and his parents feel against the middle class world whose ambivalently perceived dominating influence is felt on every hand. This is not to suggest that the middle class influence is not a good one, nor even that left to their own devices these socially deprived members of our society would do well or better. It is simply to point out that there is a contradiction in what the poor person is led to expect and what he is actually capable of achieving, and that this produces a conflict in his mind that can later lead to tension, anxiety, and aggressive acting out.*

CONCLUSION

There is no royal road to curbing antisocial acting out. The diverse ways in which it is manifested, the multi-determined ways in which it is

---

*H. Hyman has pointed out that in any society which stimulates its members toward the attainment of certain goals (money, consumer goods, etc.) while at the same time providing little opportunity or means for their attainment—"innovation" (of which *crime* is one example) will be a common phenomenon.

specifically produced, the need to meet the interrelated personal and social forces entailed all make it obvious that no simple solutions exist.

In criminal and delinquent acting out, both psychodynamic and sociodynamic influences are often inseparably linked. The many varieties of such acting out suggest that we may need to employ many modalities to understand and deal with it adequately.

REFERENCES

1. Bergler, E. Psychopathic Personalities Unconsciously Propelled by a Defense Against a Specific Type of Psychic Mechanism. *Special Issue on Psychopathy Arch. Crim. Psychodyn.*, 1961, 416-434.
2. Chwast, J. Alienation as a Factor in Delinquency. *Federal Probation*, 1964. *28*, 25-30.
3. ———. Control: The Key to Offender Treatment. *Amer. J. Psychother.*, 1965, *19*, 116-125.
4. ———. The Malevolent Transformation. *J. Crim. Law. Crimin. Pol. Sc.*, 1963, *54*, 42-47.
5. ———. Reversibility-Irreversibility: Problems in the Treatment of Offenders. *Am. J. Psychothpy.*, 1961, *15*, 221-232.
6. ———. The Social Function of Guilt. *Soc. Wk.*, 1964, *9*, 58-63.
7. Cohen, A. K. *Delinquent boys: the culture of the gang.* Glencoe, Illinois: Free Press, 1955.
8. Durkheim, E. *Suicide.* Trans. by John A. Spaulding and George Simpson. Glencoe, Illinois: Free Press, 1951.
9. Glueck, S., and Glueck, E. *Unraveling juvenile delinquency.* New York: Commonwealth Fund, 1950.
10. Harari, C., and Chwast, J. The Antisocial Crisis in Psychotherapy with Delinquents. *Corr. Psychiat. J. Soc. Thpy.*, 1964, *10*, 301-314.
11. Johnson, A.M. Sanctions for Superego Lacunae. In Eissler, K. R. (Ed.), *Searchlights on delinquency.* New York: International Universities Press, 1949, 225-244.
12. Schmideberg, M., and Sokol, J. Insensitization in the Psychopathic Personality. *J. Ass. Psychiat. Treatmt. Off.*, 1957, *1*, 4.
13. Seller, S., and Taylor, J. The Malevolent Transformation: Implications for Group Work Practice. *Soc. Wk.* In press.
14. Sellin, Thorsten. *Culture conflict and crime.* New York: Social Science Research Council, 1938.
15. Sullivan, H. S. *The interpersonal theory of psychiatry.* New York: W. W. Norton, 1953.
16. Von Hentig, Hans. *The criminal & his victim.* New Haven: Yale University Press, 1948.
17. Wilson, O. W. *Police administration.* 2nd Ed. New York: McGraw-Hill, 1963.

PART III
SPECIAL FORMS OF ACTING OUT

Acting out has many dimensions. Typically the behavior referred to involves overt aggressive or self-destructive behavior. Yet, within the context of the volume, acting out may involve any behavior which is a translation of an unconscious statement into an overt act, generally ego-syntonic.

The clinical entities represented in this part are rarely thought of as "acting out" in the usual sense of the term. But a closer look at such phenomena as drug addiction, obesity, alcoholism, psychosomatic illness (as a body language), homosexuality, and learning inhibitions suggests that these entities, too, make a statement. What is the obese person saying through his overeating? Is it different from the message given by the drug addict, the alcoholic, the somatically disturbed individual, the homosexual, or underachieving student?

The authors in this part have addressed themselves to this question by painting a full dynamic picture of each entity and labelling the unconscious statement of which the disturbance is a derivative. There is, however, diversity in theory. Although Drs. Rasor, Fox, Frazier, and Bieber are more traditionally analytic in their approach, the reader will encounter, in the papers of Drs. Dunkell and Melniker, an interesting existential point of view, particularly in the final chapter by Melniker whose "epigenetic" model encompasses many of the non-pathological aspects of acting out.

10. Drug Addiction: An Acting Out Problem

By ROBERT W. RASOR, M.D.

Doctor Robert W. Rasor looks upon drug addiction as an acting out problem in his chapter below. As Doctor Rasor makes clear, we need to have a very specific definition of drug addiction and understand not only the pharmacology of the drug or drugs used but also the deep needs and underlying problems of those who become addicted to the drugs. His chapter is an important contribution to this end.

Readers who have become increasingly aware of the scope and importance of the drug addiction problem will be interested in seeing, as Rasor does, the most common and important psychodynamic factors that appear to make for drug addiction proneness.

ABT AND WEISSMAN[1] define "acting out behavior" as the ". . . non-verbal translation of an unconscious conflict. The individual attempts to resolve an internal struggle through external action which generally is ego-syntonic, although the consequences may be ego-alien."

In studying patients addicted to narcotic drugs, one sees this form of acting out behavior quite often. Once addiction is established, the addict is compelled to perpetuate this self-destructive behavior. All his energy is expended securing the addicting drug necessary to maintain the psychological and physiological state in which he obtains satisfaction and gratification. This gratification becomes more important to him than love, or food, or sex.

The drug addict tries to reconcile his basic instinctual urges with the demands of reality through the use of an addicting drug. To reverse the process of addiction, the addict must marshal all his psychic energy on the side of his ego in abstaining from the use of narcotics and reconcile his basic instinctual needs with the demands of reality.

In discussing drug addiction, we must have a very clear definition. The definition of Vogel, Isbell, and Chapman[20] is most satisfactory: "Drug addiction may be defined as a state in which a person has lost the power of self-control with reference to a drug and abuses the drug to such an extent that the person or society is harmed." Himmelsbach and Small[8] included in their definition three distinct but related phenomena: (1) tolerance, (2) physical dependence, and (3) habituation. Tolerance is defined as a diminishing effect on repetition of the same dose of the drug, or conversely, a necessity to increase the dose to obtain an effect equivalent to the original dose when the drug is administered repeatedly over a period of time. Physical dependence refers to an altered physiological state brought about by the repeated administration of the drug over a period of time which necessitates the continued use of the drug to prevent the characteristic illness which is termed the abstinence syndrome. The abstinence symptoms include sweating, lacrimation, rhinorrhea, yawning, dilation of the pupils, gooseflesh, muscular twitching and cramps, anorexia, vomiting, diarrhea, insomnia, and increase in blood pressure and temperature. These symptoms may be rated by a system devised by Himmelsbach[8] and Kolb.[10]

Drug addiction, as discussed here, refers to the opiates and synthetic analgesics with a morphine-like action. This is the type of addiction most commonly seen at the United States Public Health Service Hospitals at Lexington, Kentucky and Fort Worth, Texas. Much that applies to opiate addiction also is applicable to other forms of addiction, particularly sedatives and alcohol.

Narcotic addiction increased following World War II. Prior to this time there was relatively little concern about narcotic addiction as a major health problem. The number of addicts prior to World War II seemed to be on the decline, judging from the number of Selective Service rejections at that time.[18] During the war there was minimal traffic in narcotics because of controls on shipping.

In 1946 and 1947 "juvenile addiction" began to increase. This increase was first noticed in our large metropolitan areas. Chein, Gerard, Lee and Rosenfeld[2] found that juvenile addicts started to use addicting drugs at age 15, usually by first taking marihuana and later switching to heroin. They would commonly start by "snorting" (inhaling) the heroin. After snorting for a rather short period, they would go on to "joy popping," meaning infrequent intramuscular or subcutaneous use. From this, they would go on to "mainlining," meaning intravenous use. Juvenile addicts as seen in the United States Public Health Service Hospital at Lexington, Kentucky had a greater representation from minority groups.[17]

It is interesting to compare the profile of the patient seen at present with those seen 25 to 30 years ago. Dr. Pescor[13] did a statistical analysis of the clinical records of 1,036 addict patients admitted to the Lexington hospital during the year July 1, 1936 to June 30, 1937. In summary, he describes a "statistical" addict composed of averages and highest frequencies:

> "Such a hybrid individual would be a white male prisoner, 38 years of age, given a two year sentence for the illegal sale of narcotics by a Federal court. . . . As an adult he would live in a deteriorated metropolitan section. More than likely he would have to resort to illegal means

of earning the additional income required to support his drug habit. He would marry, but his marriage would probably terminate in separation or divorce. . . . He would become addicted to morphine at the age of 27 through the influence of associates and curiosity. He would be given an average prognosis for permanent cure. This is a vague way of stating that he would probably relapse."

Twenty-five to 30 years later we would find that the "statistical" addict would be a much younger individual in his early twenties; he would be a member of a minority group, colored or Latin-American. He would not come from a parental home intact up to the age of 18. His choice of drug would be heroin, and he would likely have to resort to illegal means of earning the additional income required to support his drug habit. If this addict were a Federal prisoner, his sentence would be of considerably longer duration.

This youthful addict was not the only type seen at the hospital. A significant number of older addicts were also seen, but usually their addiction followed a different pattern. An example of this is the physician addict whose addiction is usually late in onset, starting with a single occasional injection of meperidine hydrochloride (Demerol) and continuing or increasing the frequency and dosage until addiction developed. The reason many of them give for their addiction was "over work." In a look beneath the surface it was usually obvious that over work had very little to do with the addiction, and the underlying dynamics were not different from those of the young heroin addict. The addict in each case found his stresses made him very uncomfortable, and he tried to reconcile these pressures with the demands of reality through the use of an addicting drug. Also seen were a significant number of older addicts who used paregoric or terpin hydrate with codeine. These patients were usually white, from urban communities, and many seemed to have more in common with the alcoholic than with the narcotic addict.

Physicians studying and classifying drug addicts have used most of the psychiatric diagnoses.[4,7,9] Psychoanalytical knowledge and techniques have been used to gain understanding of the addict's behavior, and to find economic, genetic, and dynamic meaning for the symptom formation. Weiss[21] defines psychodynamics as: "the science which describes and explains the manifestations and the consequences of the inter-action of mental forces within the human being." Economics refers to the principle of maintaining psychic equilibrium through repetitive use of a minimum expenditure of psychic energy. Genetics refers to the origin and development of the patient's personality and the current conflicts related to symptom formation. The psychoanalytical literature has been reviewed by Crowley.[3]

In the youthful narcotic addict, a particular type of individual in a particular social setting uses a particular toxic addicting drug. The addicting drug, heroin, has specific pharmacological effects on the individual. Tolerance to the drug will develop, the body will become physically dependent on the drug, and if the drug is not available after physical dependence has developed, the abstinence syndrome will appear.

Heroin in this country is available only through illegal traffic. Individuals using heroin violate Federal, State, or local laws by having the drug in their possession. The individual is committing an illegal act, and the fact that drug addiction is not socially acceptable may increase the attraction of this form of behavior. It is a rebellious type of behavior and can be considered "acting-out behavior." These individuals usually start experimenting with drugs at about the age of 15. At this period of their life, they are trying to go from boyhood to manhood or from being a girl to becoming a woman. They are experimenting with their sexual impulses, trying to make some type of satisfactory adjustment. Most of these adolescents have trouble with parental authority and rebel against it. They are in conflict with their environment, which is frequently a slum area in which they find themselves. There is conflict between what they have and what others have. The opportunities available to these individuals are different from the opportunities available to others. It is in this setting that this rebellious form of behavior expresses itself. In considering the underlying factors important in the development of an individual's narcotic addiction, one must also emphasize the social and environmental factors.

As the addiction-prone individual develops, he finds himself in an environment in which he feels unloved and unwanted. He does not feel at peace with himself or his environment. He is not attracted to the more conventional groups, such as, the athletes, the "squares," or the intellectuals, but is attracted to the groups who are experimenting with narcotics. Members of this group find themselves in conflict with their environment and rebel against it by acting out against authority.

The use of marihuana and heroin is a rebellious act. It is not accepted in our culture, and possession of the drugs is illegal. This may also be somewhat similar to experimenting with tobacco as indulged in by many youngsters at this age, and also the use of alcohol as is so common with the adolescent who may also be rebelling against a society with which he is not in harmony.

Narcotic addiction can be considered an infantile form of behavior. It is a narcissistic, hedonistic form of behaving governed entirely by the pleasure principle. The type of gratification that many addicts derive from the injection of the drug has been equated with the erotic pleasure of the sexual orgasm. Rado[14-16] has referred to this in his papers. Once addiction has been established, most individuals lose interest in sexual activity, and the gratification from the drug replaces sexual gratification. In this respect, drug addiction becomes similar to a sexual perversion, where an immature form of sexual behavior is substituted for the mature type of gratification. Many addicts experiment with all forms of homosexual and heterosexual activity. They seldom reach the level of sexual maturity, however, where they can make a mature sexual adjustment with a member of the opposite sex. They are usually unable to accept mature roles, and make poor wives or husbands or mothers and fathers. When they are asked what they want most in the world, they will usually reply, "I want to be married, to have a wife or a husband, a home and children." Their addiction, however, prevents them from ever achieving this level of achievement in any true sense of the word. The role of being a mature man or woman is not acceptable to them at an unconscious level, and their addiction will prevent them from filling these roles.

The narcotic addict remains at a very immature level of psychosexual development. His erotic gratification is obtained by the injection of a toxic-addicting drug. When the drug is injected, it gives the individual satisfaction that he has not been able to obtain in other ways. The addicting drug acts on the central nervous system, producing a psycho-pharmacological state which may progress to a stuporous, dream-like state in which stimuli arising either within or without the individual are perceived as pleasurable or less painful. When the effect of the drug begins to wear off, the existing stimuli become less pleasurable, with pain arising as a result of the abstinence syndrome; and the individual pursues his "hustling" behavior to obtain more drugs to perpetuate the desired psycho-pharmacological effect. If, for any reason, the drug is not available, the individual may experiment with other drugs, such as barbiturates, amphetamines, or alcohol, in an attempt to produce the desired psychological state.

Just as drug addiction is a way of dealing with libidinal impulses, it is also a way of dealing with hostile aggressive impulses. Nacht[11] has pointed out what man has known for centuries—that love and hate are at the very roots of our existence. It seemed to him that those he was called upon to treat had more difficulty in mastering the conflict set up by aggressive tendencies than those of other origin. In coming to these conclusions, he found that he had rediscovered what Freud[6] had already said: "I am convinced that very many processes will admit of much simpler and clearer explanation if we restrict findings of psycho-analysis in respect to the origin of the sense of guilt to the aggressive instincts."

The use of narcotics can also be viewed as an expression of a hostile destructive impulse directed against the self. The individual takes a toxic substance which is quite dangerous and injects it intravenously. If the amount of drug is great enough, it will produce a stuporous state which may progress to coma or even death. Most addicts use little, if any, septic precautions when they inject the drug, and infections, such as hepatitis, are rather common. The strength of each injection may vary tremendously since the drug is usually "cut" many times before it reaches the user. Occasionally addicts receive a supply of narcotics that is much stronger than they are accustomed to, and an overdose is not uncommon. O'Donnell[12] has pointed out that many such individuals die non-natural deaths. The exact number, however, dying from overdoses is not known and very difficult to estimate.

This form of behavior can also be viewed as a hostile act directed toward others. The hostility is most often directed toward the mother or the mother substitute. Time and time again, the struggle goes on between the child and mother. The individual uses the drug in a hostile, destructive manner against himself, but he recognizes that his mother suffers along with him. What he seems to be saying through his behavior is, "You are responsible for my suffering and because of this you should suffer also." Most addicts have had a great deal of oral deprivation during the early years of their life. Their mothers have not been able to give them the love and affection that they needed to develop a sense of security or belonging. Many of them come from disrupted homes in which their infantile needs were not provided for in an acceptable manner. As a result, relationships with love objects remained very tenuous. As they enter adolescence and start experimenting with libidinal impulses toward members of the opposite sex, drugs seem to have an unusual attraction. Through the drug they try to deal with their erotic impulses, and maintain a level of psychic equilibrium with a reasonable degree of comfort. They rebel against parental authority, and as their hostile aggressive impulses come to the surface, they are directed against the self in a self-destructive way, and are also directed toward the mother or the mother substitute in such a manner as to say that she is responsible and she too should suffer. The following is an example of this behavior:

> Samuel W. was a juvenile addict. He first came to the hospital at the age of 21, having been addicted for 5 years. He came from an intact family. His father was a merchant, operating a small store for himself. His income was very modest, and he worked long hours, having little time for his son. The mother was overprotecting and very indulgent. Both parents were foreign born, and Sam was the only child. Sam had had very little to do with girls, never having had a steady girl, and he seldom dated. At the age of 17 Sam started experimenting with marihuana, and soon went on to heroin addiction. He was able to keep his addiction from his parents for a short time, but it was not long before he was picked up

by the police on suspicion of being an addict. His mother had to appear in police court and he stated: "It almost killed her." For the next few years he was in and out of trouble because of his addiction, with his mother always coming to his rescue. He would steal anything of value from his parents to support his habit. At times when he was addicted, his mother would purchase illegal narcotics for him to keep him from becoming sick. He would build up his habit just to see how much of the drug his mother would supply him. In desperation Mrs. W. brought Sam to the hospital and related the struggle that existed between herself and her boy. They had been engaged in an indissoluble conflict for 4 years, with narcotics at the center, and both suffered the torments of hell.

Sam was a model patient and enthusiastically participated in the rehabilitative program. At the end of five months he was discharged from the hosptal, the picture of health. He took the train to New York City, but did not go home immediately. He wandered around until he was in a neighborhood where he knew drugs were available and was soon "high" on drugs. He could then return home to his parents and say: "Look Mom, I'm back on drugs." The distraught mother returned her son to the hospital, feeling that he had not remained long enough. As she left, she gave instructions that he son was not to be discharged until she could come for him. Once again, after several months of hospitalization, Sam was ready for discharge. When he learned that his mother was coming for him he left the hospital against medical advice, once again to become addicted and repeat the vicious cycle.

Addicts, in general, have a great deal of difficulty in accepting reality and are unable to substitute the reality principle for the pleasure principle. There are a few methods at their disposal for avoiding the frustrations of reality. One involves the use of a toxic agent for the distortion of reality; another is through flight into psychosis; and another, by going to sleep and dreaming. In Ferenczi's[5] interesting paper, "Stages in the Development of a Sense of Reality," he describes in the second stage of development, a period of "magical hallucinatory omnipotence." In this stage he says the child is attempting the successful reproduction of the tensionless stage of intrauterine life, and is able to do this when he goes to sleep. It seems probable that sleep in general is a periodically repeated regression to this stage of development. The pathological counterpart of this regression is in the hallucinatory wish fulfillment in a psychosis or in drug addiction.

Simmel[19] states:

"All addictions, and especially alcoholic addiction, are protections against depression (melancholia). The melancholic has introjected a disappointing object of love (basically his mother) and tends to attack and destroy the introjected object within himself. The alcoholic addict has only pseudo object-libidinous relationships with people, his drink increasingly representing his only external object. In his struggle for and against abstinence, he fights an endless, indissoluble object fixation and conflict: to draw life (love) from his mother by devouring her; to murder the one person on whose very existence his only hope for security depends."

The need for self-punishment in the narcotic addict is quite easy to demonstrate. Many patients are perfectly willing to accept the period of incarceration of many months, and in a matter of hours following their discharge may return to the use of drugs. Their hospitalization is to them a form of punishment which they are willing to accept, and once the ego has paid its debt it is free to indulge in forbidden wishes. For example, there is the addict patient who will come to the hospital supposedly to be "cured" of his drug addiction. However, before entering the hospital, he will stash his supply of drugs so that when he has completed his "cure," he will have a supply to start on again. One patient, after a prolonged hospitalization with rather intensive psychotherapy, returned to his home and immediately obtained a "shot" to prove to himself that he was "cured" and could take the drug or leave it alone. Such was his rationalization for his readdiction.

Many of these patients have received multiple operations, and for them surgery has an unconscious meaning in that it is interpreted as a form of punishment, and once they have submitted to the surgery, they feel they are free to use drugs and perfectly justified in doing so. This symptom of withdrawal in the narcotic addict, and the hangover period in the chronic alcoholic, undoubtedly are related to certain physiological changes in metabolism; but there are also psychological components of this period of suffering, and it is after this period of self-punishment that many addicts and alcoholics again feel free to gratify forbidden impulses.

In looking beyond the purely symptomatic, descriptive behavior of individuals addicted to narcotic drugs, one finds that the injection of the drug has a very subtle and imperative meaning for the addict. If drugs are available to him, he uses them in a manner destructive to himself and his loved ones. As a result of his addiction, he will never reach the level of maturity when he will be able to accept social responsibility for himself or others.

REFERENCES

1. Abt, L. E., & Weissman, S. L. Personal communication. 1964.
2. Chein, I., Gerard, D. L., Leo, R. S., & Rosenfeld, Eva. *The road to H*. New York: Basic Books, 1964.
3. Crowley, R. M. Psychoanalytic literature on drug addiction and alcoholism. *Psychoanal. Rev.*, 1939, 26, 39-54.

4. Felix, R. H. An appraisal of the personality types of the addict. *Amer. J. Psychiat.*, 1944, *100*, 462-467.
5. Ferenczi, W. *Sex in psychoanalysis.* New York: Basic Books, 1950.
6. Freud, S. *Civilization and its discontents.* London: The Hogarth Press, Ltd. & the Institute of Psycho-analysis, 4th impression, 1949.
7. Gerard, D. L., & Kornetsky, C. A social and psychiatric study of adolescent opiate addicts. *Psychiat. Quart.*, 1955, *28*, 113-125.
8. Himmelsbach, C. K., & Small, L. F. Clinical studies of drug addiction. *Pub. Hlth. Rep. Suppl.* 1937, 125.
9. Kolb, L. Types and characteristics of drug addicts. *Ment. Hyg.* 1925, *10*, 300-313.
10. Kolb, L. & Himmelsbach, C. K. Clinical studies of drug addiction. *Pub. Hlth. Rep. Suppl.* 1938, 128.
11. Nacht, S. Clinical manifestations of aggression and their role in psychoanalytical treatment. *Int. J. Psychoanal.* 1948, *29*.
12. O'Donnell, J. A. A follow-up of narcotic addicts: mortality, relapse and abstinence. *Amer. J. Orthopsychiat.* 1964, *34*, 948-954.
13. Pescor, M. J. A statistical analysis of the clinical records of hospitalized drug addicts. *Pub. Hlth. Rep. Suppl.* 1943, *143*.
14. Rado, S. The psychic effects of intoxicants. *Int. J. Psychoanal.* 1926, *7*.
15. Rado, S. The problem of melancholia. *Int. J. Psychoanal.* 1928, *9*.
16. Rado, S. The psychoanalysis of pharmacothymia (Drug addiction). *Psychoanal. Quart.* 1933, *2*.
17. Rasor, R. W. Narcotic addicts: personality characteristics and hospital treatment. In Hoch & Zubin (Eds.). *Problems of addiction and habituation.* New York: Grune & Stratton, 1959.
18. Report of Interdepartmental Committee on Narcotics to the President. Washington, D.C.: Gov. Print. Office, 1956.
19. Simmel, E. Alcoholism and addiction. *Yearb. Psychoanal.* 1949, *5*, 238-260.
20. Vogel, V. H., Isbell, H., & Chapman, K. W. Present status of narcotic addiction with particular reference to medical indications and comparative addiction liability of the newer and older analgesic drugs *J. A. M. A.* 1948, *138*, 1019-1026.
21. Weiss, E. *Principles of psycho-dynamics.* New York: Grune & Stratton, 1950.

11. Alcoholism as a Form of Acting Out

By RUTH FOX, M.D.

Doctor Ruth Fox, long recognized for her important contributions to understanding the nature of alcoholism and of the alcoholic patient, in a thoughtful and systematic presentation provides us with a way of looking at alcoholism as one form of acting out. In her formulation it is clear that no person is immune to becoming an alcoholic, given suitable needs, opportunities and situations.

Within what is essentially a psychiatric point of view, Ruth Fox develops succinctly a picture of the needs, both conscious and unconscious, in the fulfillment of which persons may turn to alcohol and become addicted to it. Although she treats alcoholism as an acting out phenomenon, she makes it clear that as a translation of conflict into behavior, acting out varies among alcoholics, and appears to depend chiefly on the underlying personality factors. In spite of the fact that this is recognized, many workers with alcoholics have not been especially concerned with understanding the latters' psychodynamics.

IT IS DIFFICULT to understand the acting out propensity of the alcoholic without first understanding something of the many and various underlying dynamisms involved. It is a mistake to consider alcoholism as an entity since all kinds of persons can become addicted to alcohol if they drink enough for a long enough period of time. Alcoholism is a disturbance of behavior with many determinants, some social, some psychological, and some physiochemical. It is also an addiction, which means that there is not only an emotional dependence on the drug but a physiological one as well, which partly, at least, accounts for the craving to resume drinking when the blood level of alcohol begins to fall. Alcohol is also an anesthetic, a poison which when taken in excessive amounts can grossly disorganize an individual's psychic processes, causing temporary psychosis. By abolishing the inhibitory functions of the cortex, it causes all sorts of repressed and unacceptable impulses to be expressed which no more represent the basic personality of the individual than would the actions of a person emerging from the anesthetic effects of ether.

Alcoholism cuts across all segments of the population, the rich, the poor, the bright, the stupid, the socially, artistically or intellectually gifted, as well as those not so well endowed. Of the five million alcoholics in the United States, only 3 per cent are on skid row. Another 20 to 30 per cent may have a psychotic, psychopathic, or severely neurotic underlying condition as well as their addiction to alcohol. This leaves then approximately 70 to 80 per cent of these afflicted individuals not noticeably different from the rest of us, persons who are working in industry, the professions, the arts, living in a family setting, and trying to carry on as normal a life as possible in spite of the devastating handicap of their alcoholism. Many do not know they are alcoholics and will vehemently deny that their drinking is any different from that of their excessively drinking companions. It is not until they get into serious difficulties because of it, with threatened or actual loss of job, or family, or prestige, or health, that they will admit they do have a problem. Many will "hit bottom" by losing fortunes, friends, social position, injuring themselves or others through accidents such as fires, drunken driving, fights, jail sentences, etc. As their disease progresses, their ostracism and isolation become progressively more painful and complete until they finally feel completely shut out from participation in the normal activities of life. No alcoholic wishes to drink the way he does, and he keeps vainly hoping that he can recapture again the ability to drink moderately. We don't honestly know why he cannot—whether the defect is constitutional, either inborn or acquired, whether it is merely a learned or conditioned response as the behaviorists would have us believe, or whether it is a blind, compulsive acting out of unconscious conflicts.

Though most psychiatrists insist that alcoholism can occur only in the neurotic individual, I myself, after working with about 3,000 alcoholics in the past 25 years, believe that it is possible for anyone who can tolerate alcohol at all to become addicted to it merely through long years of daily heavy drinking. Having then become addicted, he shows all of the psychological, social, and physical deterioration of the individual who has been alcoholic for much of his life.

CHARACTERISTICS OF THE ALCOHOLIC

No pre-alcoholic personality has ever been delineated, though a certain cluster of personality traits are found in most alcoholics during the active phase of their disease. These traits may, however, be as much a result of the years of addictive drinking as they are the cause. They have been summarized by many workers in the field.[1,4,7,9,11] The traits most frequently mentioned are an extremely low frustration tolerance, inability to endure anxiety or tension, feelings of isolation, devaluated self-esteem, a tendency to act impulsively, a repetitive "acting out" of conflicts, often an extreme narcissism and exhibitionism, a tendency toward masochistic self-punitive behavior, sometimes somatic preoccupation and hypochondriasis, and often extreme mood swings. In addition, there is usually marked hostility and rebellion (conscious or unconscious) and repressed grandiose ambitions with little ability to persevere. Most show strong (oral) dependent needs, frustration of which will lead to depression, hostility, and rage. Many patients show some sexual problems of immaturity, impotence, frigidity, homosexuality (latent or overt), sadomasochistic fixations, or confusion regarding the sexual role. It cannot be stressed too strongly that these tests were done on persons who had already become heavily addicted and may in no way represent their personalities before the addictive process took over. They may represent either fixations or regressions, and they can be considered as immature methods of coping with stressful situations.

Many alcoholics, especially those who have in their earlier lives been well adjusted and have become alcoholics at a more advanced age, have come from good family backgrounds with the normal amount of love and discipline from both parents. When these individuals recover from their alcoholism, they can return to their former good adjustment.

Many other alcoholics, however, come from homes where there have been great emotional deprivations. Family life had been scarred by death, desertion, divorce, insanity, alcoholism, poverty, quarreling, etc. Some mothers had been unpredictable, harassed, and unhappy, at times overprotecting and at other times impatient, rejecting, and controlling toward the child. Many of the fathers were passive, submissive to the dominating wife, indifferent to the children, and frequently or permanently absent from the home. Some took out their own frustrations on the children, lashing out at them with severe and unjustified punishments. Other fathers were driving successes, egocentric, selfish, overbearing, tyrannical, and belittling to the wife and children. Frequently both parents expected perfect performance from their children while breaking rule after rule themselves. Unsure of themselves, neither parent was able to set necessary limits for the child's acting out and was unable to transmit to the child the sense of responsibility needed to mature into an independent adult. As role models neither parent could be considered satisfactory nor was the child ever taught consistently what his own role should be.[5] It is significant that 52 per cent of a large series of several thousand alcoholics had a father or a mother or both who were alcoholic. Alcoholism is probably not inherited, but could certainly be considered contagious.

Children from such homes are especially vulnerable to delinquent, deviant, or alcoholic acting out. They enter adolescence heavily burdened with immature and neurotic traits, with low self-regard, shy, depressed, or with hostle, rebellious attitudes. They are often uncertain of their sex roles, are anxious, and may act out by delinquent and drinking behavior in an attempt to be grown up and manly. Feeling insecure and frightened, they may over-compensate, professing a bravado they do not feel. They may act arrogantly, overbearingly, see themselves as unique, special, and therefore justified in making inordinate demands on others, which when thwarted, drive them into vindictive rages which threaten to overwhelm them. They are in deep conflict, have little sense of their real identity, have no long-term goals, are torn between a wish to be dependent and a wish to be independent. Some retreat into a fantasy world in which they feel omnipotent and will brook no interference. Beneath this bravado lies a frightened child, no matter what his chronological age may be.

Alcohol can temporarily dispel anxiety and conflict or heighten the feeling of elation, giving the alcoholic an exalted sense of his powers, a feeling of masculinity, and a sense of belonging. He sees himself as he would like to be, omnipotent, clever, brilliant, and successful. Is it any wonder that he drinks? The rewards are great and immediate, and there is no effort involved in getting these rewards. Alcohol temporarily seems to solve all his neurotic and existential problems so that his drinking can be looked on as an attempt at self-cure. The normal, well-adjusted social drinker derives pleasure from drinking, but he does not use it as a means of dealing with deepseated emotional problems.

Behind what seems like a simple wish to drink there is, however, in the alcoholic of any age, a whole complicated structure of dynamic factors underlying it which do not occur in the moderate social drinker. To understand any of the acting out behavior disturbances—and alcoholism is one of the most frequent—requires an understanding of psychoanalytic principles, especially as regards the phenomena of the unconscious determinants of behavior, the concept of transference, and the concept of resistance to change. Silverberg[8] discusses acting out as follows:

> There is a type of patient who is forever acting out, both within the analytic situation and outside of it. By the term 'acting out' I mean that the patient, instead of discussing a specific phase of his difficulties and attempting to understand it by means of verbal formulation, gives it vivid and graphic expression in a piece of behavior. He is impelled, by motives he does not understand, to behave in the specific way involved. Sometimes, particularly after frequent repetitions of the same piece of behavior, he is aware of its irrationality or he may at least have doubts of its complete rationality. For the most part, however, patients attempt to rationalize their acting out and often have little difficulty in producing rationalizations eminently satisfactory and convincing to themselves.

Anyone working with alcoholics on either an individual basis or in a group setting has ample opportunity to see this type of rationalized acting out. The blame is a nagging wife, an unappreciative boss, a fancied slight, etc.

The repetitiousness, the futility, the irrationality, the lack of any permanently pleasurable outcome, and the flimsy rationalizations all attest to the transference nature of the alcoholic's drinking. The alcoholic transfers to current situations and persons old attitudes, feelings, jealousies, hates, loves, and beliefs from the past. To accept the fact that there are realistic forces, both human and physical, over which we have no control, is an idea foreign to the alcoholic. Yet recovery cannot take place until he does concede this.

Acting out can be regarded as a way of avoiding by psychomotor behavior the anxiety caused by conflicts, both interpersonal and intrapsychic. The patient acts rather than thinks or plans. Delany[3] states it well: "Acting out is bringing fantasy into real situations with people. It is a working out in the environment of an internal conscious or unconscious fantasy." The alcoholic acts out not only through his uncontrolled and destructive drinking, but also in many areas of his life where he may have grossly distorted relations with his spouse, his children, his parents, his employer or employees, and in his social and civic contacts. Though held somewhat in check when sober, the acting out in relation to the therapeutic situation may show itself in arriving late, missing appointments without notice, coming in inebriated, arguing about non-essential matters, being rude, leaving in a huff, etc. How these situations are handled is important, for they generally denote a state of acute anxiety in the patient. A negative countertransference can drive the patient away for good. In a group setting these negative reactions are generally well handled by the group itself. Along with condemning the act, they also give the necessary emotional support.

The type and extent of acting out depend a great deal on the background of the intoxicated individual. With the middle and upper income group of educated people, the acting out is generally not so wild or violent as it is in those of the lower stratum of society. Women of the upper classes can often hide their alcoholism for a long time even from their husbands, and because they are too ashamed to be seen, do most of their drinking in their own bedrooms. As they progress in their illness, however, there is the inevitable lowering of standards, the sense of shame, loneliness, self-hate, depression, and frustration. When the husband becomes disgusted and begins to withdraw his emotional support, the wife not only becomes frightened that he will leave her but may become vindictive as well. One wife hacked up all the furniture in their apartment after the husband refused to kiss her in the morning after she had kept him awake all night with her drunken abuse. She then slashed to ribbons all of his suits, coats, and underwear with razor blades. She was so deeply ashamed of this acting out that she forthwith joined Alcoholics Anonymous and has remained sober for the past three years. Another man, president of an important firm, chartered a plane for South America when drunk and woke up in Lima penniless and with no memory whatsoever of his trip and no inkling of why he had done it. Since he was a self-made man with a deprived background, we might conjecture that this grandiose bit of acting out made him feel important.

Patients may act out their infantile dependency needs not only by drinking, but by various acts even when not drinking—by aggressive behavior, demanding attention, refusing to work, maneuvering their family or friends into supporting them, causing confusion by infantile rage reactions and violent, angry outbursts, by truancy, threats of suicide, self-injury, throwing up a job, walking out on the family, etc.

The type of acting out among alcoholics also varies greatly, depending on the underlying personality types. A psychotic who is also alcoholic may show extremely bizarre behavior when intoxicated, whereas in sobriety he may be able to manage at least marginally. One paranoid schizophrenic when drunk would expose his genitals, chase people with knives, and showed a well-defined paranoid reaction—the food was poisoned, the living room was wired, the devil was out to get him, attendants were all monsters, etc., and he himself was God. Within hours after the alcohol had been eliminated, he reverted to his old self, rather schizoid but able to continue a job he had held for many years. Another ambulatory schizophrenic girl would fly into rages when drunk and would mutilate herself, sticking pins in her arms and hacking off all her hair, acts which she deeply regretted after the drunken episode was over. In spite of two to three short episodes of this kind a year, she is able to work fairly regularly.

Though formerly I felt that alcohol might be used as a defense against psychosis (and of course it sometimes is), I have had many ambulatory schizophrenics and cyclothymic personalities who function fairly well outside of a hospital if they can remain sober. Alcohol totally disorganizes them.

Acting out among psychopathic alcoholics can be dangerously antisocial, with beatings of the wife and children, stealing, writing worthless checks, promiscuity, prostitution, perversions, rape, homosexual experiences, etc. Such behavior should be considered as characteristic of the psychopathic personality with absence of or severe deficits in the superego structure, and not as due to the superimposed alcoholism. In my experience, even though it is possible to bring the drinking to an end, the antisocial acting out continues as before. Though the psychopathic individual may have anxiety, it is usually merely a fear that he will be caught and not an inner conviction that his behavior is in any way wrong. This is in sharp contrast to the usual alcoholic who after an episode of severe drinking feels deep remorse and an overwhelming guilt and hopelessness.

Alcoholics who have deep-seated neurotic problems, as well as their addiction, run the gamut of symptoms. Among them there are many who are phobic, hysterical, obsessive, depersonalized, compulsive, over-conforming, schizoid, helplessly dependent on a partner, masochistic, sadistic, or chronically depressed.

Most alcoholics, however, fall in the class of character disorders, a loose conglomerate of inadequate personality traits which range from the severely unhappy to the fairly well-adjusted, though often conflicted, individuals. Projective tests show many disturbances such as unbearable tension, fears of social situations, alienation from the self and others, and irreconcilable conflicts. There may be a lack of self-identification, a feeling of fragmentation, inability to judge others as friendly or unfriendly, impulsive acting out with regrets and guilt feelings, ambivalence, suggestibility on the one hand and stubbornness on the other. Many are extremely sensitive and vulnerable to criticism, which denotes a weak ego structure and an exceedingly poor and nebulous self-image. Many show confusion as to their sexual role, and some seem fixated at the pregenital level. The superego may be harsh, punitive, and archaic or it may show "lacunae," i.e., it may be effective in some areas and not in others. Instinctual drives may be inhibited, leading to restrained, cautious behavior, rigidity, a lack of spontaneity, and an inability to enjoy life. If the instinctual drives, on the other hand, are not under control of the ego, there can be gross acting out with a feeling that the world should gratify their every whim. Since this is impossible, the individual may become demanding, abusive, enraged, and threatening.

Different defenses are used in the various character disorders, the compulsive characters using reaction formations, isolation, and withdrawal from life with rigid repression of the id impulses. Occasionally the underlying sadistic and anal components may break through. The oral characters, though narcissistic and vain, can be generous and giving provided there is always a "source of supply." If not, there is depression, rage, exploitation, and revenge. The schizoid type is withdrawn, shy, and lives in fantasy in an autistic world. The paranoid type is suspicious, thinks others are out to harm him, and is generally jealous and envious.

While the individual is in the active stage of his alcoholism, there is a disturbance in the normal inhibiting function with little capacity to delay action, to tolerate aggression, anxiety, or frustration, to maintain lasting and loving object relationships, to learn from experience, and little ability to think abstractly. Life tends to be lived according to the pleasure principle, which creates difficulties in the environment. Owing to fixation or regression, the patient continues to act as he did in early childhood, and he has lost mastery over his impulses. He may revert to truly psychopathic behavior when he is drunk. When sober he often has excellent control over his aberrant impulses, can deny them, sublimate them, or change them through reaction formations. If his impulsivity can be changed into a mild compulsion neurosis, this will help him bind has anxiety and help him to desist in his acting out.

PSYCHOTHERAPY OF THE ALCOHOLIC

In treating the alcoholic, one must be aware of the many functions alcohol may have played in his life, not only in helping him to cope with his neurotic conflicts but insofar as it has often become his chief source of pleasure, allowing him to feel friendly, manly, relaxed, worthy, lovable, generous, witty, carefree, and original. We must, however, try to convince him that these feelings of well-being are not only illusory and temporary but are paid for with awful pain and misery in the long run after addiction occurs. Pointing out these negative factors alone is rarely ever effective, however, and one must put the emphasis on the fact that life can be better without alcohol than with it. One must point out and foster all the healthy elements of the personality and build up enough motivation in the patient so that he will be willing to undertake the long, hard battle toward permanent sobriety. He will need help in his struggle to overcome the ever present pressures to drink, pressures from within himself as well as from his environment.

An analytic type of therapy aimed primarily toward the production of insights into the "whys" of drinking can be spectacularly ineffective until and unless the drinking can first be stopped. Though this is a direct intervention aimed at symptom removal, it is a necessary first step before one can evaluate the underlying personality. As in most of the acting out disorders—alcoholism, delinquency, homosexuality, etc.—the aim should be to help the patient control his antisocial behavior by helping him to find a more rewarding type of life, by enhancing his sense of worth, by helping him find substitute gratifications, etc. That even deep analysis rarely helps the alcoholic unless he stops drinking early in therapy can be illustrated by one case of mine, a psychoanalyst, himself, who had had seventeen years of analysis trying to determine *why* he drank. He grew steadily worse, lost his professional standing, his family, etc., because no analyst had ever emphasized the need to stop drinking first if progress was to be made. He finally went on Antabuse, stopped drinking for the last seven years of his life and had only one slip. After sobriety he remarked that as long as he drank he couldn't profit by the analytic insights, but that with sobriety he could act on them successfully.

This direct intervention is not always possible at first, but with patience, tolerance, and the development of rapport, the patient can usually be motivated in time to give up his alcohol.

Since drinking is only one form of acting out in the alcoholic, treatment of the total personality is indicated, which may take several years. There are now many ways available to help the alcoholic which are very effective. By using a combination of therapies in a well motivated, intelligent patient, one can count on a recovery rate of 60 to 70 per cent. The available ingredients in the program of rehabilitation should include affiliation with Alcoholics Anonymous, some individual counseling of the patient and members of the family, the use of the Al-Anon Family Group (an offshoot of A.A. for the non-alcoholic members of the family), group therapy for the patients, sometimes concurrent group therapy for the spouses, and the use of Antabuse[6] as a chemical deterrent to drinking. Psychodrama, under the leadership of a trained psychodramatist,* can produce profound emotional insights and changes in the patient's concept of himself and others. Occasionally hypnosis can help the nervous, tense person to relax, get a better self-image, and improve his sleep. Interesting techniques of producing an aversion to alcohol by certain nauseant drugs, by minute electric shock to the arm, etc., are being carried out by doctors trained in the behaviorist school of therapy. A reconditioning or relearning technique has been found especially helpful in those persons who continue to be anxious and phobic even after sobriety has been attained.[10] Though the use of LSD is still controversial, it is proving very helpful in some cases, when given by qualified investigators in a hospital setting. An additional help can be given to many patients by spiritual counseling by the clergy.[2] Certain other self-help groups in addition to A.A. can add another dimension to the individual's life. Such organizations as Recovery, Inc., Parents-Without-Partners, Fathers-at-Large, AFTLI (Association Feeling Truth and Living It), etc., can be of aid.

CONCLUSIONS AND SUMMARY

Because alcohol inhibits the higher functions of the cortex anyone, alcoholic or non-alcoholic, who drinks too much will act out in some degree. The acting out in the alcoholic, however, is usually much more flagrant, disrupting, and self-defeating. Some of this acting out may be dynamically understood in terms of transference relationships. However, some can be simply due to deeply ingrained habits from childhood. In other words, alcoholic behavior is learned behavior and probably obeys the laws of learning theory. The type of acting out will, of course, depend upon the underlying type of neurosis and the nature of the conflict.

In treating the alcoholic, we find it necessary to prohibit entirely the

---

*My psychodrama groups are conducted by Miss Hannah Weiner of the Moreno Institute.

acting out which the drinking itself represents, for the alcoholic can never drink normally again. After the individual has attained sobriety, it may then be necessary to work with him to prevent other types of acting out. A combination of Antabuse to stop the drinking, group therapy, psychodrama, and A.A. will help the alcoholic not only to remain abstinent but to mature as an individual. With this multi-disciplinary type of approach in a well motivated patient, it is possible to get a 60 per cent to 70 per cent recovery rate.

REFERENCES

1. Chafetz, M. E., and Demone, H. W., Jr. *Alcoholism and society.* New York: Oxford University Press, 1962.
2. Clinebell, H. J., Jr. *Understanding and counseling the alcoholic.* New York: Abingdon Press, 1956.
3. Delany, L. T. The significance of acting out in the group treatment of the alcoholic. Presented at the annual conference of the American Group Psychotherapy Association, 1962.
4. Fox, R. The alcoholic spouse. In V. W. Eisenstein (Ed.) *Neurotic interaction in marriage.* New York: Basic Books, 1956.
5. Fox, R. The effect of alcoholism on children. *In progress in child psychiatry.* Basel/New York: S. Karger, 1963.
6. Fox, R. Antabuse as an adjunct to psychotherapy in alcoholism. *N.Y.S. J. Medicine,* 1958, *58,* 1540-1544.
7. Portnoy, I. Psychology of alcoholism. Lecture presented under the auspices of the Auxiliary Council to the Association for the Advancement of Psychoanalysis, 1947.
8. Silverberg, W. V. Acting out versus insight, a problem in psychoanalytic technique. *Psychoanalytic Quarterly,* 1955, *24,* 527-544.
9. Tiebout, H. M. The ego factors in surrender in alcoholism. *Quart. J. Studies on Alcohol,* 1954, *15,* 610-621.
10. Wolpe, J. *Psychotherapy by reciprocal inhibition.* California: Stanford University Press, 1958.
11. Zwerling, I. Psychiatric findings in an interdisciplinary study of forty-six alcoholic patients. *Quart. J. Studies on Alcohol,* 1959, *20,* 543-554.

12. Psychosomatic Illness: A Body Language Form of Acting Out

By SHERVERT H. FRAZIER, M.D.

In "Psychosomatic Illness: A Body Language Form of Acting Out," Dr. Shervert H. Frazier takes a brief but exciting look at the way in which the human being responds as a whole to anxiety and stress. For him the specific psychosomatic illness may be differentiated as the "figure" against the larger "ground" which represents the total functioning organism. Psychological factors that initiate somatic symptoms, and somatic disease with psychological overtones, in Frazier's view, constitute a continuing dialogue between psyche and soma.

From the point of view of acting out, the specific symptom formations constitute a body language that differs from one person to another but always represents communications of a person in distress. Frazier's view is an interesting one to contemplate.

PSYCHOSOMATIC MEDICINE currently is based on the premise that a human being is a unitary living organism who responds as a whole to anxiety or stress. When specific organ systems predominate in the response, the rest of the organism can be considered a "ground" against which the "figure" of the specific local response is delineated. The total nervous system (central and peripheral, voluntary and autonomic), various hormonal and metabolic systems of feedback, and the voluntary and involuntary muscles are all involved in mediation of the response.

Three distinct but interrelated types of organ system response can be differentiated. The first is the homeostatic mechanism in which the functional role of the various organs serving the internal economy of the organism is important in maintaining the *steady state* of the organism. The second involves the role of the self in utilizing the body image of the organism in a total adaptive response to anxiety. The third reflects the role of instinctual function as a determinant of responsivity to anxiety or stress.

In this framework, disorders of the total organism or of specific organ systems may be seen as the result of psychological factors initiating somatic symptoms or somatic disease in which the impact of the illness on the personality and of the personality on the illness all contribute to the total clinical picture. Thus, the mechanisms of the individual personality subserve the adaptational process.

Acting out is a direct translation of unconscious conflict into behavioral symptoms without awareness of the motivational causes of the conflict. The major thesis of this chapter considers that psychosomatic symptoms can be understood dynamically as a special case of acting out.

As a means of attempting to understand the evolution and significance of an illness, we shall use the outline of Margolin and Kaufman[6]: "an illness can be divided into the following phases with respect to the psychological factor.

1. The pre-morbid personality in terms of the social, economic, somatic, and psychosexual adaptation of the patient, including the presence or absence of frank neurotic or psychotic symptoms.
2. The onset of symptoms.
3. The latent period of the disease, i.e., the interval between the beginning of the disease process and the point at which the patient seeks help.
4. The reaction of the patient to the therapist and to therapy.
5. The reaction of the therapist to the patient.
6. The course of the disease.
7. The postmorbid state, i.e., convalescence and recovery or invalidism."

Kubie[5] in *Psychoanalysis as Science* asked the question: How does it come about that certain psychological processes of which we are *conscious* will be expressed in a symbolical language, while other psychological processes of which we are *unconscious* can also be expressed through a symbolic act but in which the link to the internal process or unconscious inner world is severed? He postulates that, since the initial stages of development every external percept must be apperceived in relation to some prior internal experience, it ought to be mathematically predictable that every unitary symbol must have both an internal and external point of reference.

Body symptoms or complaints of illness are communications of a person in distress. Disturbing physical events may be reported as vague or indefinite complaints, while disturbing life situations, human interpersonal difficulties, and intra-psychic conflict may be reported as physical symptoms in terms of the individual's personality development and the specific mode of communication which has been learned by him.

In learning the process of communication, the individual must make transitions from complete infantile dependency to the multi-variable roles of adults in a complex social system. Such a transition is fraught with many pitfalls, as we learn through retrospective reconstruction of the learning processes of a person in distress. He uses a language which is determined by many factors in the development of his personality, many of which stem from the pre-verbal period and are highly instrumental in the evolution of body language. The numerous phases encompassed in this process involve a range of mental mechanisms developed during the maturation of the personality, such as:

(a) imitation by the child of a hypochondriacal, complaining mother;
(b) learning of somatic awareness; e.g., stomach fullness is recognized as the sensation of satiety, and stomach emptiness is equated with hunger pangs and the need for food;
(c) conceptualization of the body by the mind (fatness, thinness, muscularity, size, and shape) as evidence of personality traits; e.g., large size and fatness may be equated with strength, and thinness with svelte sophistication;
(d) the body language may be symbolic and the expression of psychologic tension in terms of a specific organ system; e.g., headache may be used to mean "all of today's stresses," backache may essentially represent "my burden is too heavy," vomiting may be the internal and external expression of revulsion and disgust.

Symbolization processes are involved in (c) and (d) above; function also is involved when repressed impulses and internalized conflicts are symbolically discharged into somatic symptoms.

Ruesch[9] states that the person with a psychosomatic disease has not developed the adult processes of communication through words, gestures, and the many nuances of external body function. He has remained at a level of communication in which bodily organs are utilized. This is another way of saying that the person with a psychosomatic disease communicates through the language of his soma. The influences which lead to fixation at this level of communication rather than the normal evolution to adult forms of symbolism and abstraction are not yet fully understood.

Body language is that particular phase of communication which is the non-verbal expression of emotion. The correlation may be a simple one as between shame and blushing, or it may be a more elaborate, complex, and many-faceted one between unconscious conflict and somatic manifestations. More pertinent examples of body language are early failures in learning of perception, as evidenced in Piaget's[8] constructs and in Bruch's* hypothesis of the diminished awareness of internal visceral perceptions which have been recorded experimentally via electrogastrographs by Coddington, Sours, and Bruch[2] in anorexia nervosa and obesity patients. Many complexities of cognitive, perceptual, and psychologic development are associated with body language expression.

Psychosomatic symptoms may represent the physiological concomitant

---

*Personal communication.

of an emotional state. The usual physiological symptom accompanying a state of strong emotion may become sustained if no abreaction or release from the emotion occurs. For some time this may be a reversible process if the emotion is released, but if it is not released chronic and irreversible changes in the physiology and subsequently the structure of the organ may occur.

While varying opinions exist regarding the correlation between personality type and specifically associated psychosomatic disorder, little evidence has come to light to support such a position. In contradistinction to this concept, strong evidence exists that specific intrapsychic conflict situations produce specific physiological reactions. Increasing recognition of genetically determined organ vulnerability emphasizes the genetic role in psychosomatic disorders—a significant feature of Freud's basic statements.

The psychosomatic patient, like the neurotic, as stated by Sperling,[10] represses his dangerous impulses and internalizes his conflicts. Thus, the patient is not in conflict with his real objects, environment, or society, but discharges the repressed impulses in his somatic symptoms which represent the expression and fulfilment of specific fantasies and impulses of a pregenital nature. As an example, the specific dynamics of migraine headaches are described as unconscious fantasies and impulses to kill the frustrating object by an attack upon the head.

Kolb[5] and others[1,3] have raised the question whether the functional or psychosomatic symptom may be the defense expressed at the physiological level through the autonomic nervous system instead of at the psychological level. Certainly, phobias, compulsions, hysterical symptoms, and other mental symptoms represent partial defenses at the psychological level against unacceptable impulses. In parallel, somatic symptoms may be regarded as partial defenses against identical, unacceptable impulses at the somatic level rather than at the psychologic level. Thus, the body symptom is the emergency defense against the person's being overwhelmed by anxiety. As a consequence, the symptom is adhered to by the person because it seems essential to his structured protection of the self. The physical or physiological symptom may serve to defend against the emergence into awareness of the representation of the psychological cause of the conflict.

From the foregoing, the psychosomatic defense appears to be strikingly similar to the neurotic acting-out defense, which may be briefly defined as the direct translation of unconscious conflict into behavioral symptoms, without awareness of the motivational causes of the conflict. The unconscious resistance to the relinquishing of a defensive symptom is essentially identical in the neurotic acting-out phenomenon and in the psychosomatic symptom.

Chart

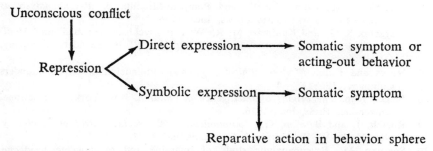

Patients often develop psychophysiological reactions through the emulation of parents, using the same mechanisms and symptoms, thus compounding the acting-out process. The mental-somatic transition specifically observed in anorexia nervosa, obesity, and asthma may be viewed as a sensitizer pathway laid down early in life by heredity and accentuated by early reinforcing experiences. The sensitization process which produces what might be termed the *ready state* is crucial for the person's method of adaptation and for his defenses against maladaptive disorganization.

If Greenacre's[4] concept that acting out originates in the impulsive acts of the infant's only means of gratification, i.e., "calling the helper," then even more basic is the imprint of the psychological need activating the biological need. Greenacre's hypothesis considers that severe trauma in the pre-verbal period of life results in persistence into adulthood of non-verbal forms of expression.

If acting out represents certain behavior which can be understood as the repetition of an unconscious conflict and as one of the available methods to communicate the conflict, then the psychosomatic analogy is pertinent. Acting out becomes a distance device to perpetuate the defensive maneuver for the unconscious conflict. Therefore, if acting out serves as a form of resistance against change or as a substitute for remembering, then the psychosomatic model becomes more credible, since the symptom "acts out" the conflict which clinically serves the resistance in an identical fashion.

REFERENCES

1. Alexander, F. *Psychosomatic medicine.* New York: W. W. Norton & Company, Inc., 1950.
2. Coddington, R. D., Sours, J. A., and Bruch, H. Electrogastrographic findings associated with affective changes. *Amer. J. of Psychiatry,* 1964, *121,* No. 1.
3. Daniels, G., O'Connor, J. F., Karush, A., Moses, L., Flood, C. A., and Lepore, M. Three decades in the observation and treatment of ulcerative colitis, *Psychosom. Med., 24,* 85-93, 1962.

4. Greenacre, P. General problems of acting out. *Trauma, growth and personality.* New York: W. W. Norton & Company, Inc., 1952, pp. 224-236.
5. Hilgard, E. R., Kubie, L. W., and Pumpian-Mindlin, E. *Psychoanalysis as science.* New York: Basic Books, Inc., 1956.
6. Margolin, S. G., and Kaufman, M. R. What is psychosomatic medicine? *Medical Clinics of North America,* Philadelphia: W. B. Saunders Company, (May) 1948.
7. Noyes and Kolb. *Modern clinical psychiatry.* Philadelphia: W. B. Saunders Company, 1963.
8. Piaget, Jean. *The origins of intelligence in children,* New York: International Universities Press, Inc., 1956.
9. Ruesch, J. and Bateson, G. *Communication, the social matrix of psychiatry.* New York: W. W. Norton & Company, Inc. 1951.
10. Sperling, M. Psychoanalytic study of migraine and psychogenic headache. *Psychoanalytic Review,* 1952, 39, 152-163.

13. Acting Out, Obesity and Existence

By SAMUEL V. DUNKELL, M.D.

In Doctor Samuel V. Dunkell's chapter, we have an opportunity to look at obesity as an acting out phenomenon both within a psychiatric frame of reference as well as an existential point of view. Dunkell was impressed with the psychodynamic parallels between obesity and acting out, and came to the conclusion that by going beyond the psychodynamics into an existential treatment of his material, he could provide the reader with an additional dimension of understanding.

The chapter that follows provides us with insight into the nature of obesity as a form of acting out behavior that is increasingly common in our culture.

OBESITY AND ACTING OUT have many parallel dynamic relationships. Both are demonstrations of the oral mode of existence; that is, a greedy, grasping, indiscriminately impulsive way of relating to the things of this world and of being-in-the-world. As a result of the essentially low frustration tolerance characteristic of the oral character, this mode of being shows marked ambivalent tendencies. The grasping character reacts to frustration with hostility, but dependency needs result in the tendency to repress aggressivity out of the fear of loss of love. Both obesity and acting out have an essentially narcissistic and regressive quality. Therefore, the objects necessary for their satisfaction are relatively unimportant as to the quality of the relationship and individual differentiation. In reality, their intended objects function only as pseudo-objects toward which a pseudo- relationship exists.[6] It is this pseudo-relationship quality and the difficulty it poses for transference that sometimes make for such difficulty in relating to and working with patients who display such patterns prominently in their pathology.

DYNAMICS OF OBESITY

The essential relationship which is significant for the obese person is the childhood symbiosis with an ambivalent, usually overprotective, maternal figure. As a reaction formation to the hostility to the child implicit in the ambivalence, these mothers show compensatory overprotection and an overestimation of the child. It is perhaps an indication of underlying hostility toward the child and other children that families of obese patients are usually smaller than average. Through the nurturing, a pattern is set up whereby feeding becomes at once a magic reliever of tension for the child, a reward for "good" behavior, and a disciplinary instrument. It becomes in the child's best interests in this situation to be "good," to settle any tension producing conflicts by eating, and to present no management problems which might cause mother's underlying hostility to emerge. The implementation and expansion of this pattern leads the child to develop an empty, passive, vegetative type of existence.[4]

Other needs of the parents may fit into the genesis of the symbiotic matrix. Often the parents come from a European immigrant background where lack of food was common. In the American transplantation, the dreams of plenty can be realized through the stuffing of the child, a visible talisman against the remnant insecurity of the parents' own childhood. Also, because of the high degree of narcissism of the parent, the child can not really be related to, and he is seen as a kind of doll, or plaything, which must be stuffed to give the surface identity a content.

The maternal ambivalence expresses itself in another way. External dangers for the child are unconsciously seen by the mother as projections of her own hostility, and she defensively tries to shield the child from situations of danger and aggression. One of the ways to achieve this is to discourage muscular activity and exploratory behavior. Thus physical and social activity and competition become tabooed. Passivity and compliance become fixated—the fat person is a jolly person precisely because he dare not be angry. But lack of exploration and lack of effort result in the crippling of personality development, and this central flaw is the pernicious feature that characterizes obesity. There is no real ego development. Body image and identity remain primitive and undifferentiated. Social skills and achievement are undeveloped, and an inner sense of emptiness, inadequacy, and helplessness pervades the personality. As a compensation for this emptiness, helplessness, and poor social image, the obese person resorts to flights into fantasy and an ineffective megalomania. But the brittle self-concept is easily shattered by even trivial frustration and leads to states of despair.

Since there is no real personality strength, there is the reparative tendency to equate physical size with strength. Fat people often see their obesity as armor. But the feelings of emptiness, nothingness, and failure continually recur, and there is then recourse through acting out, often in an impulsive and compulsive way, to fill the emptiness by means of the built-in, automatic, tension-relieving behavior of overeating.

This process is of course accelerated in times of emotional stress. It is commonly known that obesity has the function of protecting against depression[7] and psychosis. The overeating itself is often manic in character and, existentially, shows a greedy devouring of the rapidly disappearing, evanescent material of the obese patient's world. In a way there are close parallels between obesity, mania, and addiction.

In the area of sexual development as the result of the general personality impoverishment, there is usually a failure in achieving a strong sexual identity and in the ability to form mature love relationships. In the case of obese men, their fatness is confused with femininity. There may be more malignant causes for this sexual confusion and conflict since one source of the mother's hostility and ambivalence may have been the sex of her child, and the stuffing and distortion may have been meant to destroy the feared and hated sex that the child represents. In women, fatness may be seen as an exaggeration of the female form, but the fat woman is plagued by her bodily discrepancy from the currently acceptable social ideal of slenderness and as a result her feelings of deviation, unacceptability, and self-hate are increased.

This leads to the problems of aggression for the obese. The essential cause of the inability of the fat person to be openly aggressive has been described. The strongly denied aggressivity can find outlet only in distorted forms. Unconsciously, the excessive incorporation of food, seen within the context of the predominant oral fixation, becomes equated with aggressivity and cannibalism. The guilt engendered by this causes self-contempt and is often sought to be atoned for by compulsive fasting, and in extreme cases, by anorexia—a disguised form of suicide.

There may be masochistic variations in the problem of the expression of aggression. The elaboration of the masochistic "wish to be refused" may take the form of a denial of this masochistic pleasure in the form of pseudo-aggression; that is, a rebellious overeating which is seen as a denial of the fought-against infantile dependency on the mother, "I can eat as much as I want." Thus overeating itself can become a distorted form of rebellion.[1]

Another disguised form of aggression is passive manipulation of others. This is fostered by the essential inactivity and grandiosity of the obese person. This manipulation often expresses itself in the form of exhibitionism, the aim of which is to get the essential nurturance and narcissistic supplies as well as attempting a repudiation of the negative self-image.

The basic pre-oedipal mother conflict may express itself through many levels of the personality organization. There is an oral-sadistic oedipal complex with unconscious hate against mothers, and against femininity, in both sexes. From the anal viewpoint, food is thought of as something dirty and getting fat is equated with being uncontrolled and incontinent. Oedipally, to be fat may mean to have breasts or to become orally impregnated.

Eating may relax the internal tension of these conflicts through the incorporation of an object which has made the patient feel hungry or constipated or castrated or feminine and fat. Thus food may have the various psychological equivalencies of milk, of narcissistic supplies, of penis, and of child.

The genital conflict and the equivalence of food with phallus (meat), and its cannibalistic incorporation with resulting guilt, may be a factor in the denial of protein and the emphasis on starches in the dietary preferences of some obese persons.[5]

THE EXISTENTIAL ANALYSIS OF OBESITY

The two basic approaches of existential analysis to the study of human behavior are those of the phenomenological method and existential philosophy. The former attempts to apprehend phenomena naively, without prejudice or preformed judgment letting it present *itself,* so to speak. The latter sees man as always having to choose his way of being-in-the-world, of taking the raw material of the present and deciding which direction he will move toward his future (and eventual death). By accepting this responsibility for his existence he becomes free. By shirking it he becomes guilty, and the manner in which he shirks it becomes his symptoms. These concepts are exemplified in the following case histories by two leading existential analysts. In the material presented, the symptom of obesity is the result of the relinquishing of the essential requirement of existence— the freedom to develop one's implicit potentials for being to their fullest.

In "The Case of Ellen West" Ludwig Binswanger presents an elaborate existential analysis of a case of simple schizophrenia in which obesity is a central problem.[2] The life situation which Binswanger sees as the essential structure of Ellen West's existence is her conflicted attempts to achieve an ethereal ideal. This ideal is characterized by slenderness, intellectual creativity, love, and the expression of refined social values. The patient finds it increasingly difficult to achieve this ideal, or even to maintain her limited level of slight achievement because she is basically infantile and operates upon a childish, and therefore usually frustrated, omnipotence, and demandingness. As a result of the fundamental and implacable frustration, her world became increasingly narrow and empty, and nothing new could develop. This meant, for her, a loss of her sense of future, and was experienced as an increasing standstill or, at best, a crawling of her existence. She experienced herself "as a worm that moved slowly in a dark, tight circle." She was increasingly cut off from her possibilities of a future and was unable to experience the feeling of openness, wideness, and brightness before her. Her world became more and more Gestalt-less, more insignificant, with increasing loss of referential character. Her existence found less and less toward which it could design itself and out of which it could understand itself. Everything stayed the same in this world. This emptying and this standstill and vegetating of existence showed itself in its aspects as a hole-in-the-earth existence or as tomb-like (the stoppage of life). This vegetating, hole-in-the-earth existence Binswanger correlates with the

Freudian concept of anality. Ellen West sank from the height of the spirit to the lower level of almost complete vegetating. The hole must be filled and the empty feeling countered, and since Ellen West could now only exist in the world relationship of eating and devouring to fill this hole and flesh out her future, her existence became more and more an animal-like greed for food (orality). Binswanger describes greed as "characterized existentially by the closeness, narrowness and emptiness of the world, by its hole-like aspect in which the existence contents itself with whatever happens to be . . . 'at mouth'—that is, where it does not select and consider but quickly grabs or bites, swiftly throwing herself like an animal on whatever happens to be there. The form of temporalization of this being-in-the-world is no longer the expecting of the future, but solely a turning into present (a 'presenting') of the mere Now, neither born of the future nor leaving a past behind it. The 'animal seriousness' of this present shows itself in the fact that everything 'revolves' only around eating or devouring, as the only reference from which the existence can still understand itself. From everything we have set forth it must be clear that, as previously stressed, such a greed for eating, as expression of the emptying of the world of existence and making it into mere earth, is dread. When Ellen West 'throws herself like an animal' on her food, that means she is driven by dread (e.g., of loss of future), by the dread which, to be sure, she attempts to numb in the greed of eating (for in the devouring of nourishment there is still 'something doing'), only to become its slave again in the next Now. This is the inescapable 'noose' in which this existence is entangled. Thus the dread of getting fat is revealed as another expression of the dread of perpetuating the greed in the form of fattening, cramming, becoming a worm, rotting, growing shallow and ugly, and the aging and despiritualization of the existence. Being fat is the eternal reproach which the existence directs against itself, its real (existential) 'guilt.' "

As the last act in this life drama, Ellen West exercises her final reserve of freedom in the desperate existential choice to escape from her conflict through suicide.

In his book on existential analysis *Psychoanalysis and Daseinsanalysis* Medard Boss discusses the case of a patient, Maria, which is characterized by a phase of compulsive eating and obesity.[3] Prior to this phase Maria suffered from severe cardiac neurosis. Boss analyzes Maria's existence as being based upon an expansive hunger for love. This need had been expressed through her cardiac symptoms in which the expansiveness of her emotional life at the core of her physical being was arrested by the limitations of the dilation of her myocardium. Towards the end of her cardiac neurosis she had begun to feel that her physicians were losing interest in her and becoming increasingly irritated by her continual complaints (loss of love). These factors, plus the development that her mother suddenly died and that her father had become involved in a love affair, were the triggering events for the development of her hyperphagia and resultant obesity. She experienced her situation at that time as one of hopelessness and abandonment. Her hungering for love then had to be carrried out on a lower and more limited level than the organ neurotic one. She therefore inflated the mundane relationship of hunger and eating into an expansive and insatiable greed. All her possibilities for living were thus increasingly narrowed into the one possible world relationship of the incorporation of food, and practically her whole existence was absorbed by a compulsive desire to eat. Because of the extreme narrowing of this existence, her expansive need for love could only be expressed on the level of cellular and tissue metabolism; that is, by acquiring physical fatness. Because of this, her spiritual sphere became steadily emptier and she showed an increasing intellectual apathy and lack of interest in anything that could not be eaten. Diets failed because eating was now her only life relationship, and the possibility of existing for her was resolved by an inflation in the medium of the bodily tissues.

The above cases demonstrate the approach of existential analysis to obesity. Paradoxically, as seen from an existential viewpoint, the expanded body of the obese person reflects his essentially narrowed mode of being-in-the-world.

THERAPY

The therapy of obesity and acting out also shows some parallels. Usually, neither can be resolved by simple authoritarian command. In both cases, and especially where acting out is a highly characteristic defense, the development of a "reasonable," e.g., mature, ego is the best guarantee of success. For the obese patient there may be some decrease in the need to overeat during the opening phase of therapy. With increase in the therapeutic work, anxiety increases and, because of the low frustration tolerance, leads to overeating. The patients must be gradually helped—through ego strengthening—to differentiate between emotional discomfort and hunger and to face their anxiety and despair without indulging in fantasy flights and compulsive eating. When this can be done, the pre-oedipal fixations and transference relationships are worked through. The roots of their conflicts and their developmental distortions are then able to be understood, and the maturing ego make use of insight. At this point the previously ego-syntonic behavior can be transformed into ego-dystonic symptoms, and the interpretations and insight then become really effective.

REFERENCES

1. Bergler, E. Psychoanalytic aspects of the personality of the obese. *Dis. of Nerv. System*, 1957, *18*, 196-199.
2. Binswanger, L. The case of Ellen West. In R. May, et al. (Eds.) *Existence*, New York: Basic Books, 1958. Pp. 237-364.
3. Boss, M. *Psychoanalysis and daseinsanalysis.* New York: Basic Books, 1963. Pp. 155-177.
4. Bruch, H. *The importance of overweight.* New York: Norton, 1957.
5. Bychowski, G. On neurotic obesity. *Psa Rev.*, 1950, *37*, 301-319.
6. Fenichel, O. Neurotic acting out. In S. Lorand (Ed.) *The yearbook of psychoanalysis.* New York, International Universities Press. 1946, *2*, 131-142.
7. Simon, R. I. Obesity as a depressive equivalent. *J.A.M.A.*, 1963, *183*, 208-210.

14. Acting Out in Homosexuality

By Toby B. Bieber, Ph.D.

Dr. Toby B. Bieber in the chapter that follows provides us with a study of acting out behavior in homosexuality, an area in which she has collaborated as a research colleague with her husband, Dr. Irving Bieber. The author is clear that the etiology of homosexuality is to be looked upon as psychopathological, however different the emphases may be, with respect to its causation. It is nonetheless interesting to note the effectiveness of viewing homosexuality as a type of acting out behavior, and to see it within the larger context of the more general patterns of relatedness.

Dr. Bieber identifies two homosexual constellations, one of which involves a heterosexual component having to do with an incestuous aspect of maternal relationship, and the other of which concerns a homosexual core growing out of a disturbed relationship in the past between the father and son. Her chapter is an interesting one to read.

THE CONCEPT OF ACTING OUT as it tends to be understood today was suggested by Freud as early as 1905 in the *Three Contributions to the Theory of Sex*,[3] though he did not name it as such. He defined perversions as the expression of psychopathology in action, while the psychopathology in neuroses, seen as the negative of the perversions, was thought to be expressed within the self, as in somatic or obsessive symptoms. Later, his description of acting out[4] was concise, clinical, and restricted to the transference situation. He confined himself to the definition that "the patient does not *remember* anything of what he has forgotten and repressed, but *acts* it out. He reproduces it not as a memory but as an action; he *repeats* it without, of course, knowing that he is repeating it." This idea had also been made plain in Freud's postscript to his analysis of Dora where he had discussed transference.

As ideas about neurotic process evolved and changed, particularly with the elaboration of theories of character disorder, the formulation of acting out as originally conceived by Freud gave way to more descriptive usage which, in a theoretical context, has, as its underpinnings, Freud's action theory regarding perversions. In the course of the new developments, loosely defined concepts about acting out became increasingly prevalent so that currently, the term may be applied to any behavior deemed to be antisocial or self-destructive. The term is also sometimes used as a kind of clinical shorthand, and the delineation of the psychodynamic processes being acted out may be left open. The patient may be simply "acting out," meaning, of course, that his behavior is unacceptable. Inevitably, the designation has become associated with the value judgments of the therapist. For example, if an adolescent engages in sexual intercourse, and early heterosexual activity is viewed as socially undesirable, the therapist may link the behavior to the acting out of infantile sexual fantasies or to rebellion against parents, especially in cases in which there are problems about self-assertion.

The lack of precision limits descriptive usefulness. If the designation is used to describe psychopathology broadly expressed in action, the term is so all-inclusive as to become relatively meaningless. One would then have to subsume under acting out even such items as slips of the tongue and other manifestations of the psychopathology of everyday life. The problem of homosexuality as a pathologic entity illustrates the point since the effect of inversion on personality and behavior is so pervasive and anfractuous that it cannot possibly lend itself to the concept without gross oversimplification. The specifically sexual aspects, the various forms of sub-group behavior, and the wide range of activities even remotely related to homosexuality would have to be designated as acting out if one held to the broad definition, and thus would involve unproductive, circular reasoning. We view homosexuality as a pathologic *adaptation,* and shall therefore restrict ourselves to certain types of conscious or unconscious sexual role-acting and to other behavioral sequences which characterize homosexuality as a substitutive psychosexual adaptation consequent to incapacitating fears about heterosexuality.

All psychoanalytic theories about etiology and ongoing practices assume homosexuality to be psychopathologic, although varying emphases may be assigned to causation. There is agreement that the experiential determinants are mainly rooted in childhood, and that homosexuality grows out of patterns deriving from intrafamilial dynamics. In a long-term statistical-clinical study of male homosexuals in psychoanalytic treatment,[1] the parental configuration most frequently noted was the overclose, binding, overintimate, often overtly seductive mother who was in a poor marital relationship with a hostile, castrating, or detached father. The homosexual son emerged as the focal point upon whom the most profound parental psychopathology had been concentrated. Yet homosexual outcome was not a random consequence of family pathology. In a heterosexual comparison sample, marked disturbances in family relationships were apparent and psychiatric illness in many cases was severe; however, heterosexual organization remained fixed despite the presence of fears and anxiety which usually interfered with but did not extinguish heterosexuality. Characteristically, the mother of the homosexual son caught him in a double bind of sexual overstimulation on the one hand, and heterosexual restrictiveness on the other, while the father either joined in to inhibit masculine assertiveness in his son or he let his son down by relinquishing the field to the mother. The pattern of family pathology in the heterosexual sample did not reveal the concerted thrust against the patient's heterosexuality noted in the homosexual group. Where a son is overtly attached to a heterosexually restrictive, possessive mother while remaining consciously or unconsciously afraid of, hostile to, and unidentified with a competitive, unaffectionate father, a morbid resolution of the oedipus complex necessarily follows.

In the pathogenic milieu which induces homosexuality there is chronic reinforcement of fears about erotic arousal from heterosexual objects so that ultimately heterosexual cues are perceived as danger signals and are effectively repressed as sexual stimuli. An adaptive shift occurs when homosexual object choice takes over (a) as a way of achieving sexual object gratification, (b) as a defense against heterosexuality which has come to be perceived as a threat, and (c) as a means toward repairing and restoring damaged sexual functioning.

Integrated with the seeking of sexual satisfaction and associated with defensive and reparative aspects, the homosexual act encompasses a wide range of symbolic role-playing, i.e., child, parent, sibling, marital partner, and so forth. A man may choose a younger partner whom he treats as a child in ways, sexual and other, similar to the ways each would like to have been treated by his mother and father. This is often observed among pedophiliacs. In the case of a 45-year-old homosexual, whose preference was for boys between the ages of about 13 to 19, there was a tendency to seek out adolescents who were underprivileged. He would support them, take care of them, and try to reform them in cases of delinquency. The kind of tender, loving, nonexploitive parental concern the patient had missed in his own life was enacted with his young lovers. In the course of treatment psychodynamic patterns were delineated which involved multiple identifications. On one level, the patient switched identities in which the partner was the magical mother and he, the patient, was the young boy; on another level, he was the sexual mother, the source of infinite gratification; on still another level, a hostile, competitive theme was enacted in which he incorporated and displaced the father in a sexual engagement with the boy-mother; finally, the boy was assigned the identity of the male whom he, the patient, could conquer and control, yet at the same time redeem still-yearned-for paternal love. The role playing observed may be viewed as an integral part of a psychological system organized to gain lost objectives in the safety of *as if* behavior.

Lipsitt and Vallance[5] have contributed a useful concept to describe aims underlying specific acts which they term the *teleonomic trend*. It seems to be somewhat analagous to the clinical term *acting out* but more clearly distinguishes between action and underlying motives. Despite what the homosexual act purports to be for the actors—that is, erotic arousal by, and intercourse with, a member of the same sex which may or may not be accompanied by feelings of love—there are unconscious attempts to fulfill teleonomic aims such as domination, submission, identification, imitation, control, castration, dependency, and so forth. Heterosexual teleonomic trends are always identifiable whether homosexuality is expressed through a more or less stabilized "marriage" or through sporadic, casual, or impersonal encounters. Roles are mediated through styles of homosexual social interaction as well as through sexual techniques. One partner may act as if he were the wife and assume a mode of behavior he associates with wifeliness while the other, as husband, may assume a stance of complementarity. Yet in their homosexual erotic behavior, say fellatio, either may act as insertee. The act of phallic sucking may fulfill teleonomic aims such as submission, placation, and passivity for one, while for the other the trend underlying his performing the same act may be the beneficent granting of sexual pleasure in his role of benevolent, paternal figure. A heterosexual trend is well defined in anal penetration: the insertor is perceived as masculine; the insertee as feminine; the anus is identified with the vagina by both partners. The heterosexual component is a consistently appearing feature in homosexuality, though it is usually denied and repressed, but becomes clearly apparent when pursued analytically. In the study of 106 homosexual patients,[1] almost half openly reported erotic heterosexual dreams; the content included themes of sexual activity with the mother, sister, other women, and young girls.

A castration motif in fellatio is sometimes demonstrated, as was reported by I. Bieber[2] in a case by a patient who performed fellatio upon a partner, described as a masculine type, and that night dreamed that he, the patient, had blood on his teeth. An acquisitive wish for phallic power is commonly observed among male homosexuals who assign great value to size of penis. In general, the wish to have a larger penis and the seeking out of partners with a large penis indicates feelings of unacceptability and inadequacy, in particular, feelings of sexual inadequacy. Proximity to and the incorporation of a large phallus is a magical attempt at restoration of sexual functioning felt to be damaged and vulnerable. The large penis also represents the organ of the powerful, sexually aggressive father as perceived during the oedipal phase of development. In some instances the possession of a large penis may be an important claim to acceptance, as in the case of a homosexual[1] described as insecure, fearful, and blocked:

> When the patient began to go out on his own at the age of about eighteen, he felt that though he was ugly he could somehow make it up

with charm. . . . He did not feel at ease with most men, only with "gay" ones. It was when he felt defeated, frustrated or rejected that he would go "cruising." Mostly he would try to get two or three homosexuals at a bar to compete for him. It was a great pleasure to let them discover that small as he was in stature, he had a huge penis.

It has become axiomatic that the homosexual has had a singularly disturbed relationship with his mother. Our study of many male homosexuals in treatment also places the emphasis upon the father-son-relationship as a determining variable in homosexual outcome. In the homosexual liaison each may go to great lengths to gain special interest and affection from the other in order to satisfy affect hunger for paternal love. Jealousy of sexual rivals is often more intense than among heterosexuals. The derivate of homosexual jealousy is not only an unconscious association between homosexual love object and incestuous object but may also be attributed to competition for a paternal figure. A wish to restore affectional ties with a father may be inferred from data in the *Homosexuality*[1] study which revealed that 80 per cent of the homosexual sample were attracted to "masculine" qualities in another male, while the minority showed a preference for "feminine" qualities. It was found that when the patient identified the homosexual partner with the father or brother, masculine characteristics were usually sought (including the large penis); the identification of the partner with the mother or sister determined the seeking of feminine traits in the partner. Conversely, an obsessive preoccupation with destructive impulses against the father may steer the homosexual toward a masculine image with the motive of performing irrationally hostile acts against his partners. In one instance, a soldier repeatedly became involved in homosexual activity with officers. Each time the liaison wound up in the public exposure of the officer who would be court-martialed while the soldier, claiming seduction, would be let off with the mild rebuke of transfer to another installation. Not infrequently, homosexuals who know they have venereal disease will attempt to infect as many partners as possible before undergoing treatment.

The ambivalence in most homosexual relationships is a reflection of this seeking the loving paternal figure and its opposite: the attempt to destroy him. The impermanence of homosexual pairings is attributable in large part to the many inherent stresses and strains. Each tries to control and to possess the other, while at the same time, an unconscious longing for romantic heterosexuality is rarely, if ever, completely abandoned. In confirmed homosexuality, wishes for real heterosexual experience arise from time to time but remain unconscious, while the bisexual and more strongly heterosexually oriented homosexual tend to be aware of such wishes. As strength of heterosexual urge increases, certain shifts and changes in the homosexual attachment take place: (a) *Parri passu* with increasing heterosexual drive, there is a mounting hostility and anxious fear of males including the homosexual partner as transferential male figure, based upon the competitive component of the unresolved oedipus conflict. (b) Resentment grows toward the partner for failing to meet the irrational expectation of providing gratification of such heights as to extinguish the threatening heterosexual wish—a dynamic rooted in the constellation of pathologic dependency which is a general characteristic of the homosexual relationship. (c) The wish to move toward heterosexuality and away from the partner is then projected to the partner, a paranoid mechanism leading to the open conflict and quarrels frequently noted among homosexual couples. Such developments reinforce the already existing jealousy, driving one or the other into disruptive behavior which may end the liaison.

The threat of separation may precipitate depressive reactions, agitation, and profound anxiety. Rage at what is felt to be unappreciative and inconsiderate treatment may be expressed in a review of the many acts of kindness, devotion, and sacrifice for the lover; vengeful action is not infrequent. One patient, in deciding to terminate a homosexual relationship, reported that his former lover felt extremely injured and rejected. An agitated state of depression soon followed. He threatened and, in fact, carried out physical violence attempting also to expose the patient's homosexuality to his professional colleagues. Telephone calls at late hours, sudden appearances at the patient's business establishment and increasingly provocative and threatening behavior accompanied by mounting agitation, anxiety, and irrationality made it necessary to hospitalize the abandoned partner.

Some homosexuals become cynical about their own ability or that of potential partners to form a meaningful, more or less permanent relationship, and they avoid it. Instead, they seek out casual homosexual experiences in a round of "gay" living. The phenomenon euphemistically referred to as "cruising" is not limited to the uncommitted homosexual. Even in a pseudo-matrimonial arrangement, the range of transferential objects symbolized by the homosexual mate has its limits, and at times there may be a compulsive urge to find another partner with whom to act out a transference reaction. For example, a homosexual who relates to his partner as son to father may find himself in a social situation with a woman who, let us say, is reminiscent of a sister. He has been sexually stimulated by her, but there is no awareness of arousal. He may feel vaguely anxious but markedly restless—the restlessness concealing massive guilt, anxiety, and fears of reprisal. The arousal stimulated by a heterosexual cue drives him into ridding himself[6] of the excitation, which is also threatening the stabilized homosexual relationship, and induces a compulsive urge to "cruise." He checks his heterosexual drive by picking up a homosexual but one who is perceived as "feminine" in contrast to the permanent lover. Thus, the riddance phenomenon occurs within a transferential context that is heterosexual.

Our general theme has been concerned with two major homosexual constellations: (1) the heterosexual component which is linked to the incestuous aspect of the maternal relationship and manifested in certain role behaviors and other acts; (2) the homosexual core which, quite apart from the sexual gratification sought, relates essentially to defensive integrations and reparative attempts consequent to a disturbed relationship in the past between father and son. The following case is illustrative:

> Dick is a 21-year-old college student who began treatment a year and a half ago. The father, a wealthy business man, made arrangements for the initial consultation and accompanied the patient. At the end of the hour, the patient was flushed and glassy eyed; the father was in tears over his son's homosexuality. Some months previously, in a heated quarrel with his father, Dick had administered the *coup de grace* by announcing his homosexuality. This news created great turmoil in the family, an effect the patient wanted since he was involved at that time in a frenzied rivalry with his brother, four years older. The revelation was a taunt, an appeal for help, and a rivalrous play for attention. The patient's brother, not without difficulties, had managed to break away and continue his studies abroad. He was clearly the father's favorite, and everyone knew it.
>
> The mother, diagnosed as schizophrenic, is a beautiful, vain, self-centered hypochondriac who regards herself as an invalid, and for the most part is confined to her apartment. She continually complains about her health, especially in company, and embarrasses Dick when she goes into descriptions about the pains in her vagina. The mother was never interviewed. It was too much for her to come.
>
> As a child, the patient tended to be babied and the mother would show off his good looks. He remembers her asking him to show his "pretty legs" to her women friends. There is a history of heterosexual restriction and strong interference with peer relationships. The father was mainly involved in his business affairs and spent little time with the family. Occasionally he took the boys to ball games, but did not enjoy having the patient along since he would get restless and impatient. In an early interview the father confessed, "He's my son and I suppose I love him as a son but I don't like him. He doesn't wear well. He lies. He's unreliable. The difference between my two sons is the difference between day and night. Dick is superficial. He's kidding around at school. He takes silly courses (art). There's nothing to that . . . it's child's play. The only thing he's got is his good looks. I'll admit that." Yet, at a later

time, in referring to the patient, he talked with pride about the way Dick had handled himself in a social situation. "He spoke so well. I was surprised. He sounded like a philosopher."

The father's concern about his son's problem soon revealed itself to be an obsession. He would systematically go through Dick's personal effects looking for homosexual "evidence." He kept his son under strict surveillance, watching his movements and alerting trusted friends and family members to act as agents. He seemed to know exactly where the patient was and whom he was with. His hope was that the analysis would turn up information for him, and as long as he felt the analyst would serve in this role, his attitude was friendly, cordial, and communicative. When the privacy of the therapeutic relationship became apparent, he withdrew, convinced that the analyst was a naive dupe in the hands of an expert liar. The patient did, in fact, lie; but the fabrications were thinly veiled attempts at hiding opportunistic maneuvers. Since he declared a strong motivation to change, he felt guilt and shame about his continued homosexual activities which at times he concealed.

As time went on, it became clear that Dick was as obsessed with his father as was the father with him. His sessions were taken up with complaints about the father's preoccupation with him and with descriptions of out-witting machinations. The two men were locked in a colossal power struggle. The father's overt attitude toward the son's homosexuality was one of rage at a defiant child who was engaged in nefarious relationships for the sole purpose of humiliating him. Yet Dick continued to discuss the details of his life with his father, reserving sexual problems for his aunt who Dick knew carried the information right back.

In order to control and restrict the patient, the father has always used money as leverage to which Dick responds with submission. The money he has available is relatively little, and he has to beg for extras. On occasion, the father has threatened disinheritance, thus precipitating in the patient anxiety, rage, and a feeling of helplessness. He has little confidence that he can make it on his own, and is bound in a pathologically dependent tie to his successful father. Up until a few months ago, the choice of sporadic homosexual partners was primarily rich older men who gave the patient money for his sexual favors. Whenever the father turned down a request, soon after the patient was involved in a homosexual incident from which he would receive remuneration or some special consideration. In his more meaningful relationships he would test his partner to find out whether financial help would be forthcoming if he needed it.

At one point it was made quite explicit to the father that the patient's recovery required that he be given more leeway. The father cooperated for a while. It was not long before the patient was involved with a girl, though the romance did not include sexual activities other than petting. At first the father was critical of the girl for not being pretty enough to suit him, but before long he befriended her and began to include her at every opportunity. Several times during sessions, the patient would ruefully comment, "She loves my father." When the girl began to press for an engagement and Dick demurred, she accused him of having homosexual problems.

Toward the end of this relationship the patient became briefly involved with a group he referred to as the "S and M's" meaning sadists and masochists. He always took the sadistic role, but never whipped the "victim" hard. In fact during the whippings, he would whisper, "Can you take it? We'll stop if you can't." He wondered why the masochist trusted the sadists to the extent of allowing himself to be tied up. In homosexual intercourse the patient prefers to be insertee, both per anum and in fellatio.

A more recent experience involved him in heterosexual intercourse. He observed a telephone number scrawled on a public toilet door and phoned. This turned out to be a noncommercial sexual haunt. He was invited to participate in an activity which included the host, a woman, and the patient. Following some oral homosexuality, the patient had sexual intercourse with the woman which he stated he enjoyed.

Apart from these bizarre activities, the patient's more permanent homosexual relationships were had with two married men at different times. His first liaison was with an actively bisexual widower; his current relationship is with a married man who has several children. Recently he had a mild flirtation with a young married woman but hastily withdrew when her husband found out.

The pathologic attitudes and behavior in the range of this patient's homosexual adaptation demonstrate many arresting features, but several salient dynamics stand out: firstly, the inhibition of heterosexuality rests upon irrational fears of the father, given credence in reality by actual paternal hostility; secondly, the sacrifice of assertiveness, independence, and heterosexuality to the father is the foundation upon which the patient's pathological dependency on the father rests. Stemming from his renunciation, the patient chooses paternal transferential representatives who will compensate him for his sacrifice by actively providing sexual gratification, and he expects that they, as well as the father, will fulfill security needs and supply him with luxuries to which he feels entitled. An alternate course in which heterosexuality may be regained is attempted by involving himself in triangular relationships where he tries to replace the rival, gratify him, or share the heterosexual object.

In summary, the evolution of the concept of acting out was briefly reviewed. Homosexuality has been discussed as an adaptation to pervasive fears of heterosexuality consequent to a continuity of pathological parent-child relationships. Each parent participates in determining the pathogenic process specific to the sexual development of males who become homosexual. Homosexuality includes a complex of relationship syndromes, behavioral patterns, and sexual activities oriented toward sexual gratification and toward achieving defensive and reparative ends. The concept of teleonomic trends was used to elucidate the aims underlying homosexual behavior.

REFERENCES

1. Bieber, I. et al. *Homosexuality—a psychoanalytic study of male homosexuals*, New York: Basic Books, 1962.
2. ———. "Clinical Aspects of Homosexuality" In *Sexual inversion*, Judd Marmor. pp. 246-267, New York: Basic Books, 1965.
3. Freud, S. *Three essays on sexuality*, Vol. VII, (1901-1905), London: The Hogarth Press.
4. ———. *Papers on technique*, Vol. VII, (1911-1913), London: The Hogarth Press.
5. Lipsitt, L. and Vallance, T. R. "The Expression of Teleonomic Trends in Private and in Group-Related Problem Situations, *J. Personal.*, 1955, 23, 381-390.
6. Rado, S. *Psychodynamics of Behavior*, Vol. 1, New York: Grune & Stratton, 1956.

15. Learning Inhibition: A Problem of Acting Out

By ROBERT MELNIKER, PH.D.

Doctor Robert Melniker, in his "Learning Inhibition: A Problem of Acting Out," fashions for us a new theory of the learning process from the points of view of ego and existential psychology. He makes clear how complex the learning process really is, to what kinds of inhibitions it is subject, and the therapeutic implications that grow out of his point of view.

It is clear that it is useful to look upon learning problems as forms of acting out since this provides an additional dimension of understanding for the clinician concerned with the handling of learning disorders.

THIS CHAPTER REPRESENTS an attempt to formulate a tentative hypothesis concerning learning disorders and acting out, following from some theoretical speculations based on an epigenetic "self-fulfilling" model of personality function and development.

Learning disorders are variously referred to in the psychological as well as educational literature as "learning impotence," "learning inhibitions," "learning disturbance," etc. Often studies in this area are reported under the rubrics of "underachievement" as well as general "disabilities in reading". It was, in fact, this last category which was at one time most assiduously studied, because in many early cases reported, reading was primarily affected, and it was invariably involved as at least one of the academic skill areas with which children found difficulty when there was a general disorder in school progress. To delimit the problem somewhat, the learning problem will be understood to apply to children (and by extension to adults) of at least average and often of superior intelligence. There appears no evidence of neurological or other organic malfunction sufficient to account for the learning failure, and the child does not display any evidence of gross psychopathology. In addition these children are capable of learning a great deal outside of the classroom, and they do not manifest evidence of significant impairment in their capacity to relate to others. Reading is often the subject most favored for failure, but clinical experience has demonstrated that the entire spectrum of the curriculum may be involved.

The presentation of some of the pertinent literature which follows is in the nature of a brief and arbitrarily selected overview. It is an endeavor to set forth the base from which early investigations started as well as the direction in which theorizing proceeded. This short historical picture is germane to the hypothesis which will be developed. In a sense it is a development that follows from some major theoretical trends in psychoanalytic thought, including conflict theory, self-system, developmental constructs, and the creative use of anxiety in self-realization through the "search" for and productive uses of the potentials of man.

The major initial influence, as may be anticipated, was provided by Freud[9] in *The Problem of Anxiety,* in which he formulated his hypotheses on symptoms and inhibitions of ego functions. Inhibitions, he held, represented restrictions which were either precautionary in nature or resulted from the depletion of psychic energy. This point of view he further elaborated in the following three subcategories:

1. The ego might give up a function (such as the ability to learn to read) in the presence of excessive investment with sexual meaning of the organ involved in the act. Inhibition would thereby serve to obviate an ego-id conflict, and would avoid the necessity for further repressive measures.
2. The ego might fear superego punishment in the event of some successful accomplishment, and would inhibit an activity on this basis.
3. Ego inhibitions might occur where psychic energy was called away in the service of an emergency on some other front of ego activity.

In the early clinical reports and theoretical papers, these views served as rather strict guide lines. Strachey,[16] for example, proposed that since reading represented a sublimation of an oral instinctual impulse (looking equated with introjection), the function of reading could become subject to inhibition when hostile components of the oral impulse were not adequately sublimated. Blanchard[1] reported that learning difficulties in reading were involved, in part, with inadequate control over hostility which had oral components, and which had become attached to the ego process of reading. She added that the symptom was formed on the model of classical neurotic dynamics as a compromise solution in which the activity which represents a disguised expression of an instinctual wish is inhibited. The result was an avoidance of superego recrimination as well as propitiation of introjected authority by means of self-punishment, provided by academic failure and lack of achievement.

Anna Freud[6] stressed the role of sublimation in the growth of the ego and in its capacity to function effectively in academic situations. She noted that impaired parent-child relationships were a basis for faulty capacity to sublimate the infantile erotic and aggressive instincts. As a consequence of the necessity for utilizing psychic energy for repression which might otherwise be available for learning, this ego capacity suffered.

In another context, she described children who displayed restrictions of ego functions, especially in academic courses, and suggested that the symptom was a substitute for either some taboo sexual activity in the past or for some old feeling of inferiority which might be reactivated by failure in academic competition.[7] She defined an ego inhibition, such as might be present in the case of a learning disorder, as a restriction of activity in order to defend against an inner process. The transformation of a simple inhibition into a recalcitrant neurotic barrier was explained in terms of the singleness of purpose with which id impulses set out to attach themselves to available ego functions in order to achieve gratification. The ensuing struggle between the id maneuver to come out into the open and the ego defense resulted in a reduction of psychic energy. In the process, the ego at its own expense either limits or alters the gratification of the wish. In a sense this may be viewed as a self-delimitation and a surrender of some ego function to avoid an overwhelmingly painful experience which would be a threat to the organism.

Continuing along the point of view established by Freud, Pearson[13] has published extensively during the past ten years on the relationship between psychoanalytic theory and education in general and learning disorders specifically. He has presented a systematically articulated framework for explaining a wide variety of learning problems encountered in clinical work. In one of his categories (he lists seven in all), most directly related to the problem as defined in this paper, he speaks of "The involvement of the learning process itself in the neurotic conflict,"[13, p.82] and lists three subcategories:

1. A diminished capacity to *use* learning. This is based on Freud's premise concerning avoidance of conflict with the supergo. Pearson believed that the dynamic was analogous to that of sexual impotence, and he coined the term "learning impotence."
2. Diminished capacity to learn due to a disorder in the *taking in* of knowledge. Curiosity is equated with introjection, and oral conflicts are translated into learning, which represents taking in of information.
3. Diminished capacity to learn due to disturbance in the ability to digest knowledge. This is based on the premise that such cases represent severe obsessional states with regression at times from the secondary to the primary process. The consequence is difficulty in thinking, resulting from reduced ability in cataloguing, associating, and ordering data.

More recent studies are represented by a trend toward the investigation of the influence of environmental factors on learning ability, such as parental personality structure and family attitudes and values. Rubenstein, et al.[14] discuss the phenomenon of faulty symbiotic relationship, which may lead to exaggerated negativism in the child, and sustained primary identification behavior, with reduced capacity for object relationships. These authors suggest that a conflict between identification and the growth of "precarious individuality" may be involved. They conclude that for these children, non-learning stands for a striving to attain individuation, the learning tasks being experienced as a surrender of selfhood to the overwhelming demands of the mother.

The implications of their report seem to extend beyond the more traditional understandings of the ego functions, in the direction of built-in safeguards against the loss of self or major damages to the evolving self-system. One such safeguard may appear as the refusal to learn, manifested as the inability to learn, not in the attempt to escape the punishment of a harsh superego, but rather by avoiding identification with an engulfing object which threatens self-fulfillment. A position such as is implied in the foregoing research that stems from an orthodox theoretical foundation ends up closer to May's[12] expatiation of an existential formulation. May stresses that in his thinking beyond the ego is the *self* which continues to strive throughout its existence for bringing its potential to light.

Also in the current approach is a research reported by Harris,[10] in which he compared 100 emotionally disturbed boys with learning disorders with a control group containing a similar number of emotionally disturbed boys who showed no significant learning disorders. The study utilized a frame of reference of possible psychological factors which would differentiate the groups, such as: social class, family disorganization, parental ambition, birth order and parental expectation of maturity, and finally aggression and submission. Harris[10,p.142] concluded that all of the categories differentiated significantly between the two groups, and that, "One conclusion is easily evident: namely, that . . . learning problems have several causes rather than just one . . ." In the category of Aggression and Submission Harris [10,p.141] noted that "The non-learner group, in comparison to the learner group, more often showed extremes in the area of aggression: they were aggressively hostile or extremely submissive."

Finally in a recent paper Daniels[2,p.56] examined the implications of school failure within the framework of interpersonal theory rather than that of intrapsychic conflict. He points to the dynamics of "morbid envy" as well as to its consequent security operations as possible crucial factors in impaired learning, and argues that . . . "envy is always destructive to learning and to human relationships."

The sampling of the literature is based on a trend which this writer thought it reasonable to develop from the historical sequence of studies in the field, the process being somewhat as follows:

1. An ego inhibition is understood to be a symptom involving an attempt to avoid psychic pain which would arise from superego punishment for the gratification of erotic and/or destructive impulses.
2. The influence of environmental factors on the formation of attitudes and the quality of ego functioning.
3. Focus on the striving for identity representing a developmental organismic process rather than a part process such as identification with characteristics of significant persons.

It is from this last general frame of reference that I will discuss the acting out implications of learning disorders.

In the psychoanalytic literature, the concept of acting out has often been used in a rather free way. Usually it is agreed that it involves behavior in a current situation resulting from an expressive of repressed wishes striving for expression. The motive for the acting out is the need to be rid of the anxiety engendered by the conflict at unconscious levels, or to find a belated gratification for the repressed impulse. Fenichel[5] remarks that it may also represent attempts to master traumatic experiences through the mechanisms of repetition and dramatization. In our view, acting out is not intended to convey its more traditional meaning of a resistance in analysis or generally disapproved behavior.[18] What is intended by this term is current behavioral reexperiencing of some earlier need system, usually manifested in a disguised or altered form. This acting out behavior, as in the case of a charade, lends itself to translation, if the *intent* experienced in one modality can be reformulated in the experiential terms of another modality.

A number of points of view have been propounded in the psychoanalytic literature which are pertinent to the position to which I have come. In some cases these sources have a sort of indirect and basically historical relationship, and in others a more obviously direct influence in the theoretical statement which I will make.

Fenichel[5] believed that the most fundamental anxiety and the paradigm for later anxiety was connected to the infant's inability to satisfy its own imperious drives; that the first fear was a wordless terror of experiencing further traumatic states, and that it was this fear which compelled the infant to attempt to hold on to the status quo. Resistance to growth could be seen as an attempt at active mastery of psychic pressures emanating from an inner state of disequilibrium.

Escalona[4] writes that it is "experience" rather than either the outer stimuli or the organism's reaction tendencies which is the crucial factor in shaping the growing child. She stresses the developing genetic givens in the context of the availability to these of the appropriate matrix in which to unfold and grow. That writer describes the "experience" as the result of reciprocal interaction. It is in the same sense that Anna Freud[8,p.247] writes: "Whatever level has been reached by any given child in any of these respects (developmental lines) represents the results of interaction between drive, and ego-supergo development and their reaction to environmental influence . . ."

Hartmann[11] in a paper dealing with developmental psychology, cautioned against confusing a part for the whole when dealing with psychic phenomena, noting that for the purpose of understanding developmental processes and sequelae, a differential view of ego functions is preferable to the more inclusive concept of ego development as a whole. Hartmann argued that it would be useful to formulate statements as to *which* of the ego functions has experienced either retarded or precocious maturation vis-a-vis the drives and in relation to one another.

Erikson[3] in a paper in which he delineated his "eight stages of man"* employed an epigenetic model in a manner which is most directly applicable to my hypothesis, and to which model I am most indebted for the direction which my own theorizing followed. The epigenetic principle is stated generally by that writer as follows: "Anything that grows has a ground plan, and that out of this plan the parts arise, each part having its time of special ascendancy, until all parts have arisen to form a functioning whole."[3,p.52] There are corollaries deriving from this principle, among which are the following relevant four statements:

1. Each stage of development proceeds according to a genetic plan ". . . which create (for the individual) a succession of potentialities for significant interaction with those who tend him."[3,p.52]
2. Each stage progresses to a crisis point where mastery or relative failure is encountered, and where a "lasting solution" is effected[3,p.53].
3. The stages overlap, so that for example, while any given stage "B" may be in the throes of crisis, "A" is exerting its influence on the basis of how successfully it may have weathered its own critical period. In the meantime "C" (and possibly D, E, etc.) has already emerged and is proceeding to its own resolution.
4. All of the stages are interrelated and are subject not only to the external environmental medium with which they interact, but are mutually dependent for proper sequential development.

Since each stage continues to emerge despite earlier conditions which may not have been propitious, it seems warranted to comment on this principle thus: in children with "problems," there may be present at-

---

*Erikson's eight stages are given as follows: basic trust vs. mistrust; autonomy vs. shame, doubt; initiative vs. guilt; industry vs. inferiority; identity vs. identity diffusion; intimacy vs. isolation, generativity vs. self absorption; integrity vs. disgust, despair.

tenuated propensities developing alongside of, and in decisive interaction with, other more current entities, developing themselves more or less successfully, in an inexorable direction toward a series of phylogenetically determined crisis encounters, despite the lack of ontogenetic readiness.

The hypothesis I have tentatively constructed is as follows: A learning disorder (as delimited herein) may represent an acting out of a need complex, relative to an earlier phase of maturation which was excessively, but not *hopelessly,* frustrated. The following are offered as inherent extension of the major hypothesis:

1. The acting out, in relation to disorders in academic skills, represents both a continued searching for an adequate interaction with an environmental medium, as well as a resistance to proceeding further along a particular ego developmental line, in the presence of crisis failure.
2. The resistance to learning may be seen as an abandonment of an immediate source of ego power, in favor of a long term goal which exerts a more imperious pull on the organism; namely, the construction of an adequate foundation for later more complex and more highly differentiated levels of self maturation.
3. The continued acting out of the "search" is a hopeful sign that the child has not yet capitulated or settled for a "lasing solution"[3,p.53] based on despair.[17,p.49]
4. The earlier the point at which the traumatized stage appears in the maturation sequence, the greater is the potential influence on the ensuing stages, the greater is the potential insult to the overall plan of the organism itself, and the more urgent will be the pull to remain behind to repair the foundation.

The symptom which shows itself at early school age as a defect in learning is seen consequently not as a defense against anxiety flowing from fear of retaliation for taboo desires by an internalized authority representation. It is viewed rather as driven by anxiety deriving from the fight against surrendering critical needs essential to the emerging self. In this sense the resistance to learning is a defense; it attempts to apply the brakes to continuing along a predetermined line of personality growth. It is a resistance to growth which is experienced by the organism as a once and for all abandoning of hope, and with it, development of potential selfhood. Thus the symptom may be described as repetitive efforts at repair of a major, but not hopeless, trauma. The symptom picture is, however, inevitably complicated by the pressure of later developing collateral need systems. It is conceivable that the investment of words and thoughts, as well as sensory functions, with erotic or aggressive content, may be a result rather than a cause of defective learning. Traumatized need systems, struggling for fulfillment, may lend themselves to invasion by later developing functions, which themselves cannot mature and serve optimally in their own mode, because of the resistance provided by the ontogenetic lag of the earlier stage(s).

The employment of an epigenetic base for the hypothesis which is being offered follows from a conative view of man in search of himself, and the ontogenetic lag is proposed to serve a self-preservative, and by implication, a self-fulfilling function. The veritable fortress of passive resistance[18] encountered in attempting to motivate these children to learn, study, or perform in an academic setting is frustrating but impressive. The child behaves, in fact, as if giving up his symptom would be tantamount to a catastrophe, so desperately and creatively does he maintain himself in a non-learning status.

Although this model is offered as framework for an approach to learning disorders, it may prove interesting and hopefully profitable to apply it clinically as a focus for symptoms and personality "deviations" in a broader sense. The major point which is highlighted is the self-preservative dynamic inherent in the acting out. While the disorder in learning appears to inflict an obvious penalty on the immediate life situation in which the child functions, it covers an ultimate purpose and may be directed to a more urgent goal, not at once apparent. If the immediate, self-defeating and self-limiting nature of the symptom can be understood as a battle for organismic survival, the implications for treatment can be developed from an "emerging-self" rather than solely a conflict theory of personality.

From a somewhat tangential viewpoint, the philosophical roots of this position can be stated in another form. The hope for man lies not only in his ability to learn but in his absolute and obdurate insistence, in certain circumstances, of *not learning*. Acquiring cognitive mastery of the world according to one's personal style—forgetting and distorting, creative reintegration of experiences, all these may lend themselves to a view of man as containing a potential, built in to guarantee diversity, and to make for the emergence of individual variations on an evolving theme of human growth, the pattern of which can at best only be guessed at. This "nay" saying then can be at least one healthy use of aggression in the service of self-affirmation. To say "no" may be a mode of attempting to provide a proper and firm rootwork before the child begins to stretch and climb towards more precarious frontiers. It may be thought of as a rejection of conditions which range outside of "the average expected human environment," to use a phrase of Hartmann.[11] The "no" to the socially imposed expectation may in fact be the strongest and most courageous "yes" to the inner self.

In a discussion of a basic problem of the human condition, Tillich[17, p.5] sums up far better than I am able the question of the "no" and "yes." "Courage is the affirmation of one's essential nature, one's inner aim or entelechy, but it is an affirmation which has in itself the character of 'in spite of.' It includes the possible and, in some cases, the unavoidable sacrifice of elements which also belong to one's being but which, if not sacrificed, would prevent us from reaching our actual fulfillment."

REFERENCES

1. Blanchard, P. Psychoanalytic contributions to the problems of reading disabilities. *Psychoanalytic study of the child,* 1946, *2,* 163-187.
2. Daniels, M. Morbid envy in chronic learning disability, *Psychoanalytic Review,* 1964, *51/4,* 45-56.
3. Erikson, E. H. Identity and the life cycle. *Psychological Issues,* 1951, *1/1,* 50-100.
4. Escalona, S. K. Patterns of infantile experiences and the developmental process. *Psychoanalytic study of the child,* 1963, *18,* 197-244.
5. Fenichel, O. *The psychoanalytic theory of neurosis.* New York: W. W. Norton, 1945.
6. Freud, A., and Burlingham, D. T. *War and children.* New York: International Universities Press, 1943.
7. ———. *The ego and the mechanisms of defense.* New York: International Universities Press, 1946.
8. ———. The concept of developmental lines. *Psychoanalytic study of the child,* 1963, *18,* 245-265.
9. Freud, S. *The problem of anxiety.* New Yorks W. W. Norton, 1936.
10. Harris, I. D. *Emotional blocks to learning.* New York: The Free Press of Glencoe, 1961.
11. Hartmann, H. *Essays on ego psychology.* New York: International Universities Press, 1964.
12. May, R., et al. (Eds.) *Existential psychology.* New York: Random House, 1961.
13. Pearson, G. H. *Psychoanalysis and the education of the child.* New York: W. W. Norton, 1954.
14. Rubenstein, B. O., et al. Learning problems. Learning Impotence: A suggested diagnostic category. *Amer. J. of Orthopsychiat.,* 1959, *19,* 315-323.
15. Singer, E. Paper on Identification and Identity given at New York University Colloquium, February 10, 1965.
16. Strachey, J. Some unconscious factors in reading. *Int. J. Psa., 11,* 1930.
17. Tillich, P. *The courage to be.* New Haven: Yale University Press, 1952.
18. Weissman, S. Some indicators of acting out behavior from the thematic apperception test. *J. of Proj. Tech.,* 1964, *28/3,* 367-375.
19. Zanger, E. The dynamics of the passive-aggressive underachiever and ways of coping with his behavior in a classroom. Newsletter, Nassau County Psychological Association, 1965, *12/4,* 24-31.

PART IV

TREATMENT AND MANAGEMENT OF ACTING OUT

The treatment and management of acting out remain a critical issue for our society. Continuous acting out may prove detrimental not only to ongoing psychotherapy but also to all those with whom the acting out individual comes in contact.

Although Dr. Ekstein's lead chapter deals with the general treatment philosophy of acting out, the other authors essentially concern themselves with the specific management of acting out in different settings and with various age groups.

Readers of this volume will find a wide range of problems covered in this part, not all of which may be of their immediate concern or interest in the sense that they are likely to confront such special problems of acting out in their everyday clinical work. Yet it is interesting to observe that among the chapters in Part IV there is a certain conceptual unity to be found in the authors' descriptions of their areas of special competence—namely, that the acting out process represents a form of communication between two or more persons, and that the essential requirement for treatment and management is to help the acting out individual to translate his unconscious statement into a more adaptive behavioral expression.

16. A General Treatment Philosophy Concerning Acting Out

By RUDOLF EKSTEIN, PH.D.

In the chapter that follows, Doctor Rudolf Ekstein, from a broad and intensive background of rich therapeutic experience, offers us a general philosophy concerning the nature of the acting out process. It is interesting to note that Ekstein is impressed with the resemblance between acting out behavior and what he observes in the dramatic theater. He looks upon acting out as essentially one system of communication among others available to a patient for the expression of his conflicts and his translation of those conflicts, or of the anxiety associated with them, into significant behavioral expression.

Our feeling is that Rudolf Ekstein has made another important theoretical contribution which readers will find interesting and helpful in their own appraisal and understanding of acting out.

Acting out is a form of experimental recollection

WEALES,[13] A PROFESSOR OF ENGLISH, suggests in his volume: *A Play and its Parts,* that "a play is a kind of . . . playing." With Shakespeare he sees the world as a stage, and in describing a child playing, he

> used a number of words . . . *playing, performing, act, gesture* . . . which one uses automatically in talking about the theatre and about plays. Of course, these words have diverse and often complicated meanings; they are used for actions which have little to do with the stage. Still the same words can be used to describe what goes on in life and what goes on in the fictional world of the theatre. One reason is that there is a close connection between the two. 'All the world's a stage,' says Jaques in Shakespeare's *As You Like It,* 'And all the men and women merely players.' Jaques fancies himself something of a philosopher, so he goes on to explain that 'one man in his time plays many parts' and to describe the seven ages . . . from infancy to old age . . . which are the main 'acts' in each man's repertory of characters. Antonio in *The Merchant of Venice* says much the same thing; he is feeling sorry for himself, however, so his remarks are more personal than those of Jaques:
> > I hold the world but as the world, Gratiano—
> > A stage where every man must play a part,
> > And mine a sad one.

Gratiano, partly to cheer up his friend, partly because the role does fit his personality, say, 'Let me play the fool.' The comparison between the world and the stage comes naturally to the lips of Shakespeare's characters, as naturally as to your own when you say to a friend, 'Stop it; you're just putting on an act.'

Shakespeare's metaphor, Weales recognizes, antedates the psychologist's insight that the part, the role that people play, the *persona,* the mask which they carry, are but partial aspects of the total human being. It is the task of psychological research to go beyond the mask to understand the act, the play, the acting out, and to decipher the meaning behind it.

But, of course, Weales primarily thinks of acting out a part, of playing a role which is for him as conscious as the role-playing of the actor who re-enacts what he means to convey.

Much acting that is carried out in psychotherapy conveys unconscious conflicts, has a hidden message, is a part not deliberately chosen, and is referred to as acting out. To borrow an image of the Italian playwright, Pirandello, we might say that the patient who thus unknowingly plays a part as he acts out (within the context of the psychotherapeutic session or outside of its confines) is in search of a plot, the unconscious plot; in order to find the plot, he goes to a psychotherapist whom he mistakes in the transference for an author, whose interpretations he reacts to as if they were a plot created by the psychotherapist, rather than describing the patient's own past.

Acting out, according to psychoanalytic understanding, must be understood as a compulsion to repeat a symptom, and thus gives new meaning to Santayana's notion that those who do not know their past are condemned to repeat it. The philosopher's moral injunction, his demand that we are to comprehend our own history, becomes if carried into psychopathology, a technical task. The technical task of all therapy is to find, through interpretive work and through the process of working through, the hidden meaning behind the symptom, behind the acting out.

It is for this reason that Ekstein and Friedman[4] have referred to acting out as a form of recollection, a kind of trial thinking. The play on the stage is a kind of playing with acts, and acting out on the stage of psychotherapy is a kind of playing with thoughts about problems, and it must be understood as a form of communication.

Since I have introduced acting out through the simile of the play, the author's and actor's attempt to convey a meaning to the audience, I will use another simile from the stage in order to bring alive the therapeutic task one encounters when meeting up with acting-out patients. In the screen play Sayonara there are depicted a young couple, an American soldier, and a Japanese girl, whose love and marriage are put in jeopardy by the social pressures, the hate of the aftermath of the war, and who despair in trying to resolve the bitter conflict. In the movie the Americans are opposed to racial intermarriage, while the Japanese are opposed to the victorious enemy, the occupying forces. The couple, then caught in this conflict, confronted with the order that forces the American soldier to return home and forbidding him to bring the girl along, watch a subtle marionette play on a stage. The Japanese players, who act out on that stage a conflict of endangered love and who speak for the characters that they are to portray, also utilize puppets which are moved about by the actors. It is as if the voices of these actors were separated from the motor action of the puppets. The couple watches in silence, occupied with the burning and burdening conflict in them. The actors speak about that conflict, and the puppets act that conflict out. The silent depression of the young couple is reinforced by the suffering voices of the actors. These voices in turn are reinforced by the grotesque movement and actions of the puppets. One has the impression that this young couple watches a nightmare, actually a projection of its own until then unconscious "final solution," hears the voices of condemnation and sees the monsters of destruction only to wake up from that nightmare and to act on it as if the nightmare on the stage were a prophetic dream, an injunction from which there is no escape. By that time the movie-goer, having identified with the plight of the young couple and having sensed the message of the "play within a play," can have no doubt about the final outcome.

We have watched through an intrinsic system of relay and delay mechanisms the development of an affect, the depression, into a thought which spells a kind of resolution, to a trial acting-out and finally toward the total catastrophe. We realized that the Japanese actors and their puppets merely act out the secret thoughts of the young couple. They do not trigger off the suicide; they merely portray the inner thought.

May I liken the function of the therapist to the function of the audience watching that screen play? And may I suggest that the future-directed plot of the movie could be understood as the reverse of the therapeutic process which actually directs into the past? The depressive features of the actors may lead us to discover the hidden plot, the rejection by the forces of authority, the parents, and the response of the small child, withdrawal, depression, isolation and/or suicide attempt. Correct interpretation may turn the acted-out version into insight, the internal agreement of the couple with the objections of their persecutors, into healthy defiance, as was illustrated through the other couple who find a positive solution.

The wide variety of systems of communication available to patients indeed creates difficult technical problems. So difficult are these technical problems that most therapists think of acting out merely as a resistance, as an undesirable feature, as something that should be stopped, that is in the way of psychotherapeutic technique[7] which depends on verbalization, on the free flow of associations, and on the interpretive response of the therapist. The very chapter headings of this book seem to indicate that each special form of acting out, each clinical manifestation of acting out, was seen initially in the history of psychotherapy as an undesirable hindrance that had to be brought under control.

It was the genius of Freud to turn every obstacle to the analytic process into an asset. The discovery of transference, the use of resistance, the utilization of countertransference reactions, all these, at first experienced as a hindrance to the cure, became instead an essential part of treatment. I wish to emphasize that the same holds true for acting out. I want to look at acting out as a form of playing with thoughts, as an attempt at resolution of conflict, and treat it as such rather than meet it with regret and prohibition.

As a matter of fact for certain age groups it has long been recognized that acting out and playing out are normal functions.[8] When we speak about play therapy, and consider play the royal road to the unconscious of the child[6], we indeed have accepted the fact that certain age groups need to play in order to "talk" to us, and have no other way to convey their conflict to us but through the form of play. Play is not simply catharsis, and neither is acting out. Play has meaning, and is a form of playing with thoughts, as is the act on the stage. However, while the act on the stage is conscious playing (and even that is but a half-truth), the play of the child in the psychotherapeutic situation is an attempt to weave conscious and unconscious fantasies around external objects,[12] around the people who play with him, or around the toy objects which he is utilizing. These fantasies in part refer to unconscious conflicts, and they are the subject of the interpretive work.

The therapist neither encourages nor forbids the play. He makes play material available for the child who wishes to "talk" in that way, and uses his interpretive skills in order to convey to the child at the right moment what he thinks is the meaning of the play.

Play, like acting out, is not a reliable language. It is not reliable because of the implied gratifications, since it is nearer to impulse and impulse-derivatives, and because of the fact that the emotional investment in play turns it frequently into "real" life. Let us think of a little boy who wishes to play with toy soldiers. He not only works out his aggression against authority figures, or against danger and enemies of different sorts, but he works out the problems he has, the inner worries as to whether he can win or not, the issue of identification with the aggressor or the identification with the victim, and he must soon carry the play into the transference situation. He may wish to incorporate the therapist in the play situation, and may soon develop a "real" fight. Instead of moving toy soldiers and guns on the floor, the child may take the very soldiers and blocks and throw them at the therapist. Microcosmic play,[6] which allows for interpretation, suddenly becomes a form of acting out, and confronts us with serious technical problems.

It is noteworthy, by the way, that the very first example that I employ utilizes an instance of acting out which is potentially provocative, which is uncomfortable, and which is sort of in our way. So also is the suicide episode from the movie screen which I recounted earlier. But there is just as much playing out and acting out which is of a positive, socially approved nature, and which nevertheless poses similar technical problems. I think of the case of a little girl who brings a candy bar into the therapeutic hour and puts that candy bar between herself and the therapist while saying, "I will show you that I can lose weight and I will not touch the candy during the whole hour." She proceeds then to leave that piece of temptation between her and the therapist in order to fulfill the promise that she had given. This piece of acting out has overdetermined meaning, but at first glance seems to be in the service of adaptation, in the service of struggling against the symptom of overweight. It has a much more complex meaning, such as that it puts the psychotherapist into a special and awkward position. And as a matter of fact, one of the most complex aspects of acting out deals with the countertransference potential. This very example shows how easy it would be for the psychotherapist to become either the reinforcer of the conscience who strengthens the will of the girl to resist the food, or to become an indulging parent-surrogate who encourages the child to eat, or to eat at least a little bit, or half of that chocolate, so that she will love the therapist more than her strict mother. Only if the therapist can recognize the special transference meaning which is attached to this material can he rely on interpretive intervention which makes visible the hidden meaning behind this piece of acting out within the therapeutic situation, and which reflects the internal struggle between temptation and conscience, the quest for external intervention in the face of a promise one might not be able to keep.

One may look at acting out in the transference situation as a kind of acting out in which the child assigns a role to the therapist, so that the therapist is forced to join the act and counteract out. As a matter of fact, much of play therapy constantly challenges and tests the ingenuity of the therapist who is to take part in the play, such as in chess or checkers or any other form of gaming, to somehow guess what part the patient wants to have him play or "counteract out." The adroit therapist will somehow take the assigned script and play within that play in such a way that he can still interpret rather than get caught up in the play and take it seriously as a direct play commitment, as a device of gratification, of mutual participation rather than as a piece of communication.

We must look at much of the acting out and the playing out of the child as his attempt to write the dialogue of a stage plot and somehow guess what the child would have us say, so that we then in turn (rather than inventing our own plot) can still show the child what he meant to convey to us. (We may say that Hamlet certainly was not a good therapist to his uncle. He did use the traveling actors in order to convey the plot, and to provoke catharsis, but his wish was not to show the uncle the meaning of the plot in order to cure him, but rather to create evidence so that he could plot against him on his own.)

Much of the technical skill of the child psychotherapist has to do with his capacity to maintain the child's play as an interpretable play, and see to it—if the child must move the play to the acting out, a more primitive language indeed—that he still can demonstrate the meaning through interpretation rather than squash the acting out through injunction.

The point has been made that acting out is a reference to the forgotten, the repressed past. In this sense acting out must be considered an attempt at recollecting.[7] It is a sort of trial thought[4] by means of which the patient attempts to remember, and the therapist must see the act as a form of *motor reconstruction*. (Much "affecting out"—quite often a substitute for recollection—can be understood as *affective reconstruction* as well.) But not all acting out is past-oriented, and much of what will happen during the psychotherapeutic process, and I refer at this moment primarily to the psychotherapeutic work with *adolescents*, may very well be a kind of acting out which has a different function. Acting out, then, instead of being a form of recollection, a trial thought about the past, becomes a trial thought about the future, an attempt at new resolution. One may well say that much of the normal life of the adolescent has to do with the type of acting out which is future- rather than past-oriented.[4] Pumpian-Mindlin[11] has referred to this clinical fact in discussing the omnipotentiality of the adolescent. Instead of playing with *omnipotent fantasies*, as does the younger child who plays out Superman, the adolescent plays with all kinds of potential solutions for his future, acts out all kinds of identities in his quest for the true one, and gives us the feeling of constant shifts. May I suggest that the adolescent plays with *omnipotential fantasies?* None of his actions, none of his decisions are a final commitment even though they come out as quasi-acts, as the acting out of the future, forerunners of adaptation and commitment, the beginning of the adaptive process, and are future-oriented.

During psychotherapy with adolescents (of course, this holds true as well, though to a lesser degree, for work with children or adults), we find phases in which the acting out tendencies, rather than being primarily directed toward the past, the attempt to restore the forgotten memory, the painful trauma, conflict of yesterday, suddenly emerge and frequently with full pathological strength and often also with destructive implications. These tendencies have the non-genuine stamp of a symptom, but must be recognized as a "compulsion to repeat" of a different sort. These new tendencies are an attempt to measure oneself against the future, to try on a new hat, and while they carry repetitive, compulsive qualities, they are still pathological resolutions without normal commitment, and they nevertheless can be compared to a kind of rehearsal that some day may lead to a real live drama to be lived and resolved, not in terms of the stagnant neurotic past but in terms of a better future.

As a matter of fact, adolescents as they get well, frequently need to experiment through acting out with issues of separation from the family, sexual experimentation, experimentations in intimacy, search for jobs or a profession. This no doubt can be anxiety-arousing for the therapist who overlooks that such acting out is future-directed, in the sense of problem-solving, and represents the beginning of new spontaneity rather than the repetition of paralyzing compulsivity.

Ekstein and Friedman[4] have described such a case in which the search for new identity models, the moving away from the acting out of criminal impulses to the acting out of ethical, religious impulses indicated a search for new solutions. Interpretive work must be directed toward the past as well as the future, and within the context of the present transference situation, it must be oriented toward the defensive as well as the adaptive function of acting out.

So far I have referred to acting out as a form of recollection, as a form of problem-solving, and I have been occupied primarily with playing and action material which is easily translated since it goes hand in hand with the secondary process, with normal thinking. We might refer to that kind of acting and playing out as neurotic acting out.

The equivalent of *neurotic acting out* is neurotic trial thought. But there is much acting out which is of a different nature. It is the kind of acting out that is much more remindful of a dream sequence, and I refer to it as *psychotic acting out*. Psychotic acting out as my co-workers and I[3,5] have discussed elsewhere has as its equivalent the primary thought, the psychotic thought. It reveals the thought disorder, and the therapist understands it well only if he "translates it" in the same way that one would translate the manifest content of the dream as one searches for the latent meaning. One might suggest that psychotic acting out is connected with a kind of psychotic-acting-out-work—comparable to the dream work— that has to be understood analytically in order to permit interpretation. The interpretative technique frequently makes use of "interpretation within the metaphor," of symbolic gratification, of the action metaphor and the like.[2]

The older the patient gets, the more difficult does it seem to be able to cope with acting out language. As far as the child is concerned, we have frequently thought that we should encourage it. As a matter of fact, the very term "play therapy" seems to indicate that we encourage a special form of language, as if the language itself was curative. May we stress here that the language, regardless of whether the language consists of free association, of dialogue, of acting out, or of playing, is not of itself what cures. Communication itself does not represent the cure, but rather it is the question as to what is communicated which is decisive.[10]

Neither acting nor the lack of acting out does cure, but it must be looked at as a form of communication. If it is a successful form of communication, and if perhaps it is for certain stretches of psychotherapy the only form of communication, we should utilize it in order to understand the patient. Acting out is neither good nor bad; it is usable or it is not usable. The technical issue with adults, of course, is that the play of the small *child,* regardless of how destructive it may be in its intent, will do little harm, whereas the acting out of *adults* frequently leads to a catastrophe or serious disruptions in the therapeutic work.

The greatest difficulty in the treatment of acting out patients, and of course, I am referring primarily to office practice, has to do with the fact that acting out language knows no truly effective delay. All the niceties of ordinary, concise definition of terms are frequently obviated by the fact that as far as social consequences are concerned there is not much of a difference between an appropriate act and inappropriate acting out. The nicety of the theoretical differentiation that the act follows after the *thought which is a form of trial action,* the definition of thought that Freud[9] used, while acting out represents but a trial thought and cannot lead to appropriate action, is lost in the chaotic life situation of the patient and drowns out the voices of delay and reflection.

This proves anxiety-arousing to patient and family alike, and is of course an eternal source of the countertransference anxiety emerging in the therapist. Much acting out frequently, as we know, has invited *countertransference acting out,* such as the many ways in which therapists get involved with patients in strange manners which are pathological and lead to therapeutic anarchism. Acting out adult patients frequently seem to force the therapist into counter-action, into injunctions, into sharing, into all kinds of social interventions and activities which are not therapeutic and for which a quasi-rationale is all too easily found. There is but one step from a genuine rationale to the rationalization posing as an appropriate explanation.

Almost all therapeutic schools have contributed ideas to this problem, and the literature shows us that there is practically no "action" that has not been recommended by psychotherapists. How can a psychotherapist protect himself against counter-acting out and maintain the patient within the formal psychotherapeutic setting? How often is he given time to ask himself whether a certain action that he contemplates, verbal or otherwise, is truly indicated? It may be well to teach him to ask *whether this trip is necessary*. He may still experience over and over again that he was caught by the patient's acting out, and could not find an interpretive answer.

We know that much such acting out occurs in the form of emergencies: the sudden threat of quitting; the sudden asocial act; the not coming to hours; the special way of using or misusing money; the destructive actions at home with children and relatives, spouses; the embarrassing activities around the job; conflicts with the law, etc., etc. Many of these emergencies, whether they are suicide threats or homicidal threats, or the return to addictive and criminal tendencies, create a tremendous problem. It may help therapists to think of each of these emergencies as the external representation of unconscious material as it emerges to the surface. He who does not get caught in the emergency is not overwhelmed by it and does not have to rescue the patient, as it were, but can look at this emergency as material which is emerging, and hence may stem the tide through interpretation.

The way I have spoken about interpretation throughout this paper seems to give the interpretive act a kind of magic quality. I do not wish to give this impression, but rather I want to relate the interpretive act, that technical intervention, to the total therapeutic process. I do not speak about *the* interpretation but about the *process of interpretation;* that is, the analytic handling of material of patients.

I may almost suggest that the very title I have chosen for this chapter is misleading. The true psychoanalytic therapist is he who looks at the material of the patient with a sense of equidistance. He does not select certain material as more or less important, but he follows Anna Freud's dictum that the psychotherapist is to remain equidistant from ego, superego, and id. He believes that all material is equally valuable and lends itself to interpretation. Thus I am attempting to enlarge and to reflect on the Basic Rule and its modifications, on the concept of free association. In classical analysis, the patient is to tell us freely what occurs to him, and he is not to censor his thoughts or withhold. If he is to "tell us freely," he must well choose to tell us in the way that he can. Sometimes he will play things out, sometimes he will act them out, and sometimes act them in, or be silent. We "listen" to all these forms of communication and interpret them, and as we are impartial toward the *content* we must also learn to be impartial toward the *mode of communication*. And acting out is but one of these modes; is *but one of the many offspring of communication which the patient fathers*. We are to accept all these offspring, and we are to expect that all of them will fulfill their function within the psychotherapeutic task. Interpretion aims not only at making the unconscious conflict conscious, but also at the goal Freud expressed in his epigrammatic *where id was, there shall ego be,* namely at helping to let develop the capacity of the patient to solve problems, to use secondary thought processes for trial action and for the resolution of conflict on an adaptive basis.

One can also think metaphorically of the free association method on the couch as a form of acting out. The transference neurosis, after all, is but the revival, a sort of re-enactment of the infantile neurosis and thus is its replica on that stage which is called the couch. The free associations of the patient can be thought of as a kind of playing with thoughts, with words, except that there is usually no motor action, almost none, and thus we are enabled again to restore the metaphor of the play. In a recent communication on termination of psychoanalysis and working through[1], I referred to the prologue of that play called psychoanalysis in which we diagnose the patient, establish the need for analysis and watch the symtoms emerge, like the actors listed on a program, in order of appearance. Analysis, as any other form of psychotherapy, moves then to the play itself, the different acts of the play, word acts, motor acts, talking it out, playing it out, or acting it out, to the final act, the resolution of the conflict, and finally to the epilogue, the afterplay, as it were, at the end of the analysis. This ending process is characterized frequently by the resurgence of symptoms, by the resurgence of acting out, and is but the adaptive farewell of all these actors, the symptoms, who now reappear in order of importance. At first the symptoms appeared as actors who played out the past, and now they appear in order to hint at the future. The analysis has taken a full turn from the re-enactment of the past to the pre-enactment of the future. In Shakespeare's words, the past has become the prologue for the next show.

I have suggested, then, that acting out is but a special form of all re-enactment of past conflicts and of all pre-enactment of future conflicts within the context of the transference. Let us, then, react to acting out in a truly democratic way and stop its segregation from other forms of the patient's armamentarium of communication devices without denying its difference.

REFERENCES

1. Ekstein, R. Termination of analysis and working through. *J. Am. Psa. Ass'n.,* XIII, 57-78, 1965.
2. ———. Thoughts concerning the nature of the interpretive process. In Morton Levitt (Ed.) *Readings in psychoanalytic psychology.* New York: Appleton-Century-Crofts, 1959, 221-248.
3. ———, and Caruth, Elaine. Psychotic acting out—royal road or primrose path? In press.
4. ———, and Friedman, S. W. The function of acting out, play action and play acting in the psychotherapeutic process. *J. Amer. Psa. Ass'n.,* 5, 581-629, 1957.
5. ———, and ———. On the meaning of play in childhood psychosis. In Jessner, L., and Pavenstedt, E. (Eds.) *Dynamic psychopathology of childhood,* (Eds.) New York: Grune & Stratton, Inc., 1959 (269-292).
6. Erikson, E. H. Studies in the interpretation of play. I. Clinical Observation of play disruption in young children. *Genet. Psychol. Monographs,* 22, 557-671, 1940.
7. Fenichel, O. Neurotic acting out. *Psychoanal. Rev.,* 32, 197-206, 1945.
8. Freud, A. *Psychoanalytical treatment of children.* London: Imago Publishing Co., 1948.
9. Freud, S. Formulations regarding two principles in mental functioning. (1911) *Standard Edition,* 12, 218-226, 1958.
10. Loewenstein, R. Some remarks on the role of speech in psychoanalytic technique. *Int. J. Psa.,* 37, 6:460-467, 1956.
11. Pumpian-Miadlin, E. Omnipotentiality in adolescents in psychotherapy. *Amer. Acad. Child Psychiatry,* 1965.
12. Waelder, R. Psychoanalytic theory of play. *Psa. Q.,* 2, 208-224, 1933.
13. Weales, G. *A play and its parts.* New York: Basic Books, Inc., 1964.

17. Acting Out in Group Psychotherapy: A Transactional Approach

By Lawrence Edwin Abt, Ph.D.

> *"From birth to death every human being is a* party, *so that neither he nor anything done or suffered can possibly be understood when it is separated from the fact of participation in an extensive body of transactions . . ."*
>
> *Using this profound quote from Dewey and Bentley, Dr. Abt's paper departs from those who would see acting out in a private, molecular sense, and journeys into the larger land of interpersonal transactions, of which acting out is but one form. His vehicle is the group, and it is in this setting of multiple involvements that acting out transactions are observed. Rather than discourage such transactions, Dr. Abt's thesis is that they may have salutory effects on the group and, if skillfully handled, can enhance the process of treatment.*

SOME YEARS AGO, in a search for the basic conceptual unit of clinical psychology, I examined a number of possible conceptual units. Included in the group considered were *action, reaction,* and *transaction.* My inquiry[1] directed itself finally toward a consideration of clinical psychology as science conceived in transactional terms. The present paper looks at acting out in group psychotherapy and group process within a similar transactional frame of reference.

The transactional point of view in philosophy was first formulated by John Dewey and Arthur F. Bentley, originally in a series of papers in the *Journal of Philosophy* and subsequently in a book, *Knowing and the Known.*[7] They wrote as follows:

> Observation of this general (transactional) type sees man-in-action not as something radically set over against an environing world, nor yet as merely action "in" a world, but as action *of* and *by* the world in which the man belongs as an integral constituent.

Dewey and Bentley looked upon all behavior as a series of activities of the full situation, organism-environment. Writing further in *Knowing and the Known,* these authors said:

> From birth to death every human being is a *Party,* so that neither he nor anything done or suffered can possibly be understood when it is separated from the fact of participation in an extensive body of transactions—to which a human being may contribute and which he modifies, but only in virtue of being a partaker in them.

In a series of three papers entitled, "Psychology and Scientific Research," Cantril and others who associated themselves with the Ames position sought to apply the pragmatic philosophy of Dewey and Bentley to the general field of psychology[6]. Cantril and his colleagues examine the nature of scientific inquiry and of scientific method and set forth, in an important and stimulating manner, their view of transactional psychological research. In general, their position is a molar one that relies upon the past experience of the individual; and their transactional functionalism implies the importance of action and purpose in the life of the individual.

Their transactional formulation for the general field of psychology may be understood in relation to the following:

On the basis of an interactional view alone, an investigator could study the interdependence of various aspects of a perception forever and never get at the reason for such relationships until he asked himself what function such an interrelationship of phenomena served in the transaction of living. When he asks himself this question, it appears that variables such as size and difference are experientially related because it is only through their relationship in past experiences that high prognostic reliability is built up. Prognostic reliability becomes itself, then, a new dimension of experience, a new basis for a standard the psychologist can use for experimentation. And if the investigator continues, as he must, to ask the next question concerning the function of prognostic reliability in a life transaction, the apparent answer is that prognostic reliability increases effective action. So the effectiveness of action becomes another variable that can be used as a basis for a standard in experimentation. And there must follow, of course, the question: Effective action for what? We then see that we cannot understand even the simplest perception without bringing in the variable of purpose.[6,p.518]

The general transactional point of view of Cantril and his coauthors may perhaps be better appreciated in relation to the following summary of principles that are both explicit and implicit in their writings:

1. Perception is a transaction involving both the organism and its environment. It is not activity of the organism independent of the environment, nor is it the environment considered independently of the organism in its action upon that organism. *What goes on between the organism and its environment* is itself the subject of inquiry, and this is the transaction itself. Dewey and Bentley explained their notion of transaction in terms of the buyer-seller analogy, pointing out that it is virtually impossible to define the functional nature of the buyer *as buyer* apart from his series of transactions with the seller, and that it is likewise just as difficult, if not impossible, to define the seller *as seller* apart from the transactional nature of his relationship with the buyer.

Organism and environment are never conceived apart from each other, and the position of transactional functionalism is always concerned with the total situation, including the individual's past experiences and the series of expectancies that he has developed with respect to his future.

2. Perception depends, in part, upon the assumptive world of the perceiver; and this world, in turn, is significantly dependent upon the whole series of transactions of the individual prior to the present perception. In short, as the individual assumes, so he will perceive.

3. Perceptions are "prognostic directives for action" in the sense that, based as they are upon the individual's past experience and his unconscious assumption derived therefrom, they establish the likely forms of response the person will make.

4. Because of the nature of perception, there are differences in the perceptions of different persons, just as there have been differences in their assumptions growing out of different past experiences.

5. Perception is a functional process in the sense that it is always adaptive by reason of the fact that it furthers the purpose of the organism and helps establish the basis for effective action. Past perceptions that have not been validated by subsequent action tend either to be modified or extinguished as new assumptions that underlie them grow out of the individual's continuing coping with his world.

6. The specific standards and values of the individual constitute the ends to which the purposes of the organism are directed.

One of the chief values, for our present inquiry, of the transactional point of view is that it commits us to a thorough-going view of behavior, both internal and external, both molar and molecular, *as process*. Apart from this important consideration, transactional functionalism is prepared to provide us with a unit that, when suitably developed and conceptually extended, should prove useful in understanding what goes on in group process and group psychotherapy.

This unit we may designate as the *interpersonal transaction,* which may be defined as any proceeding between two or more persons, who may be either real or illusory.

Since human organisms cannot usefully be considered apart from their social environments, the interpersonal transaction is always embedded in, and is a part of, a larger social process of which it may be regarded as the most significant expression or component.

The interpersonal transaction may occur between one actor and another actor, or group of actors, in a social situation having an established and validated reality status, or it may occur in a situation in which there is no validated reality status apart from the experience of the actor himself.

We are, from this point of view, concerned, then, not alone with a study of the transactions of two or more persons who are "objectively real," but also, and significantly, with the transactions between two or more persons, at least one of whom may be illusory. Put differently, the view taken here is that, as a conceptual unit, interpersonal transaction is just as useful in investigating, describing, and understanding the fantasied interpersonal operations of individuals as it is in their similar transactions with real persons.

INTERPERSONAL TRANSACTIONS AND THE GROUP SETTING

Individual psychotherapy may be looked upon as a series of recurrent and incomplete interpersonal transactions carried on between two persons, one of whom functions in the role of the therapist and the other of whom plays the role of the patient or client. The interpersonal transactions tend to be recurrent because they are derived from material that is historically relevant to the patient that is never fully exposed, ventilated, and worked through; they tend to be incomplete because, although they have a contemporary reference point, their historical character fails to permit any given transaction to be definitive.

The patient's most psychotherapeutically significant interpersonal transactions are those, when considered from a psychoanalytic point of view, that involve transference and resistance and the countertransference operations of the therapist himself. The interweaving complex of transactions—transference-and resistance-oriented stemming from the patient and counter transference-oriented coming from the therapist—constitute the total on-going therapeutic process. When this process is viewed within the framework of the transactional point of view developed in this paper, the two operations are seen as complementary and represent the essence of the therapeutic collaboration.

The interpersonal transaction—considered not only in its verbal but also in its non-verbal manifestations—is the unit not only of individual but also of group psychotherapy. The interpersonal transaction develops from the confrontation of two or more persons that constitutes the therapeutic encounter, and the transaction represents the outcome of what each patient brings, at any given time, to the therapeutic collaboration.

The conduct of psychotherapy within a group setting affords an important new dimension to the range of interpersonal transactions characteristic of analytically oriented psychotherapy. This new dimension is *multiple transference* or target multiplicity.[11] In addition to the therapist himself, in group psychotherapy there are numerous patients, depending upon the size of the group. Each group therapy member may serve as a transference target for each other member of the group with the result that the group therapist is not the only one in the group who stands *in loco parentis*. One result of this situation may be a "dilution" of the transference, normally directed toward only the group therapist but now projected upon other group therapy members.

The multiple transference dimension of group psychotherapy provides the basis for *concurrent* and *serial* multiple interpersonal transactions among group therapy members. Such transactions may either further or impede the therapeutic process of the group, depending upon the origin, nature, and type of transaction. The presence of group therapy members, for example, may invite a decrease, rather than an increase, in a group therapy patient's libidinal investment because hostility or affection, meant for the parental figure—the therapist—may now be shared with another group therapy member and displaced on to him.

ACTING OUT IN THE GROUP SETTING

If acting out is looked upon as one form of interpersonal transaction—which is the position taken in this chapter—it does not differ significantly in individual and group therapy except in relation to the different conditions of individual and group "climate" characteristic of interpersonal fields.

According to Fenichel,[8] acting out is:

. . . an acting which unconsciously relieves inner tension and brings a partial discharge to warded off impulses (no matter whether these impulses express directly instinctual demands, or are reactions to original instinctual demands, i.e., guilt feelings); the present situation, somehow associatively connected with the repressed content, is used as the occasion for the discharge of repressed energies, the cathexis is displaced from the repressed memories to the present "derivative" and this displacement makes the discharge possible.

In a useful summary, Aronson[2] has identified four basic components of acting out:

(a) The therapeutic context, involving transference and resistance,
(b) A current action,
(c) A repressed fantasy, and
(d) A partial discharge of impulses.

A consideration of the four components together leads Aronson to the formulation of the following definition of acting out—"a manifestation of transference and resistance in which a repressed fantasy reappears in the form of a symbolically disguised current action, with a concomitant partial discharge of impulses."

Acting out as a therapeutic phenomenon always implies both a weak ego and repression. As such, acting out is therefore reflective of earlier patterns of behavior and tends to be suggestive of the difficulties in living that the patient experienced in his developmental years. Through a reinstitution of the family setting, the therapy group provides both individual-induced and group-induced anxiety that may be provocative of the kind of regression that, in combination with the patient's weak ego, will make for acting out behavior in the group therapeutic situation as well as outside of it.

Both individual and group therapists have long since rejected the notion that acting out behavior has only negative connotations. Most analytically oriented group therapists seem to look upon acting out as a process that affords the redevelopment of homeostasis in the personality after considerable regression has occurred consequent to therapeutically induced anxiety. Since the group, by its very nature, provides conflicts and anxieties, and defenses thereto, in its members, acting out offers a quick, and sometimes quite effective, means for release and discharge of the painful affects mobilized.

In transactional terms, acting out is an interpersonal response to resistance within a therapeutic context. Acting out, of course, occurs outside of individual and group psychotherapy; but its significance lies chiefly as a transference phenomenon in the service of resistance within a therapeutic framework. The group therapeutic situation often provides not only an excellent setting but also a splendid showcase for acting out phenomena of the widest behavioral range. In the formation of his therapy group, the experienced and skilled group therapist usually seeks to assign to his group patients who he believes from his experiences with them in individual therapy will represent a wide range of transactional possibilities for group therapeutic collaboration. Patients with known acting out tendencies are regularly included in such therapy groups, but they frequently need to be "balanced off" with other group therapy members who participate in such a manner as to preserve and advance the therapeutic process.

FORMS OF ACTING OUT IN GROUP THERAPY

It is clear that the range of acting out behavior is very wide. There have been several attempts to classify and put order into the types of acting out, but none of these efforts seem entirely satisfactory and some have the defect that they extend the conception of acting out behavior to the point that it embraces too wide a range of behavioral phenomena.*

---

*Slavson,[11,p.400] has offered a thorough and systematic coverage of acting out phenomena, for example, and provides a comprehensive table on the phenomenology of acting out that is useful to examine in detail.

If we take a transactional view of the acting out process—that is, one that sees it as occurring in an interpersonal context and as a response to interpersonal operations undertaken by one or more other persons—it is possible to arrive at a convenient and consistent formulation of the phenomena of acting out that has a certain operational validity.

Three types of acting out behavior in group therapy may be identified:
(a) Aggressive-destructive
(b) Aggressive-controlling
(c) Passive-resistive and assertive-dependent

Let us look in some detail at the forms of acting out behavior that may be categorized in the manner set forth above.

(1) Aggressive-Destructive

This classification embraces both verbal and non-verbal behavioral forms of acting out, and its chief characteristic is some form of aggression with destructive coloration directed either at the group therapist, members of the therapy group, or at the group as a whole.

The following are typical of such patterns of acting out:
(a) Overt physical acts: kicking, throwing of objects, shouting, etc.
(b) Acts such as failure to pay therapy fees, consistent late arrivals, failures to attend group therapy sessions
(c) Direct verbal assaults such as criticism, contempt, statements of resentment, etc.
(d) Indirect verbal assaults such as ridicule, sarcasm, demeaning references, etc.

(2) Aggressive-Controlling

This category consists essentially of verbal forms of acting out behavior that seek to permit one group therapy patient to maintain distance, enhance status, or manipulate one or more members of the therapy group as a response to some form of induced anxiety, either individual or group.

Typical of the interpersonal operations are these:
(a) By playing the role of the therapist or co-therapist, a patient acts out his need to control and dominate.
(b) Interruption of communications of other group therapy members by offering of his own dream, free association, etc.
(c) By arrogation of special knowledge and status to himself, the patient seeks to minimize the role and position of another group member.

(3) Passive-Resistive and Assertive-Dependent

This group of acting out forms covers a wide variety of avoidance reactions and methods of denial of involvement and the anxiety associated with it.

The following are suggestive of the common kinds of interpersonal maneuvers:

(a) Silence and non-participation
(b) Avoidance and withdrawal from affective involvement with the group and the therapeutic identification
(c) Complaining and resenting remarks and postures
(d) Compliant flattering remarks to placate the therapist or other group members who are inducing anxiety
(e) Masochistic maneuvers seeking to be manipulated

It is clear that the above categories are simply possible ways of classifying or looking at forms of acting out, and that any given patient's acting out behavior is capable of classification often in terms of a number of different categories that will simply seek to emphasize for the clinician the most significant patterns of the patient's relatedness to, and interpersonal operations in, the group therapy setting. Understanding the forms that acting out behavior may take, especially in the therapeutic situation, leads naturally to a consideration of the techniques for handling the acting out transactions of the patient.

MANAGEMENT OF ACTING OUT

If the clinician looks upon acting out as only one form of interpersonal transaction in group psychotherapy, he is in a better position to manage the acting out patient. There are, for example, circumstances in which the group therapist would actually want to maximize the opportunities for acting out transactions in his group in the interest of furthering the therapeutic process in one or more members of the group.

There is general agreement, I think, among most clinicians that ego-building techniques are an essential first step in the handling of acting out patients, not only in individual but also in group psychotherapy, since most acting out patients have impaired egos. Such ego-building therapeutic efforts are important because, without them, the clinician faces difficulty in offering interpretations relative to the meaning of acting out behavior since the therapeutic interventions cannot be handled by the patient.

In patients with adequately intact egos capable of responding meaningfully to interpretations, the following represents a practical method for therapeutic management:

1. Indicate as frequently as necessary the presence of acting out behavior.
2. Help the patient to bring into awareness the repressed fantasy lying behind, or presumed to lie behind, the acting out.
3. Seek to relate the present acting out behavior and the now conscious fantasy in such a manner that the patient is aware of their connection and sees that the acting out interpersonal operations are one expression of his reaction to the emergence of the repressed fantasy and the anxiety that it mobilizes.

In a group setting, members of the therapy group other than the therapist himself are often capable of inducing understanding of the kind referred to above; but it remains the principal responsibility of the group psychotherapist to determine matters of timing, form of interpretation, and an exposure of the nature of the on-going transference and resistance. It is usually helpful to offer an interpretation to the acting out patient as quickly as possible after the appearance of the acting out behavior.

Group therapy is often facilitative of the development of acting out transactions because of the multiple and simultaneous transferences common to group therapeutic membership. Since most therapeutic groups tend to be action oriented, many patients feel impelled to extend the range and nature of their interpersonal transactions, including the specifically acting out forms. Acting out behavior not expressed in regular group therapy meetings in which the therapist participates often finds special expression in alternate sessions in which the group therapist does not participate.

SUMMARY

This chapter offers a preliminary formulation of acting out behavior in group psychotherapy in transactional terms. In doing so, it suggests that the basic unit for understanding such behavior is the interpersonal transaction. It is suggested that group psychotherapy, by providing opportunities for multiple and simultaneous transferences not typical of individual psychotherapy, offers an excellent stage for the emergence of acting out transactions that, when suitably handled by the group psychotherapist, will further the therapeutic process in members of the therapeutic group. Forms of acting out transactions are set forth, and techniques for handling acting out behavior in group psychotherapy are suggested.

REFERENCES

1. Abt, Lawrence Edwin. The development of clinical psychology: a transactional approach. In Brower, Daniel, and Abt, Lawrence Edwin (Eds.). *Progress in clinical psychology,* Vol. III. New York: Grune and Stratton, 1956.

2. Aronson, Marvin L. Acting out in individual and group psychotherapy, *J. of the Hillside Hospital*, Vol. XIII, No. 1, January, 1964.
3. Berne, Eric. *Transactional analysis in psychotherapy*. New York: Grove Press, 1961.
4. ———. *The structure and dynamics of organizations and groups*. Philadelphia: Lippincott, 1963.
5. Bion, W. R. *Experiences in groups, and other papers*. New York: Basic Books, 1961.
6. Cantril, Hadley et al. Psychology and scientific research. *Science*, 1949, *110*, 461-464; 491-497; 517-522.
7. Dewey, John, and Bentley, Arthur F. *Knowing and the known*. Boston: Beacon Press, 1949.
8. Fenichel, Otto. Neurotic acting out. *Psychoanal. Rev.*, 1945, *32*, 197-206.
9. Freud, Sigmund. *Group psychology and the analysis of the ego*. New York: Liveright, 1949.
10. Gundlach, Ralph H. A technique for the analysis of process in group psychotherapy. Report submitted on NIMH Grant M-5157(A), April 1963.
11. Slavson, S. R. *A textbook in analytic group psychotherapy*. New York: International Universities Press, 1964.
12. Wolf, Alexander, and Schwartz, Emanuel K. *Psychoanalysis in groups*. New York: Grune and Stratton, 1962.

18. Problems of Therapeutic Management of Acting Out with Hospitalized Patients

By HOWARD P. ROME, M.D., AND
MAURICE J. BARRY, JR., M.D.

Doctor Howard P. Rome and Doctor Maurice J. Barry, Jr., of the Mayo Clinic, in the material that follows, are concerned with the special problems of therapeutic management of patients with acting out disorders who have been hospitalized.

These authors are especially acute in setting forth the difficulties of transition into the hospital environment, in studying the hospital as a therapeutic community, and in indicating the problems of transference not only between the patient and his attending physician, but also toward other members of the hospital staff and toward the hospital as an institution in its own right. What emerges from their consideration of the problems is a real need that exists for the establishment of a continuing dialogue among all of the persons in the hospital, both professional and non-professional, who have any kind of relationships with acting out hospitalized patients.

THE RECOMMENDATION FOR RESIDENTIAL TREATMENT in a hospital is a decision which subsumes many motivations. Patently it means that in someone's judgment, a person's present or prospective behavior is of such a nature to require more control than can be assured in a less controlled situation. The specific circumstances which prompt the recommendation and the varied interpretations of it by all the dramatis personae have a significant effect upon the events and reactions that ensue. The decision to admit a person to a hospital converts him, by formal fiat, into a patient, with all that that status entails in a medical sense. The rite of passage by which he becomes a patient has pivotal significance in an extensive psychosocial frame of reference.

The status of a patient in a psychiatric hospital has added potency as a second-order event—an event that shapes the character of subsequent events. The psychiatric hospital has kaleidoscopic qualities. It can change rapidly the character of long-established relationships. It has a mordant property too, for it can etch in high relief those traits which so often are blurred beyond recognition by the typical inattentiveness of everyday life. And because of these far-reaching influences, the decision and the behavior that follow provoke surges of affect which in turn stress the modal constraints which define ordinary conduct.

Thus, all other things being equal, the very fact of becoming a patient in a psychiatric hospital forces the adoption of those roles in relation to the hospital and its staff which reflect the patient's character as well as that of the institution. In this sense, the quality of a patient's conduct in the hospital, his relationships with fellow patients and the various members of the staff, and his acceptance of hospital routine are efforts to come to grips with a new reality. Since reality in a psychiatric hospital is manifested through events which are easily construed as symbolic of the patient's past, it frequently recalls to him and highlights his old conflicts. In a comprehensive sense, therefore, the vicissitudes of acting out can be seen in the particulars as well as the symbolic overtones of the events that lead to admission. Those which mold the patient's behavior vis-à-vis the staff and other patients are by no means more important than the effects of the social and therapeutic responsibility upon the staff and its relationships with patients.

In the course of every psychotherapeutic process, the patient passes through many phases of old conflict rekindled by the anamnestic process and its transference implications. At the same time, in adapting to the demands of an everchanging reality, he faces new anxieties which prompt his reaching out indiscriminately—sometimes to learn belatedly that the straws which he clutches are indeed straws. When anxiety increases, the patient is forced to use not only his unique mechanisms of defense but also those coping techniques of everyday life suggested by the situation itself. He does this with a varying degree of success or failure, depending upon his judgment, his prevailing affect-tone, and the quality of the pay-off. In most instances the combination of his resources and the demands of the occasion are such as to enable the patient to hold anxiety to a degree which is endurable. At the same time, a sensitive and supporting therapist has the task of increasing insight by reinforcing both external and objective reality as well as by apposite interpretations of the origins, meaning, and consequences of the subjective reality distortion. This climate of analytic retrospection conduces to regression, a state of transference dependence upon the therapist wherein the patient defensively withdraws from what he keenly feels as the hurtful hostility of a world he never made. In this state inevitably he must deal with the therapist (and pari passu with others around him) by the use of those techniques which in the past led to some diminution of anxiety generated by the re-experienced conflict between himself and figures of surrogate authority. Commonly these experiences and the techniques they mobilize impel behavior beyond the scope of internal controls, and sometimes even beyond the range of ordinary communication cathexes, where the patient's conduct enters the realm of behavior-as-a-charade.

Many of the consequences of these acted-out charades are harmless and therefore require no intervention, therapeutic or protective, other than maneuvers to further the iterative process of exposition and interpretation. There are times, however, when retributive symbolism freights the behavior so heavily as to shape it into forms dangerous to the patient or to others, warranting a more active and protective intervention.

A common danger exists in the acting out of destructive impulses wherein the edicts of an implacable retributive justice demand an eye for an eye. Inasmuch as justice in our society is an institutional phenomenon, this extreme example of individual acting out must be controlled. If its affective discharge cannot be controlled by the patient, it must be controlled by social forces; and it becomes the responsibility of the therapist to act as the social agent in substituting external controls for the deficient internal controls. The classic dispassionate, objective, analytic calm as a therapeutic instrumentality is of dubious value in a situation wherein a patient contemplates harming himself or another. By the same token, lesser forms of destructive behavior must be controlled also if the therapeutic process is not to be burdened additionally by very real social, economic, or physical health complications.

Inherent in the decision to admit the patient to the protective custody of a hospital is the assumption that less direct attempts to suggest or impose controls have failed. These attempts usually take the form of clearly communicated ego and superego reinforcements. It happens at times, for a variety of reasons, that the patient is unable either to understand the altruistic intent of these substitutes for his deficiencies or to incorporate them as an acceptable and useful part of his own set of values and checks. Consequently the constructs he employs lead to oppositional, non-conforming idiosyncratic behavior with its dangerous implications.

When ordinary control mechanisms are obviously ineffective, a therapeutic regimen designed to continue on the same plane is fitted into what is actually an antitherapeutic phase. Prior to an imposition of controls the work of therapy has relied exclusively on the use of verbal symbols to communicate the care and concern intended to produce a meliorative effect by increasing the affect of rapport. Rapport is experienced as a response to an endogenous need of the patient facilitated by the manifest interest of the therapist. When the security of this relationship falters or promises to fail, the therapist's mode of communication must take a less abstract form. His intentions of caring and helping must be demonstrated tangibly by the therapist's willingness to act out a decision to provide the patient with such controls as will give him adequate protection against the consequences of any form of noxious impulse.

Some patients accept this as a therapeutic decision with relief and gratitude, inasmuch as they are aware of and realistically fear the risks inherent in what they are impelled to do. Other patients resent and contest this decision, misconstruing its therapeutic intent as aggressive punishment motivated by impulses much the same as their own. The gross as well as the subtle meanings of this misconstruction must be dealt with, both at the time of the decision and subsequent to the patient's admission to the hospital. If the meaning of this behavior on the part of the therapist is allowed to stand unclarified, it acquires particular antitherapeutic importance, for it casts the purpose and intent of the hospital admisssion into the context of punishment and consequently places the therapist in the role of a jailer.

There are many possible reasons for entertaining such a misconstruction. The forceful deprivation of a person's freedom tacitly underscores his subordination to a totally controlling authority. This is a common problem with which many patients have struggled for years. Its latent meaning invites the muster of paranoidal defensive tactics arising from the very nature of the psychopathologic setting which engenders them. In turn these exist in parallel with and are reinforced by the realities of the situation which tangibly confirm long-held, albeit latent, suspicions. It is more likely than not that the experience easily interpreted as assaultive will call forth ancient cathexes from the repressed kitchen-middens of one's personal history. Such an action is readily interpreted as an insult to these prerequisites and mores which associate virility, adequacy, and competence with unrestricted freedom of action. The regression explicit in submission to another's assumption of the responsibility for total care may have symbolic overtones which loosen oedipal anxiety with its flood of derivative affects. Hence, a seemingly chaotic melange of symptomatic reactions often is provoked by a situation in which a decision is made to divest the patient temporarily of the unrestricted authority and responsibility for the conduct of his affairs.

In this context the hospital has additional symbolic meanings as well as those associated with its function as a realistic emergency device to be used when there is judged to be a critical juncture in on-going therapy. Since the deprivation of freedom is clear-cut abrogation of civil rights, the act has extensive socio-political connotations. It is legally permitted only if certain statutory provisions are met. Behavior which intends violence or deviates from socially approved conduct is an indication for invoking such statutory sanctions. These initiate a sequence of socially approved, legally authorized interferences with civil rights. These provisions have been enacted with the assumption that a proper hospital with facilities beyond mere custody is available to receive and treat those patients committed to it. A gloss on the word "proper" in this context requires an exposition of ideal as well as minimal standards and practices of psychiatric hospitals which, however germane to the therapeutic intent of this thesis, is beyond its compass. Suffice it to say that it is desirable that the therapist trust the hospital staff to use only that degree and those kinds of control which will assure the patient of the benevolence of their intent and maneuvers. Obviously, the continuation or the initiation of a truly therapeutic regimen is totally dependent upon such confidence.

In these circumstances the hospital staff has functions of far greater importance than its custodial or warder operations. All of its members have to become auxiliary therapists with differentiated as well as congruent roles. Their cooperative interdependence is attested by their interest in dedicating individual and collective time to understanding the patient and his personal needs.

A correlative part of this program requires that a fairly complete formulation of antecedent events be made available by the referring source. Certainly the events which prompted the decision for admission have to be known in some detail. This will shed light on at least the more obvious meanings of the acting out behavior. Armed with these cues and clues, the staff can then be more apposite in its exercise of control and in the application of appropriate adjunctive treatments. Occupational and recreational therapies, for example, can furnish acceptable and tangible outlets for the heretofore impulsive need to act—to *do* something. Such purposefully prescribed displacement activities not only facilitate control in the hospital but also provide a model for the post-hospital rehabilitation period.

The interaction between the patient and the members of the hospital staff inevitably leads to what might be thought of as transference complications. It is natural for the patient, especially in a regressed mode, to use as templates for behavior those coping patterns he knows from previous experience and relationships, disturbed or otherwise. It is this situation that he establishes the mold for new relationships, with the consequence that they are made to have an acceptable resemblance—at least symbolically—to older ones. A sophisticated staff, appreciative of the generality of this principle by which one patterns a life style and prepared by the specific details of the patient's history, can remain objective and yet empathic, attentive, and concerned, refusing to personalize unflattering allegations or to be used in any other way which would compromise the work of therapy.

Among the more common compromising traps for an unwary staff is the one in which the patient pits staff members against each other. It is required of them to listen to the alleged deficiencies and complaints with attention and realistic concern but also they are obliged to refer back the resolution of these problems. Hopefully such a confrontation under these circumstances will lead to a more meaningful communication between the patient and the staff member involved. In this therapeutic gambit the staff must appreciate the fact that its collective integrity, sensitivity and sophistication is being tested and be prepared to modify its standardized procedures in the interest of the patient. Undoubtedly this will tax the hospital's flexibility as it will test the defensive characteristics of each member of the staff. It goes without saying that each staff member's observations should be recorded and be available as part of a common data base for the conduct of continuous unified therapy.

At the level of daily operations, staff members do act as custodians entrusted with the responsibility of administering the details of the patient's life and behavior in the hospital. Experience has taught that the most effective care is the planned consequence of an integrated regimen accomplished by a system that divides the several jobs of comprehensive treatment among the staff members. Thus are shared such functions as those associated with the administration of the rules of the institution and the assumption of clinical responsibility for the supervision of the patient's physical examination and care. This shared responsibility tends to minimize the conflict which results from overlapping jurisdiction and poorly defined roles.

Within a hospital one aspires to achieve a therapeutic milieu characterized by such flexibility as is needed to facilitate the development of a program which can be individually fitted to the needs of each patient. The achievement of this end inevitably is somewhat less than ideal. The administrative essentials are those of yoking in some compatible manner the need for control and the need for treatment. In the care of the acting out patient, so-called treatment without the stabilizing influence of control has little chance of success. On the other hand, the application of controls without the objective of treatment is merely an imprisoning postponement of violence and is conducive to recidivism. There is a real need for the establishment of a continuing dialogue among the several echelons of therapists. This discussion will do much to control untoward partiality as well as to lighten the pall of an otherwise unyielding institutionalism governed by standard operating procedures. Inasmuch as the work of psychiatric treatment in large measure is the resolution of conflict between the needs of the patient and the demands for social-group consensus, therapy replicates in miniature the problems of everyday life. In this sense, the management of acting out has a universal dimension which transcends the limits of the small world of the patient and the hospital.

19. Acting Out in Family Psychotherapy

By CARL A. WHITAKER, M.D.

With the recognition that psychological illness is almost always embedded in a family situation, Dr. Carl A. Whitaker is concerned with understanding and management of acting out problems in family psychotherapy, an area in which he has done so much pioneering work.

It is clear that the multiple-therapeutic approaches characteristic of family therapy today make the problem of handling acting out one in which only the members of a therapeutic team can effectively handle. After defining the therapeutic discussion with the family, Whitaker considers not only the problems of acting out by members of the family group itself but also the problems of acting out by the therapist. What emerges is a helpful and interesting approach to the essential problems that exist in the area of family counselling and psychotherapy.

THE BEGINNING OF MULTIPLE THERAPY in 1945 as a technique of investigation and exploration of more difficult treatment problems gave us a new sense of strength so we began family psychotherapy a few years later. Since 1950, this has opened up a set of treatment problems previously kept in the shadows. Our group was so constantly involved in teaching psychotherapy and so routinely challenging each other's patterns in the multiple therapy setting, that by 1955 we had moved away from collaborative therapy and were pushing every referral toward couple or family therapy framework.

The multiple therapy supervision system makes the problem of acting out a team problem. In the one-to-one therapy effort such release for anxiety is a personal attack on the other. We have previously defined the difference between acting out and a therapeutically valuable behavioral interaction.* Acting out by any member of the therapeutic group tends to minimize the affect developing between them. In contrast, where the behavioral interaction does not tend to minimize the affect, it is a contributing force in the therapeutic process. Where it does minimize the feeling or prevent the forward movement of the psychotherapy, it should be called acting out, and is in effect the behavioral expression of a transference-countertransference disequilibrium. This does not mean that an impasse or a transference-countertransference jam exists. We clarified in the reference above the fact that any acting out to relieve the affect level is by joint agreement of the persons involved. It is probable that not only

---

*Psychotherapy of the Acting-Out Schizophrenic, *Amer. J. of Psychotherapy*, Vol. 17, No. 3, July, 1963.

is there an implicit and covert arrangement as to who shall burst the affect bind, but possibly even how it shall be done. For example, in looking back on my early work in Ormsby Village, a school for delinquents, I think it quite clear that some of the car stealing my patients did was in direct response to my vicarious enjoyment of their antagonism to the social structure. Simultaneously the acting out served as a mechanism for covering up the panic precipitated in us. They were powerful persons. I was a young therapist. Actually, I didn't feel much more adequate than they did.

THE DEFINITION OF FAMILY PSYCHOTHERAPY

"Family psychotherapy" is defined as variously as the centers that utilize it. The term may or may not include the psychotherapy of husband-and-wife couples. It may include the collaborative treatment of husband and wife by different therapists or the simultaneous psychotherapy of the entire family by several therapists, each in a separate office. Some centers include several varieties in what is called a "multiple impact approach." We operationally experience the family as a biological unit and consider that, with few exceptions, this unit is the patient. The family is an institutionalized microsociety with its own unique cultural patterns, most of which are not revealed to the outside world. It is, of course, a psychological unit and a social unit in the sense that any primary group constitutes an entity. However, for our purposes and for the purposes of this chapter, the family is a two generation group. We will discuss this group as the patient and restrict it to an artificial model consisting of father, mother, and one or more children.

In family psychotherapy, the chief complaint may vary. The son may have been stealing cars, the daughter may be shy and withdrawn, or indeed one of the adults may have become psychologically crippled. A second series of families present themselves with the chief complaint of a generalized family symptom. The adults have decided that their family is not maturing adequately, that there is not enough warmth at home or there is too much tension, or in some situations the family want to increase their own creativity. There is a third group of families who come to psychotherapy as an extension of their previous, more specific, work with a psychotherapist. Father says in effect, "I am better, my wife is better, our marriage is healthier, but we want the children to participate in this growth, and we want the family to have the kind of satisfactions we have gotten from our individual therapeutic efforts."

THE THERAPEUTIC TASK

The therapeutic task with the family should be defined accurately. Although we follow the general principle that a new experience is the significant objective, family psychotherapy highlights the complexities of the therapeutic endeavor. We have been forced to admit that family psychotherapy can be effectively undertaken only by a team of two therapists. A good surgeon can do a routine appendectomy, but even a good surgeon wouldn't attempt a major abdominal operation without a colleague of equal adequacy across the table. We believe family psychotherapy is a major operation. Moreover, we are convinced that no team is powerful enough to *"handle"* the family. Manipulative psychotherapy may be sufficient in minor operations, but it does not seem effective in major operations. Although we do manipulate transference feelings, it is impossible to gain "control" of what goes on in a family. Furthermore, it is not possible at this stage of our knowledge to *understand* the family. We do not know enough, we are not clever enough, and God knows we are not mature enough, to be subjectively involved in a family and still be objectively perceptive of our own subjective involvement and its relationships to the family process. By implication, then, our task in family psychotherapy is to be available as a team to move as participants in the psychological and social patterns of this family, and thereby to aid the family unit in its autopsychological reparative process. If we are also able to jar the psycho-biological patterns, we can have some assurance that nature will help to make this a constructive intervention.

ACTING OUT

Acting out in the one-to-one interview is carried out by the patient under an implicit doctor-patient agreement. In family psychotherapy that behavior which drains off affect can be by the therapeutic team, by the family group, or by one of the therapists, or by a sub-group within the family, or even by an individual in the family.

Acting out in the family setting has similarities to acting out in group psychotherapy. Since the dynamics in the family are to a large degree expressed interpersonally, all dynamics are in a sense behavioral. The dynamics in one-to-one psychotherapy may be within the person of the patient, and may be with or without behavioral expression in the group therapy setting. The forces at work in the family are experienced within the therapeutic group and are subtly and delicately communicated among the members of this close-knit unit. The family has been developing its covert behavior language for many years. Its exactness is phenomenal.

ACTING OUT BY THE THERAPIST

As mentioned above, we assume that any acting out is by joint agreement with the rest of the therapeutic group. Therefore, acting out by the therapist, whether by the team or one of the individuals, is by joint, usually covert, arrangement with the family. To minimize complications in our chapter, we will assume that the two therapists who make up the team are trained, experienced, mature persons and that their professional relating is stable, solid, and personal. The multiple therapy involvement with individual patients and couples serves as good training before they undertake the therapy of a family unit.

In spite of this, and with no apology, the first and most prominent pattern of acting out will often be a split in the therapeutic team. Therapist Joe will suddenly find himself saying to his co-therapist after the interview, "Bill, you were too rough on that mother today." It is as though their unity had been disrupted so that Joe was intent on making Bill protect this mother the way he wanted to himself. Of course, if the team is more open, such division can be expressed within the interview and thereby become a part of the therapeutic process. The fact that it occurred after the interview is prima facie evidence that Joe was trying to minimize the affective involvement.

Second, the acting out on the part of the therapist may become conspicuous through administrative slips. These may include poor interview timing so that one therapist is tardy, allowing the bill to accumulate so that the family is more dependent, or slips of the tongue by one or the other therapist, indicating an effort to break out of the involvement.

Third, the therapist may try to escape from the therapeutic process by an affective spill consisting of nighttime dreams about the family, fantasies between interview hours, or inappropriate bits of behavior during the interview.

Fourth, the therapists may discover they are involving one or more of the usual distancing procedures. These may include intellectual interpretative "chaff," generalized indifference, aloofness, wandering of attention, preoccupation with "scientific objectivity," or just plain withdrawal.

Fifth, one or another of the therapist team may within the interview regress technically to a more primitive form of "helping." For example, he may use reassurance, inspiration talk, haranguing, or threatening.

Sixth, a prominent pattern is the temptation to attract one of the family members into a one-to-one interaction as a way of avoiding the affective power of the family as a whole.

Seventh, the therapist within the interview may project hostility in a direct manner. For example: Joe says, "Father, you remind me of a sergeant I had overseas." Or he may project sexual feelings. For example: Bill says, "I suddenly became aware today that Susie walks just like my wife does." Finally, the therapist may, of course, retreat into guilt about his inadequacy. The fact of his impotence is a beautiful excuse for using that same impotence as a ploy.

We assume that any acting out by the therapist should best take place within the interview. It is then not only a problem to be worked through by the entire group, but is valuable since the other therapist can use it to diagnose the on-going therapeutic process. Furthermore, since not all behavior is sick, this kind of acting out honesty, if it is brought into the therapeutic relationship, may become not just a way of avoiding affect, but secondarily, a way of expressing rather than decreasing affect.

FAMILY ACTING OUT PATTERNS

With the on-going process of psychotherapy, there develops a gradual unification of the family group, an increased intimacy between its members, and concurrently a new intimacy with the therapeutic team. Their acting out serves to relieve this anxiety, and varies in character with the stage of the psychotherapy itself. In the early phase of therapy it may serve to evade the development of the relationship. In the middle phase it modifies the pressure necessary for change, and in the latter phase it is mainly a functional effort to delay the ending of the relationship itself. We will not try to separate the patterns of acting out as they apply to these various phases, since the scheme is highly synthetic, and certainly the patterns overlap to a great extent. One comment, however, seems indicated. We assume that the rubber fence patterns which Lyman Wynne talks about are probably most characteristic of the middle segment.

A—*Within The Interview:* The pattern of acting out by the family in psychotherapy is almost as variable as the culture of the family, and reflects not only the solidity and style of the family but also its group structuring. The "pseudo-mutuality" of the early interviews may be mistaken for proof of the family's unification. Nothing can be further from the truth. It is an implicit effort on the part of the family to "cooperate the therapist to death." The theme is apt to be, "Doctor, we need help, please do something." This kind of plea is exactly the same kind of ploy that the immature hysterical patient uses in saying, "I don't know what to do, please tell me." The pattern may be accentuated by masses of factual data. This is their contribution, and the resolution is left to the doctor. Next the family may develop a kind of closure against the therapists. They engage in twin talk which has a subtly paranoid character. If the therapists are not secure with each other, they may feel put upon and ostracized, as indeed they are. If they survive this test, or to put it another way, if they are ready to tolerate a greater load of anxiety, the next move may be a denial by the family of its unitary quality. The interview becomes a cocktail party, and the whole group unites in an effort to snow the therapist with a mass of one-to-one relationships. A variant of this acting out pattern is what we have come to call "group prostitution" for the therapist. Each person evacuates the problems of the week, with the anticipation that the therapist will answer all the situational questions and formulate rules for a better week than "the week that was." As the therapy frees more anxiety, the family begins a series of *role battles,* the variety of which is almost infinite. A struggle may evolve over who will be the spokesman or who will confess the family stress areas.

Scapegoating is one very frequent role. For years the entire family has developed life patterns in which one special person carries the symptom of the family illness. This is usually a child, and in the acting out defense, the family returns to this pattern. It may be varied. Annie, the oldest one, may be castigated for being withdrawn; Susie, the middle one, may be accused of being irresponsible; and Bennie, the little boy, may be attacked as "too childish." Once the general scapegoating patterns are explored and the anxiety relating to them integrated, the family may attack or even exclude the father. Margaret Mead has said that fatherhood is a social invention. It does not take much imagination to realize that in this biological unit, the mother and children have a bond which is experienced in a most profound manner, while father is merely a psychological and sociological appendage.

In family therapy this may begin a dance in which the therapists and the father are excluded together. As the working-through process continues, the family may act out the increasing anxiety by a split into subgroups. They may also unify around the protection of the "hurt one." This kind of old maid clucking about one member's limitation serves as a means for the entire family to withdraw from the therapeutic scene.

It is also easy to move from general withdrawal to the establishment of sub-group battles within the family. The children may unite to fight against the older generation, or father and mother may join to criticize the kids. It is equally frequent for the male segment of the family to get together to defend against the female sub-group. Underlying these mechanisms, there is an undercover agreement with the therapist.

The group should be developing enough integration of its anxiety and enough common cause so that acting out patterns are less a deterrent, and the therapy is moving to a more significant depth. Yet part of this effort to form a growthful therapeutic community may be interrupted by a simple jam in communication. The old network of communication within the family is breaking up, and the signals of the non-verbal network may directly counter the verbal formulations. Confusion becomes profound before freedom to be open and honest is attained.

It should be clear that any review of possible dynamic patterns of the interview setting must be incomplete. We cannot close without noting the peculiar see-saw of projections or hide-and-seek that goes on with the therapist. It is an expression of the dependent hostility patterns which emerge as therapy becomes more significant to all the persons involved.

B—*Acting Out Outside the Interviews:* We have artificially separated the acting out within the interview, which is most apparent, from the acting out which takes place surreptitiously between interviews. This second form may be very disruptive. One of the reasons for trying to thus separate these groups is the possibility that the therapists can interdict the outside behavior by direct instructions to the family. The usual problem between interviews is to continue interview talk outside the office. Families come to therapy from a life-time of talking with each other more or less openly. As the therapy increases their capacity to communicate raises the level of their anxiety, and it is natural for them to recapitulate, to argue, to debate, or to begin trying to help each other outside the interview. This process directly decreases the amount of affect brought to the interview, and is, of course, an excellent system for dissipating anxiety in the patient and in the therapist. Since some insights may accrue from this pseudo-therapy, the family may never discover that this is diminishing the amount of affect available in the professional setting.

Another frequent pattern is the escape to a surrogate therapist. The entire family may suddenly decide to go for Sunday dinner with Grandma and discuss the entire process with her; one or two members may go to talk with the pastor, or the family doctor; the kids may gossip to the school counsellor. Father may mull the whole thing over with his golf partner or his secretary and mother with a neighbor or even the maid. This dissemination of affect makes the next interview very relaxed, and, of course, almost useless. They may even bring some cute little insights picked up during the week to bribe the therapist. Then he can't be too personal.

The family may also disseminate anxiety by administrative battles with the therapeutic team. As the level of affect increases, the level of acting out takes on greater seriousness. There may be a gross explosion of affect. For example, Sonny may get into an auto accident which makes therapy impossible on the family budget. Father may lose his job. There may be serious delinquency or a new outbreak of previously latent asthma or stomach ulcer. These explosions may also be closer home and consist of a direct break with the extended family. Then it is the professionals versus the home folks.

HOW TO MEET THE THREAT OF ACTING OUT

Repairing the damage of acting out is like bringing about the correction of a transference-countertransference jam. The best method is prevention. Such prevention necessitates a clear and feeling presentation of the therapist's conviction that family psychotherapy is a struggle for both sides of the group, and that anxiety is present in both the therapists and in the family as a whole. The family must become aware that any acting out within or outside the interview is partly their responsibility. Furthermore, they must accept the fact that the correction of these recurrent pathological detours belongs to both the therapists and the family. Parenthetically, the therapists cannot communicate such a conviction if they do not believe it.

Prevention of intolerable anxiety rests upon the freedom to experience and express anxiety in the therapeutic hour. This expression is probably only possible if one is willing to bring his pathology to the interview. Intimacy necessitates a loss of pride, and most therapists are tempted by the adoration of their patients to build up more and more pride. It is not easy to say to the family, "We are in trouble," and then point out to them that it is partly your own fault. It is somewhat easier if you have already explained to them that any acting out is by implicit agreement. Further, it is difficult to limit the acting out that takes place outside the interview unless you are willing to formulate and present instructions that make the interview an isolate experience. The family's anxiety must be tied to the professional setting.

The break-up of acting out behavior is most easily accomplished when there is a continual imbalance between the therapist's acceptance of the parental role and the recurrent denial of it to the patient group. The therapist must be sure, however, that his affect to the patient has not become the center of his own world. He must always hold himself as his center. The break-up of acting out behavior usually necessitates that the therapist lead in experimenting with the patient role. His humility may make him discover his own pathology and stimulate the patients to move toward similar insights. It is important that the therapist "confess" dishonesties which he uncovers. It is also helpful to present apparently irrelevant associations or fantasies which take place within the interview, or even fantasies which take place outside the interview.

It may not seem appropriate to bring a consultant into a situation this complex, but it is sometimes amazing what he can contribute. He may discover a split between the two therapists, so that one of them has become dependent and the other isolated. He may see some dynamic pattern in the family that is not apparent to the people who are by now so immersed that they cannot see the forest for the trees. Lastly, it seems to us increasingly clear that part of the freedom to grow will emerge in the patient when the therapeutic team is willing to "give up," that is, go beyond their delusion of grandeur. We are so tempted to assume that we can "do" therapy that whenever acting out takes place that we should suspect that this delusion is one of the dynamic features behind it.

CONCLUSION

Family psychotherapy seems to be almost the ultimate challenge for the therapist as well as his great opportunity to learn about people and to grow as a person. If being is becoming, then doing is a prize system to avoid being.

The awesome stress of this work creates a severe tendency to spill affect by acting it out. This avoidance of beingness by doing must be countered in order that constructive anxiety can bring about the necessary change in the family and its members as well as in the therapists.

We have tried to describe patterns of acting out in the process of family psychotherapy. We make apology for the fact that this formulation is incomplete since the subject matter is complex. Any discussion of acting out in family psychotherapy resembles a discussion of the dynamics of the therapeutic process. The dynamics of family psychotherapy are also incomplete.

20. Treatment and Management of Acting Out in the Suicidal Patient

By HARRY JOSEPH, M.D.

> *Dr. Harry Joseph addresses himself in the material that follows to the question of how to treat and manage the acting out patient with suicidal intentions. He identifies the prerequisites for what he characterizes as the "suicidal syndrome," and finds that in each instance there is an ambivalent relation to the love object who is valued in an infantile and conflicted way.*
>
> *Through a series of cases, Harry Joseph provides the reader with the basis for a practical discussion of the indications and contra-indications with various clinical types for retaining them in office practice or confining them to hospital care.*

"DEATH BY SUICIDE" evokes an emotional reaction in each individual. Responses vary from envy to abhorrence and from respect to shame and disgust. In some cultures, the "suicide" is a hero; in others, he is disgraced, degraded, and refused a burial. The ubiquitous nature of the problem must be related to the fact that in some way every individual relates and empathizes to a "suicide." Thoughts of one's death arise from childhood through old age. They take varying forms from "If I'm dead" to "How would I commit suicide if I tried it." It seems safe to say that such thoughts or fantasies, signifying wishes, have existed in every individual at some time.

The "suicidal patient" therefore presents an unusually complicated therapeutic problem. A number of significant questions arise. How common is suicide? Which diagnostic types are more prone to end their lives? How can one know when a threat must be taken seriously? When should you hospitalize a patient? When should treatment be ambulatory? What should the treatment orientation be? We shall limit our discussion to the management of the ambulatory patient.

REVIEW OF LITERATURE AND THEORETICAL FORMULATIONS

The literature on the subject is voluminous. The religious aspect is summarized by Zilboorg.[25,27] Durkheim's[8] sociological study represents a classic in the field. Stengel and Cook[21] review suicides in England and Wales in an attempt to draw conclusions for prevention. They believe that a broken home and social isolation are prone to become strong etiological factors. Farberow and Shneidman[19,20] review clinical problems in their compendium, *Clues to Suicide*. They recommend "increasing frequency of meeting, greater activity with more discussion, telephone calls at any time of day or night, patient must be given a feeling of sincere concern and interest by the therapist in his welfare." The therapist must be able to show his willingness "to undergo the emotional strain during the period of suicidal crisis." Recommendations for prevention are made. "The basic problem is the diagnosis of depression. About half of all suicidal attempts are carried out by individuals with psychoneurotic depression."

Zilboorg's works on the subject are important in any review. In his series of articles he weighs such questions as the differences in suicide in primitive as contrasted to civilized cultures; wealthy as contrasted to poor; varying religious groups. He discusses the theoretical considerations involved and the related problems. Significantly, he describes suicide in all diagnostic categories.[25] His conclusions would indicate that suicide is a universal phenomenon endogenous not only to homo sapiens but also to other members of the animal kingdom. If we may extrapolate, Zilboorg would say that life consists of adaptation and that adaptation includes a drive to suicide. He further believes that the most dangerous type of suicide involvement met with clinically is the one who gives unconscious identification with a dead person.

Bromberg and Schilder's papers[6,7] in 1933 and 1936 review comprehensively both conscious and unconscious factors in suicidal attempts. Similar studies were done by Jamieson,[13] Lewis,[14,15] O'Neal[18] and Bennett.[4] Bromberg and Schilder used questionnaires, interviews, and therapeutic sessions. They concluded that death and suicide have several meanings —escape from an unbearable situation, need to force further affection, final union in intercourse, final narcissistic perfection granting importance to the individual, masochistic gratification and a way of expressing a composite of all instinctual drives. Findings in both neurotic patients and in "normal" individuals were similar.

Psychoanalytic research and application concerns itself with anthropological, sociological, and statistical problems as related to emotions and behavior, both in humans and animals. However, psychoanalysis is more concerned clinically with specific genetic determinants of any pathology. Abraham's[1] original studies represent an important contribution to the subject. However, Freud's paper on *Mourning and Melancholia* presented the first approach by which the significance of mourning, depression, and suicide may be understood.[10] In grief there is an actual loss of a loved object. The love for that person—the object—freed as psychic energy cannot be displaced immediately upon another object. Temporarily, the tension associated with the inability to transfer this love results in a withdrawal of any interest. There is a gradual weaning with the distribution of energy into other areas and disappearance of mourning. It is to be noted that the loss of the object is always real. In pathologic mourning or depression the picture is different. There is no actual loss of a loved person. In pathologic depression the individual acts as if there were a lost object—"he doesn't love me anymore," "nobody loves me." The ego renounces the outside world from any object within the outside world. The individual makes his own ego the object. He becomes self-centered, withdrawn, self-pitying. The anger which he is incapable of repressing turns against himself. One thinks of the elderly parent who lives with his children and who develops hypochondriachal symptoms. Angered by his dependence, incapable of expressing his anger, he spends his days suffering in order to control and disturb the children with whom he lives.

In the depressions, a harsh, severe, punitive and sadistic superego cannot express its anger at an outside object. The aggression is then internalized and expressed by turning the sadism onto oneself, or more precisely, on the introjected object within oneself. Fenichel's[9] paraphrasing thesis "nobody kills himself who had not intended to kill somebody else" has been repeatedly shown. Menninger has studied suicidal drives and their emotional determinants.[16,17]

Our thesis rests on the statement "nobody kills himself who had not intended to kill somebody else," and the primary problem then concerns the vicissitudes of aggression and hostility. Nevertheless, specific fantasies are elicited in the analysis of specific patients which show other precipitating phenomena. Warburg[23] in a most interesting paper shows how suicide, pregnancy, and rebirth fantasies can be precipitants in a neurotic patient. Here it is not the struggle between the superego and the ego which is important. Hendrick,[12] Lewis,[14] and Zilboorg[24] cite other cases. Friedlander[11] describes a case of "longing to die," where the primary desire is one for protection by mother. Thorner[22] describes two interesting cases in which the modes of suicide were genetically determined by fantasies arising in childhood.

The review of the literature on suicide therefore presents many problems of concern. The literature and associated recommendations for prevention—representing many facets, ethnic problems, religious differences, cultural and sociological differences—may be valid but are not helpful in coping with the individual of concern. Statistics are meaningless since it is our opinion that a great number of suicides are never recorded as such. It is even questionable whether "Organizations for Prevention of Suicide" perform any truly valid function.

TREATMENT AND ACTING OUT IN THE MANAGEMENT OF THE SUICIDAL PATIENT

Our previous theoretical discussion raises the questions—who precisely should be prone to suicidal attempt, who is clinically suspect? We would say that the first step rests in the increase of "narcissistic needs," manifested by the complaint of the patient "nobody loves me-wants me, nobody needs me, I am useless." Clinically there has been a definite change in "involutional depressions" during the past 25 years. Twenty-five years ago, "Involutional Depressions" were associated primarily with the "Agitated Depressions" of the female menopause. Drugs developed were usually oriented towards women. Today when one reads an ad starting with "when the change comes," it is directed more towards men. What precisely has created the change? A generation ago, women's position in the home was generally devoid of modern conveniences, of freezers, frozen and instant foods. Women spent their days without leisure time. In the fifth decades the children left, for marriage or in search of careers. Suddenly the "need to be needed" appeared. There were no outlets since none had ever been available. The fact that this occurred during the menopausal period was a matter of coincidence.

We find today, as a result of increased leisure time among women, a search for social and intellectual outlets. There has been a marked diminution in the female menopausal depressions and an increase in the "Male Involutional Depressions." Why has the change occurred? Increasing security, pension plans, and retirement are all socially necessary. However a paradox arises. More and more individuals seek security in their jobs and professions, looking forward to retirement. However, shortly after the age of fifty, the presence of a young man in the office is a constant reminder of the fact that shortly one will be retired, being not needed and useless. Few indeed are those individuals who have any interests other than their work. The emotional response is simple. "Soon I shall be retired. They don't need me. He can do the work as well as I. I am not needed, wanted." Male "menopausal depressions" are found frequently. There is, by definition, no menopause in males. The syndrome results from a narcissistic withdrawal in search of the "need to be wanted and/or loved." We see similar symptoms in the loss of a friend, failure to achieve in school, failure to have a satisfactory marriage, illness, financial reverses, and other emotionally adverse experiences.

The second prerequisite for the "suicidal syndrome" is an ambivalent relation to the "loved object." In each instance the person is loved in an infantile and ambivalent way. The mother loves her children but is constantly angered because they do not satisfy her emotional needs. The young man loves his fiancee, but is constantly preoccupied and angry with her inability to satisfy his emotional needs. The "Involutional Executive" is delighted with the growth of his trainee, the junior who will displace him, but critical and angered at minimal provocation, for he knows that he is being replaced.

Finally, the anger, the hostility, the aggression is displaced onto oneself. The ambivalence is resolved in the formula "The love, I love him—the hate, I hate myself. It is I who am worthless." The sadism of the conscience is insatiable, the more the ambivalence toward the objects.

It is precisely the externalization of the "sadistic impulses," the anger and hostility, which is the focus in the prevention of suicide.

Case 1

A 47 year old woman, the wife of a patient called at approximately 2:00 A.M. awakening the doctor with whom her husband was in treatment. She herself was also in treatment. Although she professed a love for her husband, her complaints were constant. She felt deprived in this "man's world." She was "unfulfilled." She had pride in her husband's accomplishments, but derogated him publicly. She was ever critical and suspicious, constantly dissatisfied. On the 'phone she stated, "I'm going to commit suicide." Assuming that the threat was a serious one since there were prior suicidal attempts, the doctor was concerned as to what should be done. One might say, "Don't do it. I shall be down immediately." This appears artificial and imposes an obligation on the patient to show that she actually meant her threat by a suicidal attempt, which even though abortive may have serious consequences. One might say, "Wait a moment" as one goes to another 'phone to call the police. One may argue with her. But each of these responses seems inadequate. Reminded of the need for the "externalization of aggression," the doctor said, "I'm sorry you arrived at the decision." The next morning she was present at the door, furiously denouncing her husband's therapist for "lack of heart."

It is difficult to evaluate the correct response in any given similar situation. Any scientific method consists not only of objectively gathered recommendations but also the art in its application. We believed that the response on the phone was sufficient to arouse the patient's anger and pride sufficiently to prevent the suicidal attempt.

Case 2

A 35 year old male was seen in psychoanalysis for chronic anxiety and tension states associated with periods of depression. He had been hospitalized on three previous occasions for periods of three to six months when he threatened suicide. He had received psychotherapy and two courses of shock treatment.

His life history was associated with constant concern over all bodily functions requiring discharge of tension. He was encopretic until the age of eight and recalls running home from school with "loaded trousers," interspersed were long periods of constipation. His early years in school were spent in constant preoccupation with his "bowels." He suffered from nocturnal enuresis until the age of ten. His "compulsive masturbation" began at about the age of eight and has continued. The home was described as a constant tension-ridden battleground between mother and father, with mother usually the winner. Although he dreaded "tension," he became a comedian in a burlesque show and later in theatre and night clubs because he loved the "excitement." At the age of 21 he married a quiet home-loving woman five years his senior who catered to his every need. She worked to support the family. He continued to have affairs with women throughout his marriage. Each relationship was intense and the "greatest," but always terminated precipitously in a quarrel. In these affairs he would have his partners dress or act as "call girls." He stated "after a while I would realize that I loved my wife and would return to her. After a few months I couldn't stand her." In the course of the transference it was noted that he expected the analyst to take care of his needs just as his wife did and just as mother had not. At a critical point, rejected by his "girl friend," incapable of finding a job, he demanded an answer to a question. When this was not forthcoming, he arose and stated, "Doc, I've threatened before—this time I'll do it—you better send me to a hospital." The response was "I'm sorry the hour is up. I'll see you tomorrow." He walked out stating furiously, "this time it's the end." In view of the previous hospitalizations, we needn't state that despite any questions of countertransference, there was concern. The next day the patient came for his hour, furiously complaining of the lack of interest. "You don't care what happens to me or what I do." The episode and its further comprehension were the turning point in the patient's analysis.

The problem of hospitalization will be discussed later. It is, however, important to note that here also the externalization of aggression, rather than support or tender understanding, served as the therapeutic measure.

Case 3

A 55 year old scientist was found in the kitchen with all gas jets turned on. An ambulance was called, and he was taken to a hospital. Recently he had been concerned about his potency, and had begun to have an affair with his wife's friend. When his wife discovered the matter, she insisted on a showdown as did his mistress. Actually the patient knew that the gas from the stove was natural gas and not carbon monoxide, but he also knew that everyone would be upset by his behavior. As a result of the episode, his wife promised to allow him to do whatever he wished;

his mistress promised never to abandon him. He enjoyed torturing both with repeated suicidal threats.

Case 4

Here we include a number of individuals who, prior to an actual suicide, visit old friends, throw parties, act in a most tender manner to the husband or wife immediately prior to the suicide. A 40 year old attorney called a classmate whom he hadn't seen for many years, asking to have dinner with him. They met and had a most pleasant time discussing the past. That night he committed suicide. At the funeral it was learned that in the past two weeks he had had similar appointments with ten other classmates.

Case 5

Upon the death of her husband, a 40 year old widow, Mrs. K., and the mother of two children, refused to leave her bedroom and refused to eat. The anorexia was so severe that she lost approximately 40 pounds in a month, neglected her home and children completely. Briefly, the history was one of overindulgence from infancy. She was extremely narcissistic, spending most of her time in the beauty parlor or shopping for dresses. A brother two years her junior was considered the "smart one." All decisions were made by him. Her husband assumed a position of an "appendage." The details of his death were learned from other members of the family. Mr. K. had had serious heart disease for about two years. On the night preceding his death, Mrs. K. remarked to members of her family that her husband appeared seriously ill and that she was afraid "the end was coming." The next day Mrs. K. watched her daughter taunt and tease him. She said nothing. He began to run after the daughter and died precipitously. The family had spent the next few months caring for Mrs. K. tenderly, constantly expressing concern. Mrs. K. insisted that she wanted to die.

She was told on consultation that her behavior was merely selfish, showing no love for either her husband or children, and that hospitalization was recommended. She became furious, left her bed, and immediately insisted on running her husband's business. She refused any further treatment. She was again seen five years thereafter socially, by coincidence, and stated, "I still mourn for my husband and will never love a man again. I never told you, but a week prior to his death he banged his head against a door. That's why he lied. I'm running the business. It has given me a chance to prove myself." The narcissism, the ambivalence, the turning of the aggression on herself during the period of mourning are clearly manifested. The denial of the events of the death are an expression of the infantilism of Mrs. K. Parenthetically, Mr. K.'s death and his daughter's involvement were a family secret never mentioned again.

At the suggestion of the brother, the daughter was sent to a private school because she found it impossible to remain with her mother whom she professed to hate. The daughter made three subsequent suicidal attempts. She stated that at each time she believed that her father was calling her to come to him and abandon the mother. The libidinous gratification in reunion with her dead father, whom she took from her mother, is to be noted. The suicidal attempts were withheld from the mother because it might upset her and she might not function in the business.

Prolonged mourning is associated with ambivalence, guilt, and hostility toward the death of the individual mourned. "Why did this happen to me" is its simplest manifestation. It becomes pathologic when it persists beyond the weaning period of any normal "mourning."

DISCUSSION

1. *Hospitalization:* Suicidal trends are common in any clinical practice, and one is readily tempted to hospitalize such patients. We believe patients are hospitalized too frequently and that the chances of a suicidal attempt after discharge are increased. Few hospitals offer adequate psychotherapeutic measures. Except for schizophrenics and unmanageable psychotic depressives, we rarely hospitalize a suicidal patient. It is uncommon for a patient under adequate therapeutic measures to commit suicide. The hope for "cure" rests in resolving the problem and not in isolation from the community.

2. *Prediction-Prognosis:* It is difficult, if not impossible, to predict which person will commit suicide and which one will not. It is true that a narcissistic, ambivalent, demanding individual who has made several suicidal attempts would be more prone to repeat his attempt. But such attempts occur in all diagnostic groups. Every suicidal threat must be taken seriously. It is in fact impossible to quantify such threats for prediction purposes.

3. *Psychotic Depression:* When the individual is so depressed that he sits motionless, incapable of taking care of himself, there is little danger of suicide. There seems inadequate energy for such an attempt. When, however, the depression is "lifted" and the patient begins to feel his "old self," the danger of suicide rises.

4. *Schizophrenia:* Suicidal attempts in the schizophrenic are common and often assume most violent and bizarre forms. When a depression is present, the dynamics are similar to those previously described. In addition, we find two other factors which precipitate suicidal attempts:

(a) The loss of contact with reality is disturbing, but especially so in a patient with previous remissions. A 40 year old accountant attempted suicide. He had had several previous schizophrenic episodes for which he had been hospitalized. He stated, "I just don't want another episode. I know when it's coming. It's as if the dams in my mind break. The thoughts just keep coming. I lose my hold on the world."

(b) Suicidal attempts may be made in response to hallucinatory commands. A 25 year old woman jumped in front of a train but fell into a pit between the tracks. She later stated, "God talks to me. He tells me that if I die, the world will be saved."

Disturbed schizophrenic patients with suicidal trends should be hospitalized.

5. *Psychopaths:* It is rare for a psychopath to seek help unless it is required as a result of an antisocial act. Psychopaths cannot tolerate frustration and incarceration. Unless watched, they will make attempts at violent suicide.

6. *The Aged:* Suicide in the aged occurs in response to emotional demands previously discussed. With increasing life span there will be an increasing number of "Aged" or "Senior Citizens." This perhaps is one of our most important social problems. The majority of this group has little interest in any activities after retirement. They remain narcissistically parasitic on their children. Institutionalization, change of environment, unfamiliar surroundings destroy any interest in life. Although not diagnosed clinically as a suicide, the change to a chronic institution prognosticates a life expectancy between three and six months. There is an increasing recognition of this problem with the establishment of Senior Citizens' Centers in which they may continue to live a useful, active, and social life. Brill[5] refers to "psychic suicide" which he associates with the loss of desire to live.

7. *Pregnancy:* Suicidal attempts in pregnancy are not uncommon. The question of therapeutic abortion arises. It has been our experience that this most serious problem is too frequently denied. We have also seen a masochistic desire for a criminal abortion in such women as an expiation of guilt. One is guided by the emotional trends of the woman and her previous history.

CONCLUSION

Suicide is a universal problem and has existed in every period of human history. In our culture it occurs most frequently in an individual with increasing narcissistic needs, with an ambivalent relation to a love object, and with increasing guilt resulting from unexpressed hostility. Adequate therapeutic management of various problem situations is the best prevention of an unnecessary termination of a life.

REFERENCES

1. Abraham, K. A. *Selected papers on psychoanalysis.* London: Hogarth Press, 1948.
1a. ———. Notes on the Psycho-Analytic Investigation and Treatment of Manic-Depressive Insanity and Allied Conditions 1911, 137-157.
1b. ———. A Short Study of the Libido Viewed in the Light of Mental Disorders, 1924, 418-503.
2. Batchelor, I. R. C. Management and prognosis. *Geriatrics,* 1955, *10,* 291-293.
3. ———, and Napier, M. B. Attempted suicide in old age. *Brit Med. J.,* 1953, *2,* 1186-1190.
4. Bennett, A. E. Prevention of suicide. *Cal. Med. J.,* 1954, *81,* 396-401.
5. Brill, A. A. Concept of psychic suicide. *Int. J. Psychanal.* 1939, *20,* 246-251.
6. Bromberg, W., and Schilder, P. Death and dying. *Psychanal. Rev.,* 1933, *20,* 133-185.
7. ———. Attitudes of psychoneurotics towards death. *Psychanal. Rev.* 1936, *23,* 1-25.
8. Durkheim, E. *Suicide.* Evanston: Illinois University Press, 1951.
9. Fenichel, O. *Psychoanalytic theory of neurosis.* New York: W. W. Norton, Inc., 1945, 400.
10. Freud, S. Mourning and Melancholia. In *Collected Papers.* London: Hogarth Press Ltd., *4,* 152-173.
11. Friedlander, M. K. On the longing to die. *Int. J. Psychanal,* 1940, *21,* 416-425.
12. Hendrick, I. Suicide as a wish fulfillment. *Psychiat. Q.,* 1940, *14,* 30-43.
13. Jamieson, G. R. Suicide and mental disease: a clinical analysis of one hundred cases. *Arch. Neuro. and Psych.,* 1936, *36,* 1-11.
14. Lewis, N. D. C. Studies on suicide. *Psychanal. Rev.,* 1933, *20,* 241-273
15. ———. Studies on suicide. *Psychanal. Rev.,* 1934, *21,* 146-153
16. Menninger, K. A. Psychoanalytic aspects of suicide. *Int. J. Psychanal.,* 1933, *14,* 376-390.
17. ———. *Man against himself.* New York: Harcourt Brace and Co., 1938.
18. O'Neal, P. E., Robins, E., and Schmidt, H. A psychiatric study of attempted suicide in persons over sixty years of age. *Arch. Neuro. and Psychiat.,* 1956, 275-284.
19. Shneidman, E. S., and Farberow, N. L. *Clues to suicide.* New York: McGraw Hill, 1957, 119-131, 187-194.
20. ———. Clues to suicide. *U. S. Pub. Hlth. Rep.,* 1956, *71,* 109-114.
21. Stengel, E., and Cook, N. G. *Attempted suicide: its social significance and effects.* Maudsley Monographs, Chapman & Hall Ltd., London, 1958.
22. Thorner, H. A. Suicide as a management of fantasy. *Int. J. Psychanal.,* 1939, *20,* 246-251.
23. Warburg, B. Suicide, pregnancy and rebirth. *Psychan. Q.,* 1938, *7,* 490-506.
24. Zilboorg, G. Differential types of suicide. *Arch. Neuro. and Psychiat.,* 1936, *35,* 270-291.
25. ———. Suicide among civilized and primitive races. *Am. J. Psychiat.,* 1936, *92,* 1347-1369.
26. ———. Considerations on suicide with particular reference to that of the young. *Amer. J. Ortho.,* 1937, *7,* 15-31.
27. ———. Fear of death. *Psychanal Q.,* 1943. *12,* 465-475.

21. Management of Acting Out Adolescents

By ERNST PAPANEK, ED.D.

Dr. Ernst Papanek, who writes from long experience as the former director of the Wiltwyck School for Boys and from his present position as a Professor of Education in the City University of New York, gives us an insight into the practical and difficult problems of handling the acting out adolescent. In a deeper sense, Papanek seeks to set forth a philosophy for understanding the problems of adjustment of young people in the United States at the present time. In doing so, he provides the reader with an insight into the many conflicting points of view about growth and development in adolescence and the problems that young people have in making the difficult transition between childhood and adulthood in which there is an everpresent danger of an acting out solution.

Professor Papanek offers us a chance to observe how many of his ideas found fruition in an institutional setting in which problems of acting out among adolescent boys were extremely common.

THERE IS FAR MORE fantasy and fancy than fact in what we grown-ups think we see going on in and with our adolescents. We interpret their actions inadequately, we look at them with prejudiced eyes; what is worse, we put our own out-of-date labels on the men and women of the future. We judge adolescent acting out from our adult point of view and reminisce about our own bygone adolescence—and our reminiscences are likely to contain fewer facts than biases and defenses. We expect today's adolescents to conform to our conception of what adolescents should be, without realizing that we—now adults—make them the objects of our outdated thinking, while they—still adolescents—make themselves the subjects of their own visionary thinking. Often we do not even try to find out what makes them act out, what they are acting out, why, or against whom they are acting out.

We are still under the notion that childhood, youth, and adolescence are merely preparations for adulthood. But if we want our young people to live in—that is, inside—our society, we must accept them as equal partners in that society; in return, we must demand that they accept us as equal partners. All this is not so complicated as it sounds; it is the self-evident foundation of every democratic group composed of members who each form a part of the group, each one influencing the group, each one influenced by it.

We have difficulties with the adolescent who *acts out* because we do not let him *act* on his own responsibility, because we believe, as he does, that he is acting out against us and our society—whereas, in truth, both we and he should realize that he is acting out against the society we share and against the concept of co-existence of adult and adolescent.

All behavior is purposeful, motivated by a goal. No one will strive toward a goal without some promise of success. There is much confusion in the adolescent's mind when he is searching for a new road. He is overwhelmed by new physical and emotional discoveries, and he is influenced by these discoveries to new activities. As a child he was quite often merely a reflector, reacting without much thought. He started thinking as soon as he was born, of course, but he had not enough symbols, he misunderstood them, or was confused by them. His responses were egotistic and appropriate only in rather limited relationships. Later on, stimuli became motivations that were challenging and complicated. Rather complex social responses were demanded, and if he did not learn by imitating acceptable examples or by trial and error, the "sources of acts," the "results of acts," and his "capacity to learn"[7] got all mixed up and henceforth only served to create more confusion, insecurity, and insufficiency of satisfaction or lack of satisfaction.

Desperate not to lose prestige, he will be driven by anxiety and fear to try to avoid anything new. Once he has started on the course he believes is the best one, relatively speaking, he will stick to it even after he has recognized it is not the best. An acting out adolescent who is met head-on by a stronger, more violent counter-action will only try to act out more forcibly; his accustomed pattern is at stake, and the way of life he believes is the only one he can travel. Even if our counteraction is so strong that the youngster has to give in, our success will be limited to situations in which we can continue to exercise constantly increasing terror. The cowardly young person may give in, but even with him we shall have achieved nothing more than a temporary victory. And what is worse, the adolescent who is seeking for ideals will grow more and more afraid of them.

Youth has an emotional need for self-assertion. These are years of transition from irresponsibility to responsibility—responsibility for living with others, working, creating a family, participating in community life. Yet, despite these burdens which are heaped upon our young people, their status within the community is at best ill-defined. They cannot learn from any constructive example set by their environment, because it has none to offer. All that is available to them are social institutions which were outdated a generation ago. If they want the respect of others, self-respect, friendship, acceptance, a place for themselves, a feeling of belonging and social status, they often feel they have to join what we call gangs to find it; our society does not provide enough of it elsewhere. If they are looking for an ideal, a conviction worth working for, living and dying for, they are not likely to find too much of it in our present society. The all-embracing, all-supporting, all-understanding ethical and religious ideas are badly underdeveloped

Adolescence and youth is the most marvelous and the most frightening period of life. Between puberty and maturity, youth is the time when the conflict between the dependency of childhood and the responsible and self-reliant maturity of adulthood give rise to insecurity and doubts for individual, internal reasons. It is the time when emotionally determined behavior patterns must be checked by intellectually controlled concepts; when idealistic aspirations, justice, and sincerity, are confronted with realistic obstacles. It is the time when independent creativity must be integrated into cooperative social action; when filial love, the childhood 'buddy' and childhood 'play' are replaced by enduring relationships, by friendship, love, interest in work, community affairs, national, and international problems. It is the time when interest in, and devotion to, the old family of childhood as well as to the new family of parenthood are struggling for dominance.

The acting out adolescent is most generally defined as one who differs from normal children mainly in socially violent and destructive emotional actions and reactions. Concepts of management—such as they are—are still too often conventional. Even where new concepts are adopted, they rely heavily upon basic philosophical ideas and practical considerations other than those of treatment: for instance, the need to protect society against offenders, the hope of deterring other potential delinquents, etc. These other considerations—important as they are for other reasons—may actually conflict with the interests of successful treatment, and precisely for this reason they are in many cases unsuccessful, both in their efforts to protect society or to deter other potential delinquents.

Our concepts are also influenced in many cases by our not so noble desire for revenge or retaliation, by our traditional impulse to inflict punishment, by the sense of helplessness and guilt created by our own bias and egotism. Sometimes—too often, I fear—it is not acting out or juvenile delinquency we are fighting; often we simply hate the young people who dare to do what we ourselves did not dare to do at their age.

More is involved than analyzing the young person's social background, the environmental, biologic, and emotional factors and their historical interpretation, the hopes and fears of the court or therapist if we really would like to manage the acting out adolescent successfully. There is, for example, the degree of the adolescent's dependence upon past experiences and frustrations, which may have helped to shape what we call his character or personality; actually it is no more than a defense mechanism. In the interplay between his wishes, potentialities, and insights, this so-called character is formed, and once formed, it resists change. To take an Adlerian approach, we might even say that the individual tries to escape into a "character" that is not based upon his real and social interest, but serves as an excuse that this *is* his character (he believes) and he cannot do anything about it. Acting out, delinquency, and crime, on which he now believes he depends, are desperate and inadequate solutions of a bewildered and frightened youth. Adler called crime the heroism of the coward. Confidence, security, and courage, and not anxiety and fear or the reckless heroism of the coward, are constructive factors which enable us to manage the acting out adolescent.

Children and youth of today, themselves endangered physically and spiritually, by a frightened and bewildered society, in turn, frighten, bewilder, and endanger that society. From the more and more or less normal rock 'n' roll youngster, the rebellious or withdrawn or aggressive child, a direct line of ever-increasingly severe emotional disturbance leads to the acting outer, the delinquent, the neurotic, and the psychopath. Juvenile delinquents or acting outers are not just emotional or psychiatric deviates; they are also social deviates or are both emotionally and socially handicapped or retarded.

Their social reeducation is, therefore, important not only for the protection of the community in which they live—an importance we cannot underestimate and which we will have to impress also on the acting outer and on the juvenile delinquents in their treatment—but it is also an important part of the new treatment and reeducation. Without a new social orientation no real rehabilitation of any offender can be complete, and without helping the emotional deviate to find his place in society, we cannot help those either. But do we have satisfactory tools for it, anything to build on emotionally?

THE USE OF PUNISHMENT AND REWARDS

For centuries men have been searching for incentives to motivate human beings to adopt socially acceptable, constructive behavior; for centuries they have imagined that reward and punishment are the best tools for the job. As such, reward and punishment both have proved to be unreliable and unsatisfactory. If we regard justice as simply revenge for wrongdoing, then reward and punishment may still be an efficient stimulus to portend better conduct and a corrective of faults and mistakes. With our present knowledge of psychology, however, in our present democratic society, reward and punishment are pretty well outdated; they should certainly play a far less important role than heretofore, and, if possible, they should be dropped entirely.

Deterrence, another reason given for the use of punishment, appeals only to selfish fear, not to insight or morality. It may sometimes succeed with cowards, but actually it fosters cowardice.

In his natural struggle to overcome external difficulties through his own personal endowments, the child or grown-up threatened with deterrent punishment will be inclined to overcompensate for his inferiority feeling toward the punisher and to try to outwit him, to be smarter than the victim he has just seen punished, to do everything not to get caught.

Even the desire to avoid punishment will not serve as sufficient deterrent. It will work only where patterns of social response have been well established by emotional and intellectual factors and not as a conditioned reflex.

Some people believe that Pavlov's dog experiments with conditioned reflexes and other similar animal experiments, important as they are, prove that at least temporary success can be achieved with deterrent punishment, and that repeated periodic application can bring lasting results.

We maintain that to reward a dog with food for secreting saliva at the sound of a bell, or to punish him for not obeying his master, is quite all right for a dog. Obedience is all we expect of him; from a human being we expect more, and we cannot get it by taming him through fear. Education and, where necessary, reeducation, must enable human beings to respond with more than reflexes, reactions, and repressions of instinct and drives. Education or reeducation must help the unsocialized youth or adult to become an understanding, cooperative, yet independent and happy member of human society, for if he is not part of that society, he is not a human being.

Freud, in *Civilization and Its Discontents,* states that "the need for punishment is an instinctual manifestation on the part of the ego, which has become masochistic under the influence of the sadistic superego, i.e., which has brought a part of the instinct of destruction at work within itself into the service of an erotic attachment to the superego."

We do not believe this over-all generalization is correct; we would rather limit ourselves to Adler's more specific observation that "Many criminals are not very fond of their lives; some of them at certain moments are very near suicide."[1] But, if there were such a thing as an instinctual need for punishment, we would have to discard completely deterrent punishment; such punishment would satisfy a need of the individual—it would not deter him, nor could it be superego-forming either, as Freud assumed.

Nor can we accept Freud's statement in the same book that "the price of progress in civilization is paid for by forfeiting happiness through the heightening of the sense of guilt." Rather do we believe no progress of civilization is real if it does not contribute to the happiness of the individual, and that no individual can achieve real happiness without contributing to the progress of civilization.

Mankind is not trapped, as Freud pessimistically tells us, between aggressions prompted by instincts and their repressions or sublimations. If we were actually in this dilemma, of course, our only means of forwarding civilization would be the multiplication and strengthening of repressions by a "heightening of the sense of guilt," "social anxiety," and the "need for punishment."

But neither the "need for punishment" nor a "heightening of the sense of guilt" nor "social anxiety" is a constructive factor in education or in therapy. Each may sometimes be helpful in preventing further wrongdoing when other, more ethical, more constructive and more beneficial emotional and intellectual reactions to wrongdoing, and other, more ethical and fruitful motivations for rightdoing cannot be immediately attained. But such negative motivations always lead to unhealthy responses, and we often have a hard job undoing and mitigating the mischief they have done—before we can start our proper treatment. And guilt feelings and social anxiety do not always repress or sublimate aggressiveness; they sometimes arouse it. Repression can never help build, develop, or promote civilization; it can at best sometimes help achieve a sterile conformity which we can consider only as an unhealthy adjustment to society.

If punishment is an expression of the pessimism and lack of self-confidence of the punisher in its own educational and therapeutic abilities, rewards—in the form of tokens of distinction, concessions, premiums, gifts and favors—are hardly less so. This sort of compensation for creditable performance deprives the performer of his natural joy in accomplishment. This appeal to other, unrelated, not highly moral instincts through illogical bribing does not offer constructive stimulation or improve motivation.

Encouragement by approval and assent to the efforts made, acclaim, and praise are not only highly appreciated, but they are often necessary to help disheartened and tired youth. It gives them confidence in themselves, stimulates them to make greater demands on themselves and to rise to a higher level of self-judgment.

Of course, praise must be earned or it loses its value. If it conflicts with the adolescent's self-evaluation, it only belittles his work or makes him accessible to bribes not related to his efforts and achievements.

There is a lot of satisfaction for every human being in the feeling of accomplishment in overcoming difficulties in the fact of successfully finishing a job. If we teach our youth how to overcome difficulties, these difficulties can even exercise a stimulating and strengthening effect.

A child, an adult, and especially an adolescent confronted by situations which they have not learned to expect and to master feel lost, insecure, upset, aggressive. To meet these situations, to escape difficulties they create many symptoms. They may become delinquent, acting out, they may become neurotic and withdrawn. Frustration imposes and increases this pattern.

We certainly do agree that our society, our social and economic system should take a cure, for as Erich Fromm[3] puts it in his *Sane Society:* ". . . mental health cannot be defined in terms of the 'adjustment' of the individual to his society, but, on the contrary . . . it must be defined in terms of adjustment of society to the needs of man, of its role in furthering or hindering the development of mental health."

There is another particularly important phenomenon; if we neglect it, we shall not have too much chance of success in our treatment. Neither acting out nor juvenile delinquency is merely a medical, emotional, or social disease contracted by one or another youngster; it is a phenomenon in which individuals, families, communities, nations, the entire world are actively involved. All are responsible for the disease, and all are its victims. The problem is not only: What is the acting out adolescent doing to us, and what are we doing to him? The problem is rather: What are we doing to ourselves, to our society by our handling of him? Our educational, treatment, and correction concepts have to take into account all the active and passive manifestations of the individuals involved *and* those of his environment and society. We must study the character-forming values—*our* social values as we see them; we must ask ourselves what are the attractive models our young people are asked to identify with, what is the right community spirit—should it be a spirit of helpfulness and cooperation? Can a society which bases its values on insecurity and murderous competition request and expect that its most active members, its adolescents, be successfully treated for their acting out, which we so often provoke?

It is not the acting out adolescent—not even all adolescents at a given period of life—we are concerned with. It is the eternal regimenting process of growing up, it is the co-existence of generations, it is progress of mankind at the most promising time of life.

Once we have defined without hypocrisy the value system we believe in and desire to set for all, we have to find out how to best communicate it to our young people.

"In preindustrial society, with its stable or static social structure, conditions of work, public opinion and political affairs conformed to the pattern of the family. In modern industrial society, whose chief characteristics are industrialization and mechanized production, bureaucratization and urbanization have created large-scale political, economic, and social organizations controlled by modern methods of mass communication and often impersonal management. The contradictions between the economic structure of a worldwide and modern industrial society and the social structure of a former competitive preindustrial, sometimes even still feudal, society have increased tensions and conflicts which create feelings of great insecurity in the individual. A resulting consciousness of crisis in the mind of modern youth arouses keen dissatisfaction with their social relationships and ultimately alienation and hostility, which are only surpassed by fear of no escape from nuclear destruction.

"Urbanization lessens our onetime sense of community; morality is threatened. The current decline of traditional authoritarianism is another result which has caused a certain popular confusion as to our sources of standards, ideals and principles of action.[4]"

Sometimes the course of development is determined by some unhappy experience—frustration, jealousy, sibling rivalry, rejection, hopelessness. It goes without saying that we find individual qualitative and quantitative differences in reactions and acting out even in an absolutely normal, inherited endowment. But there are also many inborn potentialities for creativity, intelligence, courage, or tenacity, and these can be constructively or destructively guided, channeled, and shaped into psychological patterns which decisively influence human development. Our treatment or education must promote socially constructive patterns because man is dependent upon them. These patterns will vary remarkably according to the needs of individuals born in a particular period of history, in a particular country, or class.

Many fallacious interpretations and conclusions in this connection prove most dangerous. It is an error, and sometimes it is malice, to assume that juvenile delinquents, withdrawn, or acting out adolescents became that way because they were born into an uneducated family or a slum environment. It is not simply the bad examples set in a slum environment that make it so difficult for the middle-class teacher, social worker, or therapist to deal with these young people. Their contempt for middle-class values, and their rebelliousness, stem rather from being deprived of higher standards, excluded from the advantages of higher values, of better learning opportunities and better living conditions. These attitudes flow from their being *not wanted* as participants in such benefits—not from their not wanting, or their parents' not wanting, to participate. Only the more courageous and creative of these young people act out rebelliously against those who are depriving them and against a society that is biased against them, which does not want them because they are poor or of a different color.

Not every adolescent who acts out, of course, belongs in this category. As already mentioned, acting out is a reaction to a variety of unsolved adolescent problems. It is only one among many possible reactions—like withdrawal or delinquency, which may also result from deprivation of "normal" development. But we must make a clear and concrete distinction between a class that allegedly cannot or does not wish to participate in community development, and a class whose children are prevented from doing so. Differential diagnosis and differential treatment and approach to the problem must be considered; above all, we shall have to make up for the destructive consequences of discrimination and inferiority feelings that have become part of their daily lives. These young people do not belong; they are made to understand clearly that the good things are not for them, that their teachers have little understanding or liking for them or their parents or their aspirations—and since the good things are not for them, and since they are consistently kept out as just "no good," as Negroes, as Jews, or as paupers, they cannot be interested in supporting this way of life. Rather are they inclined to hate it, to fight it; their desire is to destroy it. In their acting out they are seeking to rationalize the way of life they have been made to feel is their own. They would much prefer the way of middle class ideology—if that choice were open to them.

Acting out, like doing nothing, or doing something, or withdrawing, is adjustive behavior. Often enough it is the only road left open to them—so they believe; for such adolescents believe that all they are expected to do is adjust to deprivation, frustration, rejection—yet they too want a little happiness.

More than 150 years ago the great Swiss educator Johann Heinrich Pestalozzi[6] wrote (in *How Gertrude Teaches Her Children*): "Man is good and wants to be good; but in so doing he also wants to be happy; if he is bad, you may be sure that someone has blocked the road on which he wished to achieve this goal."

The first aim of therapy is usually to halt the progress of the illness. We naturally want to stop the acting out, since we realize that it makes trouble and difficulty for the individual who is doing it and for both his immediate environment and the larger society affected by it. But in the interests of all we do not, or should not, try to stop *acting* per se because to us it may look like dangerous acting out. Unfortunately there are many adults who just want the young person to "cut it out"—for the sake of convenience they would like the adolescent not to act at all, as the lesser evil. And very soon they begin complaining that the youngster is lazy, that youth today is not interested or involved in anything.

Acting out does not contribute constructively to socialization; frequently it alienates the adolescent more and more from himself and from his environment. He feels threatened in his search for identity by a society which he defies; in return, he threatens that society.

There are no longer many people—at least not in the fields of education, treatment, and correction, I hope—who are ready to equate the acting out adolescent with the juvenile delinquent. Perhaps we should assume that every juvenile delinquent is an acting out kid—but even where the nature of the acting out adolescent is seriously misunderstood, we are no longer prone to charge every one with juvenile delinquency. Nevertheless, these young people baffle and frighten us, and we are often content to manage them in what we should like to believe is the best interests of the environment and society at large.

But the fact is that we expect any success at all in our treatment if we believe our business is to change an *object*—the adolescent—in his own interests and the interests of a society to which he must conform. But psychotherapy is a process whereby the patient tries to grow up with the help of an understanding and knowledgeable person, the therapist.

All psycho-social illnesses are adjustment problems, whether we believe that some inborn instinct is responsible for the trouble, or that certain inborn potentialities must be developed, or that the source of difficulty is the outside world. There is not just one patient—in our case the acting out adolescent. We may give him the best treatment and he may still be unable to adjust. The family, the school, his peers and siblings, his immediate environment, society as a whole—all are patients, and at the same time all are co-therapists, both as individuals and as a community of co-human beings. For instance, there is not just the problem of R.S., "who was scheduled to die on the following day"; upon the Governor there weighs with almost unbearable weight the problem of his decision: to prevent or not to prevent the execution of a death sentence which it is in his power as Governor to prevent. It is to be hoped that the members of the Tennessee Assembly or State Senate regard as a grave problem their vote on the abolition of capital punishment; their decision and the Governor's action are surely serious problems to us who want our adolescents not to act out furiously but to accept wholeheartedly a society that by democratic process enables every individual to become a true member, and enables every member to rely upon the assumptions of justice and fair play and humanity—whether he himself is a "good guy" or a "bad guy." The prisoners to whom the Governor spoke had to take their first step toward confidence in society in order to begin to raise themselves; our adolescents likewise, not yet able to distinguish between acting and acting out, need our understanding and "permissiveness," but also our firmness, especially when treatment is just beginning. Another factor to be considered in our treatment: What attraction can our society be offering its youth, what help can they be expecting from us, when four of every 100,000 commit suicide, and a hundred more try to without success, or disguise the attempt as an accident?

Education has for too long been what Mark Twain once called "the organized fight of the grown-ups against youth." It has always pretended to be educating for the future, but more often it has been oriented toward adjustment and sterile conformity to the norms of the present—nay, still more often to the norms of the past. That child has seemed to us the best child who has learned from history the great fallacy that his future, the future of the human race, lies in unquestioning acceptance of what seemed greatest in the past—whereas we should in truth be educating them to see the past as the indispensable stepping-stone to a future that they, the youth, must create for themselves.

"The child," Edouard Claparede once wrote, "is not a child because he is lacking in experience; he is a child because he has the natural drive to acquire that experience." In his *Functional Pedagogy* Claparede demands that we place the child at the center of our education; he regards as desirable the development of certain functions of the child, depending upon the requirements of the environment in which education takes place. This theory can be interpreted only in the positive sense that experience should be acquired on the basis of constructive drives, not on the basis of repression or sublimation of certain socially unacceptable instincts. Neither in the forming and development of the individual human mind, nor in the forming and development of our civilization, can we rely upon a psychology of one or two basic instincts so anti-human that Freud, who proposed them to us, believed that human and interhuman growth and development demanded stern repression or sublimation of those instincts. In *Civilization and Its Discontents* Freud says pessimistically; "It almost seems it would be best for the creation of a great human community if we did not have to consider the happiness of the individual at all."

More than 300 years ago Comenius realized that "every human being is endowed with potentialities suitable for acquiring knowledge of all things." That is why youth in a highly competitive society has been able to acquire also the needed competitive emotional attributes, and why, in a democratic society, they are able to acquire also the now needed cooperative emotional attributes.

Now as always, of course, human beings have been driven to master difficulties emotionally and intellectually when they cannot cope with those difficulties by natural reflex. But it is an unjustified assumption that there is in man some mysterious inherited instinct of rebelliousness. We should rather recognize this impulse of rebellion as the product of the interaction of certain human and socially quite constructive needs, common to one and all—the need to overcome inferiority, to conquer obstacles, to remove anti-social impediments on the road to an individually happy and socially useful life.

Children want to grow up into able and responsible adults. They love the sense of accomplishment they get when adults whom they respect take notice of their growth and give them the privileges that go with a developing sense of responsibility. Such development of responsibility in young people depends upon the patience, time, understanding, and love they receive. There are always regressive periods, and these involve most often the adolescent in danger of losing his natural courage and optimism. These youngsters need trust and respect from grown-ups if they are to learn how to assume responsibility with success.

The attitude and behavior of adults with respect to their own responsibilities will influence the development of responsibility in children and youth. It is important that grownups expect and accept imperfection and variability while the child is learning. Too much responsibility placed on the child all at one time can do serious harm. His sense of responsibility should be seen as a developing faculty. And we should properly differentiate between true responsibility, which involves initiative and decision, and a mere passive submission to the demands of others. Freedom and responsibility should go forward hand in hand, from the very beginning of any societal group, large or small. If we want a free and democratic society, we will have to have a free and democratic education and reeducation, where necessary.

Adolescence is a cultural accident; it was not deliberately planned or achieved. Real social inventiveness is required, however, if we are to provide satisfactory outlets for the creative urges and energies of a prolonged childhood and adolescence that is denied adult status. If the younger generation is not permitted to develop in accordance with its creative needs, or to attain status commensurate with its development, it must act out or degenerate.

You will hear the frequent statement that "at one point in history every country has been able to show a marked decrease in juvenile delinquency—that was when compulsory education was first introduced." You will also hear: "The more and better the schools, the fewer the prisons." These statements are true enough; and William Kvaraceus's[5] study on delinquency in Paterson, New Jersey, disclosed that during vacation time children with nothing to do can easily turn into juvenile delinquents. But his study also found that children and especially adolescents of junior high school age who had been truants and delinquents during the school months, finding it no longer necessary to be truants, dropped their delinquent activities during vacation and became peaceable. In those free months they were no longer forced to act out against every indication and constant reminder that they were not smart enough to go to school.

Kvaraceus interpreted this remarkable fact—correctly, I believe—as the result of the lessening or total lack of challenge, during the vacation weeks, of the school and academic competition which these problem children were not able—or thought they were not able—to cope with. What appears to be contradictory in this case actually proves as in nearly every case of acting out youth or of juvenile delinquency—that the same factors which in one instance and under one set of circumstances lead to delinquency, in another instance and under another set of circumstances lead to a courageous, socially constructive life.

There are many varieties of responses to the concept of "no punishment but consequences," and we will have to try not to degrade this method to a pattern which is logical first but could become a meaningless routine after a while.

"In the history of human culture," says Alfred Adler[2] in *Die Formen der seelischen Aktivitat,* "there is not a single form of life which was not conducted as social.

Never has man appeared otherwise in society."

Since society played an essential part in this striving for adaptation, the psychological organ had from the beginning to reckon with the conditions of society. All its abilities are developed on a basis which embodies the component of a social life. Every human thought had to be so constituted that it could do justice to a community.

Natural interest for other human beings, the desire to belong to them, the growing insight and understanding that alone man is the weakest and most vulnerable creature, but that as an organized community, in cooperative building up increasing wisdom of the race and providing application of it, he will be able to master much of beast and material; the inherited predisposition toward community feeling will be developed.

Children and youth who have not known understanding, social acceptance, significance, friendship, or love, or who have misinterpreted or misused them when offered in an overprotective and unchallenging way, will often suffer, as they grow up, from frustration, insecurity, anxiety, and tension. These explode into aggressive, anti-social behaviors. Unguided guilt feelings, following upon such behavior, engender still more insecurity, still more anxiety and tension, which in turn explode into vengefulness and more aggressiveness, the reaction to their own hopeless frustration. Punishment or the demands for repressing "justified or injustified desires" can only aggravate the condition of frustration which has produced this pattern of disturbance or delinquency. Psychotherapy and reeducation, based on friendly understanding and the inherited potentialities for social interest and community feeling, can help to interrupt this "vicious circle."

We too often overlook the "response" in responsibility. Youth of all ages like to have something asked of them. Responsibility comes more easily and naturally to the child whose efforts have been appreciated, even though they have not been wholly successful.

The sense of belonging and social feeling for other human beings are not understandable and are without meaning if they are not interrelated with, not derived from, and do not lead to social and psychological responsibility.

It is no over-statement to say that many children, adolescents and grown-ups as well, become delinquent because they were considered "still children" or inadequate in comparison with others, and were prevented from taking a responsible place in their family or community, and so overcompensated their feeling of social and emotional inferiority by acting it out in neurotic or delinquent fashion. Perhaps even some psychopath is only a deviate who uses strong asocial fixations to escape serious frustrations which he suffered in early childhood, when he tried to assume responsibilities which he associated with his sense of belonging and social interest in interpersonal and over-all community relations.

Man, as a behaving organism is, as we all know, stirred to action by his needs and wants. After the conflicting wants in any given situation have been critically weighed against one another, and one has won out over the others as promising to take best care of all the pertinent considerations, the want thus critically evaluated and found most worthy of choice ceases to be a mere want; it becomes what we call a value. As John Dewey says, a value is "whatever is taken to have rightful authority in the direction of conduct."

If we offer young people an easily understandable, easily inspiring idea of mutual understanding, cooperative living, a democratic and social ideal of unwavering devotion to the principles of peace, liberty, equality, and fraternity of all human beings, they will also find solutions to the eternal conflict of generations without violence; old and young will not only co-exist but live together and, through mutual guidance, achieve technical, social, and ethical progress.

We shall never be able to treat or to "manage" acting out youth, withdrawn youth, or juvenile delinquents until we recognize that commitment to the spiritual-moral is an essential element in the effort. Respect for personality, wherever found, regard for the rights and feelings of others, commitment to the common good—these are in the final analysis moral and spiritual values and must be so treated. Effective moral commitment is our only safe hope for meeting the social needs of the world, and for meeting the needs for individual happiness of its members.

SOCIAL INTEREST AND COMMUNITY FEELING

In our search for a theoretical foundation upon which to build a promising reeducation and treatment program for the asocial and anti-social child and young person, we cannot rely either on the theory of instinctual repression and sublimation, Eros and Thanatos, or that of freedom for the instinct of rebellion. I personally like Fritz Redl's[8] lively interpretation that "defiant behavior . . . . is not the outcropping of a corrupt or morbid personality but the defense of a healthy one against the kind of treatment that should not happen to a dog but often does happen to children." If we wish to shape our own destiny and help disoriented or misoriented so-called juvenile delinquents to shape theirs, consciously and openly, rather than allow them to feel they are victims of dark and mysterious drives, we shall find more hope and encouragement in a school of thought which teaches that social responses develop through the logical interplay between the individual and his society.

Shall we not better understand rebelliousness if we base it upon social causes to which an innate potentiality for defense reacts when provoked?

Shall we not do better to assume the existence of another potentiality, also inborn, the positive social sense, "gemeinschaftsgefuehl,"[1] which can be developed into a free, voluntary, enjoyable, and constructive cooperativeness with other human beings, with the human society? A friendly interpersonal, constructive relationship, founded not on fear, anxiety, and repression, not on cowardly conformism and meek adjustment, but on well-understood social interest and well-developed social feeling?

The democratic community cannot function without the cooperation of its young people and their spirit of social interest; this alone justifies us in demanding the sacrifices youth makes. The local, national, and international community must give youth not only opportunities for studying and working, but also a place in the democratic process and status according to their contribution. The participation of youth in the public life of the community must be insured. We must find a way of acknowledging and fulfilling the emotional needs of young people for their own forms of organization—a democratic Youth Movement, as an element of their participation in public life and as an element in their purposeful mental hygiene and their psychological treatment when this should be necessary. Only by learning by doing can the younger generation acquire confidence and socially constructive strength for the exercise of their rightful place in present and future society instead of a destructive acting out.

Most of us are still unwilling to concede that youth has a role in society equal to our own; we still insist that *they* must adjust or conform to society in total accordance with our own ideas of reality. I am well aware, of course, that we adults have trouble enough with our own social concepts and our own role in society; we are disturbed enough by our own divergent or utterly antagonistic beliefs, by the varying interpretations we put upon society and its functions, by the biased and sick, egotistic use we make of them even when considering only our own interests as adults. I am aware also that, in principle, grown-ups always want to do what is best—as they see it—for their children and other young people. And I understand that it is very difficult for the young to recognize what is best for them— especially the adolescent, who is both child and youth and, in addition, believes himself to be very nearly adult and must, in consequence, struggle seriously to become a responsible adult.

If the adolescent can be actively and constructively involved in our community, the management of the few remaining adolescents who still act out will become the joint enterprise of adults and young people working together with good prospects of success. What a promising undertaking, no longer to have the emotional conflicts provoked by our demand that the young *conform* to our preconceived, outdated ideas, but to have them *commit* themselves, with an involvement perhaps even deeper than our own, to a society no longer alien to them, a society in which adolescents, as adolescents and not merely as adults of the future, form an important segment of a community made up of children, adolescents, adults, and old people.

Such a voluntary commitment in itself will already be in contradiction to what we would colloquially call "management." It will be a democratically worked out insight, a channeling of interests and responsible cooperation of therapist and patient. Only by misunderstanding an atavistic point of view could we compare the relationship between therapist or teacher or parent with the adolescent with the structural division of labor in our present era of coercing and coercive economic and social life— the manager who knows best and the worker who is supposed to execute the manager's ideas and orders without questioning and without emotional involvement. This scheme of a management isolated from those who are to be managed no longer works in economics and sociology; it does not work in psychotherapy and education either. Therefore the consequences of this structure are in every case alienation and not constructive integration.

If we hold to the belief that adolescents act out under the compulsion of certain mystic instincts—of such wide dominion and of such evil that they must be repressed or sublimated before society can accept them—then, of course, we would have to apply our management of these youngsters based mainly upon repression due to social anxiety and fear of punishment. And if we agree that there are no instincts other than the two Freud recognized, then the threat of rather severe punishment will be necessary to combat and repress these most powerful drives. Bribery may also be tried—but what tempting bribes they must be if the adolescent is to be persuaded to trade for sublimation the gratification of these most urgent, allegedly supreme and dominating, all-important instincts.

But the fact is that adolescents do not act out under pressure from any such primordial instincts—sex or death instincts, or rebelliousness, which Robert Lindner added to the first two. There are usually very good, concrete reasons for adolescent behavior arising from the interaction of environmental factors and one or many inherited potentialities with which nearly every human being is endowed to some degree. Different potentialities predominate in different individuals, but there is a great general similarity in such endowments. These potentialities can grow stronger and more active, or they can wither away, depending upon the creative power of the individual, upon other inherited characteristics, and upon the dominant environmental factors and trends and its teaching in any given period.

Another important element of misunderstanding in the treatment of adolescents is responsible for much frustration and defeat among adults who work with them. They believe that education or therapy for adolescents must be in accordance with the character and personality of the *past child* or the *future adult,* while it should be in line with the daily changing, developing character and personality of the adolescent. To grow up is a dynamic and perpetual process of living in the present plus integrating the past and looking forward to a hopeful future.

What a child is born with is not so important as what he wants to do with whatever he was born with; what we can do to help him is to promote the factors which are socially constructive and which enable him to have a happy life, to let him profit from the accumulated wisdom of the human race and, in return, to contribute proudly to his society that which he has inherited and what he has learned with its help.

When children and youth who seem intelligent do not keep up to their grade level in school, we must consider whether their achievements are being retarded by emotional rather than intellectual disturbances. It will often prove the case that they believe themselves to be "stupid." Seriously upset by this conviction, they do everything possible to hide it, and feel they must find a way out of their dilemma.

One of the boys at Wiltwyck, a 12 year old, could not read or write. He expressed contempt for the boys who studied hard: those sissies just didn't know any better. He was constantly bragging about his own superior insight and judgment, and his professional outlook to become a gangster who would have to know how to handle a gun, but not how to read and write. We didn't give him up; we tried again and again for two years, always another new method, another therapist.

One day he came to see me secretly and said with tears in his eyes: "Papanek, give it up, don't try any more. I'm too stupid, I'll never learn how to read and write. But don't tell the other kids or I'll kill you."

We wouldn't agree to that. We told him over and over again that he was not stupid, that he could learn; and for all of us it was a deeply gratifying day when he actually did succeed in writing two words, his own name. Thereafter, that name decorated all our walls, every spot he could lay his pencil to; and his ambition to become a gangster was forgotten.

In the process of education and treatment, understanding and "permissiveness" are only a first step, and we understand under this unfortunate term only that we knowingly, but not approvingly, disregard their deviate behavior and still accept them, still like them, and are still willing to help them to get rid of it, in spite of so many failures. Reorientation and reeducation will often dictate that the adolescent experience the consequences of his actions, beneficial only if constructive help is given which will enable him to face these consequences. There is only a negligible danger that such an offer of help will be abused or misinterpreted, whereas almost always, deliverance from anxiety and tension may be expected in the "offender," a feeling of relief at being given a way out, at finding a helping hand. These are the best bases for treatment and constructive education.

Let me here present to you an example to illustrate this statement.

Danny came to Wiltwyck when he was 11 years of age. He was part Indian and part white. He had quite a reputation as a runaway. He was removed and rejected by 27 agencies before he came, and he had managed to run away from wherever he had been, even from a police station.

When our caseworker brought him up from Youth House, he missed the train, as he said for the first time in his life; everybody in Youth House had to kiss Danny "Goodbye" because he was such a cute boy and each one said, "Thank God you take him away. This boy is a devil. You will not keep him. He will run away."

On the very day of his arrival before I had met him, I was discussing some matter with our resident director in the dining room when a cute young man came in who could be only Danny and said, "Papanek, I want to talk to you."

I said, "That's fine. Please sit down and wait until I have finished with Mr. Norris."

"I want to talk to you *now*," Danny remarked.

"I can't right now. I have to finish with Mr. Norris, but wait for a few minutes."

"I want to talk to you now and if you don't talk to me, I will break all the windows."

"You are not supposed to break any windows. You will have to wait until I have finished with Mr. Norris. If I were talking to you, and he would come in, he would also wait until we had finished."

So Danny took a stick and started to break windows while Mr. Norris and I told him not to do it. After he had broken more than 30 windows, we restrained him by holding his two hands, which was easy enough, but he also tried to kick us and bite us. After a while he quieted down. I asked him to sit down until I had finished the conversation with Mr. Norris, which Danny did. We did finish it, though I assure you that we were very fast about it.

When I asked Danny then what he wanted to talk about, he had forgotten already. As is usual in such cases, he was much too excited and worried and not tough at all, as he pretended to be—only too glad to be restrained and still to be accepted. So we talked for a few minutes about everything, and then I said goodbye and reiterated the rule of courtesy and practical efficiency that you have to wait if you want to talk to someone who is just talking to somebody else.

Danny agreed and started to leave when I called him back and reminded him casually that, of course, he would have to pay for the broken windows. Now hell started again, and he felt very happy to have a reason for his tantrum, shouting to me that he was told that there was no punishment at Wiltwyck, and he also had no money for paying at all. I assured him that there was no punishment, but who else should pay for the broken windows which had to be replaced? He suggested that I should do it or the "city" which had sent him to Wiltwyck, which I refused because I didn't break the windows nor did the city. I told him that he would receive an allowance of one dollar and that he would have to repay one-fourth of it, 25 cents, until the whole was paid. He objected at first, but accepted it when he saw that we were firm about it and assured him that not to punish did not mean we were suckers who would pay for damage he had done purposely.

For six weeks Danny paid his share very "faithfully." He had no other choice because we deducted it in quite a ceremony before giving him the allowance. The counselor would say, "One dollar allowance, Danny. You owe us 25 cents, so here is your 75 cents." After six weeks I called him in and said, "You have been very faithfully paying your share. Do you know how long you would have to pay? and explained that it would take about seven years until everything was paid that way. This did not impress him too much. It impressed him much more how many bottles of Coca-Cola he could buy for that money.

Then I assured him that we were his friends and wanted to help him to pay and he, therefore, should pay two or three more installments and we would pay the rest. Danny was speechless about this offer and started to cry, because he did not believe that we would help him that way. His mother told us that she did not remember that he had ever cried before. Danny repeated almost verbatim my words of six weeks before—"Why should you pay? You didn't break the windows?" When I said I wouldn't pay—that the city would pay—he said, "Why should the city pay? They didn't break the windows?" "No, but you are our friend, and we want to help you." It was the beginning of the treatment which was made possible by showing him that we were willing to help him, although we were not willing to be suckers who would just accept his misdeeds without letting him feel the consequences involved—consequences which we were willing to help him to carry.

We must not see consequences only in a negative way. Not less important are what I would call positive consequences, either for things well done in the line of accomplishment, or just to dramatize illogical behavior. All therapeutic or educational consequences have in their main importance the meaning of dramatizing the logical results of the youth's action and in no way of revenge or punishment.

As an example, the following episode:

We were not very much plagued at Wiltwyck with the problem of runaways. Sometimes for many months not one boy would try to leave, but there are two seasons when it happens almost epidemically. One is the time when we change in the fall from the summer camping program to the academic school program and the second period is spring. I leave the explanation of why at that time to the poets.

One sunny spring day three boys ran away just before some of the groups were about to leave for shopping trips in Kingston, New York. We had to use cars which would have otherwise taken the boys there now for going after the runaways. When we brought them back after about two hours, it was too late to go out for the shopping trip.

It was the day of our general assembly, so when all the boys and staff were together, I apologized to the boys for their not having had a chance to go to Kingston, and explained to them that we had to go after the boys because we believed that runaways do not have to be punished, but that we have to bring them back under all circumstances, because running away does not solve any problem. We told the boys that we had to use all the means at our command to bring them back, and if we were not successful, we would have had to inform the police, and if the police had not found them, we would even have had to ask the Army to help us. The boys laughed, and I tried to explain that there was nothing funny about it, because it was not only the question of running away not solving any problem, but also the possibility that a boy would be up there somewhere in the woods with a broken leg, and we would have to find him to help him. Therefore, I said jokingly, we would also ask for help from the Air Force in such a case.

Two days later when I came to the school, a counselor whom I met at the entrance of the institution said, "Mr. Papanek, you forgot the Navy in the discussion of runaways." At my surprise, he told me that four boys had run away, stolen a boat, and crossed the Hudson. Since we had no Navy at our command, they got to the other side, and on the train, and only from there did we get them back.

Some students of New York University who were doing their field work at Wiltwyck at that time and who did not approve of our treatment without "punishment" suggested that now we would have to punish, because this could not be tolerated. A little bit annoyed, I asked them what the difference was between running away on the Hudson or on the Mississippi, because one of our greatest writers, Mark Twain, had immortalized the famous flight of Tom Sawyer and Huck Finn on the Mississippi, and we gave this book with great delight to our boys to read. When one of the students said, "You have a point there," I said, "No, there is a difference, because the Hudson and the boat the boys stole was much more dangerous than the adventure in Mark Twain's book." On this basis, we discussed the incident with the four boys and, apparently, dramatized the whole story so vividly that one of them started to cry and said never in his life would he do such a thing any more.

But one of the other boys said he didn't care how dangerous this trip was, he had to try to get to New York. His mother had not written to him for more than two months, and he was sure that she was dead or very sick in a hospital.

When we said that this also is no reason for running away because he could have asked his caseworker to arrange for a home visit, and he would have been given a ticket to New York—and that if he still believed this was necessary, we would do so now—the N.Y.U. student remarked that this was going too far, because now we were even rewarding running away instead of punishing it, and from now on, he was convinced, every boy who ran away would have a story of being concerned about his mother. We assured him that we were not suckers, and the boys knew it, and knew that we would not just believe such a story, but it would have to be proved, and for that reason, and because of the honor they have when nicely treated, it would not often happen that a boy would pretend such a reason. Over six years went by without one boy pretending such a reason for running away, and then in the last week I was at Wiltwyck, a boy used this excuse!

Sometimes our boys ask what the difference is between consequences and punishment. We explain to them—if you jump out from the third floor window, in spite of our telling you not to do it, and explaining to you why, and break your leg, this is a consequence, and you have to take it and feel it, even if we would like to help you. You will not be punished for jumping out of the window, and we will even try to put your leg into a plaster cast and help you correct the trouble, but you will have to suffer the consequences of your unreasonable action. If you break windows just because you feel like it, you will have to pay for them exactly what they cost—this is a consequence. You will not be punished for it. If you offend the community by stealing, by acting out in doing harm to the community, the community will react to protect itself with consequences which you could not escape, and you have to learn this.

CLINICAL TREATMENT: PSYCHOTHERAPY

So-called "clinical services" should not be separate from other services but a part of the whole treatment process. We will have to try to surround and encircle the child with all necessary services available and integrate them so that there is no other escape for him possible than to get well again.

Harmonious life requires a successful relationship to society, work and love, all three closely interwoven. All work has economic, social, and psychological implications. Human beings, until misuse, misinterpretation, and misguidance have corrupted their attitude toward work, enjoy working and enjoy achieving mastery over materials and tools.

They like to promote their own well-being and that of their community by their work. To pay off with rewards is to negate the ethical, psychological, and social character of work, achievement and duty.

But even more important is that work and worker should never be dishonored by being forced to work under penalty. We therefore offer an opportunity simply to work and accomplish, to contribute to community needs by working without payment, and opportunity to earn money by additional work.

Every child and adolescent should receive a weekly allowance, before he is a wage-earner, to use as he pleases. He, of course, will need advice and help on how to spend it, and he will need advice, help, and opportunity for hobbies and leisure time.

It seems to us that the most important role of any psychotherapist is to make clear to his patients, adolescents and grown-ups, what their role in society is, and what the role of others is, so that they understand the division and variety of functions and accept them. Socializing the anti- or asocial adolescent consists mainly of showing him, interpreting for him, making him understand, accept and respect the role and function of others and himself in society. Every pretense or wrong fact or interpretation is especially dangerous here.

Participation in administration—not the pretense of "self-government"—

must be meaningful in the daily life of the adolescent if it is to be educational and constructive. We believe that imitation of the organizational setups or other social institutions, such as the government of a republic, town or village, even if the words "junior," "boys," or "children" are set before them, are of no use here.

An example from the Wiltwyck School setup: We had functional committees necessary to handle projects of the daily lives of the boys. We had a Canteen Committee, a Food Committee, a Paid Job Committee, a Sports Committee, and had a committee to handle the allowance of the dogs.

This committee was formed when one day a boy suggested that "Butch" (our dog) should also get his allowance in the same way as the boys had it. "Butch," he said, was an intelligent dog. He went to school with the boys and, therefore, was entitled to an allowance. The whole assembly, boys and staff, decided against my opinion that a dog was not entitled to an allowance. Defeated by this decision, I asked maliciously what would "Butch" now do with the allowance; he did not know how to handle it. One boy suggested having a committee appointed consisting of three boys and one counselor to handle the allowance for the dog, and so it was decided.

One special contribution to the therapy form often and successfully used with acting out adolescents is psychodrama or sociodrama. Here the *re-enactment* by different people shows the patient alternative solutions in more relaxed and, therefore, more thought-provoking situations. In an organized and constructive way the acting outer sees his own mishandling of the problem and the reactions of others to his behavior.

In the re-enactment the "actors" can take roles of persons with whom they conflicted before; by this method they will better understand the motivation of the people they oppose, without being afraid that to do this would make them lose prestige or friendship or love.

The generalizations that will come as a result of the discussion of the play lead to a sharing and formulation of principles of conduct in daily affairs. The unique quality of this form of learning is that in it the student can re-do his actions and change them where he thinks they were not what they should be.

All adolescents have lost the old structure and discipline of childhood without having yet found the new one of the adult; they belittle its importance while they are longing for help in finding it. They are sometimes able to "escape" into a temporary solution as they see it by joining a gang, a club, the Boy Scouts, the Camp Fire Girls. Unfortunately, some get stuck there, get fixated in this state. But most of them move ahead to the next step of development, even when still holding fast, at least sentimentally, to what they learned of human relationships.

If nothing else were acquired than patterns of positive interrelationship, adolescence would be an important enough period in the life and development of men.

INSTITUTIONAL CARE AND MILIEU THERAPY AS A TREATMENT APPROACH FOR JUVENILE DELINQUENTS

We do not believe that institutional care, with emphasis on milieu therapy, is the only possible treatment, but we believe that in its complex approach, many aspects of other methods based on social interest and community feeling are embraced and other methods in turn reveal their influence in this broad approach.

The one-to-one therapeutic relationship between patient and therapist is in most cases of social deviation not enough. Group therapy and so-called milieu therapy can give a patient a better chance to:

(a) see himself mirrored by more than just the therapist who is also permissive. He will see the reactions of the more critical members of the group, in whose understanding and acceptance he is deeply interested, while the therapist continues to protect him against too heavy demands by the group and its individual members;

(b) he can test the interpretations and orientations received from the therapist by the reactions of his peers and check on his own reactions to them; and

(c) he can test and learn to control the consequences of his behavior in a sheltered environment, and he can try out his interpretations of his own and others' behavior among equals who are in the same boat with him.

Milieu therapy, constructively structured in a very active community of children or young people, guided and counseled by well-trained and experienced adults, gives the juvenile delinquent or acting outer an opportunity to learn by experiencing, by living, and by doing, in an understanding, non-threatening, moderately challenging and moderately competitive, accepting, friendly, and cooperative environment that his concept of a hostile world, which he thought he had to fight, is wrong. Here he can gain new perceptions that are less biased; he can find new incentives and motivations to tolerate more frustrations, to make positive choices, to take on responsibility and at the same time to practice, to experiment and to learn by trial and error how to make responsible use of what he has learned for his daily living.

Let me state immediately that that means only the right to err, not that he will have to do so; he also can and must learn by errors made by others and from advice offered by adults whom he trusts. We do not live long enough to make all the errors by which we are supposed to learn by ourselves.

This is why I believe that in most cases of adolescent acting out and of juvenile delinquency where thorough treatment and reeducation are necessary, these should be given in an institutional setting which provides an environment which surrounds them with all the facilities and limitations which permit the juvenile delinquent or acting outer no other escape but recovery.

We live on the eve of a new era. This century will shake the world to its very foundations. Will this great epoch which is evolving from hitherto unheard of technical and economic development find a generation educated in the spirit of already outdated, outgrown pedagogical principles, and left in emotional turmoil because our psychotherapy of troubled and acting out youth is not developing in accordance with the permanently changing patterns of culture; or will this fateful epoch find a generation ready to handle their inheritance in a social and emotional frame of mind which will enable them to use it to the benefit and advantage of each and all members of the human race?

REFERENCES

1. Adler, A. *What life should mean to you.* New York: Grosset & Dudley, 1931.
2. ———. *Psychiatric aspects regarding individual & social disorganization,* 1937.
3. Fromm, E. *The sane society,* 1955.
4. Kilpatrick, W. H. and Papanek, E. "Interim Report of the L.I.D. Study Commission on Youth and the Social Order", *White House Conference,* 1960.
5. Kvaraceus, W. *Juvenile delinquency in the schools,* New York: World Book Co., 1945.
6. Pestalozzi, J. H. "Leonard and Gertrude," *Collected Papers,* L. W. Seyfarth, *Liegnitz,* 1781, 1899-1902.
7. Riessman, F. *The culturally deprived child,* New York: Harper & Row, Inc., 1962.
8. Redl, F. Our Trouble With Defiant Youth, *Children,* Washington, D.C., 1955.
9. Rodman, H. On Understanding Lower Class Behavior, *Social and Economic Studies, 8,* 1959.

22. Management of Acting Out Problems in School

By Julia Vane, Ph.D.

Professor Julia Vane in her chapter on the handling of acting out problems in a school setting asks for a reasoned and careful approach to the evaluation and understanding of the child who acts out his conflicts in the classroom. She makes it clear, through a series of discussions of cases that have come to her attention, that there are many non-recognized as well as recognized dimensions of acting out behavior in school, that each requires careful study in its own right, and that an important role of the school psychologist and of the school guidance person is that of ascertaining how the acting out child can be helped to function more effectively in school.

ACTING OUT, defined as the nonverbal expression of unconscious conflict, is one of the most disturbing problems a child can display in school because acting out usually interferes with the school program to a marked degree. The child who is acting out often is unable to learn, frequently prevents other children from learning, and in addition may encourage similar behavior in other children.

Teachers generally cope with routine acting out problems in the classroom on a day to day basis. In most cases they are successful in eliminating the behavior or in ameliorating it to such an extent that it does not interfere with the school program. Acting out that has not responded to the usual methods of classroom control suggests that the conflict that has precipitated the behavior is likely to be deepseated, and the acting out may be filling a meaningful need of the child. The behavior may be the only way the child knows of solving his conflict. It is unlikely, therefore, that the child can easily give up the behavior or that an increase in the same kind of controls already attempted will be successful. Steps beyond the usual school procedures must be considered.

The first step should be an initial exploration designed to determine why the behavior is being displayed. An accurate report from the teacher is essential. The report should cover a description of the behavior, its initial occurrence, its frequency and intensity, the methods used to control the behavior, and the child's reaction to these methods. Hidden problems are sometimes discovered by noting the discrepancy between the child's actual response to the method of control and the expected response. The teacher often arrives at a fairly adequate estimate of the sequence of behavior and an awareness of some of its causative factors by answering such questions.

A teacher, who had referred eight-year-old Gary for help because during daily reading he had begun to throw his book on the floor and to cry, arrived at an understanding of his behavior in this way. Gary behaved this way only in reading, not in arithmetic or other studies, yet he was a good reader. If the teacher remonstrated or talked to him, he cried harder and sometimes threw himself on the floor. The teacher had found no effective method of control. Gary would not move if told to go to the principal's office. If the teacher tried to lift him from the floor, he became stiff and resistant. As the teacher answered the questions, she noted that this behavior was most intense on Mondays and Fridays and that Gary often fought with and threw things at other students on Monday. The teacher wondered whether something was occurring at home that might be precipitating the behavior. A conference was held with the mother who admitted that Gary's father, from whom she had recently separated, promised Gary to take him out on the weekends, but he rarely kept his promise. Each Saturday Gary was up early waiting at the window for his father. On Sunday night Gary was still waiting, would eat no supper, did not get to sleep until late, and by Monday morning was in a difficult mood. This information helped the teacher understand Gary's behavior, but did not explain why he acted as he did in reading. When she noted that the stories in the reader related to a family in which the father and son were pictured doing many things together, she realized this was too much for Gary to bear in his state of deprivation, and that he was acting out his conflict regarding his father by throwing away the book in which a good father-son relationship was pictured.

Another step necessary in evaluating the behavior is an interview with the parent in order to determine whether the behavior is displayed at home as well as in school and to determine the parent's attitude toward the behavior. The interviewer should be alert for signs that indicate the parent is covertly or unconsciously encouraging the behavior. Children have a need to make the predictions of their parents come true. Many a child behaves a certain way in school for this reason. The parent who says "this year you will have that nasty Mrs. Brown, I never could get along with her," will have a child who cannot get along with Mrs. Brown, even though the parent may tell the child to behave in school. Such contradictory statements by the parent place the child in a conflict situation. If he misbehaves, he will be reprimanded or punished by teacher and parent, but how can he be expected to get along with his teacher, if his parent could not get along with her? If he does get along with his teacher, he may think he is betraying his parent and may feel guilty about this. Getting along with his teacher also interferes with his need to identify himself with his parent, and this creates anxiety. In such circumstances the child may act out his confusion. Such dynamics operate to some extent when a child displays undesirable behavior in school but not at home. Similar factors often operate with children from lower socioeconomic homes who daily must face the conflict arising from differences in standards between their homes and those of the school.

Another essential step is an evaluation of the personality of the child. Psychological testing is needed to determine the child's ego strength, his self-concept, his view of the environment and the authority figures in it, and his capacity to interact with others. A recent report from the family physician should be available. A neurological examination may be necessary if signs suggestive of neurological impairment are present in the psychological tests. A psychiatric evaluation may also be necessary.

The evaluation phase may be lengthy, and by the time all the material has been collected, some children may have ceased to display the acting out behavior for which they were referred. This is often attributed to the influence of the psychological examination, the psychiatric evaluation, or the parent interviews. The most valid explanation is that the increased attention given to the child's problem has in some way altered the situation that precipitated the behavior. During the evaluation process, the exchange of information, opinions, and suggestions among parents, teacher, principal, school psychologist, and others has no doubt resulted in changes that may have influenced the child to alter his behavior. This occurs often with a child who is in conflict about whether his parent really cares and who needs a concrete demonstration that the parent and other adults in his environment will act with more concern for him than they will for the average child.

It may also occur with children such as Gary where acute acting out has followed a traumatic home situation. Gary had not shown difficult behavior before his father separated from the family. When the father responded to suggestions that he be more dependable in visiting, Gary's acting out diminished. It did not entirely disappear because his father never became completely reliable. The teacher was usually able to tell from Gary's behavior when his father had disappointed him. In order to help Gary adjust to the separation from his father, Gary was seen in a group with three other boys, all of whom had fathers missing from the home. Meetings were held on Monday, and were structured so that the boys were able to ventilate their feelings toward their parents without disrupting the class and without feeling too guilty about their hostility. They were able to displace some of their aggression and to gain help from the group leader in controlling their own acting out when it became too intense. These sessions helped to eliminate some of the acting out in class and gave the teacher more opportunities to reinforce Gary's good behavior.

Once the material has been collected, it should be integrated and a school conference held to consider the basis of the behavior and the most effective plan of management that will be in keeping with the welfare of the child. If success is to be achieved at this stage, those who are involved must be willing to think in new areas, to formulate or accept new ideas, and to discard favorite notions. The solutions most frequently suggested are psychotherapy, suspension from school, or transfer to a special school.

None of these methods should be applied routinely. There should be an awareness that psychotherapy has been found to be less effective with dull children than with bright children and less successful with children and adults from low socioeconomic backgrounds than among those from the upper and middle classes. The author's experience has been that young children from all social classes are responsive to play therapy conducted in a school setting, but that there are class differences in structure. Children from low socioeconomic backgrounds seem to have a need for sessions in which there is food, physical contact, and inexpensive items they may take home. Their orientation is toward the group leader rather than toward one another. Middle class children have little interest in food or items to take home, are competitive toward one another, and casual toward the therapist. These differences in behavior are consistent with the experimental findings of Maas,[8] who noted differences between adolescents from low and middle class backgrounds with respect to their approach to the group leader and toward one another. These differences were also demonstrated in two experiments[3,10] which showed that middle class children responded well to praise, but not to food rewards, whereas the situation was just the reverse with children from the lower classes. A finding somewhat similar by Levin and Simmons[7] indicated that not only was praise ineffective with a group of institutionalized delinquent boys, but that it actually acted as an aversive stimulus. With these facts in mind it may be unrealistic to recommend psychotherapy for an acting out child from a low socioeconomic background.

If a decision has been made to recommend psychotherapy, it is important to prepare the parent for the type of structure he may experience. A parent often agrees to bring the child for psychotherapy, but may stop going after the first or second session because the therapist did not act like the family doctor.

When the suggestion is made that the child be transferred to a special school, almost all parents react negatively. Parents from low socioeconomic levels consider this discriminatory, and middle class parents object on the grounds that their children will become worse if they associate with "those bad children." If this method is the one indicated, the school will usually be most successful in implementing it if the family physician is convinced that this is a good plan for the child. In such a situation it is also desirable to have a psychologist or psychiatrist from outside the school involved, so that the parent will feel the situation is being appraised from a non-school viewpoint and that the major concern of all is the welfare of the child. The parent must be convinced the transfer will be helpful to the child if the child is to benefit from the transfer.

If it is decided that none of the foregoing methods will be helpful in managing the acting out behavior, what other methods are available? Imaginative use of some of the results in the field of learning theory and operant conditioning are open to investigation. A number of reports[1,4,5,6,9] tell of the successful application of these methods to human behavior problems.

A study by Williams[11] tells of the elimination of tantrum behavior in a two-year-old by means of extinction procedures. No punishment was used. This technique is often used intuitively by teachers to eliminate disruptive attention seeking behavior. Such a method might be used more often if teachers were aware of the laws of learning upon which it is based so that they might anticipate the rate of extinction and also be able to cope with the phenomenon of spontaneous recovery.

A study by Burchard and Tyler,[2] who used operant conditioning to modify the acting out behavior of 13 year old Donny, who had been in an institution for delinquents for four years, is also pertinent. The authors found that five months of operant conditioning in which Donny was rewarded for good behavior, and routinely and unemotionally punished by isolation for acting out behavior, was more effective than the conventional types of psychotherapy utilized during the previous four years. Essential to the success of the plan was a method to prevent the institution personnel from reinforcing Donny's behavior. Even though the staff suffered from his behavior, they tended to feel guilty when they punished him, and did things to compensate for the punishment. In doing this, they reinforced the feeling of power Donny obtained through his acting out and thereby encouraged repetition of the behavior. This factor must be considered in a school situation. Frequently the teacher or parents may be reinforcing the very behavior about which they complain.

A situation in which operant conditioning was used effectively related to a fifth grade boy who had never been a problem. The acting out began when James' teacher noted he had soiled his trousers in class. The teacher quietly suggested to James that he go to the boy's room, and he notified the school nurse who helped him clean up, took him home for clean clothes, and returned him to school. The mother had no explanation for the situation, but when it occurred two days later, she had James examined by the family physician who found nothing physically wrong. The soiling continued about every two days in class. Each time James remained in his seat until told by the teacher to go to the boy's room, and each time the nurse took James home and brought him back again. When James was asked why he did not leave the room when he felt an accident might occur, he merely cried. Although he cooperated with the school psychologist in the testing, he cried when questioned about the soiling. After three weeks James was asked to remain home for a week, and the parents were urged to give him extra attention. Psychotherapy had been recommended, and the family was on the waiting list at a local clinic. When James returned to school, the soiling continued. Two weeks later a conference was held to determine what to do with James. The evaluation material indicated he had normal intelligence, was working to capacity, and was generally popular. He had been an only child until six months previously when a brother was born. The regressive nature of James' behavior, the projective test material, and the fact that the parents admitted the new brother was receiving a lot of attention, pointed to jealousy of the baby as a possible cause, despite the fact that both the parents and James claimed he loved the baby. The fact that the behavior occurred only in the classroom indicated that the attention James was receiving from the teacher, nurse, and children might be reinforcing his behavior.

The psychologist suggested that a different method of handling, based on the principles of operant conditioning, be tried. It was decided that when the teacher noted James' behavior, she would take him to the door without expressing any emotion, and ring for the nurse who without expressing any emotion, would send him home immediately. He would not be permitted to return to school that session. Plans were made to keep the attention of his classmates to the behavior to a minimum. It was also decided that the teacher would reward James for every half day he remained in school without soiling. At the end of each morning and afternoon session the teacher was to tell James she was happy he had no accidents and give him candy, which he loved, to act as a reinforcement for not soiling. If he went a whole day without soiling, James would receive one of a set of special coloring pencils which the teacher had noted he desired. Although the school staff had doubts about the plan, they agreed to try it for two weeks. The first week James soiled twice, the second week once. This was less than he had during the previous two week period. It was decided to try another week. Monday of the third week he soiled again, and then there were no more accidents. As the time went on the rewards were spaced more widely and finally discontinued with the exception that

James continued to receive a coloring pencil every Friday. By the end of the school year, seven months later, James had soiled in school only twice more.

Although this method treated only symptoms, removal of the symptoms permitted James to remain in school and avoided the emotional disturbance that would have accompanied exemption from school and disruption of his school work. Many schools that have accepted programmed learning and teaching machines, both based on the principles of operant conditioning, would also accept such methods of handling acting out behavior if the dynamics of the situation were made clear.

This type of management was also successful in a case of school phobia. In this instance, Arthur, a seventh grade student, had moved into a new school district after his father had died. Because Arthur and his mother were extremely upset at the father's death, the mother permitted Arthur to remain at home with her for ten days to get adjusted to the new home and neighborhood. When it was necessary for the mother to return to her job, Arthur would not go to school. The mother sought help from the psychotherapist she had been seeing for six months and from the school. A plan was worked out by the school in conjunction with the psychotherapist in which it was agreed that the mother would return to work leaving Arthur home alone, to be looked in upon by the landlady. The latter was instructed not to socialize with Arthur. It was felt that when the mother remained at home with Arthur she was reinforcing his behavior. The school psychologist visited twice a week to talk to Arthur and to get him to walk part of the way to school with him every day. During the first week, Arthur would not move from the couch in front of the television set, but by the end of two months he had accompanied the psychologist to school to visit him in his office. Arthur finally began to go to see the psychologist on his own, and after ten weeks was spending part of every day in the classroom. Six months later Arthur was attending school on a full time basis and showing no unusual symptoms. Consultations with the school psychologist continued on a weekly basis until the end of the school year.

The schools will continue to face many realistic problems and challenges in the management of human behavior. Essential for successful handling of these problems is a knowledge of psychological and educational dynamics and the principles of learning as well as an interest in trying out new ideas. If the schools are to obtain scientific answers to their problems, there should be a resource person on the school staff with an extensive background in psychology and education. Such a person would be able to impart to the school personnel the results of recent research in pertinent areas and to bring to the attention of those working in the fields of research the problems encountered by the schools. Cooperation between those working directly with children, teachers, and parents, and those working in behavioral research, is the cornerstone to more successful management of school problems.

REFERENCES

1. Bentler, P. M. An infant's phobia treated with reciprocal inhibition therapy. *J. child Psychol. Psychiat.*, 1962, *3*, 185-189.
2. Burchard, J. D., and Tyler, V. O. The modification of delinquent behavior through operant conditioning. Read at American Psychological Association Meeting, Los Angeles, Calif. 1964.
3. Douvan, Elizabeth M. Social status and success striving. *J. abnorm. soc. Psychol.* 1956, *52*, 219-223.
4. Jones, Mary C. A laboratory study of fear: the case of Peter. *Pedagog. Sem.*, 1924, *31*, 308-315.
5. Lang, P. J. Experimental studies of desensitization psychotherapy. In J. Wolpe, A. Salter, and L. J. Reyna (Eds.) *The conditioning therapies,* New York: Holt, Rinehart and Winston, Inc., 1964. Pp. 38-53.
6. Lazarus, A. A. The elimination of children's phobias by deconditioning. In H. J. Eysenck (Ed.) *Behavior therapy and the neuroses.* New York: Pergamon Press, 1960. Pp. 114-122.
7. Levin, G. R., and Simmons, J. J. Response to food and praise by emotionally disturbed boys. *Psychol. Rpts.*, 1962, *11* (2), 539-546.
8. Maas, H. S. The role of member in clubs of lower class and middle class adolescents. *Child Develpmt.*, 1954, *25*, 241-251.
9. Schwitzgebel, R., and Kolb, D. A. Inducing behavior change in adolescent delinquents. *Behav. Res. Ther.*, 1964, *1*, 297-304.
10. Terrell, G., Durkin, Kathryn, and Wiesely, M. Social class and the nature of the incentive in discrimination learning. *J. abnorm. soc. Psychol.*, 1959, *59*, 270-272.
11. Williams, C. D. The elimination of tantrum behavior by extinction procedures. *J. abnorm. soc. Psychol.*, 1959, *59*, 269.

PART V

PREDICTING ACTING OUT BY MEANS OF PSYCHOLOGICAL TESTS

The prediction of overt behavior is both one of the most essential and difficult tasks set before anyone working in a diagnostic therapeutic setting. A correct prediction may lead to the employment of appropriate safeguards, as in the case of the suicidal or homicidal patient, and prevent a tragic occurrence. Is it any wonder, then, that the clinical psychologist is so often called upon to answer one important question from his test protocols: "Is this patient likely *to act out* his frightening fantasies"?

Were it not important to answer this question, studies involving *prediction* would be justified since prediction involves a scientific inquiry toward the validation of psychological hypotheses underlying our test constructs and the development of valid and reliable criteria.

The various instruments represented in this Part make up the typical psychodiagnostic test battery and have, therefore, often been referred to as "the first string."

To a large extent the authors who have contributed papers to this Part were given the most difficult assignment, for as scientists each is keenly aware of the fact that no single test can answer all, nor can human behavior be placed in a linear relationship to a single sign. Each author, although writing independently, has in some way cautioned against over-generalizations, and has advised a healthy skepticism for the reader, until further validating research is presented to support our diagnostic claims.

It is still worth remembering the final statement put so well by Dr. Fred Brown in the last chapter:

> ". . . the clinician's worth to patients who call upon his diagnostic skills, insights, and sensitivities would be sadly diminished if he always waited for the statistical green light before crossing the Rubicon of diagnostics."

23. The Wechsler Scales and Acting Out

By SIDNEY J. BLATT, PH.D.

Dr. Sidney J. Blatt in this chapter is interested in considering in which manner the Wechsler Scales may be diagnostically employed to detect the potential for acting out behavior. Though Dr. Blatt elsewhere* has taken the position that the prediction of overt behavior is not a goal of diagnostic assessment, his thoughtful review of the literature makes it clear that pattern analysis of the Wechsler Scales is capable of helping in the assessment of the potential for acting out.

He is interested in considering the role of language, introjection and identification, anxiety, and the general problem of anticipation and planning in relation to understanding the nature of acting out behavior. Clinicians who use the Wechsler Scales in their diagnostic studies are almost certain to find Blatt's contribution important and helpful to them.

THE CONCEPT OF ACTING OUT was originally used by Freud in his "Postscript to a Case of Hysteria,"[10,p.119] and later expanded in one of his technique papers[11] to describe the tendency of some patients to communicate aspects of their past experiences in a non-verbal form. Memories unavailable for recollection in the treatment process were expressed by the patient, and observed by the therapist, in the acting out within the transference or in the patient's current actions and life activities. The patient, unable to remember and to communicate in thoughts and words some early experiences, expresses these repressed memories and experiences in a more primitive, primary process dominated mode with strong pressure for discharge. Freud conceptualized the force which activates these repressed experiences into action as the "compulsion to repeat".[11] The acting out of a specific, focused, and repressed memory during the treatment process has generally been seen as a secondary form of a more primary tendency to "act upon impulse."

More recently the term acting out has been extended to include a variety of impulse disorders and more generally any actions which have anti-social features. In this chapter the term acting out will be used in this broader sense to include impulsivity and anti-social behavior.

Both primary and secondary acting out represent varying degrees of ego inefficiency with a reduction in the capacity for delay, control, and verbalization and a heightened responsiveness to external provocation and

---

*Engel, Mary and Blatt, S. J., "Clinical inference in psychological assessment." Paper read at American Psychological Association Meetings, Philadelphia, September, 1963.

internal drive states. Kanzer[14] in a report of a panel discussion on the relationship of acting out to impulse disorders summarizes many of the features of acting out. In the acting out individual there is an impairment in the usual developmental sequence which proceeds from action to fantasy to mature, goal-directed and purposeful thought, and there is a tendency to continue to use non-verbal modes of expression. Language and verbal skills are relatively poorly developed, and motor activity is ego syntonic. Appropriate goal-directed action based on thought, planning, and anticipation is lacking, and action per se is highly cathected. Feelings, wishes, fears, and impulses generally are not adequately reality tested and modulated, but tend to be experienced directly, and are not integrated with an understanding of the current situation and earlier experiences. There is also a relative lack of meaningful object relationships, identifications, and internalized control structures. The relative deficiency of object ties and identifications leaves the individual open to environmental stimulation and influence. There is usually also a high degree of narcissism and either a relative lack of anxiety or an inability to tolerate anxiety. The emphasis is upon the sensory, concrete, and immediate rather than on the abstract and conceptual; and this emphasis results in a heightened expression of instinctual life. The lack of control mechanisms results in a lowered threshold for stimulation, and since the binding potentials of identifications and of language are underdeveloped, there is little capacity for delay, fantasy, and planning. These various characteristics and features of primary acting out (or acting on impulse) manifest themselves in a variety of ways on the Wechsler Intelligence Scales.

ACTION AND PURPOSEFUL THOUGHT

Impairment in the developmental sequence progressing from action to purposeful thought is reflected in the balance between the Verbal and Performance Scale IQs. Relative disruption of verbal skills and the preference for action result in an elevation of the Performance Scale IQ as compared to the Verbal Scale IQ. This relative elevation in Performance Scale IQ, however, must be qualified somewhat depending on the individual's general intellectual level. In the lower IQ range, below an IQ of 100, the Performance Scale IQ is generally expected to exceed the Verbal Scale IQ by at least a few points. A slight imbalance favoring the Performance Scale IQ in the lower range, therefore, does not necessarily suggest acting out; it is only when the Performance Scale IQ exceeds the Verbal Scale IQ by approximately five or six points or more, in the low IQ range, that the potentiality for acting out should be considered. In the upper IQ range (above 110 IQ) the Verbal Scale IQ usually exceeds the Performance Scale IQ from two to eight points. In the above average intellectual range, therefore, a Performance Scale IQ equal to or exceeding the Verbal IQ would suggest tendencies toward acting out. There is extensive research support for the observation that Performance Scale IQs tend to be higher than Verbal Scale IQs in acting out individuals. Wechsler[23] with adolescent psychopaths; Foster,[8] Diller[6] and Field[7] with adolescent delinquents; Wiens, Matarazzo and Gavor[26] with sex offenders and Graham and Kamano[12] and Panton[17] with prisoners all report Performance Scale IQs are generally higher than Verbal Scale IQs. The consistency of these findings may be somewhat exaggerated by the lower IQ of the subjects in several of the studies. The data, however, offer considerable support for the hypothesis about the Verbal-Performance Scale IQ imbalance in acting out.

The potential for impulsive acting out rather than for planned, purposeful action can also be expressed in the qualitative features of the responses on each of the subtests. On the Performance scales, the behavior may be characterized by impulsivity, rapid trial and error, and a lack of persistence. Responses to the Verbal scales may be immediate, imprecise, and with little reflection on the various possibilities implicit in the question or the various alternate responses.*

CONCRETE, FUNCTIONAL, AND ABSTRACT MODES OF THOUGHT

Indications of an impairment in development of language can be seen in the tendency to think in concrete and functional terms, rather than on an abstract or conceptual level. On the Similarities subtest, the similarity between *orange* and *banana* might be "You eat them both," rather than "Both are fruit;" or the similarity between *piano* and *violin* might be that "You play both of them," rather than "They are both musical instruments." The extensive use of functional categories suggests that the ideational processes do not have a major role in delay, organization, and planning, but rather that there is a general emphasis on activity. Even further, within the Similarities subtest one can identify a potential but tentative binding power in the quality of the verbalizations. A response to *orange* and *banana* such as "You can eat them both" or to an *ax* and *saw* as "Both are used for cutting," contains the conditional phrase "can" or "used for" which implies that some delay is imposed between the stimulus and action.

Definitions to the Vocabulary subtest can also reflect a tendency to respond with action-oriented phrases rather than with conceptual definitions. The word *slice* might be perceived as a verb, as in "to cut," rather than as a noun with a definition of "a thin piece of." *Sentence* might be

---

*Weissman[24] found a similar tendency toward quick reaction times on the TAT with a group of adolescent aggressive acting out subjects.

something imposed on a criminal rather than a grammatical structure, or, *hasten* might be defined as "rush" rather than as "to go faster." The implicit quality of action in a definition suggests that words are not experienced as concepts which serve to organize and direct experience, but rather they are stimuli which seem to have all too easy access to the motor system. Though the differentiation of the various levels of thought ranging from action to abstract thought is consistent with the conceptualizations of Werner[25] and Piaget[18] relatively little research has been conducted with this particular dimension of the Wechsler protocol.

IMPULSIVITY AND DEFIANCE OF SOCIAL CONVENTIONALITY

The impulsivity and lack of persistence discussed earlier as a deficiency in delay and planning also represent an inability to work toward a goal. Persistence, dedication, and general attitudes toward work are frequent expressions of ego and superego organization which are usually deficient in acting out. The development of the superego and of a moral code can on occasion be assessed on the Comprehension subtest of the Wechsler. The Comprehension subtest presents a series of more or less conventional social situations, and in asking about appropriate behavior and its rationale, the test assesses the grasp of social conventionality and social judgment.[19] A lowered score on Comprehension would suggest a possible impairment in judgment or a defiance of social conventionality. Thus a record in which this scale is lower than many of the other scales suggests anti-social trends and the possibility of acting out. The qualitative features of responses to the Comprehension subtest can also be particularly valuable in assessing anti-social tendencies. For example, a response to the *bad company* item such as, "Most people would say they might influence you, but I really don't believe there is such a thing as bad company," not only indicates an intrigue with deviant groups and behavior, but even the juxtaposition of comments within the response itself suggests a defiance of conventional modes of thought. Acting out and anti-social tendencies in a naive and repressive defensive organization might be suggested by the misinterpretation of "bad company" as "dull company."

A struggle for control which may not be fully effective can be seen in Comprehension subtest responses such as to the *fire in the theater* item. Instead of responding "Tell the usher," or "Yell fire," the response might be "I wouldn't yell fire, I would tell the usher" or "I know I shouldn't yell fire but . . .". These latter responses suggest that controls do not operate efficiently and automatically, and that there is a lability and impulsivity which the individual is attempting to control secondarily. Tallent,[22] however, found that 9th grade boys judged to be behaviorally impulsive by their teachers did not have any greater tendency to "yell fire" on the theater item than a control group. Tallent's study is, however, limited in at least two respects. There is no clear indication that the teachers were adequately assessing impulsivity, and an attempt to differentiate impulsivity should not be limited to a single item but should be assessed on at least the total subtest and preferably on the entire Wechsler protocol.

IMMEDIACY AND THE LACK OF ANTICIPATION AND PLANNING

There is considerable evidence that at least in delinquency, and probably in acting out more generally, there is a strong present orientation with only a limited awareness of concern about the future.[1,3,4,15,20,21] The primary subtest which assesses planning and anticipation on the Wechsler is Picture Arrangement,[19] and there is recent evidence which supports this conceptualization that Picture Arrangement is related to anticipation, planning, and future time perspective.[2,5]

The Picture Arrangement subtest, much like the Comprehension subtest, presents stimuli which are concerned with social interaction. In requiring an understanding of the inter-relationships between a series of interpersonal events, the Picture Arrangement assesses the grasp of the essentials of social interaction. An ability to understand the cause and effect relationships between a series of discrete pictures seems to reflect a capacity to anticipate or understand a sequence which extends through time into the future. The ability to see the inner connections between a sequence of continuing and causally related events reflects the capacity to recognize continuity and to anticipate from one moment to the next. It is the capacity for anticipation which permits integration and understanding of a complex array of stimuli and the organization of these stimuli into a related and coherent sequence. The understanding of possible antecedents and consequences of an event is essential for planning. If this capacity for anticipation is lacking, each event occurs in isolation, and there is no organization or continuity. The Picture Arrangement subtest, in limited form, seems to assess the capacity for anticipation and planning; and a relatively poor performance on this subtest reflects a propensity for impulsive and unreflective action.*

A valuable additional procedure with the Picture Arrangement subtest, in addition to noting the time and placement of the cards, is to ask for stories to those series which are failed and to the last two problems, whether they are correct or incorrect. In asking for the stories, one removes the pictures and asks the subject "what was that story?" This

---

*Psychopathy, to be discussed later, is a form of acting out which can present a general exception to this observation about an inefficiency on Picture Arrangement in acting out. This exception can also occur on the Comprehension subtest.

material is valuable in evaluating the distortions in thinking which may underlie an incorrect sequence, or it may indicate specific idiosyncratic interpretations even though the item was responded to correctly. The stories on the eighth item, *the taxi,* for example, are frequently helpful in evaluating sexual difficulties and the possibility of sexual acting out. Typical of such a response is a story told to item 8 by a patient where one facet of the pathology was extensive sexual acting out as a defense against underlying homosexual concerns: "The man was carrying a statue and called a taxi, and he moved the statue closer and closer to him so that people would think he was on a date and was making out."

A performance on either the Comprehension or Picture Arrangement subtest which is lower than many of the other scales of the Wechsler suggests a propensity for acting out with possible anti-social features. The relative impairment on the Comprehension subtest primarily reflects a difficulty in understanding, or a defiance of, social conventionality because of the lack of meaningful object ties and adequate identification and introjects. Relative impairment on the Picture Arrangement subtest indicates that there may be acting out primarily because of a relative inability to anticipate and plan. This inefficiency in anticipation and planning is consistent with the observation that impulse disorders frequently have a disturbance in the sense of time and that there is an urgency to many of their reactions.

THE ROLE OF ANXIETY

Anti-social behavior not only occurs in the impulse disorders but it may also occur in a more controlled and calculated context. The socially adroit and usually verbally facile psychopath can manipulate individuals and situations, and these tendencies are frequently expressed in Wechsler protocols by an elevation of the Picture Arrangement subtest[19]. The clever manipulative orientation usually occurs around specific issues, but more long range anticipation and planning are generally lacking.* Anxiety and guilt which can function as important deterrents and constraints for inappropriate and dangerous activity are frequently not present. The Wechsler scales usually impaired by anxiety, such as Digit Span and Block Design, along with Picture Arrangement, are frequently elevated in comparison to other scales in the psychopath.

Though the research on Digit Span as a measure of anxiety is inconclusive, Moldawsky and Moldawsky[16] report findings which support this as-

---

*The reason for this paradox on the Picture Arrangement of Psychopaths is generally not well understood. The elevated score on this subtest may be an expression of heightened sensitivity to immediate interpersonal situations independent of any capacity for temporal extension.

sumption as does Hiler,[13] who reports that patients who tend to remain in psychotherapy beyond the initial contacts have lower Digit Span scores.

Indications in a Wechsler protocol that anxiety can be experienced and tolerated are an important evidence of the capacity to contain acting out and anti-social behavior. Anxiety can represent the capacity for recognizing inappropriate and dangerous aspects of behavior, the capacity to identify with society and its controlling agencies, and the potentiality for eventually internalizing values and controls so that they operate automatically and efficiently. The performance on the Digit Span subtest, therefore, is important in evaluating the potential for impulsive or anti-social behavior. If Digit Span is higher than many of the other subtests, it suggests that the usual constraints and restrictions of social pressure are not fully experienced. Conversely, a Digit Span score significantly lower than many of the other subtests would suggest a high level of anxiety. Particularly with impulsive rather than manipulative individuals, heightened anxiety can increase the tendency toward action and discharge. Thus, either a marked lack of anxiety or heightened anxiety can result in acting out, depending on the context as indicated in other aspects of the protocol.

NEGATIVISM

Within the Digit Span there is a secondary feature which can also be seen in acting out. Usually the number of digits remembered in the forward order exceeds the number of digits remembered backwards. Remembering more digits backwards than forward occurs relatively infrequently and primarily in negativistic individuals.[19] This negativism can be expressed in a variety of ways including defiance of authority and in unconventionality. Research on this dimension has also been lacking but a recent study[9] indicates a significant positive correlation between this measure of negativism on Digit Span and the conventional Rorschach measure of negativism, the white space responses. Though this convergence of two independent expressions of negativism lends support to the hypothesis that digits backwards superior to digits forwards is a possible indication of negativism, more definitive research is necessary with this dimension of the Wechsler protocol.

CONTROLS

Thus far a number of indications of acting out, as they are seen on the Wechsler Intelligence Scales, have been presented. Though these diagnostic indications can be valuable in assessing acting out, a full evaluation requires an assessment of the indicators within the total context of the diagnostic battery. The specific indications of potential impulsivity and anti-social behavior must be considered in relation to the available controls and the organization of defenses as manifested in a complete psychological battery. Some controls operate smoothly and efficiently, and impulses rarely have full access to the motor system without intervening delay and modulation. Such controls are usually derived from well integrated identifications with adequate parental figures. In such instances there is relatively little indication of impulsivity or anti-social preoccupation on the Wechsler. There are other types of controls which do not operate so efficiently and automatically, and which operate only secondarily to regulate labile and impulsive action. These control processes are indicated in the Wechsler by the individual's attempts to contain an inappropriate or impulsive response and by the heightened level of anxiety produced by the struggle between impulse and control. This struggle for containment may be seen on the Wechsler, but a fuller assessment of these controls must be gained from other procedures within the diagnosic battery. Impulse, defense, and self-integrative functions should be considered across a wide range of psychological levels and functions as they are expressed in the various procedures of the diagnostic battery.

SUMMARY

Some of the major indications of acting out on the Wechsler scales include:

1. An imbalance between Performance Scale and Verbal Scale IQ's, where the Performance Scale IQ usually exceeds the Verbal Scale IQ to a significant degree.

2. Behavior and responses during the test which are impulsive and unreflective.

3. Action-oriented verbalizations rather than conceptual and abstract definitions.

4. Impaired judgment, defiance of social conventionality, or lack of anticipation and planning as reflected in either low Comprehension or low Picture Arrangement scores.

5. Qualitative aspects of the response to the Comprehension items or stories told to the Picture Arrangement sequences which indicate impaired judgment or a defiance of social conventionality.

6. Impulsivity may be indicated by heightened anxiety and a diminished tolerance for this anxiety.

Digit Span and secondarily Block Design are usually sensitive to anxiety and acting out which may be indicated by inefficiency on these scales. Conversely, a general lack of anxiety, indicated by a relative elevation of Digit Span and Block Design, may be seen in the more calculated psychopathic anti-social behavior. Thus, depending on the context of the record, scores on Digit Span and Block Design may be relatively impaired or elevated in acting out.

7. Negativism suggested in digits backwards equal to or greater than digits forward.

8. More controlled and calculated anti-social orientation can be expressed in a marked elevation of the Picture Arrangement and, on occasion, the Comprehension subtest.

The Wechsler scales can be a valuable source of inference about the role of action in psychological organization, but these observations must be integrated with observations gained from other procedures and from other vantage points. There must be a convergence of observations gained from a variety of sources, which lead inevitably toward similar conclusions. The utilization of the Wechsler scales as an evaluation of the role of action in psychological organization is still relatively unexplored, and much research is needed to validate, clarify, and elaborate the assessment of acting out on the Wechsler Intelligence scales. Such clarification will enrich the use of the Wechsler not only as a diagnostic instrument, but in turn, it will also enrich our understanding of the role of action in personality organization and development.

REFERENCES

1. Barndt, R. J., & Johnson, D. M. Time orientation in delinquents. *J. abnorm. soc. Psychol.,* 1955, *51,* 342-347.
2. Blatt, S. J., & Quinlan, P. Planning and anticipation in early and late volunteers. Unpublished manuscript, 1965.
3. Davids, A., Kidder, Catherine, & Reich, M. Time orientation in male and female juvenile delinquents. *J. abnorm. soc. Psychol.,* 1962, *64,* 239-240.
4. Davids, A., & Parenti, Anita. Time orientation and interpersonal relations of emotionally disturbed and normal children. *J. abnorm. soc. Psychol.,* 1958. *57,* 299-305.
5. Dickstein, L., & Blatt, S. J. Death concern, futurity, and anticipation. *J. consult. Psychol.,* (in press).
6. Diller, Juliet C. A comparison of the test performance of male and female juvenile delinquents. *J. genet. Psychol.,* 1955, *86,* 217-236.
7. Field, J. G. The performance-verbal I.Q. discrepancy in a group of sociopaths. *J. clin. Psychol.,* 1960. *16,* 321-323.
8. Foster, A. L. A note concerning the intelligence of delinquents. *J. clin. Psychol.,* 1959, *15,* 78-79.
9. Fox, Elizabeth, & Blatt, S. J. WAIS digits backwards and forwards and Rorschach white space responses. Unpublished manuscript, 1965.
10. Freud, S. Fragment of an analysis of a case of hysteria. *The standard edition of the complete psychological works of Sigmund Freud,* Vol. 7, London, Hogarth, 1953 (1905), 3-124.
11. Freud, S. Remembering, repeating and working through. *The standard edition*

of the complete psychological works of Sigmund Freud, Vol. 12, London, Hogarth, 1953 (1914), 145-156.
12. Graham, E. E., & Kamano, D. Reading failure as a factor in the WAIS subtest patterns of youthful offenders. *J. clin. Psychol.*, 1958, *14*, 302-305.
13. Hiler, E. W. WB intelligence as a predictor of continuation in psychotherapy. *J. clin. Psychol.*, 1958, *14*, 192-194.
14. Kanzer, M. Report of a panel on acting out and its relation to impulse disorder. *J. Amer. Psychoanalytic Assoc.*, 1957, *5*, 136-145.
15. Mischel, W. Preference for delayed reinforcement and social responsibility. *J. abnorm. soc. Psychol.*, 1961, *62*, 1-7.
16. Moldawsky, S., & Moldawsky, Patricia C. Digit span as an anxiety indicator. *J. consult. Psychol.*, 1952, *16*, 115-118.
17. Panton, J. H. Beta-WAIS comparison and WAIS subtest configurations within a state prison population. *J. clin. Psychol.*, 1960, *16*, 312-317.
18. Piaget, J. *The origins of intelligence in children.* New York: International Universities Press, 1952.
19. Rapaport, D., Gill, M., & Schafer, R. *Diagnostic psychological testing.* Chicago: Yearbook Publishers, 1946.
20. Roth, D., & Blatt, S. J. Psychopathology of Adolescence: Spatio-Temporal parameters. *Arch Gen. Psychiat.*, 1961, *4*, 289-298.
21. Spivak, G., & Levine, M. *Self regulation in acting out and normal adolescents.* Research report, Devereux Foundation, 1963, Devon, Pa.
22. Tallent, N. Manifest content and interpretive meaning of verbal intelligence test responses. *J. clin. Psychol.*, 1958, *14*, 57-58.
23. Wechsler, D. *The measurement of adult intelligence,* (3rd ed.). Baltimore: Williams & Wilkins, 1944.
24. Weissman, S. L. Some indicators of acting out behavior from the Thematic Apperception Test. *J. Proj. Tech. & Pers. Asst.*, 1964, *28*, 266-275.
25. Werner, H. *Comparative psychology of mental development.* New York: International Universities Press, 1948.
26. Weins, A. N., Mattarazzo, J. D., & Gavor, K. D. Performance and verbal IQ in a group of sociopaths. *J. clin. Psychol.*, 1959, *15*, 191-193.

24. Acting Out Indicators on the Rorschach

By Joseph Levi, Ph.D.

In the brief chapter that follows, Dr. Joseph Levi sets forth, largely from his own clinical practice, a group of four patterns of Rorschach protocols that constitute for him, acting out indicators. As he makes clear, other clinicians will want to consider their own clinical experiences with the Rorschach Test in relation to his findings as a basis for seeking their validation.

In the meanwhile, these indicators represent promising suggestions for techniques for the evaluation of Rorschach records in the search for indications of acting out potential.

THE TERM "ACTING OUT" was first used by Freud, in 1905, in reference to the case of Dora.[2] At this time, Freud used the term only in connection with the transference neuroses. The writers who followed Freud expanded and altered his theory, and they described acting out as a type of personality structure. In this paper, I will discuss acting out in this sense; that is, viewing acting out as part of the character structure of the individual, rather than as merely a phase of the analytic situation.

The later definition of acting out states that it is an immediate discharge of impulses *onto the environment,* when the character type is one whose controls of motility (an ego function) are not efficient in maintaining affect. It occurs when the ego does not have control over its actions. It, therefore, follows that the energy used is primary process energy, since the ego, having available only bound secondary process energy, is unable to be mobilized. Since acting out is due to an impulse disturbance, the cognitive awareness of reality is momentarily hampered by an inability to maintain affect.

At this point, we must distinguish acting out from normal, free-flowing behavior, which can also produce immediate satisfaction. Uninhibited behavior *doesn't* show affect while acting out, which is best described in the words of Ogden Nash, "When ah itch, ah scratch," does. In other words, when one shows affect, one has not acted out. This holds true even if the affect is that of signal anxiety which causes delay via an inner charge of anxiety.

The criteria for acting out are quite different. Acting out occurs when the action increases extra-psychic conflict, thereby creating additional guilt feelings for an unacceptable act. If both conditions are absent, the behavior *cannot* be labelled "acting out," since it is probably uninhibited and free-flowing. Thus, there must be a conflict, either within the individual, (intra-psychic) or with society (alloplastic), for behavior to be termed "acting-out."

A set of criteria for the purpose of distinguishing acting out from schizophrenic behavior and neurotic behavior (neurotic symptom formation) should also be set up. The most important distinction is that the acting out character type actually discharges in a direct motor way *onto* the environment, while the schizophrenic's motor apparatus seemingly draws the inner perception away from the environment, causing a mainly *visual* hallucination. The difference between schizophrenia and acting out is, therefore, one of cognition. Whereas the schizophrenic misinterprets reality, the person who acts out finds that the cognitive awareness of reality is momentarily hampered by an inability to maintain affect.

When we contrast acting out and neurotic behavior (neurotic symptom formation), a similar distinction can be drawn. The acting out process involves an immediate perception leading to a *direct* motor action onto the environment. This *direct* or impulsive motor activity aims at the direct gratification of a basic instinctual drive, ruling out symptoms, symbolic acts, etc., *which are compromise formations*. Neurotic behavior, which involves symbolic acts, is not directed *onto* the environment, nor does it grant immediate satisfaction, as acting out does. Neurotic behavior, and other pathological defenses of the ego, are disorders which represent compromise formation with symbolic gratification, preventing instant satisfaction of an impulse.

Let us now trace the development of controls against acting out. A basic psychoanalytical concept is that behavior begins with immediate discharge, and as Freud puts it in the *Interpretation of Dreams,* shortly after birth, perception leads to direct motor action and that this immediate discharge is the prototype of all human behavior. In the process of development, our defenses for motor control are established. These immediate discharge controls may be due to neurological growth or psychological development.

The neurological factor which prevents the organism from discharging free-unbound energy is development of the central nervous system, especially the cortex. Organic injury to the central nervous system, or arrested development, causes an inability to control motility; thus, acting out, an immediate discharge of impulses onto the environment, occurs.

The ability to maintain affect, an inner discharge which is both psychic and somatic, is another control against acting out which we develop. The inability to maintain affect causes impulse disturbances and acting out.

Defense mechanisms also serve to control motility. From a person's defenses we can see if he is working against acting out. Depression, a qualitatively different type of defense from that of normal defense mechanisms, is a *direct defense* against acting out. This is clearly demonstrated by the mechanism involved in manic-depressives. The emotional paralysis and psychomotor retardation are defenses against impulsive discharge of energies; the rapid switching from one activity to the next is indigenous to the manic phase. When we see depression, then, we know it is a defense against acting out.

RORSCHACH TEST INDICATORS

Our next task is to see how the personality structure of an individual who acts out reflects itself on the Rorschach Test. There are no set rules for one type of acting out. What we can do is postulate Rorschach indications for acting out by the following methods: First, through empirical findings in which the Rorschach patterns of people who have shown clinically the behavior of an acting out personality structure are known. Second, through a priori, or deductive reasoning, Rorschach indications for acting out can be postulated. If we accept the psychological meaning of the various Rorschach determinants or patterns, we may infer the type of behavior pattern. These types of inferences must, of course, be tested experimentally.

The patterns that we will propose are based primarily on empirical findings and are the results of my experiences of the last fifteen years.

The first Rorschach pattern presented is the *"Dd"* pattern. An individual who is extremely perceptive and who seems to pay attention to unimportant details (who is, in other words, a picayune, obsessive-compulsive person) is a *"Dd"* type. I gave this interpretation of the *"Dd"* pattern in cases of all such records. Two cases came to my attention in which the behavior was not obsessive-compulsive. Actually, it was typical *acting out* behavior.

The histories of the two such cases are briefly as follows:

Case A

A young man of 28, whose outstanding difficulty was that he could not control his impulses when he got angry at his employer. Once, showing no restraint, he attacked him physically. Therapy did not help him curb his escapades and all the types of acting out behavior which he exhibited, nor did it help him correct the sexually promiscuous activity he had been involved in since early adolescence. This individual gave about 75 responses to each card. All were *"Dd's."* His Rorschach was never finished since it took him one hour to respond to each card.

Case B

A young woman of 24 who cannot control her behavior as long as she remembers. During her adolescence she went to religious school, hoping her impulses would be controlled; but it was to no avail. She was sexually promiscuous, impulsive, and lost many jobs because she couldn't control her impulses. She gave more than 100 responses to each card. She spent one hour on each card, for each of four cards, and at this point the examiner stopped her. All her responses were *"Dd's."*

Case C

After having worked with the above-mentioned two cases, I took from my files a very similar case of a Rorschach record of responses, 60 of which were *"Dd's."* I questioned the therapist, who handled the case, in regard to the behavior of this patient. (The case had been written up as obsessive-compulsive individual). The therapist described this patient as an acting out type. The patient had made many "slips" of the tongue, which caused her great embarrassment since she was a radio announcer. She was alarmed at the great number of "slips," and began therapy.

Case D

As a result of my experience with the above cases, I have changed my interpretation of the significance of *"Dd"* responses and I now consider an excess of *"Dd"* responses or an apperceptive type of *"Dd"* as an indication of acting out behavior. This hypothesis was tested by Herbert Jones[3] in his doctoral dissertation,[2] for which he used children, ages eight to 11, who gave *"Dd"* perceptions of 15 per cent or over. His results show that such children were all diagnosed as having character disorders, or as showing acting out behavior.

The second Rorschach pattern we shall present is the *"M"* response. *"M"* responses on the Rorschach are usually interpreted as an indication of behavior with inner controls or resourcefulness. What happens when all or almost all of the responses are *"M"?* Three such cases have come to my attention during the past three years. These were Rorschachs of young girls, ages 16-22, who were acting out in a very extreme manner. They were sexually promiscuous, addicted to drugs, and had made suicidal attempts, when only slightly frustrated. A reevaluation of the meaning of *"M,"* when shown in excess, is called for. We suggest that whenever excess of control is given, as in this case, there is really an extreme degree of underlying discharge behavior. In other words, the extreme discharge behavior is the basis of the excess of control. We infer such behavior by the extremity of the defense against it.

The third pattern is *"F+."* A 100 per cent *"F"* record, of which all of them are *"F+"* responses, is usually found in cases of extreme depression. It has been pointed out in the theoretical section of this chapter that part of depressive behavior is really a defense against acting out. It is, therefore, reasonable to assume that 100 per cent *"F"* responses, all of which are *"F+,"* is another defense against acting out. Once again, this has been found empirically.

The last pattern is the *"C' "* sample. Black, as a color, may be considered indicative of the acting out individual. Piotrowski claims that *"C' "* is an indication of intermittent depression. For this pattern the empirical findings are as follows:

A student in my advanced Rorschach class presented five cases, all of which had given at least three responses using *"C' "* as a determinant. Each patient had been arrested for an impulsive act, which indicated unpredictable behavior. Acting out was the outstanding personality characteristic, as described by the attending psychiatrist.

It is therefore suggested that a record with three or more *"C' "* responses is an indicator of a personality structure in which acting out is likely to occur.

SUMMARY

We have presented four patterns that indicate acting out behavior. It is interesting to note that the four patterns all constitute defenses against acting out. This is in line with Anna Freud's[1] statement that "there is a regular connection between particular neuroses and special modes of defense."

REFERENCES

1. Freud, A. *The ego and the mechanisms of defence.* New York: International Universities Press, 1946.
2. Freud, S. Fragment of an Analysis of a case of Hysteria. *Standard Edition, VII,* p. 1190.
3. Jones, H. The Rorschach and Acting Out in Children. Unpublished Doctoral Dissertation, Yeshiva University, 1962.

25. Detection of Suicidal Risks with the Rorschach

By MARGUERITE R. HERTZ, PH.D.

Professor Marguerite R. Hertz as early as 1948 became impressed with the possibilities of employing the Rorschach Test in studying the detection of suicide potential. In what was essentially a nomothetic inquiry, she developed evidence of "suicidal configurations" in Rorschach protocols that have been well validated by other workers in the intervening period.

In her contribution, Dr. Hertz makes reference not only to her original research and the pertinent material but also to the whole body of information presently available to Rorschach psychologists. The chapter is a systematic, definitive, and unusually clearly stated contribution to the problems and possibilities of predicting suicide with the Rorschach Test. Virtually every clinician will welcome it, not only because it will directly help him in his work, but also because it is likely to broaden his horizons with the Rorschach Test as an instrument useful in many other diagnostic by-ways.

SUICIDE MAY BE VIEWED as a violent aggressive form of acting out behavior resulting in self-destruction. It is a problem of tremendous magnitude because of needless loss of life. Despite differing opinions as to the causal factors involved, there is general agreement on the urgent need to understand the psychodynamic factors operative in suicide, to determine under what circumstances people are impelled toward self-destruction, and to increase the effectiveness of the early recognition of suicidal potentiality.

Any technique, then, which gives insight into the personality dynamics of the suicidal individual and helps predict suicidal behavior can be of invaluable service.

In recent years, efforts have been intensified by psychologists and psychiatrists to evaluate the degree of suicidal danger present in an individual at a given time. Many procedures have been devised. These include psychiatric assessment, use of social histories, study of suicidal notes, diaries and other personal documents, the analysis of dreams, fantasies, and communications of suicidal individuals, and the use of psychological tests, especially the projective methods.

It is my purpose to focus on one of these projective methods, the Rorschach, first to summarize the Rorschach correlates which appear to reflect the differing personality constellations behind suicidal behavior, as hypothesized by clinicians on the basis of experience and as reported in empirical studies, and second, to assess the value of the method in detecting suicidal risks.

Before we appraise the value of any method for detecting suicidal potentialities, however, we must keep in mind that suicide is a multifaceted term, involving different kinds of personalities, with differing motivations and experiences.[10,11,39,41,50] It includes different kinds of behavioral acts, suicidal gestures, threats, attempts, suicidal "equivalents" such as drug and alcohol addiction, and actual suicides.[12,34,46,51] The multidimensional nature of the term is reflected in the many theories of suicide which have been proposed.

Thus theorists explain some suicides in terms of intentional acts, logically thought out to relieve intractable pain, for example, or to advance a cause.[9,34,47]

Again many psychiatrists and psychologists base self-destruction on individual maladjustment or psychopathology, emphasizing depression, aggression turned against self, accumulated self-contempt, guilt, loss of identity, feelings of being worthless and abandoned, helplessness, hopelessness, disillusionment, disappointment, and a host of other factors.[1,8,12,17,19,32,47]

Again suicide is explained in terms of unfortunate experiences in early life, as deprivation of love or rejection, or the loss of a love object, or current difficulties and intolerable life situations as family disorganization, loss of health, home, money, status, or prestige.[8,27,47,51,52]

Other authorities, sociologically oriented, view suicide as the response to frustrations and difficulties which are socially and culturally determined. Thus "anomie" or "normlessness" is seen as the common basis of all suicidal behaviors, a social and psychic state which arises from social disorganization, from conflicts and ambiguity in one's position in society, or from frustrations because of lack of opportunity to achieve cultural goals valued by the social group in a society where the social structure fails to provide the means for achieving them.[9,18,20,21,33,37]

Finally, other workers view suicide as communication to others, the "cry for help" in order to effect changes in the life situation.[39,42,48,56]

It is obvious, then, that behind the diverse manifestations of suicidal behavior there is a multiplicity of factors involved in pushing an individual toward self-destruction. These vary in nature, strength, and significance from one person to another.

Thus any tools which are utilized to understand the personality of the suicidal person must yield information on drives, dynamic constellations, ego strength and ego defects, and on the impact of environmental pressures on the individual. More important, they must be interpreted in conjunction with the social and cultural context, the sequence of experiences that lead up to a particular kind of behavior, and the precipitating factors which incite it at one particular time.

Many clinicians believe the Rorschach is such a tool since it penetrates deep into the personality, reveals underlying motivations, anxieties, defensive operations and adjustive resources, and captures the more elusive factors with respect to the range and interplay of personality characteristics and dynamics and the social environment.

RORSCHACH HYPOTHESES

As a result of clinical experience, Rorschach workers have identified specific responses, patterns, and themes which appear characteristic of individuals with suicidal proclivities.

Lindner[29] for example singled out Card IV as the "suicide card," viewing dysphoric responses such as "decaying tooth" or "rotted tree trunk" as keys to depressive states with suicidal overtones. For Phillips and Smith,[35] Shock in Card I may reflect hostility which may be acted out directly through assault, stealing, or suicidal threats.

Other authorities study the ratio of color to shading responses to determine suicidal trends. For Klopfer,[25] the preponderance of chromatic over achromatic responses suggests acting out tendencies which may take the form of non-destructive behavior or suicidal, homicidal, or antisocial behavior, depending on the content, the balancing effect of human movement, and the stability of the form level. According to Piotrowski,[36] the preponderance of dark shading over color reflects the existence of acting out tendencies which may push the individual to self-destruction. Similarly other workers emphasize shading patterns in certain contexts, although in some suicidal pictures, few dysphoric responses and shading anxiety indicators appear.[3,7,38]

Other patterns considered crucial in the determination of suicidal tendencies include:

hostile M and M projected into animals,[36]
space responses with an Introversive *Erlebnistypus,* dysphoric content, and lack of control,[26]
space responses with M, reflecting "inhibited aggression" or constricted *Erlebnistypus* with high %F+ reflecting "repressed aggression,"[6]
patterns reflecting an "insufficient ego" and "bound" and "free" anxiety,[4]
imbalance between %F, movement, and color and shading scores, Fm and mF greater than M and FM, many texture, crude C,[55]
color and shading shock,[23,38]
behavior and attitudes reflecting self-depreciation, impotence, agitation, depression,[4,5,35,45]

terminal statements reflecting hopelessness, impotence, and resignation.[5,35,45]

Rorschach workers likewise find important clues to suicidal ideation and affect in the content of Rorschach responses, certain themes of death, depression, mutilation, aging, destruction, passivity, change, emptiness, dependency, and the like being associated with self-destructive thought content.[22,55]

In addition, other themes, while not specifically associated with suicidal ideation, frequently suggest certain personality dynamics and preoccupations of the suicide-prone individual. The number and quality of the human forms, for example, reveal much about identity problems.[14,28,45] Similarly, the number and kind of anatomy themes, especially with dysphoric elaborations, permit clues as to body preoccupation, hypochondriacal brooding, and the degree to which destructive impulses will be acted out.[26,35]

Again, themes centering on sadism-masochism, weakness, subjugation, negative identity, aging and death, suggested by Schafer,[45] and themes of religion and morality, depersonalization, oral reunion, rebirth and destruction, discussed by Beck,[5] all may give leads to suicidal ideation. Finally, responses which emphasize barriers and penetration, analyzed by Fisher and his colleagues,[14-16] may give clues not only to negative feelings toward the body but to salient personality characteristics and styles of behavior of the potential suicide.

CURRENT RESEARCH

A few case studies of suicide-prone individuals and of actual suicides have been reported.[3,5,24,38,53] They serve to illustrate how the Rorschach can identify dominant personality trends, underlying motives, basic conflicts, and modes of solution. More important, they give clues as to how Rorschach clinicians integrate and weigh Rorschach data.

Empirical studies utilizing the Rorschach to detect suicide-proneness are also few in number. For the most part, three approaches are utilized—the identification of specific patterns, the development of batteries of "signs," and the identification of Rorschach configurations which suggest suicidal proclivities.

ISOLATED PATTERNS AND SCORES

Color and shading patterns, considered singly and in combination, were analyzed by Hertz[23] in the records of 178 consecutive clinical cases, differentiated into suicidal and non-suicidal groups on the basis of evidence of suicidal ideas, attempts, threats, and actual suicides as reported in case histories. Significant differences were obtained between the groups in only a few of the patterns.

Reliably more suicidal than non-suicidal subjects gave low color scores, reflecting repression of emotional responsiveness to the environment, higher minus scores on the "Emotional Stability" formula,* which suggested that aggression was turned in upon self rather than directed against the world, and higher plus scores on the "General Anxiety" formula,† implying greater sensitivity to unpleasant moods and more severe self-evaluation.

Fisher[13] was even less successful in obtaining differences in the individual Rorschach factors when he compared records of 20 paranoid suicidal schizophrenics who had attempted suicide with 20 non-suicidal paranoid schizophrenics, as evaluated by three judges. No differences were obtained with the shading categories, with self-destructive and self-depreciatory content, and with C and CF.

Sakheim[43] compared the protocols of 40 suicidal hospitalized psychiatric patients who had attempted suicide with a matched group of non-suicidal patients for diagnostic scores, signs, and specific content advanced in the literature as indicators of suicide. Of 27 variables, only two, Dark Shock in Card IV and the number of responses in which animals behaved like humans, significantly differentiated his groups. Numerous dark color responses showed a tendency toward statistical significance.

Recently Appelbaum and Holzman[2] identified a specific score, the color-shading determinant, which they report reflects suicidal tendencies in hospitalized psychiatric patients compared with non-suicidal patients. This score combines color and shading in one determinant, as for example, the response "bluish crocheted material" to the blue area in Card VIII. The authors hypothesize that this score reflects "a sensitivity to nuances of feeling." In psychiatric patients, it may point to attempts to penetrate "beyond the obvious," a tendency which may lead to a loss of perspective in reference to certain relationships to their life situations. No cross-validation studies are included.

Taking a different approach, Sapolsky[44] analyzed Rorschach responses to a specific area, the lower center part of Card VII, commonly viewed as the "mother card." This area is frequently seen as a vaginal area. He set out to test the psychoanalytic hypothesis that suicide can represent an unconscious wish to return to the maternal womb or to be reborn. Comparing 20 patients with functional psychiatric disorders who responded to this area ("responders") with 20 control schizophrenic patients, matched for sex, age, and diagnosis, who did not respond ("non-responders"), he found statistically more responders than non-responders evidenced suicidal thinking.

*[FC - (CF+C)] wt.

†[FSh - (ShF+Sh)] wt., Sh referring to shading in general, including all varieties of shading.

RORSCHACH "SIGNS"

A few studies employ the "sign approach," grouping certain patterns into clusters and identifying those reliably associated with the records of suicide-prone persons. The presence or absence of these indicators permits inference as to suicidal tendencies in an individual. Attempts have been made to develop predictive scales with these signs.

Martin's[30] checklist of 17 signs* based on a comparison of records of suicidal psychiatric patients and those of non-suicidal patients have been applied by Daston and Sakheim[7] to the records of three groups, those who committed suicide, those who attempted suicide, and controls, 36 in each group, all hospitalized patients with functional psychiatric disorders. The suicide-prone patients could be differentiated from the non-suicidal. Six or more of the signs successfully identified 72 per cent of the attempted suicides and 83 per cent of the successful suicides, while only 17 per cent of the controls showed this many signs. The checklist could not, however, differentiate the successful suicides from those who had attempted suicide.

Weiner[54] also applied Martin's signs to the records of 71 adult psychiatric patients. He reported that the number of signs were relatively independent of age, sex, hospital status, and Rorschach response total of the subjects. In an additional study, he compared the records of 24 suicidal and 63 non-suicidal patients. The former received significantly more of the signs than the controls. The best cutting score for predictive use was the incidence of eight or more signs. This correctly classified 79 per cent of the suicide attempts and 60 per cent of the controls. Examining the signs individually, however, the investigator found that only two of the 17 reliably differentiated the suicidal from the non-suicidal group.

Many clinicians criticize the molecular approach which is involved in research with isolated scores, patterns, and signs. The most conspicuous limitation upon such score-oriented research is, of course, the omission of the qualitative features of the patterns, which influence them in differential ways. Some critics insist that scores must be evaluated in research as they are in clinical application, applied in a variety of ways, each of which must be considered in the research.

The sign approach may appear "objective" and may be attractive because scores may be obtained in a short time and with a minimum of effort. Signs have not, however, been carefully cross-validated in terms of different clinical groupings, nor have they been considered in terms of base rates with suicides in clinical populations.[31,40] As yet, single scores and batteries of signs do not have the status of practical or reliable predictors of suicidal potentialities.

---

*For the list of signs, reference should be made to the original work[30] or to Daston and Sakheim.[7, p. 357]

RORSCHACH CONFIGURATIONS

A few studies are reported utilizing the configurational approach, in which research units involve interpretation in the form of personality characteristics or dynamic behaviors. A series of characteristics associated with suicide-prone individuals are formulated and then translated into Rorschach correlates in terms of scores, sequence of scores, summarized score patterns, formulas, test behavior and attitudes, and content analysis, all integrated. The presence or absence of these configurations in a record permits inference as to suicidal tendencies in the individual. The entire record is scrutinized, and final determination as to whether or not a configuration is present depends upon the subjective estimate of the interpreter. As in clinical practice, he identifies his own clues, weighs them, and on the basis of their consistency, makes his final inference.

Hertz[22] described 14 such configurations, which, on the basis of clinical experience and reports in the literature, appeared to reflect tendencies suggestive of suicide. The records of groups of 229 clinic patients, 113 neurotic and 116 psychotic cases, and 96 normal subjects were analyzed for the presence of these configurations. Clinic cases were divided into suicidal and non-suicidal groups, suicidal status determined from case histories and psychiatric records where the presence of suicidal ideas, suicidal attempts and actual suicides were recorded. No selective principle operated in the choice of normal records, except there was no evidence or suicidal ideas.

Ten configurations reliably differentiated between suicidal and non-suicidal groups. These included *neurotic structure, depressed states, active conflict and deep inner struggle, deep anxiety* evaluated especially from reactions to shading elements in the blots, *constriction* seen as a symptomatic effect of anxiety and reflecting the immobilization of ego functions, *ideational symptomatology* referring to special kinds of content in the context of certain Rorschach patterns, *sudden and/or inappropriate emotional outbursts,* suggesting unexpected changes in mood and behavior, *withdrawal from the world, resignation trends,* and *agitation.* Reference must be made to the original study for a detailed description of the component items which comprise each configuration.[22,pp.3-21]

While 74 per cent of the suicidal groups showed six or more configurations, this was true of only 5 per cent of the non-suicidal and none of the normal subjects. Again, 94 per cent of the suicidal groups, 22 per cent of the non-suicidal, and 1 per cent of the normal subjects showed five or more configurations.

In a cross-validation study[23] already referred to, the records of 178 consecutive cases were identified as suicidal or non-suicidal on the basis of the presence of five or more configurations. Again the group was differentiated into suicidal and non-suicidal according to the criterion classification used in the previous study. Agreement between the Rorschach identification of suicidal trends and the clinical criterion occurred in 84 per cent of the cases. With this cutting score, 17 per cent of the suicidal cases and 15.7 per cent of the non-suicidal were misclassified. The results corroborated the significance of the configurations originally identified. They are all the more significant in this study because they were obtained from a sample of consecutive cases rather than from a preselected sample divided into suicidal and non-suicidal subjects as in other studies.

It was concluded that the Rorschach may be used to infer or predict suicidal tendencies when the configurational approach is used. Six or more of the ten configurations associated with suicidal behavior in a Rorschach record point to suicidal trends, and five or more are highly suggestive of proneness to suicide.

It should be stressed that since we now have evidence that there are considerable differences in personality dynamics between those who attempt, threaten, and complete suicide,[10,11,34,49,50] there is need to define and delimit more carefully suicidal groups which are studied. As Farberow[10] suggests, possibly the differences between our groups might have been sharpened, if the groups had been more strictly delimited.

Fisher,[13] failed to discriminate his 20 suicidal schizophrenics from 20 non-suicidal by the application of the Hertz "suicidal" configurations. While a greater proportion of the suicidal patients manifested six or more of the configurations, 25 per cent of the non-suicides likewise showed this number and 80 per cent showed five or more.

On the other hand, when Holzberg and his colleagues[24] applied our configurations to a specific case of an individual given a Rorschach three days before the act of self-destruction, eight of the ten "suicidal" configurations were identified in the record. Utilizing the configurational approach, we could have identified the patient as a suicidal risk, prior to his self-destruction.

More significant is the study by Sakheim[43] in which the records of his 40 suicidal patients were compared with those of his matched group of non-suicidal patients for the presence of the Hertz "suicidal" configurations as well as for the other 27 diagnostic signs considered indicative of suicide. In order to "objectify" our procedure and to have a "constant frame of reference," he credited a configuration with being present in a record when at least one-half of all the component items listed were present or when one-third of the factors comprising the most valid patterns associated with the configuration were present.[43,p.338]

Five configurations distinguished between the groups. Two others bordered on statistical significance. Five or more configurations were given by

87 per cent of the suicides and 27 per cent of the non-suicides. With this cutting point, however, 27 per cent of the non-suicides gave five or more configurations, and 12 per cent of the suicidal patients were missed. Six or more configurations were given by 60 per cent of the suicides and only 10 per cent of the controls.

Thus of the 37 variables investigated, besides two items referred to above, only the configurations differentiated reliably between the groups.

Sakheim's study supports the writer's view that only the configurational technique has some validity in the accurate diagnosis of proneness to suicide.

In similar fashion, White and Schreiber[55] describe their special clinical technique of interpretation for diagnosing suicidal risks. They report a study in which 105 out of 1250 Rorschach records were judged suicidal risks by their procedure of interpretation. Of the patients judged suicidal by the Rorschach, 77.2 per cent showed adequate evidence of suicide, as gleaned from their clinical histories.

Criticism has been directed at our configurational approach. We are told, for example, that many items are enumerated ambiguously in each configuration. We have not stipulated numerically what constitutes normal ranges. Relative weights have not been assigned to the items associated within each configuration. In addition, a large element of clinical intuitive "feel" is involved in applying the configurations to individual records.[13,43]

In the clinical application of the Rorschach, the question of quantity and weighting of the various factors involved in the determination of a personality trend has to be answered in terms of *each* record. This also holds in the application of the configurations to determine suicidal risks. It is obvious that available normative data must be utilized and applied appropriately for interpreting the quantitative scores. Further, they must be qualitatively evaluated in terms of the total record.

Similarly, each inference which is made on the relative weight of the items within a configuration depends on the study of all the items in their various interrelationships and in the context of the total picture. In some cases, a configuration may be considered present when a few of the items complement and reinforce each other and stand out in bold relief. In other cases, certain malignant indicators may be counterbalanced by more favorable patterns. Here many of the items subsumed under a configuration may be required before the configuration is credited as being present in a record. As yet, we have no basis for assigning weights to the items. The procedure utilized by Sakheim[43] in which he arbitrarily assigned cut-off points for the component items listed in a configuration is unwarranted until his criteria have been established through research.

In the last analysis, it is the clinician who must determine the relative quantity and weighting of the items associated within a configuration. This introduces a high degree of subjectivity, but the procedure closely resembles the way in which the Rorschach is usually applied in clinical practice.

There can be little doubt that research is needed to determine how we weight and give hierarchic position to the items within each configuration and to the configurations themselves. It would be more objective if we could develop a weighting system for the items within the configuration, perhaps develop a "suicide-proneness" scale based on the configurations. Indeed, this is needed for Rorschach interpretation in general. Future research must be directed toward specification and quantification of the subjective judgments and the clinical cues which combine to produce the inferences which we make when interpreting a record.

In the absence of such research, however, we must depend upon our clinical skills, and we must be guided by published case studies which demonstrate some of the processes which are involved in interpretation.

RORSCHACH INTERPRETATION AND LIFE CONTEXT

Finally it should be emphasized that the Rorschach per se does not and cannot predict specific suicidal behavior. Every clinician knows that there are many underlying personality traits which in combination may lead to a number of different outcomes, depending upon the situation to which the individual is exposed. Certain personality constellations may give rise to a host of problems which may take different forms—mental illness, suicide, delinquency, or crime, depending on a diversity of factors—constitutional predispositions, developmental difficulties, accidents of rearing, environmental demands and pressures, and the like. These variables interact and have different weightings in different personality combinations.

Thus while inferences may be made from Rorschach data as to the presence of dominant trends and how and to what extent they may help or hinder the individual in his adjustment, the specific form of behavior which these tendencies may take depends on multiple interrelated and interacting socio-cultural and situational factors.

In reference to prediction of suicide, we make tentative hypotheses. We say that the Rorschach indicates that there are certain personality trends and motivational patterns which in combination may lead to a certain outcome, self-destruction, depending upon the situation and the pressures to which the individual has been and is now exposed. Whether or not he will be impelled to suicide depends not only upon personality structure and dynamics, but also on his developmental history, his past experiences, and his current life situation.

Hence another direction which our research must take is to identify not only personality configurations which reflect suicidal proclivity, but also configurations conjoined with clusters of situational and socio-cultural factors which promote the development of these patterns or serve as precipitating circumstances in encouraging them.

In the absence of research, the clinician must keep in mind the complex problems of interacting variables. Once the question of suicidal potentialities is raised by the Rorschach, it is important to weigh Rorschach results against life context before making predictions as to probable suicidal behavior.

For example, information in the case history reflecting excessive demands of the environment, unfortunate life events such as losses in money, health, success, or occupational status, loss of a loved one, strained relationships with parents, or other severe interpersonal conflicts would heighten concern lest suicidal potential be translated into suicidal behavior. Again knowledge concerning the individual's life goals, his perspective on life, his hopes, his proneness to overestimate his difficulties or to underestimate his resources, would help predict more specifically the kind of overt behavior to be anticipated.

Thus additional information about the individual permits not only the identification of underlying personality constellations and the diagnosis of suicidal proclivity, but also the prediction of suicidal behavior.

SUMMARY

In summary, the Rorschach offers a systematic approach to the evaluation of suicidal risks.

The configurational technique appears to be useful toward achieving an insight into the individual's potentiality for suicidal behavior. The configurations which have been empirically derived, however, must be repeatedly cross-validated. More important, they must be sharpened and refined so that the bases for subjective judgments may be more explicitly described and so that the configurations may be related to more meaningful personality dimensions describing and predicting suicidal behavior. This appears to be our chief task.

Even now, the Rorschach, when interpreted by a skilled clinician, can provide information on the basic personality dynamics of the suicidal individual. Suicidal trends, though not manifest, may be disclosed. Suicidal threats, gestures, and attempts may be identified as genuine or false. "Suicidal crises" met in the course of psychotherapy can be evaluated as may be the "reactivation" which frequently appears when the patient is deemed to have improved. In addition, the Rorschach may be useful in furnishing leads for making clinical decisions regarding focus and procedure of treatment.

Finally, when the Rorschach is utilized in the clinical fashion here outlined, with emphasis on the interaction of psychic forces and external pressures, the method may help bridge the gap between those theories of suicide relating it to maladjustment and psychopathology and those which emphasize the influence of the social environment. The Rorschach may then contribute to the development of a theory of suicide where the psychological and sociological factors are combined and integrated within a single conceptual framework.

REFERENCES

1. Appelbaum, S. A. The problem solving aspect of suicide. *J. proj. Tech.* 1963, 27, 259-269.
2. ———, and Holzman, P. S. The color shading response and suicide. *J. proj. Tech.*, 1962, 26, 155-162.
3. Beck, S. J. *Rorschach's test. II. A variety of personality pictures.* New York: Grune and Stratton, 1945.
4. ———. *Rorschach's test. III. Advances in interpretation.* New York: Grune and Stratton, 1952.
5. ———. *The Rorschach experiment. Ventures in blind diagnosis.* New York: Grune and Stratton, 1960.
6. Bohm, E. A. *A textbook in Rorschach test diagnosis.* trans. Anne G. Beck and S. J. Beck, New York: Grune and Stratton, 1958.
7. Daston, P. G., and Sakheim, G. A. Prediction of successful suicide from the Rorschach test, using a sign approach. *J. proj. Tech.*, 1960, 24, 355-361.
8. Dublin, L. I. *Suicide: a sociological and statistical study.* New York: Ronald Press Co., 1963.
9. Durkheim, E. *Suicide.* trans. J. A. Spaulding and G. Simpson, Glencoe: The Free Press, 1951.
10. Farberow, N. L. Personality patterns of suicidal mental hospital patients. *Genet. Psychol. Monogr.*, 1950, 42, 3-79.
11. ———, and Shneidman, E. S. Attempted, threatened, and completed suicide. *J. abnorm. soc. Psychol.*, 1955, 50, 230.
12. ———, and ——— (Eds.) *The cry for help.* New York: McGraw-Hill, 1961.
13. Fisher, S. The value of the Rorschach for detecting suicidal trends. *J. proj. Tech.*, 1951, 15, 250-254.
14. ———. Relationship of Rorschach human percepts to projective descriptions with self reference. *J. proj. Tech.*, 1962, 26, 231-233.
15. ———. Further appraisal of the body boundary concept. *J. consult. Psychol.*, 1963, 27, 62-74.
16. ———, and Cleveland, S. E. *Body image and personality.* Princeton: Van Nostrand, 1958.
17. Freud, S. *Mourning and melancholia.* London: Hogarth Press, Ltd., 1925.
18. Gold, M. Suicide, homicide, and the socialization of aggression. *Amer. J. Sociol.*, 1958, 63, 651-661.
19. Hendin, H. Psychodynamic motivational factors in suicide. *Psychiat. Quart.*, 1951, 25, 672-678.
20. Henry, A. F., and Short, J. F., Jr. *Suicide and homicide: some economic, sociological and psychological aspects of aggression.* Glencoe: The Free Press, 1951.

21. ——, and ——. The sociology of suicide. In E. S. Shneidman and N. L. Farberow (Eds.) *Clues to suicide.* New York: McGraw-Hill, 1957.
22. Hertz, Marguerite R. Suicidal configurations in Rorschach records. *Rorschach Res. Exch.,* 1948, *1,* 3-58.
23. ——. Further study of "suicidal" configurations. *Rorschach Res. Exch.,* 1949, *13,* 44-73.
24. Holzberg, J. D., Cahen, Eleanor R., and Wilk, E. K. Suicide, a psychological study of self destruction. *J. proj. Tech.,* 1951, *15,* 339-359.
25. Klopfer, B. *Rorschach technique.* New York: World Book Company, 1956.
26. ——, Ainsworth, Mary D., Klopfer, W. G., and Holt, R. E. *Developments in the Rorschach technique.* New York: World Book Company, 1954.
27. Kobler, A., and Stotland, E. *The end of hope: a social-clinical study of suicide.* New York: Free Press of Glencoe, 1963.
28. La Fon, F. E. Behavior on the Rorschach test as a measure of self acceptance. *Psychol. Monogr.,* 1954, *68,* (No. 10) Whole no. 381, 1-14.
29. Lindner, R. M. The content analysis of the Rorschach protocol. In L. E. Abt and L. Bellak (Eds.) *Projective psychology.* New York: Knopf, 1950.
30. Martin, H. A. A Rorschach study of suicide. Unpublished doctoral dissertation, Univ. Kentucky, 1952.
31. Meehl, P. E., and Rosen, A. Antecedent probability and the efficiency of psychometric signs, patterns, or cutting scores. *Psychol. Bull.,* 1955, *52,* 194-216.
32. Menninger, K. *Man against himself.* New York: Harcourt, Brace, and Company, 1938.
33. Merton, R. K. Social structure and anomie. In L. Wilson and W. Kolb (Eds.) *Sociological analysis.* New York: Harcourt Brace and Co., 1949.
34. Neuringer, C. Methodological problems in suicide research. *J. consult. Psychol.,* 1962, *26,* 273-278.
35. Phillips, L., and Smith, J. G. *Rorschach interpretation: advanced techniques.* New York: Grune and Stratton, 1953.
36. Piotrowski, Z. *Perceptanalysis.* New York: The Macmillan Company, 1957.
37. Powell, E. H. Occupation, status, and suicide: toward a redefinition of anomie. *Amer. sociol. Rev.,* 1958, *2,* 123.
38. Rabin, A. I. Homicide and attempted suicide: a Rorschach study. *Amer. J. Orthopsych.,* 1946, *16,* 516-524.
39. Robins, E., Gassner, S., Kayes, J., Wilkinson, R. H., and Murphy, G. E. The communication of suicidal intent: a study of 134 consecutive cases of successful (completed) suicides. *Amer. J. Psychiat.,* 1959, *115,* 724-733.
40. Rosen, A. Detection of suicidal patients: an example of some limitations in the prediction of infrequent events. *J. consult. Psychol.,* 1954, *18,* 397-403.
41. Rosen, S., Halles, U.M., and Simon, W. Classification of "suicidal" patients. *J. consult. Psychol.,* 1954, *18,* 359-362.
42. Rubenstein, R., Moses, R., and Lidz, T. On attempted suicide. *AMA Arch. Psychiat.,* 1958, *79,* 103-112.
43. Sakheim, G. A. Suicidal responses on the Rorschach test: a validation study. *J. nerv. ment. Dis.,* 1955, *122,* 332-344.
44. Sapolsky, A. An indicator of suicidal ideation on the Rorschach test. *J. proj. Tech.,* 1963, *27,* 332-336.
45. Schafer, R. *Psychoanalytic interpretation in Rorschach testing theory and application.* New York: Grune and Stratton, 1954.

46. Schechter, M. D. The recognition and treatment of suicide in children. In E. S. Shneidman and N. L. Farberow (Eds.) *Clues to suicide.* New York: McGraw-Hill. 1957.
47. Shneidman, E. S., and Farberow, N. L. (Eds.) *Clues to suicide.* New York: McGraw-Hill, 1957.
48. ———, and ———. *The cry for help.* New York: McGraw-Hill Book Co., 1961.
49. Stengel, E. Recent research into suicide and attempted suicide. *Amer. J. Psychiat.,* 1962, *118,* 725-727.
50. ———, and Cook, Nancy G. *Attempted suicide: its social significance and effects.* London: Chapman and Hall, 1958.
51. Toolan, J. M. Suicide and suicidal attempts in children and adolescents. *Amer. J. Psychiat.,* 1962, *118,* 719-724.
52. Tuckman, J., and Connon, Helene. Attempted suicide in adolescents. *Amer. J. Psychiat.,* 1962, *119,* 228-232.
53. Ulett, G. A., Martin, D. W., and McBride, J. R. The Rorschach findings in a case of suicide. *Amer. J. Orthopsychiat.,* 1950, *20,* 817-822.
54. Weiner, I. B. Cross validation of a Rorschach check-list associated with suicidal tendencies. *J. consult. Psychol.,* 1961, *25,* 312-315.
55. White, M. A., and Schreiber, H. Diagnosing suicidal risks on the Rorschach. *Psychiat. Quart. Suppl.,* 1952, *26,* 161-189.
56. Yessler, P. G., Gibbs, J. J., and Becker, H. A. On the communication of suicidal ideas: I. Some sociological and behavioral considerations. *Arch. gen. Psychiat.,* 1960, *3,* 612-631.

26. Predicting Acting Out by Means of the Thematic Apperception Test

By ZYGMUNT A. PIOTROWSKI, PH.D.

As the instrument of choice for the rich investigation of the interpersonal field and the patient's interpersonal operations in that field, the Thematic Apperception Test has long been regarded as an important addition to psycho-diagnostic test batteries. Readers are especially fortunate in having the counsel of Dr. Z. A. Piotrowski, in the chapter that follows, when they think of the special problems of estimating the likelihood of acting out manifestations of their patients, and in turning to the T.A.T. for help in the process of making such a study.

In a systematic and thorough review of the entire body of pertinent literature, Piotrowski raises the crucial issues that are involved in going from what a clinical psychologist sees in his T.A.T. protocols to a consideration of the patient's likely behavior and more general problems in the interpersonal field.

There is little doubt that the skilled and experienced judgment of Piotrowski, especially in relation to the test under examination, will have the merit of extending the usefulness of the procedure in the ascertainment of acting out potential.

PUBLISHED EVIDENCE rather overwhelmingly contradicts the possibility of reliably and validly predicting an individual's specific manifest behavior on the basis of his TAT responses.[30,39,58] Some psychologists, however, manage to predict rather well certain types of manifest behavior under certain circumstances.[22,79] The determining factors in making satisfactory predictions seem to be the manner of interpreting the TAT raw data and the psychologist's ability to apply sound knowledge of human personality and social relations to the test data. In this brief survey it is impossible to record all TAT studies in the field. We have a perceptive and penetrating report and evaluation in Murstein's book[58] and pertinent comments and selected reviews in the book edited by Kagan & Lesser.[30]

Since the greatest asset of the TAT, as of other projective personality tests, is to reveal the subject's inner self, one might ask why try to predict overt behavior. For one thing, there is our belief that inner attitudes are somehow related to overt behavior.[23] We hope that the TAT may alert us to behavior of which we have no knowledge, or may help in deciding whether or not an individual is likely to perform desirable actions or to refrain from repeating an undesirable action. Finally, we feel better whenever we predict overt behavior because we view such predictions as more trenchant tests of the TAT's validity than inferences regarding only inner attitudes.

Observations made during prolonged psychotherapy support the conclusion that, when well handled, the TAT can provide a good personality inventory of inner attitudes or potential behavior. Changes in the TAT parallel changes which occurred during psychotherapy.[51,47,86,75,18,23] Murstein's[58] review of the literature supports the use of the TAT as a measuring aid of the effects of psychotherapy.

Predictions of overt behavior have been attempted for a great variety of actions: interhuman relations, gratification of bodily needs, solving of arithmetical problems, predicting suicide, etc. The results have been contradictory. The contradictions are greatly reduced if one limits the function of the TAT. As in other projective tests, the TAT's main, if not exclusive function, is to throw light on the role the subject plays in interhuman relations important to him.[67] When predictions were limited to this psychosocial role and the changes occurring in it, they tended to be statistically significant in both normal and experimental situations.

Bellak[5] went out of his way to irritate his subjects by criticizing them unfairly and harshly. The hostility he caused was evident in the post-irritation repeat TAT. Poorly adjusted individuals displayed more hostility in such an experiment than the better adjusted ones.[72,9] Feshbach[15] conducted a similar study, also using a control group. The insulted group projected significantly more aggression in the second TAT than did the control group. Hokanson & Gordon[25] confirmed the ease with which subjects can be disturbed deliberately and show it in their TATs. (See also Hammer & Piotrowski).[20]

Milam[48] behaved toward one group in a positive, toward another in a neutral, and toward a third in a negative way. Again his results confirmed that the stressful irritation manifests itself by an increase in aggressive or hostile themes.

On the other hand, the number of aggressive themes in the test is not related to overt physical aggression in disturbed boys, aged 9 to 14, at a summer camp.[49] The TAT reflects the habitual role in interhuman social relations much more directly and validly than it does overt bodily behavior.

Stone[82] obtained significant correlations between TAT fantasied aggression and overt behavior in the case of army prisoners whose aggression was a matter of public record.

Eron's[13] hospitalized mental patients produced stories which were emotionally flat and unimaginative, regardless of psychiatric diagnosis. His non-hospitalized patients gave more happy as well as sad TAT stories. The marked differences in the patients' overt social relations reflected the TAT differences.

As clinicians well know, the TAT is successful in revealing the subject's attitude toward his parents. Relations with parents are the earliest, longest, and least variable social attitudes. Little has been published on this specific and successful application of the TAT.[22,23]

Predictions of fatal suicide have never been better than chance.[78] One might describe suicide as a breaking off of all social relations. McEvoy[45] compared 61 suicidal cases with 50 non-suicidal ones. The TAT failed to demonstrate significant differences, including the frequencies of suicidal or dysphoric themes.

A number of studies[73,74] indicated that under certain conditions there was some positive association between the degree of hunger and the amount of hunger-related TAT themes. In the experiment with the longest time of food reduction, however, the TAT-like Rosenzweig Frustration test failed to reflect the increasing and conspicuous preoccupation with food. In this experiment, volunteers, who were conscientious objectors, stayed on a diet of 1500 calories a day for about 24 weeks. They became a close-knit group with a strong esprit-de-corps; some of these young men did not even want to see the girl friends who visited them. The experiment did not increase social pressures; on the contrary, it lightened them. The subjects knew they would not be allowed to die or risk illness. Thus the uncomfortable aspect of the experiment, the reduction of food intake, was an intraindividual matter which did not at all unfavorably influence their social relations.

Sanford[73] found that children in a group produced more names of foods, names of meals, and verbs meaning "to eat," before eating than after eating. Since the meals had been a regular procedure, the children may have been looking forward to the excitement accompanying the group meals. In a later study[74] college students behaved similarly. The number of their food responses, given after hours of deprivation, was slightly greater than at the end of the normal eating cycle. Hungry psychology students mentioned less food in their group TAT than did non-hungry students on high relevance cards, but mentioned more food on cards of low relevance for food.[12] In a subsequent experiment Epstein et al.[11] failed to obtain the same results when somewhat different cards were used. Atkinson and McClelland[37] found no increase in food imagery when deprivation of food increased from one, to four, and to 16 hours.

The results are similarly ambiguous with sleep deprivation. E. J. Murray[54] kept soldiers awake for 96 hours; Nelson[62] for 16 to 40 hours. Both of these studies showed a significantly inverse relation between deprivation of sleep and sleep imagery. It is possible that sleep, being primarily an intraindividual physical need, would not affect that TAT which, like other projective tests, is not sensitive to bodily needs not involving others.

Experiments with frustration and the achievement motive were varied in results, according to the involvement of the subject in the experiment and the significance which the testing had for the subject's social relations, overt or covert. When the task which served as the independent criterion was presented as an important measure of ability, the TAT scores of the achievement need were associated positively with achievement on the task.[2,44,53] Children, eight to ten years old, with high TAT achievement imagery were rated by their teachers as being more strongly motivated than others, more independent, and taking greater pleasure in success.

Many diverse investigations have been made to test the achievement motive theory of McClelland and its modification by Atkinson. They are well covered by Atkinson[2] and Murstein.[58] The findings are complex and rather inconsistent, hardly ever impressively positive.[43,88,50] When the competitive spirit was aroused and the subjects became aware of their standing within their group, the correlation between the TAT content and external independent criteria increased. The creativity of outstanding physicists and biochemists was not reflected in their TAT[88]; but what fascinates physicists is inanimate matter and abstract theoretical formulas, not interhuman relationships, and thus the TAT failed to reflect their special interests. Young social scientists, on the other hand, who are intensely interested in emotional relationships produced imaginative TATs.

How seriously does the subject take the action-tendencies revealed by the TAT? If lightly, predictions of their manifest appearance in behavior are likely to be more difficult than when he takes them earnestly. Superficial drives are more easily deflected and suppressed than deep-seated ones. Moreover, superficial action-tendencies can sometimes be gratified in fantasy, which is not so in the case of the earthy and stronger drives. When subjects were angry while viewing a fight film, the number of aggressive word associations decreased by comparison with testing after witnessing a non-aggressive and non-violent film.[16] The anger was mild in this experiment: it was assuaged by looking at a violent film, and it was aroused (when absent) by a violent film for a short period. When the subjects were not angry while viewing the fight film, the number of their aggressive words increased afterwards. The rise in the association was far more striking than the decrement.

That in many of the tests of the achievement motive, it was the independent criterion which was faulty and not the TAT is suggested by the significant correlation between TAT achievement scores obtained in childhood and ratings for actual achievement realized in adulthood.[52]

The TAT responses are, in part, a function of the willingness of the subject to disclose information about himself. Murstein[57] demonstrated this in relation to hostility, Wallace and Sechrest[91] for hostility and somatic complaints, and Clark[7] for sex content. Murray's point[55] that socially accepted drives have a better chance to appear in records of normal subjects than do drives of which society disapproves has been confirmed. Subjects can deliberately control themselves and manipulate TAT responses to a higher degree than responses to inkblots.

Responses measuring attitudes toward father and mother, especially to cards 6BM and 7BM, seem to be relatively least censored. Shatin[77] found a significant association, $p < .04$, between a Rorschach Adjustment Index and "parental figures, benign and nurturant". He also found that the absence of benign parental figures in TAT protocols indicated maladjustment. Interaction in the TAT, even if negative and disappointing is more healthy than absence of interaction between parents and children in the TAT. Interaction with benign parental figures was associated with emotional stability.

Some drives may cause so much anxiety that they will not be reflected in the test at all.[64] Henry[23] calls it "negative evidence."[57] Sometimes, the absence of a particular content may be a sign of intense conflict.[2] It is also true that a drive is expressed in a TAT story only when it is not satisfied in reality. The TAT cards, on the whole, suggest more unhappiness and distress than happiness and calm. Therefore, absence of a particular drive, where it would be expected according to statistical norms, indicates avoidance of that drive (likely to be aggressive or sexual) and may mean "much with guilt" or "little with no guilt." To feel that one has society's approval reduces guilt even when one destroys life. Service men, policemen, etc., may behave destructively without being illegal or feeling guilty. Prediction of overt behavior in these special cases presents particular difficulties.[19] This applies also to some children. Mother's attitudes have a great influence upon their children's TAT.[23] Lesser[34] demonstrated a significantly positive correlation between TAT aggression and overt aggressive acts of children when their mothers approved of overt signs of anxiety. By contrast, children of mothers who disapproved of overt manifestations of anxiety showed a significant negative correlation between TAT aggression and overt aggression. In army prisoners, including some murderers, who had long histories of aggression,[70] TAT fantasy was not a substitute for direct action but was correlated with overt behavior. These men could not hide their past and apparently did not try to do it. Their social code, that of the lower socio-economic class, does not disapprove of aggression as much as does the code of the middle class.[23]

The different effects of varying test instructions upon the TAT content prove how sensitive the test is and how complicated is the problem of predicting overt behavior. Certainly, the administration of the test is of great importance, a point stressed by Henry.[23] Subjects can adapt to the demands of the examiner with apparent ease.[16,61,83]

Sex differences also must be kept in mind in making predictions of overt behavior. Men surpass women in TAT admission of aggression and sex interest; women admit more readily abasement and nurturance needs.[40] In summarizing results in this area, Murstein[58] indicated that most women show sharp increases in desire for personal achievement when the test situation changed from a relaxed one to one involving social acceptability, while men displayed no change; men projected more desire for achievement when incitements to leadership and intelligence were given, while the average woman was unmoved. Women told sadder stories than men, were verbally more productive, projected more into their stories, and were generally more involved in the testing than were the men.[58]

Symonds[84] tested his male subjects in adolescence and 13 years later. The TAT remained essentially the same when the subject had stayed at or near his home. Those who traveled and moved into different socioeconomic circles produced different TAT stories on reexamination. In general, depression and realistic perception of social interaction increased with age.

The TAT does not cover the same personality aspects in every examination of the same individual or in simultaneous examinations of different individuals. If one subject associates achievement and another hostility, it does not necessarily mean that the former is the more ambitious and the latter the more hostile of the two. It is possible that both are equally ambitious or hostile, but that the first is more ambitious than hostile and the second more hostile than ambitious, etc.[16]

Application of general psychological principles can help in making predictions. The appearance of weakness and fear in a subject makes unlikely the overt manifestation of any signs of hostility that may be perceptible in the TAT. The mutual strengthening and weakening of compatible and incompatible drives can be used with success.[22,23]

The ease with which the TAT responses vary for a multitude of reasons does not trouble clinicians because they are interested in the subject at the time they are examining him, and the knowledge of what is troubling him at the moment may be of greater importance than his personality structure. It does, however, complicate the problem of validating the test.

Henry[23] and Murstein[58] discussed the importance of specific TAT cards and the problem of high relevance versus low relevance of cards for the eliciting of various action-tendencies. Kenney and Bijou,[31] Epstein and Smith,[12] Jensen,[28] Murstein,[58] etc., all showed that the medium relevance cards, on the whole, work better than the high relevance cards. Thus, the specificity of the cards influences directly the process of making predictions. Paratroopers produced more fear stories when tested with the standard TAT cards before jumping than when tested with specially designed pictures of jumping.[14] Projection works best when it alleviates anxiety.[67] A highly relevant stimulus is likely to stimulate anxiety, thereby affecting the associations. Leiman and Epstein[33] found a positive relation between the number of TAT sex themes and actual sex outlet only with low relevance pictures; when the stimulus cards were highly relevant to sex, the group differences between high and low sexual outlet males disappeared.

The problem of relevance is related to the problem of ambiguity. Ambiguity should be defined not in terms of the objective physical aspects of the stimulus, but in terms of diversity of responses elicited by the stimulus from different viewers. The indeterminateness requirements of a TAT card do not basically differ from those of an inkblot.[67]

Murstein[59] experimented with four different types of stimulus cards. The set in which the figures were quite ambiguous as to sex and age, but in which the interaction between the figures was deliberately definite, elicited, by far, the highest correlation between the TAT conclusions and the psychotherapists' evaluations of subjects. The correlation of $+.70$ proved this set to be the most meaningful. Complete ambiguity of both figures and interaction turned out to be the poorest means of obtaining valuable personality data, the r between TAT conclusions and the independent criterion was only $+.17$. The increase in "pleasantness" of stories with increase in ambiguity or indeterminateness[57] agrees with the responses prompted by the most ambiguous stimulus, the blank card, which usually elicits pleasant stories, superficial wishes for a more comfortable and less distressing life.[23,27,64] The relatively high validity of action tendencies elicited by cards on which nearly all subjects identify the figures as plainly differing in age (and thus readily take them for parents and children) is an exception. Usually it is the ambiguous figures that evoke the more valid though indirect self-descriptions. The exception is not surprising considering the lasting influence of early child-parent relations.

Subjects can deliberately modify their responses without difficulty. Weisskopf and Dieppa[92] employed three different instructions: standard, asking the subjects to give the best possible impression of themselves on the test, and asking for stories which would put the subjects in a very bad light. Hospitalized neurotic males succeeded in changing their stories in the required directions significantly. The same results were obtained by Lubin[42] with standard, facilitating, and inhibitory instructions. Van Lennep and Houwink,[87] using the Four-Picture-Test, asked their male subjects to deliberately reinterpret the test from the standpoint of a woman. They did so easily. Transient moods can also cause a marked change.

Henry[23] reported highly successful "blind" TAT estimates of intelligence; the correlation coefficient between these estimates and objective test I.Q.s was .85. This result was obtained by "relying upon the examiner's own set of standards."

The sense of reality is much less challenged by the TAT than by inkblots, and this may be the reason why psychotics rarely reveal their dereistic thinking on the TAT, while manifesting it frequently on the Rorschach inkblots. Apparently, only when the examination session is unusually long, the schizophrenia becomes manifest.[1] Although Eron[13] was not able to find any differences among various diagnostic categories, he observed that a widespread deviation of a mild degree shown in many cards seemed to indicate a more serious psychopathology than a conspicuous deviation on only one or two cards. Eron reported perceptual distortions in all diagnostic categories, while Holt[26] and Wyatt[94] concluded that such distortions are hardly present in non-pathological cases. Using three formal diagnostic criteria: perceptual organization, perceptual range, and perceptual personalization, Dana[10] differentiated well groups of normals, psychotics, and psychoneurotics. The Little and Shneidman[41] extensive study of "blind" TAT analyses proved that neuropsychiatric diagnosis was the TAT's outstanding weakness.

Neurotics' TATs contained more hostility than those of equally hostile psychotics.[76] This result may be due to the psychotics' frequent desire to keep people at a safe distance. The neurotics' hostility is a much better organized drive aimed clearly at others. Paranoid schizophrenics, depressed patients among whom were schizophrenics, and the normals were significantly differentiated by a very simple measure, the initial reaction time. Both the difference between the longest and the shortest IRT and the ratio obtained by dividing the longest IRT by the shortest IRT differentiated these groups from one another.[17]

Once the main diagnosis has been determined, psychosis or neurosis, it is possible in many instances to specify the dominating mental mechanisms, obsessional, hysterical, anxious, phobic, etc. In general, this differentiation is based on the same clues as those used in clinical assays.[4,21,64,65] The psychopathology of the patient is frequently exaggerated in TAT conclusions, especially "blind" ones. The main reason seems to be the neglect of formal test aspects.[68]

Having evaluated "blind" analyses of the same TAT record by 17 psychologists, Henry A. Murray (in foreword to Shneidman, Joel, and Little[79]) exclaimed that "those who laughed at probabilities and stretched inference to the limit succeeded in seizing the fruits of truth," while those who limited themselves to descriptive statistics were "less triumphant." "Stretching inference" consisted of employing, in addition to whatever statistical information was available, psychopathological principles and of interpreting the test record in the light of these principles, the applicability of which is not limited to the TAT. Henry's[22,24] success is due to the same approach which cannot be learned by following textbook prescriptions. Selected aspects of the test, however, can be objectified and serve as a basis for a more systematic as well as valid analysis of the TAT for the purpose of predicting overt behavior. The rules which follow are tentative until adequately checked against dependable evidence, but they are more than hunches. They were described in greater detail and illustrated in two extensive case studies in *The Psychoanalytic Review*.[64,65]

Rule 1. The TAT seems to reflect, with greater freedom and lesser distortion, the subject's attitudes and activities than the actual individuals toward whom his activities and attitudes are mainly and habitually directed. Since people love their desires more than objects of their desires, they change the objects of their desires more readily than the desires themselves. One conclusion from this statement is that verbs appearing in the TAT can be treated at greater face value than the nouns.[69] (Piotrowski, 1964). Weissman's[93] second best single sign differentiating between overt physical aggressors and non-aggressors was the ratio of the number of verbs to the sum of verbs and nouns. It is easier to deflect an action than to suppress it. The displacement of the action from the person who was the original target toward one who is less likely to respond unpleasantly may suffice to alleviate anxiety.

Rule 2. Every TAT figure seems to reveal some aspect of the subject's personality. This rule removes the "hero," i.e., the need to search for the sole TAT figure with whom the subject presumably identifies. It is very difficult to find the "true hero." Murray et al.[56] and Lindzey[38] suggested methodological refinements to strengthen the hero concept, but the refinements succeeded only in retaining the word while logically eliminating the concept.[66] (Piotrowski, 1952 b). To avoid embarrassment or anxiety, the subject can project some of his action-tendencies on TAT figures which, by virtue of their sex, age, or other physical attributes, would be a more suitable person to carry out the action-tendencies. Infantile wishes can thus be ascribed to children and physical limitations to old people.

Rule 3. The greater the physical similarity between the subject and the TAT figure to which a drive is attributed, the more acceptable is the drive to the subject. It is assumed that the most acceptable drives are projected on figures of same sex, same age, etc., and that the most unacceptable drives are projected on figures physically most unlike the subject. The term unacceptable is used advisedly because the drives attributed to the other-sex and other-age figures may be conscious and cause only tension or guilt when they press for expression in overt behavior; they signify conflict. Acting overtly is a function of desires and inhibitions. Desires attributed to the other-sex and other-age figures are, as a rule, the more inhibited ones. Sometimes the other-sex or other-age figures are presented as attractive and desirable; they seem then to indicate what the subject would like to be.

Army men with controlled antisocial tendencies (they had no criminal records) ascribed hostility to TAT female figures rather than male figures.[70] Fearful soldiers, close to the site of an exploding atom bomb, expressed their fears more readily viewing pictures of women and children than pictures of soldiers.[90] There is a significant relation between the degree of displacement and inhibited overt behavior.[35,36] When subjects were asked to use the first person pronoun, they produced impoverished TAT stories with longer initial reaction times; when they used fictitious characters or the third person pronoun, the number of impoverished avoidance stories decreased.[80,81] When there were more than one figure in the card, the stories were richer, and even more rich when the figures differed in sex.[59]

The explanation for the failure of Negroes to produce more revealing stories on special Negro cards than on the standard TAT set of cards,[58] suggested by rule 3, would be that the special Negro cards only increase their feeling of being an underprivileged and alienated minority; the special cards probably were too challenging, and thus dampened imagination, while the standard cards helped to alleviate anxiety through the mechanism of displacement. The predictive success of that type of card in which the figures were indeterminate but the interaction between them definite[59] also supports the value of rule 3.

Rule 4. The degree of generalization of TAT conclusions affects their validity: the more specific they are, the easier it is to contradict them and the harder to confirm them, while the more general and restrained they are, the greater their chance of agreeing with independent criteria. The most general conclusions would be formulated in terms of attraction to others, repulsion for others, or indifference toward them. These attitudes could then be specified by suggesting the manner in which they are likely to be experienced by the subject inwardly and displayed outwardly, etc.

Henry[23] pointed out the necessity of qualifying predictions of work output and work quality. If someone seeks individually centered pursuits, the conditions of his work and the degree of freedom which he receives may be much more important for his occupational success than if he works only for money and the type of work is not important to him. It is crucial to predictions of overt behavior of the great majority of subjects to know the people with whom they live and work and other environmental and occupational details.

The judicious use of symbols can result in a higher percentage of correct predictions. Mention of suicide rarely signifies a desire to commit suicide, but nearly always implies loneliness and a fear of remaining lonely. Playing the violin can symbolize any pleasurable activity and frequently relates to genital activity. Food and eating symbolize dependency with a wish for greater support rather than actual food consumption. Sleeping indicates passivity in interhuman relations rather than a desire to rest; at any rate, "sleep," "food," etc., stand for psychological attitudes and hardly ever signify physical objects or actions. When a group of college men had been exposed to sexual stimulation, they produced significantly less manifest, but significantly more symbolic, sex responses in the post-arousal TAT than the controls.[7,8] The symbols reflected both the sexual interest and the conflict created by the experiment.

Rule 5. The TAT sometimes reveals superficial and stereotyped attitudes and fails to reflect genuine and important ones. Socially approved attitudes, rather than socially disapproved attitudes, expressed on the TAT are much more likely to be signs of real but insincere conformism. The socially disapproved attitudes frequently remain unrealized wishes or fears.

When a subject spontaneously puts himself into the story and announces it, he is most likely revealing an important action-tendency that he repeatedly manifests in overt behavior.[46,47] The blank card is also sometimes interpreted in the first person.[27] This card, the most indeterminate of all, however, usually elicits frank and pleasant but rather superficial wishes for greater comfort and security[64] (Piotrowski, 1950). Some psychotics respond with morbid and frustrating sadomasochistic stories to the blank card.

Rule 6. The TAT frequently seems to reflect what the subject feels and thinks about persons represented by the TAT figures, old, young, male, female, parent, child, etc. Rules 3 and 6 complement each other because the knowledge of others and the knowledge of ourselves are interdependent. A man producing hostile women would be said to repress his own hostility (rule 3) and would also be said to believe that women are hostile (rule 6). The more repressed an individual is, the more readily does he harbor preconceived and distorted ideas about people. Since no TAT record ever gives a survey of the whole personality, it is possible for the subject, through (unconscious) selection to raise the similarity between his unacceptable action-tendencies and the action-tendencies he ascribes to the TAT figures of opposite-sex and different-age.

In application of this rule, the implications of rule 4 should not be overlooked. A story in which the relationship between an elderly man and a young woman is described may be interpreted as reflecting various relationships, depending on the degree of generalization which is used in abstracting the TAT story. In the most general terms, the story may be taken as reflecting the testee's ideas about relationships between two people, regardless of their sex. At a less general level, the story illustrates the subject's ideas about relationships between man and woman. At a still more restricted level of generalization, the interpretation indicates the subject's ideas on the relationships between a parent and a child of the opposite sex. Next it may demonstrate his notions about the relationship between father and daughter. Finally, if the subject giving the story is a female, the story may reflect her relationship toward her father; and if the subject giving the story is a male, the story may be said to indicate his relationship toward a daughter or a younger sister.

Rule 7. It seems that the more varied and incompatible the action-tendencies are in a subject's TAT, the greater the possibility of poor personality integration, indecisiveness, and anxiety. Drives and counter-drives do not usually cancel one another but create a new action-tendency.

A sense of guilt associated with a particular action-tendency, anticipation of punishment or other forms of retaliation for acting out a particular drive, is an important sign that the individual is hesitant in overtly manifesting the drive. Anxiety, guilt, fear, and expectation of retaliation suggest that the action-tendency is at least slowed down and manifested in a limited degree of overt behavior. In the TAT record, it is frequently possible to separate the description or expression of a definite action tendency from references to guilt, anxiety, or inhibition associated with a possible overt manifestation of that action tendency. The separation of the two is very definitely helpful in predicting overt behavior.[2,23,29,51,60,65,86] An index combining expression of an action-tendency and expressions of anxiety, retaliatory punishment, or other inhibitory agents, predicted overt behavior better than action-tendency alone or inhibitory tendencies alone.[23,35,63,70,86] Levitt, Persky, and Brady[37] hypnotically induced anxiety and were able to demonstrate its effect physiologically and clinically as well as on the TAT.

Rule 8. It seems that the chances of a TAT action-tendency being manifested in overt behavior are correlated with the frequency of appearance of the action-tendency, its degree of originality and the emotional intensity accompanying the expression of the action-tendency, subject to the qualifications of the other rules.

The persistence of a drive in the TAT, especially when it is expressed in a variety of modifications, with reference to the past and particularly to the future, raises the probability that the drive is strong. The frequency principle was found useful for religious interest, achievement drive, hostility and somatic preoccupations, but the intensity of a response to a particular TAT card was, at times, a much more important guide than the frequency with which the response appeared in the entire record.[91] "Perceptual facilitation" was positively correlated with aggressiveness as well as with rating on a special hostility questionnaire.[32] A negative correlation was found between TAT achievement scores and anxiety questionnaire scores[71] and between personal achievement and TAT somatic complaints.[91] Statistically rare responses always contain important clues concerning the subject producing them and concerning his manner of motor behavior.

Rule 9. All rules proved valuable in the study of association disturbances should be applied: uneven pace of interpretation, differences in elaboration of stories elicited by different cards, disregarding obvious details, bizarre notions, etc.* The basic action-tendencies seem to reflect the lasting personality traits better than the imaginative elaborations of the basic action-tendencies.

Weissman[93] found the initial reaction time or the uneven pace of interpretation to be the most important single factor in predicting overt aggressive behavior; the type of behavior studied was uncontrolled and detrimental either to the individual or to society. All forms of disturbances in the flow of associations[85] are helpful in the analysis of test records even when applied to tests other than the TAT.

The nine rules are of major importance not only for predictions of overt behavior, but also as procedures of validating the TAT.

REFERENCES

1. Arnold, Magda B. *Emotion and personality.* 2 vols. New York: Columbia Univ. Press, 1960.
2. Atkinson, J. W. (Ed.) *Motives in fantasy, action, and society.* Princeton, N. J.: Van Nostrand, 1958.
3. ——— & McClelland, D. C. The projective expression of needs: the effect of different intensities of the hunger drive on thematic apperception. *J. exp. Psychol.,* 1948, *38,* 643-658.
4. Balken, Eva R., & Masserman, J. H. The language of fantasies of patients with conversion hysteria, anxiety state, and obsessive compulsive neuroses. *J. Psychol.,* 1940, *10,* 75-86.
5. Bellak, L. The concept of projection; an experimental investigation and study of the concept. Psychiatry, 1944, *7,* 353-370.
6. Brozek, J., Guetzkow, H., & Baldwin, Marcella V. A quantitative study of perception and association in experimental semistarvation. *J. Pers.,* 1951, *19,* 245-264.
7. Clark, R. A. The projective measurement of experimentally induced levels of sexual motivation. *J. exp. Psychol.,* 1952, *44,* 391-399.
8. ———. The effects of sexual motivation on fantasy. In D. C. McClelland (Ed.) *Studies in motivation.* New York: Appleton-Century-Crofts, 1955. Pp. 132-138.
9. Crandall, V. S. Induced frustration and punishment-reward expectancy in thematic apperception stories. *J. consult. Psychol.,* 1951, *15,* 400-404.
10. Dana, R. H. Objective TAT scores and personality characteristics: perceptual organization (PO). *Percept. mot. Skills,* 1960, *10,* 154.
11. Epstein, S., Nelson, Jane, Berger, M., & Leiman, A. Food-related thematic responses as a function of time without food, stimulus-relevance, and ego-

---

*Formal features referring to "how" one reports rather than "what" is reported often correlate with overt behavior because the manner of reporting *is the overt behavior.*

strength. In S. Epstein (Principal Investigator) *The influence of drive strength upon apperception.* Progress Report NIMH Grant M-1293, 1958, 4-7.
12. Epstein, S., & Smith, R. Thematic apperception as a measure of the hunger drive. *J. proj. tech.,* 1956, *20,* 372-384.
13. Eron, L. D. A normative study of the thematic apperception test. *Psychol. Monogr.,* 1950, *64,* No. 9, (whole No. 315).
14. Fenz, W. D., & Epstein, S. Measurement of approach-avoidance conflict by a stimulus dimension in a test of thematic apperception. *J. Pers.,* 1962, *30,* 613-632.
15. Feshbach, S. The drive reducing function of fantasy behavior. *J. abnorm. soc. Psychol.,* 1955, *50,* 3-11.
16. ———. The influence of drive arousal and conflict upon fantasy behavior. In J. Kagan & G. S. Lesser (Eds.) *Contemporary issues in thematic apperceptive methods.* Springfield, Ill., Charles C Thomas, 1961. Pp. 119-152.
17. Foulds, G. A method of scoring the thematic apperception test applied to psychoneurotics. *J. ment. sci.,* 1953, *99,* 235-246.
18. Fry, F. D. A normative study of the reactions manifested by college students and by state prison inmates in response to the MMPI, the Rosenzweig P-F study, and the TAT. *J. Psychol.,* 1952, *34,* 27-30.
19. Gundlach, R. Research with projective techniques. *J. proj. tech.,* 1957, *21,* 350-354.
20. Hammer, E. F. & Piotrowski, Z. A. Hostility as a factor in the clinician's personality as it affects his interpretation of projective drawings. *J. proj. tech.,* 1953, *17,* 210-215.
21. Hartman, A. A. An experimental examination of the thematic apperception technique in clinical diagnosis. *Psychol. Monogr.,* 1949, *63,* No. 8, 48.
22. Henry, W. E. The thematic apperception technique in the study of group and cultural problems. In H. H. Anderson & G. L. Anderson (Eds.) *Introduction to projective techniques.* New York: Prentice Hall, 1951. Pp. 230-278.
23. ———. *The analysis of fantasy: the thematic apperception technique in the study of personality.* New York: John Wiley & Sons, Inc., 1956.
24. ———. The thematic apperception test. In A. C. Carr (Ed.) *The prediction of overt behavior through the use of projective techniques.* Springfield, Ill.: Charles C Thomas, 1960. Pp. 18-29.
25. Hokanson, J. E., & Gordon, J. E. The expression and inhibition of hostility in imaginative and overt behavior. *J. abnorm. soc. Psychol.,* 1958, *57,* 327-333.
26. Holt, R. R. Formal aspects of the TAT—a neglected resource. *J. proj. tech.,* 1958, *22,* 163-172.
27. ———. The nature of TAT stories as cognitive products: a psychoanalytic approach. In J. Kagan & G. S. Lesser (Eds.) *Contemporary issues in thematic apperceptive methods.* Springfield, Ill.: Charles C Thomas, 1961.
28. Jensen, A. R. Aggression in fantasy and overt behavior. *Psychol. Monogr.,* 1957, *71,* No. 16.
29. Kagan, J. The measurement of overt aggression from fantasy. *J. abnorm. soc. Psychol.,* 1956, *52,* 390-393.
30. ——— & Lesser, G. *Contemporary issues in thematic apperceptive methods.* Springfield, Ill.: Charles C Thomas, 1961.
31. Kenny, D. T., & Bijou, S. W. Ambiguity of pictures and extent of personality factors in fantasy responses. *J. consult. Psychol.,* 1953, *17,* 283-288.

32. Kohn, H. Some personality variables associated with binocular rivalry. *Psychol. Record*, 1960, *10*, 9-13.
33. Leiman, A. H., & Epstein, S. Thematic sexual responses as related to sexual drive and guilt. *J. abnorm. soc. Psychol.*, 1961, *63*, 169-175.
34. Lesser, G. S. The relationship between overt and fantasy aggression as a function of maternal response to aggression. *J. abnorm. soc. Psychol.*, 1957, *55*, 218-221.
35. ———. Conflict analysis of fantasy aggression. *J. Pers.*, 1958, *26*, 29-41.
36. ———. Population differences in construct validity. *J. consult. Psychol.*, 1959, *23*, 60-65.
37. Levitt, E. E., Persky, H., & Brady, J. P. *Hypnotic induction of anxiety: a psychoendocrine investigation.* Springfield, Ill.: Charles C Thomas, 1964.
38. Lindzey, G. TAT: assumptions and related empirical evidence. *Psychol. Bull.*, 1952, *49*, 1-25.
39. ———. *Projective techniques and cross-cultural research.* New York: Appleton-Century-Crofts, 1961.
40. ——— & Goldberg, M. Motivational differences between male and female as measured by the TAT. *J. Pers.*, 1953, *22*, 101-117.
41. Little, K. B., & Shneidman, E. S. Congruencies among interpretations of psychological test and anamnestic data. *Psychol. Monogr.*, 1959, *75*, No. 6.
42. Lubin, B. Judgments of adjustment from TAT stories as a function of experimentally altered sets. *J. consult. Psychol.*, 1961, *25*, 249-252.
43. McClelland, D. C., Clark, R. A., Roby, T., & Atkinson, J. W. The projective expression of needs: the effect of the need for achievement on thematic apperception *J. exp. Psychol.*, 1949, *39*, 242-255.
44. ——— & Lieberman, A. M. The effect of need for achievement on recognition of need-related words. *J. Pers.*, 1949, *18*, 236-251.
45. McEvoy, T. L. A comparison of suicidal and non-suicidal patients by means of the Thematic Apperception Test. *Dissertation Abstracts*, 1963, *24*, 1248.
46. Masserman, J. H., & Balken, Eva R. The clinical application of the fantasy studies. *J. Psychol.*, 1938, *6*, 81-88.
47. ——— & ———. The psychoanalytic and psychiatric significance of fantasy. *Psychoanal. Rev.*, 1939, *26*, 343-379.
48. Milam, J. R. Examiner influences on TAT stories. *J. proj. tech.*, 1954, *18*, 221-226.
49. Miller, L. C. Relationships between fantasy aggression and behavioral aggression. Unpublished doctoral dissertation. Harvard Univ., 1953.
50. Mitchell, J. V. An analysis of the factorial dimensions of the achievement motivation construct. *J. educ. Psychol.*, 1961, *52*, 179-187.
51. Morgan, C. C., & Murray, H. A. A method for investigating fantasies: the thematic apperception test. *Arch. neurol. & psychiat.*, 1935, *34*, 289-306.
52. Moss, H. A., Kagan, J. Stability of achievement- and recognition-seeking behavior from early childhood through adulthood. *J. abnorm. soc. Psychol.*, 1961, *62*, 504-513.
53. Moulton, R. W. Notes for a projective measure of fear of failure. In J. W. Atkinson (Ed.) *Motives in fantasy, action, and society.* Princeton, N. J.: Van Nostrand, 1958, Pp. 563-571.
54. Murray, E. J. Conflict and repression during sleep deprivation. *J. abnorm. soc. Psychol.*, 1959, 95-101.

55. Murray, H. A. Uses of the thematic apperception test. *Amer. J. Psychiat.*, 1951, *107*, 577-581.
56. ——— et al. *Thematic apperception test manual.* Cambridge: Harvard Univ. Press, 1943.
57. Murstein, B. I. The role of the stimulus in the manifestation of fantasy. In J. Kagan & G. S. Lesser (Eds.) *Contemporary issues in thematic apperceptive methods.* Springfield, Ill.: Charles C Thomas, 1961.
58. ———. *Theory and research in projective techniques* (emphasizing the TAT). New York: John Wiley & Sons, Inc., 1963.
59. ———. The T.A.T.: fact and fantasy. *CASSP Conf. on projective techniques, Apr., 1964.* Sect. 2, Newington, Conn.: Conn. Offset & Rydingsward, 1964.
60. Mussen, P. H., & Naylor, H. K. The relationship between overt and fantasy aggression. *J. abn. soc. Psychol.*, 1954, *49*, 235-240.
61. ——— & Scodel, A. The effects of sexual stimulation under varying conditions on TAT sexual responsiveness. *J. consult. Psychol.*, 1955, *19*, 90.
62. Nelson, C. Thematic sleep responses as a function of time without sleep, stimulus-characteristics, goal availability, and set effects. In S. Epstein (Principal Investigator) *The influence of drive and conflict upon apperception.* Progress Report NIMH Grant M-1293, 1961. Pp. 8-9.
63. Petrauskas, F. A TAT and picture frustration study of naval offenders and non-offenders. In Magda B. Arnold *Emotion and personality.* 2 vol. New York: Columbia Univ. Press, 1960.
64. Piotrowski, Z. A. A new evaluation of the thematic apperception test. *Psychoanal. Rev.*, 1950, *37*, 101-127.
65. ———. The thematic apperception test of a schizophrenic interpreted according to new rules. *Psychoanal. Rev.*, 1952a, *39*, No. 3, 230-251.
66. ———. (TAT newsletter). *J. proj. tech.*, 1952b, *16*, 512-514.
67. ———. *Perceptanalysis.* Philadelphia: Ex Libris, 2nd print., 1965.
68. ———. The relative pessimism of psychologists. *Amer. J. Orthopsychiat.*, 1962, *32*, 382-387.
69. ———. Projective tests—theory and research. *CASSP Conf. on projective techniques,* Apr., 1964. Sect. 1. Newington, Conn.: Conn. Offset & Rydingsward, 1964.
70. Purcell, K. The TAT and antisocial behavior. *J. consult. Psychol.*, 1956, *20*, 449-456.
71. Raphelson, A. C. The relationships among imaginative, direct verbal, and physiological measures of anxiety in an achievement situation. *J. abnorm. soc. Psychol.*, 1957, *54*, 13-18.
72. Rodnick, E. H. & Klebanoff, S. Projective reactions to induced frustration as a measure of social adjustment. *Psychol. Bull.*, 1942, *39*, 489.
73. Sanford, R. N. The effects of abstinence from food upon the imaginal processes: a preliminary experiment. *J. Psychol.*, 1936, *2*, 129-136.
74. ———. The effects of abstinence from food upon the imaginal processes: a further experiment. *J. Psychol.*, 1937, *3*, 145-159.
75. Saxe, C. H. A quantitative comparison of psychodiagnostic formulations from the TAT and therapeutic contacts. *J. consult. Psychol.*, 1950, *14*, 116-127.
76. Scodel, A., & Lipetz, M. E. TAT hostility and psychopathology. *J. proj. tech.*, 1957, *21*, 161-165.
77. Shatin, L. Rorschach adjustment and the TAT. *J. proj. tech.*, 1953, *17*, 92-101.

78. Shneidman, E. S., & Farberow, N. L. Clues to suicide. In E. S. Shneidman & N. L. Farberow (Eds.) *Clues to suicide.* New York: McGraw-Hill, 1957. Pp. 3-10.
79. Shneidman, E. S., Joel, W., & Little, K. B. *Thematic test analysis.* New York: Grune & Stratton, 1951.
80. Solkoff, N. Effects of a variation in instructions and pictorial stimuli on responses to TAT-like cards. *J. proj. tech.,* 1959, *23,* 76-82.
81. ———. Effects of a variation in instruction on response to TAT cards. *J. proj. tech.,* 1960, *24,* 67-70.
82. Stone, H. The TAT aggressive content scale. *J. proj. tech.,* 1956, *20,* 445-452.
83. Sumerwell, Hariet C., Campbell, Mary M., & Sarason, I. C. The effect of differential motivation instructions on emotional tone and outcome of TAT stories. *J. consult. Psychol.,* 1958, *22,* 385-388.
84. Symonds, Percival M. *Adolescent fantasy.* New York: Columbia Univ. Press, 1949.
85. Tendler, A. D. Significant features of disturbance in free association. *J. Psychol.,* 1945, *20,* 65-89.
86. Tomkins, S. S. *The thematic apperception test.* New York: Grune & Stratton, 1947.
87. Van Lennep, D. J., & Houwink, R. H. Projection tests and overt behavior. *Acta Psychol.,* 1953, *9,* 240-253.
88. Veroff, J. Thematic apperception in a nationwide sample survey. In J. Kagan, and G. S. (Eds.) *Contemporary issues in thematic apperceptive methods.* Springfield, Ill.: Charles C Thomas, 1961. Pp. 83-118.
89. Veroff, J., Wilcox, Sue & Atkinson, J. W. The achievement motive in high school and college-age women. *J. abnorm, soc. Psychol.,* 1953, *48,* 108-119.
90. Walker, E. L., Atkinson, J. W., Veroff, J., Birney, R., Dember, W., & Moulton, R. The expression of fear-related motivation in thematic apperception as a function of proximity to an atomic explosion. In J. W. Atkinson *Motives in fantasy, action, and society.* Princeton, N. J.: Van Nostrand, 1958. Pp. 143-159.
91. Wallace, J. & Sechrest, L. Frequency hypothesis and content analysis of projective techniques. *J. consult. Psychol.,* 1963, *27,* 387-393.
92. Weisskopf, E. A. & Dieppa, J. J. Experimentally induced faking of TAT responses. *J. consult. Psychol.,* 1951, *15,* 469-474.
93. Weissman, S. L. Some indicators of acting out behavior from the thematic apperception test. *J. proj. tech.,* 29, 1964, 366-375.
94. Wyatt, F. A principle for the interpretation of fantasy. *J. proj. tech.,* 1958, *22,* 173-180.

27. Acting Out and Its Prediction by Projective Drawing Assessment

By EMANUEL F. HAMMER, PH.D.

In his consideration of the perceptual and graphomotor processes involved in projective drawing assessment, Dr. Emanuel F. Hammer takes the psychodiagnostic clinician on an interesting and rewarding journey that culminates in the latter's deeper appreciation of the many factors that enter into projective drawings. Hammer, who has a special sensitivity for and competence with the interpretation of graphomotor expressions, suggests the intriguing ways in which such projective procedures, with due caution on the part of the clinical psychologist, may make their significant contribution to the assessment of acting out likelihood.

There is little wonder, as one explores Hammer's approach and conclusion, that projective drawings continue to be an important component in the psychodiagnostic test battery that so many clinical psychologists use.

PROJECTIVE PSYCHOLOGY has, by now, established the concept that every act, expression, or response of an individual—his gestures, perceptions, selections, verbalizations, or motor acts— in some way bears the stamp of his personality.* In projective drawings, the subject's psychomotor activities are caught on paper. The line employed may be firm or timid, uncertain, hesitant or bold, or it may even consist of a savage digging at the paper. The difficulties of capturing and recording the transient qualities of overt movement are thus met by the innovation of graphomotor techniques.

Wolff[30] has made an interesting contribution to the area in his concept of the "rhythmic quotient," based upon careful measurements of drawings made by children, blind persons, epileptics, and even by a sample of African subjects. He has discovered that there are definite proportional ratios in the size of form elements which are characteristic of each individual, which do not vary much with his age, and which appear relatively early in life, thus demonstrating the reliability of expressive movement.

In assessing acting out potentials, the clinician may use any technique

---

*In fact, the pressing forward of facets of self-portraiture in art, the earliest form of "projective drawing," actually has been recognized for hundreds of years. Leonardo Da Vinci, the genius of so many spheres of activity, is credited with one of the early observations of this process of projection. The person who draws or paints, he recognized, "is inclined to lend to the figures he renders his own bodily experience, if he is not protected against this by long study."[18]

which taps personality via the psychomotor, as opposed to the verbal, modalities and has the distinct advantage of requiring less of an inferential leap in making predictions. Projective drawing, with its infinitely subtle language concerning body image and its motor tendencies, comes closer than do the Rorschach, TAT, and other verbal-expressive tools to *directly* sampling motility phenomena.*

Now, when a subject cooperates consciously and does not resist on a subconscious level, it is generally agreed by clinicians that the Rorschach usually provides a richer personality picture, but when the subject is evasive or guarded—as are those referred for assessment because of getting into acting out difficulties—projective drawings have been found to be the more revealing device.[21]

A particular individual's Rorschach may not yield nearly so much dynamic or structural material as does his projective drawing, or vice versa. The former condition, the writer has found, is more likely to occur in concrete-oriented, more primitive personalities, along with the occurrence of the Performance Scale I.Q. on the Wechsler-Bellevue exceeding the Verbal Scale I.Q. The latter condition, of the Rorschach (or TAT) protocol providing a richer yield than the projective drawings, occurs more frequently in verbal, "intellectual" subjects, with Wechsler-Bellevue Verbal Scale I.Q.'s exceeding Performance Scale I.Q.'s.[13]

The bulk of what the Rorschach yields of the subject's personality comes by way of a relatively indirect route. The subject's Rorschach percepts must, first, be translated into and, second, be communicated in, verbal language. In drawings, on the other hand, the subject expresses himself on a more primitive, concrete, motor level. In addition to the writer, Landisberg[20] has also found that patients exhibiting guardedness seem more likely to reveal their underlying traits and psychodynamics in the drawings. She states, "They are able to exercise more control over their verbal expression, seem to be more intellectually aware of what they might be exposing on the Rorschach. They tend to lose some of this control in their creative, motor expression (employed in drawings)."

An incident was related to the writer by a psychiatrist-colleague who had undergone a psychological examination in being screened for psychoanalytic training. Whereas he was able to withhold Rorschach responses and TAT themes, he felt might be damaging to his chances for admission to the psychoanalytic program, he was not able to manipulate his projective drawing production in a similar manner. While drawing the female

---

*Such motility phenomena include psychomotor tempo, flow of movements, smoothness, and integration versus jerkiness and irascible unpredictability of action, speed of response, naturalness of motion, impulsiveness, rate and intensity of expressive movements, dimensions of constriction versus expansiveness, and dimensions of withdrawal versus charging forward into the environment.

person, for example, he tried to place a smile on her face. But she turned out looking strict and forbidding. Attempting to present his relationships with females in as benign a light as possible, he proceeded to erase and redraw, but each new rendition only gave her face a more formidable and menacing expression than before. In spite of all his efforts, in the end she wore a stern expression. In his own words, "I just couldn't control the way she turned out."

Another case in point was that of an adolescent boy who was brought before a juvenile court on five charges of breaking, entering, and larceny and three charges of entering and larceny. Clinically, he appeared as a hostile, aggressive lad who, however, in his Rorschach and drawings attempted to give a benign impression. In the interview following the drawings, he offered the information that he had been "trying to draw a school boy, but the way it came out, it looks like a tough guy that hangs around the river."

These performances underscore the words of Machover[23, p.85]: "Stereotyped defenses are less easy to apply to graphomotor than to verbal projections."

The present writer's experience with inmates at Sing Sing Prison[12] further supports this view. Incarcerated subjects, for example, because of their basic mistrust and bitter resentment of authority figures in general, remain somewhat suspicious of all personnel employed at the institution, even after years of "public relations" effort on the part of the psychiatric and psychological staff. Loaded down with pervasive fear of revealing themselves to an authority figure even remotely associated with the prison setting, they manifest defensiveness, and the inmates dare not "see" anything off the beaten track. The number of their Rorschach responses, for example, tends to drop to a meager ten to 12, with the most frequent record consisting of one noncommittal response given to, and thus dismissing, each card. Their TAT themes assume a barren quality, remaining for the most part on a relatively superficial and descriptive level. Expressions become stereotyped, and the inmate sticks to the "safe" response. Attempts at conformity and undeviating acceptability in voiced Rorschach and TAT percepts are the rule. Richness of imagination is stifled, and real feeling is hidden behind an obscuring curtain of constant control. The scanty record thus obtained loses the pith and the subtle nuances necessary for full or for accurate assessment of the individual type of personality reaction pattern.

In addition, inmates as a group are generally among those subjects who cling, for various reasons, to the concrete. They become anxious and threatened when confronted with the ambiguous stimuli of the Rorschach, and attempt to steer clear of real involvement with this type of projective situation, at least insofar as communicating and explaining verbally what it is that they may see.

To illustrate, sex offenders, for example, who are seen psychotherapeutically after psychological examination often confide to their therapist, once rapport has been cemented in a transference setting, that on the Rorschach they did not reveal everything they saw, e.g., "especially those dirty sex pictures that were there." In responding to the projective drawing task, on the other hand, these patients must reveal something of their sexual adaptation in one of two ways: either in their manner of handling the direct or symbolic sexual areas of the House, Tree, Person figures or else, all the more, by their omitting to draw areas that carry sexual implications, for example, the genital zone or secondary sex characteristics of the drawn person, the chimney on the house, and the branches on the tree.[11,12]

Fox,[10, p.249] also reports, "drawings, relative to other projective techniques, are . . . difficult to falsify, and in its application there is no barrier to education or language." Bellak's[4, p.292] experience is in the same direction: "The verbal expression of aggression may be successfully controlled when its muscular expression is clearly seen . . . in tests probing the subsemantic area."

But if the above demonstrates the *relatively* more appropriate utility of projective drawings to the problem of assessing acting out potentials, such cues on projective techniques, in general, remain a most elusive cluster of data to catch.

First, it should be emphasized that at this time a high degree of accuracy in our generalizations from projective drawings to life situations cannot be expected. It does appear, however, that we can achieve gross accuracy, particularly if we use a battery of tests, but we must always assume that the projective techniques have not revealed all major personality variables and their patterns of interaction. Also, "We must always make the limiting assumptions that fate often tips the scales of external circumstance one way or the other, regardless of the individual's character structure and intentions, and that to a significant extent the prominence of character features and pathological trends depend on external circumstance."[29]

Murray[25] goes even further by pointing out that, "The patterns of the imagination (as revealed in projective tests) and the patterns of public conduct are more apt to be related by contrast than by conformity."

There are several examples in which the latent and the manifest levels of behavior are inversely related. Oral dependency needs may, for example, be conspicuously evident in the projective drawings. While such a finding may occur in an alcoholic subject who more or less acts out his oral dependency needs, it may also occur in the projective drawings of a striving business executive who is attempting to deny these needs in himself by proving quite the opposite in his behavior.

It is only by integrating the behavioral picture with the projective technique data that the full personality evaluation can be derived. When we view the frustrated oral needs evident in the drawings alongside of the driving, overstriving behavior in the business executive's overt behavior, it is the viewing of these two levels side-by-side which may allow for the speculative prediction of eventual ulcers, but we can not always predict from the presence of dependency needs on the projective drawings the overt form of these needs.

Homoerotic elements reflected in the drawings may be considered as another example. Whether the homosexual orientation, suggested by these drawings, results in inhibited heterosexuality, compensatory Don Juanism, or overt homosexual activities depends, in part, upon the interaction of the basic potential of the subject with the influences in his environment, the latter factors being generally outside the scope of those tapped by projective techniques.

To mention one more example, if the projective drawings suggest extreme aggressiveness, and the patient behaviorally assumes the role of a meek, docile, self-effacing and submissive individual, a *comparison* of the two levels of data may permit the valuable inference that this subject must suffer from the effects of suppression and/or repression of a significant amount of aggressive impulses. The mild exterior he presents, we may then deduce, is at the expense of creating considerable tensions within him.

Another handicap which interferes with clinicians' attempts to predict overt behavior exists in the fact that manifest behavior of any importance is invariably highly over-determined, the resultant of numerous interacting factors: identification figures, superego pressures, social and cultural settings, type and strength of defenses, traumatic experiences, and possibly constitutional predisposition would all have a great bearing on the ultimate overt pattern.[29] Often, we are able to infer the presence of a powerful trend, kneaded deeply into the personality, but cannot say which of several possible manifest forms it may assume. While it is true that at times the clinician can be impressively successful in predicting overt behavior, he cannot with confidence assume that he can consistently so interrelate the indicated factors as to predict, very specifically, the future behavior. The subject's resources and limitations with respect to adaptive, sublimatory activity, and achievement are often difficult to take into account. These factors tend to depend so much on situational support and threats, and on other external elements over which the subject frequently has little control (and which themselves cannot be predicted).

The broadest common denominator, then, which interferes with prediction of future behavior and postdiction of genetic events is the operation of *multiple determinism,* both internal and external. Projective tests merely elicit feelings (and a small sample of behavior), and any conclusions derived from the projective test data are made predominantly by way of inference. Psychodynamic inference "is not something which is built into the tests, but enters the realm of general personality theory."[17] Inferences from projective drawings, then, are not only bound by the extent of the clinician's knowledge of this clinical tool, but also by the limits of our present-day knowledge of psychodynamic principles.

Nevertheless, in spite of all of the above, in that which follows we will see that *clues* to acting out are at times available in projective drawings, to be picked up, if only tentatively and speculatively, if one is sentitized to such subtleties.

To start, however, with the grosser and less subtle indications brought to eye-level in drawings, let us consider several instances of "acting out" *directly* on the drawing page itself.

DIRECT ACTING OUT ON PAPER

An adolescent boy, referred to the writer because of excessive truancy, the flaunting of rules in school, and generally rebellious behavior, reflected his characteristic role in life in his drawing of a person as presented in figure 1. The drawn male is dressed in a soldier's outfit as a reflection of the subject's need for greater status and recognition as a male than he feels he possesses. The drawn person turns his back on the world, much as the subject himself has done, and *introduces a regulation into the picture merely to break it.* His adding the sign, "No Spitting," just so that the drawn person may disobey it, clearly parallels the subject's seeking out rules and regulations merely to break them, to prove to himself and others that they do not apply to him, that he is outside the sphere that authority encompasses, that he is bigger and better than the rules and the people who make them.

For his drawing of a female, he offers us figure 2, a female whose face is smeared and debased. He describes her as, "A young girl, flat as a board, trying out her new non-smear lipstick, and it smears." Here, again, we note that he directly acts out his anger on the drawn page, besmirching the figure's face in an aggressive laying on of the crayon. (We note, also, that he amputates one of her hands where it should attach to the arm.)

When we get to the Unpleasant-Concept-Test (the subject is asked to draw the most unpleasant thing he can think of) we note that he once again *acts out,* and this time all the more directly, his need to debase and vent his acute rage (see fig. 3). Where subjects popularly offer the concept

PERSON

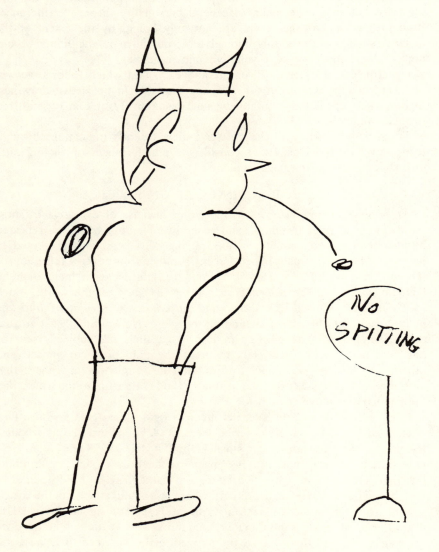

Figure 1

FIGURE 2

Figure 3

of war, disease, or death, this subject instead draws a man with a ludicrously elongated nose, a huge penis hanging out of his open pants, and then stabs him with a long sword running through his body. He then adds the tag, *Dad*.

In clinical practice, we may generally assume that a subject who acts out this violently on paper—and particularly when this acting out reaches such inappropriate extremes—that he would be prone to also act out the same needs to depreciate others, to search out rules and regulations to break, and to release his accumulated anger at the immediate world around him.

Figure 4 represents another case of intense and multiple statements of a theme, mounting up to suggest the likelihood of this theme bubbling over into acting out. This figure was drawn by an adolescent boy who happened to be one of a group of subjects studied in an effort to get a normative population from a local high school.

The expansion of the shoulders into exaggerated, sharply-pointed, aggressive corners, the knife in the hand, the gun carried in the belt, the rough clothing and cap, the piercing eye, the sharp nose, and the mustache pulled down into a depiction of walrus tusks more than soft hair all add up to a reflection of an individual who is drastically motivated to prove himself aggressive, dangerous, and prone to violence. The fact that the feet are particularly out-sized and the shoes taken off suggests the primitiveness of his impulses, and that the subject appears to have shed considerations of social constraint and more sublimated behavior. When we add to this the fact that the entire figure seems to be pulled off balance by the aggressively pointed shoulder, we get a picture of an individual who suffers from a feeling of emotional instability which may quite easily be triggered into aggressive behavior.

After seeing so vocal a rendition of a compensatory and hostile theme, the writer consulted the school records and found that this youngster was indeed an acter outer, having gotten into trouble for numerous fights in school, once having thrown a blackboard eraser through a closed school window, and recently having mugged a fellow student for money in the school bathroom.

To turn to an example provided in the drawing of a tree, figure 5 was offered by a 12-year-old boy who had been referred because he had been observed picking up baby pigs with the prongs of a pitchfork, throwing down baby chicks and crushing them under the heel of his shoe, and at one time setting fire to a bale of hay underneath a cow. On top of this, he had recently released a tractor to roll down a hill onto some children. (Fortunately, the children dodged the vehicle in time.)

His drawn tree speaks as eloquently as does his behavior. It is a graphic

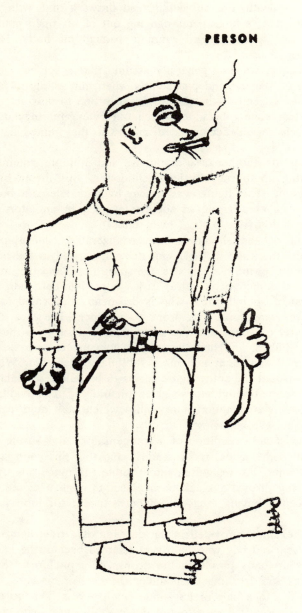

Figure 4

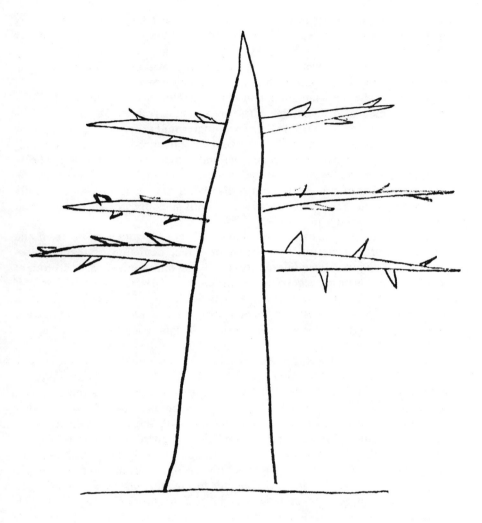

FIGURE 5

communication, saying in distinct and unequivocal language: "Keep away from me!" Spear-like branches with thorn-like "leaves" decorate a sharply pointed tree trunk. The branches reach out aggressively in a premise of inflicting significant harm to all those who come within reach. The drawing is steeped in sadism, aggression, and angry resentments.

Similarly, the drawing of a house in the House-Tree-Person (H-T-P) technique may also catch the clues to potential acting out. One 12 year old boy (see fig. 6) heralded his eventual running away from home by drawing a house in which a child was escaping through the top window, and a lower window as depicted slammed down on the mother's neck, pinning her there. In spite of the family's beginning to involve itself in therapy at that point, four months thereafter the youngster did actually run away from home, and it was not until a couple of days later that he was found asleep in a park.

At times the implications for acting out may be gotten more from the strained efforts at control than from the direct depiction of the impulses themselves. Figure 7 was offered by a 15 year old youth who was brought to the clinic because, according to his mother, he had threatened to kill her. The initial question which raised itself in our minds was of a differential diagnosis between vocalization on the part of an adolescent who merely wanted to get his mother off his back versus an actual homicidal potential.

The projective drawings administered at the time to the youngster provided rather vivid evidence on the side of the actual possibility of serious capacity for violence pressing forward in him. The strained facial expression, the exaggerated attempts to maintain control over bodily impulses, the head pulling tensely to the side with the eyes reflecting acute inner strain and efforts at control are all brought to focus by the hands presented almost as if to carry the suggestion of being manacled together to provide *external* controls against his lashing out in angry fury. To experience the actual kinesthetic feeling, the reader has only to reproduce the entire body position and twisted pull of the head on the neck along with the facial expression to feel in one's own musculature the struggle of control versus intense aggression within. Such a kinesthetic verification of the visual data may also convey a feeling of the almost vivid immediacy to this potential eruption.

The fact that his drawn tree was presented as conspicuously off-balance adds all the more to the personality picture of a youngster whose felt equilibrium was very much in jeopardy and who was shaky in maintaining defenses against his volcanic violence within.

Following the emerging of this tension-flooded picture, the boy was referred to a mental hospital for more detailed observation. The impression

FIGURE 6

FIGURE 7

of his therapist there later supported the implication that this was indeed a youngster who carried the active seeds of matricide.

The next case adds a second illustration of the principle of *overemphasized control* in the drawings, providing the clues to potential acting out in overt behavior. Figure 8 was drawn by an exhibitionist. We see in the hand drawn as tucked-in under a belt which anchors it—and keeps it from moving to engage in forbidden acts (of exposing himself?) —the strong conflict of impulse versus control. When, however, external controls have to be resorted to (such as, in this instance, strapping the hand down), we may presume that internal controls are insufficient and the likelihood of acting out all the more probable. This is supported by the fact that while he draws the person with hands pinned, at the same time the drawn person does engage in the exhibitionism of the extremely long, phallic-shaped nose. The impulses circumvent the efforts at control.

At times, issues of life-and-death import themselves may be picked up by the projective drawings.* Figure 9 was drawn by a man suffering from an involutional depression. He drew the large figure first; then when he saw that he could not complete the entire figure on the page, he drew the smaller figure. He momentarily paused, looked at both figures, said that the larger figure lacked a collar, picked up the pencil he had laid down, and drew the "collar" by slashing the pencil across the throat of the drawn male. It was almost as if, the writer got the eerie feeling, the patient were committing suicide on paper. Along with this, the patient offered a story to TAT Card 1 which consisted of the boy's picking up and smashing the violin. We recall Bellak's theory of the violin's representing the body image and here find consistency with the suicidal impulses acted out on the drawing page. The witnessing of this man slashing his drawn throat on paper was too vivid a demonstration to take lightly. Conferring with his psychiatrist resulted in the patient's being institutionalized. Some time later the patient actually made a suicidal attempt, but fortunately, owing to the protective surroundings of the institution, this was detected, and the bathrobe belt with which he attempted to hang himself was cut down in time.

In summary of this section, then, we may see in the cases presented that *the stronger, the more frank, the more raw and unsublimated the expression of impulses which break through in the projective drawings, the more the defensive and adaptive operations of the ego may be presumed to be insufficient in their assimilative function, and the more the likelihood of acting out may be taken to mount.*

---

*As they were in the case of the youngster who suffered matricidal impulses.

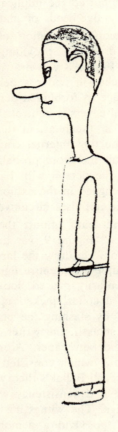

FIGURE 8

Figure 9

SIZE

Of the variables employed by subjects to express their aggressive patterns, one of the most frequent ones is the handling of space on the paper. The drawing which is too large, which tends to press out against the page's edges, denotes a similar tendency to act out against the confines of the environment.

Figure 10 was drawn by a 28 year old male. The most conspicuous aspect of the subject's drawing performance is the large size he gives the drawn male, causing it to crowd the drawing page at both top and bottom. Along with this, the firm line pressure, the overextended, broadened shoulders, and the stance (with the feet spread apart and the arms hanging away from the body, ready for action) all reinforce the impression one gets of someone who is trying "to prove himself." The subject cannot prove himself big enough in stature (that is, there is not room enough on the page to draw the person as large as he would wish it to be), nor generally impressive enough. The zoot-suit treatment, the stern, hard facial expression, and the almost ape-like, long arms that extend too far down the body length all emphasize the subject's attempt to prove himself on paper—to prove himself manly, active, deserving of status, and one not to be taken lightly.

When we learn that the subject was examined because of a rape offense for which he had been convicted, we then see the close parallel of his trying to prove himself more manly than he actually feels, on paper as well as in real life.

Precker,[28] too, found that exaggerated size may be considered as evidence of aggressiveness or motor release. Zimmerman and Garfinkle[31] as well found that lack of restraint in the size of drawings correlated with aggressiveness and a tendency toward the release of this aggressiveness into the environment.

SEQUENCE

By analyzing drawing test data in terms of the sequential emergence of drive derivatives, defense, and adaptation, we may witness dynamic and economic shifts which at the same time lay bare structural features of the personality of the subject. By examining samples of ongoing drawing processes, we have an opportunity to study in slow motion, as it were, the structural features of conflict and defense.

In the microcosm of the interaction between a subject and the drawing page we may, for example, see a subject give tiny shoulders to his drawn person, then erase them, and finally endow the drawn person with compensatory, overly-broad shoulders. Such a subject then looked at his drawing in a perplexing fashion as if some automatic phenomena had

Figure 10

taken over, and he couldn't understand how this process got away from him. He commented, "I guess the shoulders expanded a little too much" as if *it* rather than he did it. From this we may postulate that the subject's first reaction to a new situation is one of inferiority feelings which he then quickly attempts to cover-up with a facade of capability and adequacy, which, however, he overdoes to the point of compensatory acting out which breaks away from him.

In a study of sex offenders sent to Sing-Sing prison,[13] lack of ego-strength and inadequate control of impulses have shown up as forming an important factor in the total picture. By this is meant the relative concept of a weak control mechanism for an approximately average amount of impulse strength, or else a control mechanism of about average strength, given the overwhelming task of keeping in check, pressures building up from excessive push. The majority of the sex offenders studied fell into the former category.

In fact, the vast majority of rapists and pedophiles studied had ego pictures of *rigid* control by weak control mechanisms, a control so inflexibly and tightly spread that it manifested a capacity for sporadic breakthrough of impulses. Only the incest group harbored a predominance of individuals in whom consistently *inadequate* control, as a result of a shattered ego, was the basic longstanding situation.

To illustrate the attempts at rigid control of the rapist and pedophile group, punctuated by short erupting interludes, the following excerpt from the psychological report on a rather representative case is cited:

> In reproducing the Bender-Gestalt figures, the subject started out by making them noticeably small, but ended with the last two figures growing excessively large; this would tend to reflect strong needs at constrictive control over emotional impulses which, however, cannot remain successful for a prolonged time without cracking and allowing an impulsive release of uncontrolled affect and/or behavior.

Conversely, defenses gaining dominance over impulses, and hence a contra-indication to acting out are conveyed by the opposite sequence: for example, a male, 38 years of age, first drew a large, threatening female with feet placed in a broad stance and with face wearing a stern expression. She was clothed in a riding habit and carried a large whip in her hand. Following this depiction of a threatening, stern, and punitive female figure, the subject gazed at his drawing for a long time and then hesitantly reached for the next sheet of paper and drew a small, puny male who stood with shoulders drooped dejectedly, head bent, arms behind the back: all-in-all a most submissive, subjugated posture. The subject thus views females as menacing, and then attempts to placate them by assuming a passive, appeasing role.

Sequential analysis of the set of drawings may provide clues to the amount of drive or energy of the subject, and it may also provide data which allow an appraisal of the subject's control over this drive. Does the subject, for instance, break down under the emotionally-tinged associations that are presumably aroused by the different drawing concepts, or is he able to handle himself well in these spheres? Does energy maintain itself, peter out, or erupt? Progressive psychomotor decrease, as he proceeds from one drawing to the next in the set of projective drawings, suggests high fatiguability. Progressive psychomotor increase suggests excessive stimulability and potentials for acting out. A modulated, sustained energy level reflects more healthy personality integration.

Frequently subjects are somewhat disturbed initially, but soon become calm and work efficiently as they proceed from the first to the last drawing. This is presumably simply "situational anxiety," and is not indicative of anything more serious.

PRESSURE

Pressure of pencil on paper has been found, like size, to be an indication of the subject's energy level.[14,15,28] In regard to reliability, it was found by Hetherington[14] that subjects are rather remarkably constant in their pressure.

Alschuler and Hattwick[1] reported that children who drew with heavy strokes were usually more assertive and/or overtly aggressive than other children.

Consistent with this, Pfister, as reported in Anastasi and Foley,[3] found that psychopaths, one of the most troublesome of the groups who act out, characteristically employ heavy pressure.

One youth, examined by the present writer at a reformatory, drew his house, tree and person with so fierce a digging at the paper that his pencil actually tore through the paper at various points along the line drawn. Several months later he stabbed a fellow inmate, in a dispute over a card game, with a "knife" he had fashioned from a spoon.

STROKE

Alschuler and Hattwick[1] found that children who drew with long strokes stood out for their controlled behavior, whereas children who worked with short strokes showed more impulsive behavior.

Mira[24] also writes, "In general, the length of movement of a stroke tends to increase in inhibited subjects and decrease in excitable ones."

Krout[19] found that straight lines were associated with aggressive moods. Jagged lines (which incidentally appeared as the symbol of the most aggressive unit in Hitler's army) were associated with hostility, usually overt and acted out.

DETAILING

Children or adults who have the feeling that the world around them is uncertain, unpredictable and/or dangerous tend to seek to defend themselves against inner or outer chaos by creating an excessively-detailed, rigidly ordered, highly structured world. The drawings of these subjects will be very exact. These people tend to create rigid, repetitious elements in their drawings. There is nothing flowing or relaxed in the lines, the drawings, or in their total presentation. Everything is put together by force, as though they feel that without this pressure everything would fall apart.

Too perfect a drawing performance, executed with unusual, exacting control and care, is offered by patients who range from obsessive-compulsive to incipient schizophrenics or early organics. But whatever the diagnosis, the "too-perfect" performance reflects the effort of these patients to hold themselves together against the threat of imminent disorganization. It is a direct manifestation of their hyper-vigilance, and implies the presence of a relatively weak ego, so afraid of acting out a breakthrough of forbidden impulses that it dares not relax its constant vigilance.

The most frequent emotional accompaniment of the excessive detailing of one's drawing is a feeling of rigidity. Stiffly drawn trees or animals parallel the same quality in the drawn person. In this regard, the latter may be presented as standing rigidly at attention, with body and head very erect, legs pressed closely together, and arms straight and held close to the body. The kinaesthetic emphasis, in these projections, is on the erect posture and on the rigid tension with which the posture is held, keeping impulses in. These drawing performances often express a most unfree, and hence uncertain but rigidly-controlled defensive attitude. This is the characteristic drawing performance of people to whom spontaneous release of emotions is an acute threat. Impulses, when they are released, are not smoothly integrated, but tend toward the eruptive and uncontrolled.

SYMMETRY

Symmetry has long been regarded as one of the most elemental Gestalt principles. It is not surprising, therefore, that drawings which display an obvious lack of symmetry have been found to indicate equivalent feelings of personality imbalance, diminished integration, and hence increased chances of acting out.

PLACEMENT

In regard to placement on the horizontal axis of the page, Buck[8] hypothesizes that the farther the mid-point of the drawing is to the right of the mid-point of the page, the more likely is the subject to exhibit stable, controlled behavior, to be willing to delay satisfaction of needs and drives, to prefer intellectual satisfactions to more emotional ones. Conversely, the further the mid-point of the drawing is to the left of the mid-point of the page, the greater is the likelihood that the subject tends to behave impulsively, to seek immediate, frank and emotional satisfaction of his needs and drives, and to act out. Koch[16] independently, on the basis of his projective drawing work on the "Tree Test" in Switzerland, identifies the right side of the page with "inhibition," which is consistent with Buck's concept of emphasis on the right side of the page suggesting control. Wolff's[30] finding that subjects who were attracted to the right side of the page in their drawings showed introversion, and those to the left side of the page extroversion, is also consistent with Buck's findings, in that introversion is associated with the capacity to delay satisfaction, and extroversion the seeking of more immediate gratifications.

DISSOCIATION

Suggestions of dissociation, which are offered by incongruities between the graphic drawing and the verbal description of it (i.e., a clash between the two communication media) are perhaps the most pathognomonic of the clues to acting out tendencies.

This can best be conveyed by an example.

The patient, a 17 year old white male, was referred to the clinic because he had been arrested for involvement in fights on the beach on several occasions and charged with felonious assault during racial riots. He had been transferred from high school to high school because of inability to relate to the Negro population in school, and hence was referred to the clinic with the idea of appraising his potential assaultiveness.

The essential problem for which we were asked to appraise this youth, namely his dangerousness, gains focus as we examine his performance as he moves through the projective drawing figures. He draws his first person, a female, as an extremely puny figure, and then comments that it is "pretty skinny." He had left the top of the head out, and it now comes through that this was so that he could delay choosing whether to make it a male or a female. He decides to refer the question to the examiner and asks, "It doesn't matter, does it, whether I make it a male or a female, does it? . . . Which shall it be?" When this question was referred back to the patient, he elected to make it a female and added a curlicue of hair and earrings below. He then commented, "Holy Sweat, *it* looks like *it* went through the mill". Here, in addition to the feeling of debasement, we note that he chooses the neuter gender in which to refer to the figure.

The feelings of insufficiency, punyness, unimpressiveness, and confusion about psychosexual identification which come through in the first person drawing are then handled in a passive-aggressive, compensatory maneuver in the following Person drawing (fig. 11). He emphasizes the shoulder muscles and then opens the person's mouth wide in a sort of savage roar, where facial muscles strain, the arms go out to intensify the energy he is expelling, and the teeth are bared. To add to the aggressive quality, he then makes the nose quite sharp. The demonstrative efforts to convey himself as angry, noteworthy, and certainly someone to be reckoned with are somewhat denied by the subtleties of the figure being empty, and thus without substance or the power he attempts to convey, and the fact that one arm appears as if grafted at the elbow. Thus we get an image which is essentially empty and attempts to play a role of aggressive savagery and anger.

In regard to the question concerning his potential aggressiveness, the important quality which comes through is not so much the aggressiveness of his character armor but rather the *dissociated* aspects of this aggression. This dissociated ingredient is discerned when he describes the drawn figure. When asked what the figure is doing, the subject commented, "just standing there." This comment cannot be dismissed as mere evasiveness, for the subject is frank, even vividly expressive, in his graphic communi-

FIGURE 11

cation. It is as if, rather, consciousness does not recognize the clearly angry quality which comes through around the edges of his awareness. When we then move on to a consideration of his drawn tree, we find a sharp and somewhat unintegrated branch structure exists in among the foliage. This sharp, hostily-pointed branch is not blended with the tree but rather again appears to be a thing apart. Once more we get the feeling that aggressive qualities can be dissociated in him and surge outward, away from his control. In summary, then, the uncertain quality conveyed in the first person drawing gives way to the compensatory masculine posturing of the second. This posturing is re-enforced by anger to make it all the more impressive. But this rage is, in turn, handled by dissociation—unfortunately making it all the more dangerous and prone to be acted out.

Sometimes the clues to a state of dissociation of hostile impulses will come through within the drawing level alone, without involving a disharmony between the drawing and its verbal description. Figure 12, with its massive, highly-aggressive, and mechanical-like hands, attached as mere appendages at the end of the arms, illustrates this type of projection. The automation quality, particularly in the area of the aggressive urges, suggests that these impulses are acted-out automatically and without adequate integration with the personality proper.

CHROMATIC DRAWINGS

Now for the last, and perhaps most dramatic, of the variables. The introduction of color to the projective drawing task, by asking for a new set of drawings, this time in crayon, adds an additional affective element. It has long been established that color symbolizes emotion. The many experiments establishing this are too numerous to mention singly. The most abbreviated sample will have to suffice.[1,3,5-7,9,11,13,15] Common parlance supports the experimental data. We speak of someone "red with rage," we associate "yellow" with cowardice and fear, "blue" as depression, "green with envy," and refer to someone as "colorful" if he is in various ways freer in expressing unique personality ingredients and is generally at the opposite pole from the emotionally subdued or constricted personality.

Color stimulates people, as every fine arts painter or even advertising man well knows. Asking a patient to draw in crayon tends to supply an additional affective impact, and thus moves closer to sampling reactions to, and tolerance for, emotional situations—just those situations in which acting out, if it is to be released, is apt to be triggered.

Moreover, the chromatic series of drawings is designed to supplement the achromatic series, to take advantage of the fact that two samples of behavior are always better than one. But the chromatic series is more than a second H-T-P sample because the subject who produces it must,

PERSON

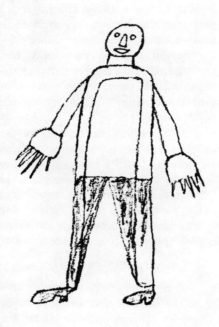

FIGURE 12

I believe, be in a somewhat more vulnerable state than he was when he produced his achromatic drawings. Even to the best adjusted subject, the achromatic H-T-P and the subsequent searching Post-Drawing-Interrogation are an emotional experience, for many memories, pleasant and unpleasant, are aroused, at the least.

Thus the chromatic series becomes a behavioral sample that is obtained with the subject at a level of frustration that is different from that which obtained when the achromatic series was sought. If the achromatic (as it frequently is for the well-adjusted subject) was a welcome catharsis, the subject may be far less tense than he was at the beginning. In the average clinical case seen for differential diagnosis, however, this will scarcely be the case. Such a subject will almost inevitably be emotionally aroused enough so that his chromatic series will reveal still more about his basic needs, mechanisms of defense, etc., than the achromatic.

In the achromatic series, the subject is afforded every opportunity to employ corrective measures: he may erase as much as he likes, and the pencil is a relatively refined drawing instrument. In the chromatic drawings, the only corrective measure available is concealment with heavy shading, and the drawing instrument, the crayon, is relatively crude.

Thus, at the beginning, with the subject in relatively fuller possession of his defensive mechanisms, he is given tools which permit expressive defensiveness; in the second phase, by which time the subject will be more likely to have lost at least part of his defensive control (if he is going to lose it all), he is provided with a grosser instrument, and with an opportunity to express symbolically (through his choice and use of color) the emotions, the controls, and lack of controls which have been aroused by the achromatic series and Post-Drawing-Interrogation.

Thus, when aggression is *relatively* more mildly conveyed in the achromatic rendition, as in figure 13, but is then presented by the subject in his chromatic expression (fig. 14) in frank and unvarnished fashion, our experience has been that such subjects can more-or-less get by in ordinary relations but tend to erupt into violence in emotionally-charged situations.*

---

*The patient had been charged with sexual assault, following a necking and petting session with a girl he had met at a dance and was now taking home. As he tried to advance to slipping his hand under her blouse, the girl objected; he, in an excited state, drew a knife and threatened her. The Probation Officer's report described the incident as follows: "He asked her to open her blouse, and she refused again. At this point the defendant ripped open her blouse with his hand. With the knife he cut her brassiere in the middle and fondled her breast. He made her bend down and he put his finger in her vagina. During the whole episode he made threats, and at one point banged the complainant's head against the side of the building. This knocked her down. He pulled her up, and wanted her to open his zipper." At this point the victim was able to break away and run to safety.

316   ACTING OUT

FIGURE 13

FIGURE 14

As we follow this particular subject from his achromatic to his chromatic person drawing, we observe that the facial expression becomes more menacing, the hands now become so large that they are elongated, pointed, spear-like entities which fairly shriek "hostility" This time the shoes turn into a sort of Army boots affair which go up to almost the knees in conveying a feeling of brutality. All in all, the body-image gives way to the pressing forward of a chromatic depiction of a monster. His raw feelings of aggression and rage are similarly apt to come charging forward in emotional situations.

A word of caution: Examples here were presented as illustrations, as samples only. In actual clinical practice, the dangers of basing interpretative deductions on isolated bits of data are obvious. In practice, confirmation of interpretative speculation on the basis of one drawing must be checked against not only the other drawings, but the entire projective battery, the case history, the clinical impression gleaned during the interview with the subject, and all other available information.

SUMMARY

Clues, but only *clues*, then to the possibility of acting out may be reflected in projective drawings by strong, open, and unsublimated expression of impulses breaking through to flood the drawing page; by too large a size of the drawing so that it presses out against the page's edges as the subject himself will similarly tend to act out against the confines of the environment; by sequential movement from expression of controls to exaggerated expression of impulses (in contrast to the opposite sequence); by pressure and savage digging of the pencil at the paper; by stroke; by detailing, dyssymmetry, placement, evidence of dissociation, and by the triggering-off of the impulses in the chromatic expression.

As to the type of impulses apt to be released in the acted out behavior, this can be discerned in the content more than in the structure of the drawings, whether aggressive, exhibitionistic, suicidal, and so on.

The pencil or crayon stroke, at the moment of contact with the paper thus carries, in the words of the American artist Robert Henri, "the exact state of being of the subject at that time into the work, and there it is, to be seen and read."

REFERENCES

1. Alschuler, A., and Hattwick, W. *Painting and personality.* Chicago, Univ. Chicago Press, 1947.
2. Anastasi, A., and Foley, J. A survey of the literature on artistic behavior in the abnormal. *Psychol. Monographs,* 1940, *52,* 71.
3. Anastasi, A., and Foley, J. P. An analysis of spontaneous artistic productions by the abnormal. *J. Gen. Psychol.,* 1943, *28,* 297-313.
4. Bellak, L. A study of limitations and "failures": Toward an ego psychology of projective techniques. *J. Proj. Tech.* 1954, *18.* 279-293.

5. Bieber, I., and Herkimer, J. Art in psychotherapy. *Amer. J. Psychiat.*, 1948, *104*, 627-631.
6. Brick, M. The mental hygiene value of children's art work. *Amer. J. Ortho.*, 1944, *14*, 136-146.
7. Buck, J. N. The H-T-P technique: A quantitative and qualitative scoring manual. *Clin. Psychol. Monogr.*, 1948, *5*, 1-120.
8. Buck, J. N. Richmond Proceedings (mimeographed copy) Calif., Western Psychological Services, 1950.
9. England, A. O. Color preference and employment in children's drawings. *J. Child. Psychiat.*, 1952, *2*, 343-349.
10. Fox, R. Psychotherapeutics of alcoholism. In Bychowski, G. and Despert, J. L. (Eds.). *Specialized techniques in psychotherapy.* New York: Basic Books, 1952.
11. Hammer, E. F. The role of the H-T-P in the prognostic battery. *J. Clin. Psychol.*, 1953, *9*, 371-374.
12. ———. A comparison of H-T-P's of rapists and pedophiles. *J. Proj. Tech.*, 1954, *18*, 346-354.
13. ———. *The clinical application of projective drawings.* Springfield, Illinois: Charles C Thomas, 1958.
14. Hetherington, R. The effects of E. C. T. on the drawings of depressed patients. *J. Ment. Sc.*, 1952, *98*, 450-453.
15. Kadis, A. Finger painting as a projective technique. In Abt, L. E., and Bellak, L. (Eds.). *Projective psychology.* New York: Knopf, 1950.
16. Koch, C. *The tree test.* Berne: Hans Huber, 1952.
17. Kerner, A. Limitations of projective techniques: Apparent and real. *J. Proj. Tech.*, 1956, *20*, 42-47.
18. Kris, E. *Psychoanalytic explorations in art.* New York: International Universities Press, 1952.
19. Krout, J. Symbol elaboration test. *Psychol. Mono. A.M.A.*, 1950, *4*, 404-405.
20. Landisberg, S. Personal Communication, March 1951.
21. ———. Relationship of Rorschach to the H-T-P. *J. clin. Psychol.*, 1953, *9*, 179-183.
22. Lindberg, B. J. Experimental studies of colour and non-colour attitudes in school children and adults. *Acto. Psychiat. Neurol*, 1938, *16*.
23. Machover, Karen. Human figure drawings of children. *J. Proj. Tech.*, 1953, *17*, 85-91.
24. Mira, E. *Psychiatry in war.* New York: Norton, 1943.
25. Murray, H. Uses of the Thematic Apperception Test. *Amer. J. Psychiatry*, 1951, *107*, 577-581.
26. Napoli, P. Fingerpainting and personality diagnosis. *Genet. Psychol. Monogr.*, 1946, *34*, 129-231.
27. Payne, J. J. Comments of the analysis of chromatic drawings. In Buck, J. N. The H-T-P techniques: A quantitative and qualitative scoring manual. *Clin. Psychol. Monogr.*, 1948, *5*, 1-120.
28. Precker, J. Painting and drawing in personality assessment: Summary. *J. Proj. Tech.*, 1950, *14*, 262-286.
29. Schafer, R. *Psychoanalytic interpretations in Rorschach testing.* New York: Grune & Stratton, 1954.
30. Wolff, W. *The personality of the pre-school child.* New York: Grune and Stratton, 1946.
31. Zimmerman, J., and Garfinkle, L. Preliminary study of the art productions of the adult psychotic. *Psychiat. Quart.*, 1942, *16*, 313-318.

28. The Bender Gestalt and Acting Out

By FRED BROWN, PH.D.

In "The Bender Gestalt and Acting Out" Dr. Fred Brown provides us with an insight into both the difficulties and promises of using a combined perceptual and graphomotor technique for ascertaining acting out potential. As the longtime head of the Division of Psychology at the Mt. Sinai Hospital in New York City, Brown has been in the unusual position, both as practicing clinician and research worker, to have worked with many psychodiagnostic problems in which the prediction of therapeutic or hospital management difficulties became a matter of great importance.

What emerges from his efforts to show the usefulness of the Bender Gestalt Test is a masterful and skillful statement of the general problem of studying acting out behavior and the specific merits of the Bender toward this end. Clinical psychologists in particular, but also all those concerned with a briefer assessment procedure, will welcome Dr. Brown's contribution.

EVER SINCE HE SEVERED the umbilical cord that attached him to philosophy, the psychologist has longed desperately to become a full-fledged and accepted member of the scientific community. In order to achieve the accolade of "scientist" and to be granted membership, he has known that among the stringent entrance requirements embodied in the general matrix of operations known as scientific method none loomed so large and forbidding as demonstration of the capacity to make *predictions*. The clinical psychologist, throwing in his lot with medicine as a father figure despite his adolescent rebelliousness, and demonstrating this in his free use of such medical terms as *diagnosis, treatment* and *patient,* is even more conscious of his blurred professional identification and role concepts. On the one hand he is regarded with disdain by the thin-skinned experimentalist who feels safer in the sterilized domain of his laboratory than in the treacherous marshes of psychodynamics where ignes fatui offer deceptive attractions that must be contended with by the tough-skinned clinician, and on the other hand he feels himself to be, in his more moodily introspective moments, excluded from the good company of the physical and biological scientists who have achieved respectable predictive competence that enables them to photograph the moon, survey Mars, and expose the secret templates of heredity.

There are those of us who feel that a psychodiagnostician's skills reside in his ability to *understand* another human being in depth and to communicate this understanding to the therapist who will utilize it to good advantage in his work with the patient, and that the therapist's skills will enable him to ameliorate distressing symptoms and guide the patient toward wholesome and socially acceptable self-fulfillment. While the concept of prediction is implied in another medical term which the clinical psychologist has borrowed, *prognosis,* the predictive element is more muted in these formulations of professional role. There are others of us, and with considerable overlapping of views, who strive for predictive accuracy and cannot suppress a Little Jack Horner surprise and gratification when a prediction is confirmed. Despite persistent and disheartening published negative findings concerning the predictive validity of projective and objective tests used by the clinician in his daily work, he is continually asked to predict suitability for one or another type of therapy, suicidal potential and risk, presence of organicity, outcome of therapy, the most likely course of a disease process, and acting out potentials. Even though he is called upon to "appraise," "evaluate" or "estimate," he is never exempted from the predictive challenge as an ultimate touchstone of the validity and reliability of his services. The "no better than chance" conclusions reported in the literature will harass him and necessitate denial, rationalization, intellectualization, and perhaps more private defense involved in repairing breaches in the wall of his self-confidence and of his faith in his techniques and instruments.

Puzzling, no doubt, but part of the psychodiagnostician's credo, is his generally conceded success in dealing with the ideographic complexities of the individual personality outside the confines of an experimental design. Were it not for this case-by-case demonstration of worth in hospital and clinic, the clinician would long since have gone the way of the dodo.

No projective test has escaped direct or implied criticism for its "unsupported" claims, and the Bender Gestalt test, used as a projective technique, is no exception. To enter into an extended discussion of research findings on various assumptions concerning the utilization of the Bender as a clinical tool is outside the scope of this chapter, but will be found in the Tolor and Schulberg[26] recent critical survey of such studies. My purpose here is to discuss the use of this technique in predicting acting out potentials.

THE NATURE OF ACTING OUT

To do so requires an understanding of what is meant by the term "acting out." To begin with, the concept itself is unclear because of its many dimensions and degrees that range from an angry outburst to homicide. The man who has a record of several successive marriages and divorces may be acting out his oedipal fantasies; the "underachieving" adolescent may be acting out his rebellious resentments against a tyrannical father or an emotionally cold mother; the drivingly over-ambitious tycoon may be acting out his competition with a father figure or his defensive fantasy of phallic grandiosity; the motorist with a history of many accidents may be acting out his destructive hostility and aggression; the psychosomatically afflicted patient may be acting out the role of a disadvantaged and helpless child; and the suicidal patient may be acting out his hostility toward a hated introject. These represent only the barest minimum of possibilities that embrace the broad spectrum of socially criticized or disapproved human behavior. It is interesting to note that the connotation is always a negative one, implies harm to the individual or society (more often the latter), and takes no cognizance of the acting out implications of an individual's far-reaching philanthropic activities, the hazardous exploits of explorers and astronauts, or the extraordinary heroism of some soldiers in combat.*

The concept of acting out was first applied by Freud[11] to manifestations of resistance to psychoanalytic therapy, and was specific to this situation only. It has now come to mean any form of behavior that tends to be typical of the individual under conditions of stress that would be minimal for others and which is characterized by uncontrolled and aggressive actions. To qualify for classification in the category of acting out, the behavior pattern must be detrimental either to the individual or to the society in which he lives. Such a definition seems to narrow the scope of the term by excluding a variety of covert behavior patterns of the type mentioned above, but makes it possible to focus upon observable behavioral phenomena of a relatively unambiguous type.

Various writers have contributed theoretical formulations of the psychodynamics underlying acting out behavior. Fenichel,[9] referring to neurotic acting out, states that such behavior is not always well rationalized and results in a surrender to every neurotic impulse without any introspective search for motivations. He equates individuals who act out with impulse neurotics and emphasizes their intolerance of tensions as a consequence of oral fixations and early life traumata. He writes, "They cannot perform the step from acting to thinking—from an immediate yielding to all impulses to reasonable judgment. Their aim is avoidance of displeasure rather than attainment of pleasure." Through acting out[10] the individual reacts in conformity to a central dynamic that evolves from early deprivation and frustration of external needs necessary for the development and maintenance of self-esteem. This results in a fixation at the oral phase of psychosexual development and causes violent reactions to frustration

---

*There is no doubt that the concept of "acting out" has been generally in the hands of psychopathologists. Chapters such as those of Kanzer, Robertiello, and Melniker in this volume represent a step in a different direction.

on the assumption that what was not given freely will be taken by force. Hughlings Jackson[16] postulates a neurological basis for such outbursts on the assumption that the phylogenetically more recent higher centers of the brain are either structurally defective or traumatized in unrestrained individuals, and therefore the ordinary inhibition of action is lacking. This results in a life pattern characterized by an infantile need for immediate satisfaction. The multidetermined implications of this concept have been given critical attention by Duffy[8] in her comprehensive assessment of activation. It would appear that individual differences in activation and arousal thresholds exist from the earliest days or hours of life and are perhaps associated with constitutional factors that merge with early life experiences and determine the individual's frustration tolerance level. Bellak[1] calls attention to excessive overstimulation of all sense modalities in the early life history of the acting out character which results in a "lifelong excessive stimulus hunger matched only by the inability for containment and the constant need for discharge." It is Greenacre's[13] contention that the groundwork for aggressive acting out is laid during the second year of life at the time when speech is developing. Traumatic experiences may inhibit speech development and throw the individual back upon bodily expressions of feelings with the accompanying belief in the magical power of action to get things done, and with consequent continued use of action as a medium of communication and expression. Michaels[22] comments that individuals who act upon impulse show a "retardation in language . . . related to an overcathexis of the tactual sphere and preverbal states and a lack of differentiations of the ego and super-ego systems." Carroll,[4] in his discussion of duplicity, summarizes this admirably in the following statement: "Because early in life real facts have seemed to the child to differ from what was said about them, orientation to reality through action and orientation to reality through language have developed relatively independently of each other and without adequate integration between them. In the normal person, in whom proper integration has occurred, thought and language are used to sample and test reality and action. In the person who acts out, failure to assimilate language as a concise method of conceptualization and communication is associated with the tendency to act out complete dramatic sequences rather than to select some detail for symbolic representation."

BASIC ASSUMPTIONS UNDERLYING THE BENDER GESTALT TEST

In the light of these theoretical formulations it can be hypothesized that the sheet of paper presented to the patient about to be tested with the Bender represents the boundaries of a miniature world within which he is expected to confine his activities. Each design, regardless of whether or not it has a connotative and symbolic meaning,[12,15] requires nonverbal compliance with an implied external directive. Demands for control vary from less to more bounded figures, thus allowing variations in the extent to which regressive modes are permitted, e.g., Figures 1 and 2. The designs range from simple to complex and from repetitively routine to more "interesting" and challenging configurations (Figures 1 and 2 versus 7 and 8), thus duplicating in this figurative spatial microcosm presumptive paradigms of the individual's life space. Pascal and Suttell[23] regard the test as ". . . a work sample, which involves certainly the cortical capacity to perceive the designs as presented and the psychomotor capacity to reproduce them; but it involves, also, and more importantly with subjects of normal intelligence, a factor that seems to be best described as an attitude. The test situation for the individual, once he is subjected to it, becomes a bit of reality with which he has to cope," and Bender[2] writes: "The whole setting of the stimulus and the whole integrative state of the organism determine the pattern of the response."

It stands to reason, therefore, that basic modes of adaptation and defense comprising such polarities as impulsivity-restraint, expansion-constriction, plasticity-rigidity, and compliance-oppositionalism will manifest themselves and should warrant inferences concerning the relationship between the microcosmic work sample and its macrocosmic correlates. It would be naïve to expect a perfect one-to-one relationship between Bender Gestalt performance and predicted overt behavior, however, since many contingencies must be taken into consideration within the framework of a defensive operation. Tripp,[27] for example, attempted to establish and cross-validate some of the graphomotor features which discriminate between delinquency and non-deliquency in Bender Gestalt performance. Working with white adolescent males who were all charged with felonious crimes, he reports: "The results of this study point to delinquent's impulsiveness and problem of self-control. In other instances the guardedness and over compensation with which delinquents struggle to control their actions results in compulsive overdoing of the concrete elements in a task." In this instance the examiner might ask: "Why such excessively emphasized control?" If he is an experienced clinician, he will postulate that defensive over-control implies very strong impulses and that such impulses are likely to erupt into action with a higher probability than would be the case if there was more expressive leeway. What is true of other projective techniques when used for screening purposes is also true of the Bender; namely, that the chances of making a correct prediction increase as one deals with the extremes of test behavior and productions (e.g., extremely plastic and extremely rigid reproductions with very few false positives on the former and more false negatives on the latter). Furthermore, the clinician always deals with *probabilities* rather than neat dichotomies, a factor frequently disregarded in most validation studies. Tripp[27] presents statistical evidence in support of his contention that "even very powerful discriminators cannot be safely used to diagnose individual delinquency."

BENDER GESTALT STUDIES OF ACTING OUT

There have been remarkably few experimental attempts to evaluate the Bender's ability to predict acting out behavior. In the study already mentioned, Tripp found that six out of 15 measures significantly differentiated delinquents from non-delinquents. These were Collision, Dot Crudity, Closure Problem, Loopy or Springy Vertical on Figure 6, Placement of the First Figure, and Disturbed Line Quality. Zolik[28] compared the Benders of 43 adolescent delinquents with 43 non-delinquents who resided in a high delinquency area, and found that the two groups differed significantly on all comparisons made. Zolik used the Pascal and Suttell scoring system, which is oriented only towards diagnostic membership assignment (i.e., is he or is he not a "patient"; is there considerable or little ego strength, is he "disturbed" or healthy?) and makes no commitments on the problem of acting out. Zolik's study indicates that the Bender differentiates between disturbed and non-disturbed adolescent delinquents (nature of delinquent behavior not given), but throws no light on our own interests. Curnutt and Corotto[7] report poor predictive efficiency of the Pascal and Suttell scoring system in differentiating delinquent behavior from non-delinquent behavior, whether one utilizes the higher cut-off score suggested by Pascal and Suttell or the lower one suggested by Zolik. In another study that seems to implicate the acting out factor, Corotto and Curnutt[6] tested the efficiency of the Bender in differentiating between a flight group and an aggressive group of adolescents. Using Pascal and Suttell scoring, they found that girls reacting with aggressiveness tended toward higher (poorer) scores than did those who resorted to flight. Boys who ran away made poorer scores than those who reacted with aggressiveness. This study suggests the need for further investigation of impulse vectoring and its relationship to sex differences.

Koppitz[17] observes; "Expansiveness or the use of two or more sheets of paper for the drawing of all nine Bender designs is not infrequently found among preschool children and among very impulsive and acting out school children with poor inner controls." Clawson's study[5] supports this observation.

In my own approach to the Bender, which I have used routinely in my own practice and with all hospital cases for over 19 years, I am primarily concerned with projective aspects on the one hand and with estimation of the *probabilities* of acting out on the other. These approaches overlap within the framework of a configurational evaluation that extends to the test battery as a whole and requires considerable intra- and inter-test scanning and cross-checking.

INDICATIONS OF ACTING OUT IN THE BENDER PROTOCOL

The individual who is prone to act out has, by definition, a low tolerance for restraint and inhibition and an impelling need to discharge his impulses. He is unlikely to set long-range goals for himself, is "immature" in this respect, and will be more concerned with his own immediate needs and demands than with the comfort and convenience of others. His psychomotor development may lag far behind his chronological and mental age, and his test performance is often characterized by deviations present in the Bender designs of children under the age of nine years.[23] This implies a regressive orientation and/or a low threshold for retrogressed behavior.

Narcissistic traits are conspicuous in such individuals and comprise avoidance of difficult and exacting tasks, overt or covert unwillingness to comply with authority imperatives, strong riddance needs, and a tendency to deal with phenomena in a gross and over-simplified manner. Under certain circumstances the acting out individual is likely to utilize compulsive defenses against the discharge of impulses in the Bender. This is likely to occur in the test records of incarcerated subjects,[27] acting out patients who have been in treatment for some time, children and adolescents with a history of acting out who are examined while in a disciplined and structured special school setting, drug-tranquillized patients, and those hospitalized for control breakdown. In most cases where the Bender protocol shows excessive compulsivity and literalness of reproduction marked by guide lines and guide points, counting and re-counting, requests for a straight-edge or attempts to use another card for this purpose, and excessive erasures, the clinician should be alerted to the danger of acting out. A poor recall protocol characterized by significant weakening or collapse of integration in such cases reinforces the impression of a precarious defensive position.

All who work with the Bender Gestalt test are indebted to Hutt[14,15] for his bold and original conception of the Wertheimer figures as valid elements for projective interpretations. Since the inception of this approach, others have enriched the technique with their own insights and experiences in the same manner that Rorschach interpretations have gone beyond those delineated by Rorschach, himself.[3,19,20] In the rest of this chapter I shall outline some indications of acting out that may be regarded as guiding hypotheses for research investigations but which are presented here as a communication from one psychodiagnostician to another. These indicators are based upon extensive clinical experience, have in general held up well, and increase the probability that a specific patient will act out when there is an accumulation of them in a single protocol. The *total patterning* must always be given primary consideration.

Heavy line pressure

This is often associated with overt hostility when the lines are drawn in a rapid and impulsive manner, almost as if the pencil were being used as a slashing knife. In some cases the pressure is so strong that the pencil point is broken as an indication of tensions that are barely controlled in the testing situation. There is a difference here between the firm lines of an individual with a great deal of drive and ambition and a high energy level,[18,21] and pressure of such intensity that it seems to seek penetration of the paper.

Substitution of circles for dots

This is a manifestation of regression that tends to coincide with behavior commensurate with that of children below the age of nine. Not infrequently present in the protocols of very immature and narcissistic individuals, it assumes significance as an indicator of acting out potentials when combined with supplementary signs.

Collision

Overlapping of designs suggests an indifference to the life-space boundaries of others and a disregard for their rights and comfort. The collision variable varies from a cautious and tentative probing into the environment of an adjacent figure (as when the vertical of Figure 6 is drawn from bottom to top and enters the space bounded by the curved areas of Figure 4 or 6) to an aggressive thrust that ploughs through another figure. The former is more apt to be associated with indirect forms of exploitative behavior; the latter with more blatant hostile and aggressive manifestations.

Spikes on curve

Sharp angles or spikes on the curves of Figure 6 indicate difficulty in holding aggressive drives under restraint and have frequently been noted in the records of individuals with chronic psychosomatic complaints and low irritability thresholds. There seems to be no direct correspondence between the number of spikes and the intensity of the aggressive impulse, since even a single spike or angle in an otherwise flattened copy warrants alertness to the danger of acting out. Hutt and Briskin[15, p.84] regard Figure 6 as "a direct portrayal of emotionality", but even though Prado, Peyman and Lacey[24] found no relationship between flattened curves and/or decrease in angulation and flattened affect in experimental and control groups, clinical experience supports the assumption that distortions in this figure are often associated with affective disturbances.

Dot distortions

(*a*) *Transformation into "z" forms:* This distortion of dots has high validity as an indicator of severe tension and control difficulty in individuals who have strong acting out impulses, draw back from a direct thrust into the environment, and then thrust out again. They find it very difficult to remain within the tightly confined space of the dot and to constrict all their inner turbulence in such a miniscule area. A compromise is sometimes reached by regression (circles) and restitutive efforts (filling in) that results in a large black blob as an indication of tension and anxiety generated by the tenuousness of controls. At other times Figure 1 will begin with dots, change to circles, and end with "z's" as a graphic manifestation of the progressive weakening of controls. The reverse sequence is suggestive of restitutive capacities similar to the impulse-defense sequence described by Schafer[25] in Rorschach protocols.

(*b*) *Dashes:* This substitution is a reliable indicator of impulsivity and indifference to control imperatives imposed by the environment. It is important to note whether the stroke is drawn vertically (toward the patient) or horizontally (toward the right). In the former there is apt to be a strong egocentric personality component associated with self-defeating and self-destructive acting out patterns, whereas in the latter the probabilities are greater that impulses will be acted out against others. This observation also applies to *overshooting* on the diamond of A, the angular component of 4, and on Figures 7 and 8; i.e., extending lines beyond joining points.

Compression-expansion placements

As a general rule, compression of figures within a small segment of the page may be regarded as an indication of repressive controls. Expansive placement characterized by the use of more than one sheet of paper, excessive use of space between any two successive figures, or progressive increase in the size of figures, are frequently indicative of precarious controls and strong acting out tendencies. I have found that patients who copy the first three or four figures in reduced size, compress them into a constricted cluster, and hug the margin of the paper, and who follow this with progressive increase in size of the remaining figures are likely to be extroversive in their behavior with underlying introversion, masochism, and vulnerability to psychosomatic symptoms. Irregular sequences indicate fluctuating ego functions and poorly controlled impulses characterized by externalized tensions and a low acting out threshold, especially when accompanied by expansiveness. Patients of this type are apt to be unpredictable in their behavior and may show paroxysmal features if a single figure is magnified out of all proportion to the others. This is even more likely if Figure 6 is so expanded.

Crossing difficulty

This will be manifested largely on Figures 6 and 8, and represents basic difficulties in coordinating drives with demands for stable and realistic object relationships. When crossing difficulty is accompanied by heavy lines and excessive overlining within an expansive framework, the possibility of violent acting out should be considered. The probabilities rise sharply if either arm of Figure 6 runs off the paper, if Figure 8 is at least twice the size of other figures in a vertical direction, (suggestive of acting out against authority figures), and if the total configuration involves excessive use of space.

Integration difficulty

There are three types of integration difficulty that indicate the probability of acting out. These pertain to Figures 3, 4, and 7 and are based upon the postulate that Figure 3 symbolizes aggressiveness or assertiveness, that Figure 4 has oral-receptive implications, and that Figure 7 symbolizes interpersonal relations involving the father and/or male authority figures. A marked dissociation of the point of the arrowhead has been observed in the records of individuals who have difficulty in keeping assertive behavior within conventional bounds and lose control over their aggressive impulses when moderate and socially acceptable assertiveness is called for. The probability of control failure is increased when the dots in this figure are drawn as circles and when this is accompanied by expansion of the entire gestalt.

Figure 4 has shown a peculiarity often associated with suicidal acting out against the self. This consists of an overlapping of the open square and the curved figure so that a portion of the former, the lower right-hand corner, is incorporated into the area of the curved figure. Hutt and Briskin[15] state that the open square represents the male and the curved figure the female. My own experience prompts me to consider the curved figure as a representation of the breast and the interpretation of the figures as an hypothesized wish to reunite with the mother figure at a very early psychosexual level, possibly representing regression to an intrauterine plane of existence and suggesting that the integration failure is motivated by unconscious symbiotic cravings that favor a suicidal solution in some cases.

Figure 7 suggests acting out potentials when the leaning figure seems to be pushing against the vertical one in such a way as to give the impression that the latter is tilting to the right. This pattern seems to be associated with an aggressively demanding attitude towards authority figures, and is even more likely to denote acting out when line pressure at the top of the leaning figure is heavily accentuated and the figure itself is noticeably larger than the vertical one. Another characteristic of acting out individuals is more often noted on recall and consists of the leaning figure drawn horizontally and thrusting against the vertical one so that it leans markedly to the right. This is a more striking manifestation of the characteristic noted in the copying phase.

Splitting and reduplication

This phenomenon has been noted in the Bender records of individuals who exhibit a low threshold for dissociation and are likely to act out rather violently either against themselves or against others while in such a temporary fugue-like dissociated state. The Bender characteristic occurs most frequently on the circle of Figure A, the curve of Figure 4, and on Figure 6. It consists of splitting or fraying the ends of the curved lines and/or overlining them so that multiple lines or circles result.

Boundary violation

This differs somewhat from use of space, and is manifested by a figure that fails to stop at the margin of the paper and runs off beyond this natural boundary. This flight-to-nowhere is most likely to be elicited by Figure 6, usually involves the horizontal axis, but has also been noted in cases where the vertical axis is drawn from top to bottom and runs off the bottom of the paper. The affective significance of Figure 6 suggests that emotional restraint is difficult for individuals who perform in this manner, and that they are more likely to flee from a stress situation than to come to grips with it.

CONCLUSION

In this chapter I have attempted to present some of the basic assumptions underlying the use of the Bender Gestalt Test as a projective technique, with special reference to the detection of acting out potentials. I am fully cognizant of the need for painstaking statistical and empirical research in this area, and it would be presumptuous of me to admonish conscientious clinicians to approach the qualitative analysis of the Bender with scientific circumspection and sophisticated skepticism. On the other hand, the clinician's worth to patients who call upon his diagnostic skills, insights and sensitivities would be sadly diminished if he always waited for the statistical green light before crossing the Rubicon of diagnostics.

REFERENCES

1. Bellak, L. Acting out: Some conceptual and therapeutic considerations. Delivered at Emil Guthiel lectures, New York, 1962.
2. Bender, L. *A visual motor gestalt test and its clinical use.* New York: *Amer. Orthopsychiat. Assoc. Res. Monogr.*, 1938, No. 3, p. 4.
3. Brown, F. An exploratory study of dynamic factors in the content of the Rorschach protocol. *J. proj. Tech.*, 1953, *17*, 251-279.
4. Carroll, E. J. Acting out and ego development. *Psychoanal. Quart.*, 1954, *23*, 521-528.
5. Clawson, A. The Bender Visual Motor Gestalt Test as an index of emotional disturbance in children. *J. proj. Tech.*, 1956, *23*, 198-206.
6. Corotto, L. V., and Curnutt, R. H. The effectiveness of the Bender Gestalt in differentiating a flight group from an aggressive group of adolescents. *J. consult. Psychol.*, 1960, *24*, 368-369.
7. Curnutt, R. H., and Corotto, L. V. The use of the Bender Gestalt cut-off scores in identifying juvenile delinquents. *J. proj. Tech.*, 1960, *24*, 353-354.
8. Duffy, E. *Activation and behavior.* New York: Wiley, 1962.
9. Fenichel, O. *The psychoanalytic theory of neurosis.* New York: W. W. Norton and Co., Inc., 1932, p. 507.
10. ———. Neurotic acting out. *Psychoanal. Rev.*, 1945, *32*, 197-206.
11. Freud, S. Further recommendations in the techniques of psychoanalysis: recollection, repetition and working through. In *Collected Papers* (1914). New York: Basic Books, (II), 1959, p. 366.
12. Goldfried, M. R., and Ingling, J. H. The connotative and symbolic meaning of the Bender Gestalt. *J. proj. Tech. & pers. Assesm.*, 1964, *28*, 185-191.
13. Greenacre, P. General problems of acting out. *Psychoanal. Quart.*, 1950, *19*, 455.
14. Hutt, M. *A tentative guide for the administration and interpretation of the Bender Gestalt Test,* U. S. Army, Adjutant General's School, 1945.
15. Hutt, M. L., and Briskin, G. J. *The clinical use of the Revised Bender Gestalt Test.* New York: Grune and Stratton, 1960.
16. Jackson, H., and Lindner, R. M. A formulation of psychopathic personality. *Psychiatry*, 1944, *7*, 59-63.
17. Koppitz, E. M. *The Bender Gestalt Test for young children.* New York: Grune and Stratton, Inc., 1964, p. 102.
18. Levy, S. Figure drawing as a projective technique. In Abt, L. E., and Bellak, L. (Eds.), *Projective Psychology,* New York: Knopf, 1950, Pp. 257-297.
19. Lindner, R. M. Content analysis in Rorschach work. *Ror. Res. Excg.*, 1946, *10*, 121-129.
20. ———. The content analysis of the Rorschach protocol. In Abt, L. E., and Bellak, L. (Eds.), *Projective Psychology,* New York: Knopf, 1950, Pp. 75-90.
21. Machover, K. *Personality projection in the drawing of the human figure.* Springfield, Ill.: Thomas, 1957, p. 281.

22. Michaels, J. J. Character structure and character disorders. In *American Handbook of Psychiatry.* New York: Basic Books, 1959, (I) p. 366.
23. Pascal, G. R., and Suttell, B. J. *The Bender Gestalt Test.* New York: Grune and Stratton, 1951, Pp. 5, 44.
24. Prado, W. M., Peyman, D. A., and Lacey, O. L. A validation study of measures of flattened affect on the Bender Gestalt Test. *J. clin. Psychol.,* 1960, *16,* 435-438.
25. Schafer, R. *Psychoanalytic interpretation in Rorschach testing.* New York: Grune and Stratton, 1954.
26. Tolor, A., and Schulberg, H. C. *An evaluation of the Bender Gestalt Test.* Springfield, Ill.: Thomas, 1963.
27. Tripp, A. Some graphomotor features of the Bender Visual Motor Gestalt Test in relation to delinquent and non-delinquent white adolescent males. Unpublished doctoral dissertation, New York University, No. 24, 988, 1957.
28. Zolik, E. S. A comparison of the Bender Gestalt reproductions of delinquents and non-delinquents. *J. clin. Psychol.,* 1958, *14,* 24-26.

Index

Abstract thinking, 244
Achievement motive, 273-274
"Acting-in," 20-29
  definition of, 20
Acting out
  and acting, 10
  adaptive aspects of, 10-11
  Bender-Gestalt, 320-332
  bondage in, 12-13
  cathartic interpretation of, 14
  as catharsis, 9-10
  causal factors in, 104-106
  character, 74
  character neurosis, 5
  child, 48-67
  clinical varieties of, 4-6
  concept of, 3-19
  and correctional measures, 13
  and creative imagination, 30-39
  criminological aspects of, 12-13
  definitions of, 3, 20, 77, 110
  and delinquency, 49-51
  and depersonalization, 10-11
  and deprivation, 65-66
  description of, 142
  direction of, 103
  duration of, 103
  dynamic aspects of, 9-10
  economic aspects of, 11
  ego-alien and ego-syntonic aspects of, 12, 14
  family patterns of, 193-195
  and family psychotherapy, 189-197
  and fantasy life, 39
  and Figure Drawings, 288-319
  forms of, 101-102
  genetic aspects of, 8, 17
  and general overstimulation, 9
  and group psychotherapy, 173-182
  and hysteria, 42
  and impulse disorders, 6
  locus of, 102-103
  metapsychology of, 6-13
  minimal forms of, 81
  and multiple diverse identification, 8
  neurotic forms of, 168-322
  and "neurotic character," 7
  and oral fixation, 8
  and psychopathy and sociopathy, 5, 17
  psychotic forms of, 168
  and Rorschach Test, 252-266
  in school, 233-240
  and situational manipulation, 14
  sociological aspects of, 11
  structural aspects of, 11
  summary of, 18
  and Thematic Apperception Test, 271-287
  treatment and management of, 13-18, 162-172, 180, 183-188, 198-207, 208-232
  topographical aspects of, 11
  and transference, 81-82
  varieties of, 81-84
  and visual sensitization, 8
  and the Wechsler Scales, 242-251
  and "working through," 40-45
  and "working through," definitions of, 42
Acting out in adolescence, 68-75, 208-232
Action, 173
Action tendency, 281-282
Adolescence, definition of, 68-69
Adolescent and culture, 69-71
Adolescent ego, 68-69
  education, 225-226
  institutional care and multiple therapy, 231-232
  treatment and management, 229-231
Affective reconstruction, 167
Aggression, 155, 202
  destructive aspects of, 179
Aged, 206
Agitated depression, 201
Alcoholism, 83, 119-128
Antabuse, 127-128
Alcohol and anxiety, 122-123
Alcoholics, characteristics of, 120-126
  personality types of, 124-126
  and socio-economic status, 123-124
  therapy of, 126-127
Alienation, 105
Alloplastic Reactions, 5, 10

Ambivalence, 205
Anxiety, 247-248
Assertive-Dependence, 180

Basic Rule, 170
Bender-Gestalt Test, 320-332
  assumptions, 323-325
  boundary violations in, 320
  collision in, 327
  compression-expansion in, 328
  crossing difficulty in, 329
  dot distortions in, 328
  and expansiveness, 325
  and heavy line pressure, 327
  and impulsivity, 328
  integration difficulty in, 329
  spikes in, 327
  splitting and reduplication in, 330
  studies, 325-326
  substitutions in, 327
  suicide and, 329
Birth of Hero fantasy, 30

Case of Sammy, 52 ff.
Castration anxiety, 37
Cathexis, 177, 184
Children, treatment techniques with, 51-52, 65
Classical analysis, 170
Concrete thinking, 244
Conformism, 281
Conflict, alloplastic, 252-253
  intra-psychic, 252-253
Control, 105-106, 248-249, 302
Counteraction, 23, 27
Counter-transference, 23, 165, 169
Creativity and crime, 36-37
  and exhibitionism, 38
  and pregnancy, 35
"Culture conflict," 101

Death Instinct, 224
Defense mechanisms, 131, 133, 184, 253-254
Delinquents, 190, 246-247
Depression, 199, 254
  pathological, 200
  psychotic, 205
Direct psychoanalysis, 23 ff.
Delinquency and criminality, 100-108

Desensitization, 104
Displacement, 202, 280
Drives, 105
Drug addiction, 110-118
  characteristics of, 113-116
  definition of, 111
  and hostility, 115-116
  and juveniles, 111-113
  and reality, 116-117
  and self-punishment, 117
Durham Rule, 12

Ego strength, 235
Ego weakness, 83, 177-178
Epigenetic principle, 157, 159

Figure Drawings detailing, 310
  and chromatic drawing, 313-318
  and dissociation, 311
  and placement, 310
  and pressure, 309
  and sequence, 306-308
  and size, 306
  and stroke, 309
  and symmetry, 310
Family romance, 30-31
Feedback, 73

Gide, Andre, 30-39
Group setting, 176
Group therapy, 178
Guilt, 105, 205, 213, 235, 275

Hero and criminal, 36
Homosexuality, 142-151
  ambivalence in, 146-147
  description of, 143
  dynamics of, 143-144, 150-151
  role playing in, 144
Homeostasis, 178
Homicidal threats, 170
House-Tree-Person Test, 313-318
Hypochrondriacal symptoms, 200

Identification, 292
  with aggressor, 165
Impulse disorder, 242, 245-246
Inhibited behavior, 280
Involutional depression, 201
Insight, 253
Intra-family disharmony, 92-95

Juvenile delinquency, 232

Language and verbal skills, 243
Learning disorders, 154
Learning inhibition, 152-160
  and acting out, 156, 158
  and ego, 153-154, 156
  and parent-child relationships, 153
  and resistance, 158
Learning theory, 27
Love objects, 201-202
LSD, 127

Malignant masochism, 82
Malevolent transformation, 104
Manic-depression, 254
Manipulative psychotherapy, 191
Masturbation, 31 ff.
McNaughton Rule, 12
Menopause, 201
  "male," 201
Minnesota Multiphasic Personality Inventory, 89
"Mother," 22 ff.
Motor reconstruction, 167
Mourning, 200
Multiple determinism, 293
Multiple impact approach, 190
Multiple therapy, 189, 192
Multiple transference, 176

Narcissus myth and art, 39
"Negative evidence," 275
Negativism, 248

Obesity, 135-141
  and aggression, 137
  dynamics of, 135-138
  existential analysis of, 138-140
  and maternal ambivalence, 135-136
  therapy of, 140
Operant conditioning, 239
Outside values and supports, 105-107
Over-cathexis, 323

Passive-resistance, 180
Perception, 175, 253
Permissiveness, 217
Phenomenological method, 138

Play, 165
Play action, 50, 56-57, 59-60, 63
  microcosmic, 166
Poison Control Center, New York City, 89
Prediction and prognosis, 205, 241, 251, 321
  with Rorschach Test, 252-256
  with Wechsler Scales, 242-251
Pregnancy, 206
Programmed learning, 239
Projective drawings, 288-319
  and homosexual activities, 292
  and oral dependency, 291-292
Projective tests, 238
Psychiatric hospitals, 183
Psychodynamics, definition, 112
Psychological autopsy, 76
Psychological testing, 235
Psychopaths, 206, 221, 246
Psychosomatic illness, 129-134
  figure-ground differentiation in, 129
  phases of, 130
Punishment and reward, 211-212, 217, 220, 234, 282

Reaction, 173
Rebelliousness, 222, 224
Recidivism, 188
Repression, 178, 213, 218, 222
Residential treatment, 183
Resistance, 165
Rorschach Scales, 252-256
  configurations in, 263-266
  current research with, 260-267
  "Dd" responses in, 254-255
  F plus responses and, 255-256
  "M" responses and, 255
  signs and, 262

Schizophrenia, 82-83, 205, 253, 278
Search for identity, 33
Sensory overload, 17-18
Scapegoating, 194
School management, 239-240
  phobia, 239-240
Self-concept, 235
Sex, 224
Social conventionality, 245-246
Social anxiety, 213

Social interest, 222
Social status, 210
Spontaneous recovery, 237
Stimulus hunger, 323
Sublimation, 153, 218, 222
Submission, 155
Suicide, 76-86, 87-99, 164, 198-207
   in children and adolescents, 87-99
   acts, psychology of, 79-81
   casual statement of, 89-90
   crisis in, 267
   depressive aspects of, 84
   fantasy systems in, 80
   forms of expression of, 89-92
   gesture in, 90-91
   hospitalization and, 205
   inability to communicate and, 96-97
   incidence of, 87-89
   and inner conflicts, 93-94
   and plan thereof, 84-85
   prevention and treatment of, 95-97
   "proneness," 266
   and Rorschach Test indicators, 257-270
   syndrome, 201
   threats of, 91-92, 170
Suicide Prevention Center, Los Angeles, 76, 82
Superego, 153, 292
   strengthening, 15
Symbiotic unions, 83-84

Symbols, 280-281
Symptoms, compromise formations of, 253

Target multiplicity, 176
Teaching machines, 239
Teleonomic trends, 144-145
Thematic Apperception Test, 271-287
   blank card of, 281
   "hero," and, 279
   and Negroes, 280
   and punishment, 282
   and Rorschach Test, 275
   rules for, 279-283
Transaction, 173
   interpersonal aspects of, 175, 177
Therapeutic milieu, 188, 231-232
Transference, 165
   multiple, 181
   simultaneous, 181
Trial and error behavior, 71
Trial thought, 167

Underachievement, 152
Use of prediction in treatment, 15

Wechsler Scales, 242-257
   performance scale of, 243-245
   and Rorschach, 248
   verbal scale of, 243-245
Working through, 171